VOLUME NINE

ADVANCES IN TRANSPORT POLICY AND PLANNING

Urban Transport and Land Use Planning: A Synthesis of Global Knowledge

VOLUME NINE

ADVANCES IN TRANSPORT POLICY AND PLANNING

Urban Transport and Land Use Planning: A Synthesis of Global Knowledge

Edited by

XINYU JASON CAO

Humphrey School of Public Affairs, University of Minnesota Twin Cities, Minneapolis, MN, United States

CHUAN DING

School of Transportation Science and Engineering, National Engineering Laboratory for Comprehensive Transportation Big Data Application Technology, Beihang University, Beijing, China

JIAWEN YANG

School of City Planning and Design, Peking University Shenzhen Graduate School, Shenzhen, GD, China

ELSEVIER

ACADEMIC PRESS

An imprint of Elsevier

Academic Press is an imprint of Elsevier
50 Hampshire Street, 5th Floor, Cambridge, MA 02139, United States
525 B Street, Suite 1650, San Diego, CA 92101, United States
The Boulevard, Langford Lane, Kidlington, Oxford OX5 1GB, United Kingdom
125 London Wall, London, EC2Y 5AS, United Kingdom

First edition 2022

ISBN: 978-0-12-824080-9
ISSN: 2543-0009

For information on all Academic Press publications
visit our website at https://www.elsevier.com/books-and-journals

Publisher: Zoe Kruze
Acquisitions Editor: Sam Mahfoudh
Developmental Editor: Naiza Ermin Mendoza
Production Project Manager: James Selvam
Cover Designer: Matt Limbert

Typeset by STRAIVE, India

Contents

Contributors

John Edward Abraham
HBA Specto Incorporated, Calgary, Canada

Laura Aston
Urban Planning and Design, Monash Art, Design and Architecture (MADA), Monash University, Caulfield East, VIC, Australia

Xinyu Jason Cao
Humphrey School of Public Affairs, University of Minnesota Twin Cities, Minneapolis, MN, United States

Chuan Ding
School of Transportation Science and Engineering, National Engineering Laboratory for Comprehensive Transportation Big Data Application Technology, Beihang University, Beijing, China

John Douglas Hunt
Intelligent Transport Systems Research Center, Wuhan University of Technology, Wuhan, Hubei, China; Department of Civil Engineering, University of Calgary, Calgary, Canada

Md. Kamruzzaman
Urban Planning and Design, Monash Art, Design and Architecture (MADA), Monash University, Caulfield East, VIC, Australia

David A. King
School of Geographical Sciences and Urban Planning, Arizona State University, Tempe, AZ, United States

Jonathan Levine
Taubman College of Architecture and Urban Planning, The University of Michigan, Ann Arbor, MI, United States

Petter Næss
Professor of Planning in Urban Regions, Norwegian University of Life Sciences, Department of Urban and Regional Planning, Ås, Norway

Lipi Bhavesh Patel
Urban Planning and Design, Monash Art, Design and Architecture (MADA), Monash University, Caulfield East, VIC, Australia

Farjana Shatu
Freelance Researcher, Narre Warren South, VIC, Australia

Guang Tian
Department of Planning and Urban Studies, University of New Orleans, New Orleans, LA, United States

Bert van Wee
Faculty of Technology, Policy and Management, Delft University of Technology, Delft, The Netherlands

C. Erik Vergel-Tovar
Department of Architecture, School of Architecture and Design, Universidad de los Andes, Bogotá, Colombia

Rui Wang
National Engineering Research Center for Water Transportation Safety; Intelligent Transport Systems Research Center, Wuhan University of Technology; Engineering Research Center for Transportation Safety, Ministry of Education, Wuhan, Hubei; School of Foreign Language, Wuhan University of Technology, Wuhan, China

Wanle Wang
National Engineering Research Center for Water Transportation Safety; Intelligent Transport Systems Research Center, Wuhan University of Technology; Engineering Research Center for Transportation Safety, Ministry of Education, Wuhan, Hubei; College of Air Traffic Management, Civil Aviation University of China, Tianjin, China

Jiawen Yang
School of City Planning and Design, Peking University Shenzhen Graduate School, Shenzhen, GD, China

Yuling Yang
School of City Planning and Design, Peking University Shenzhen Graduate School, Shenzhen, GD, China

Ming Zhang
School of Architecture, University of Texas at Austin, Austin, TX, United States

Yiming Zhang
National Engineering Research Center for Water Transportation Safety; Intelligent Transport Systems Research Center, Wuhan University of Technology; Engineering Research Center for Transportation Safety, Ministry of Education, Wuhan, Hubei, China

Ming Zhong
National Engineering Research Center for Water Transportation Safety; Intelligent Transport Systems Research Center, Wuhan University of Technology; Engineering Research Center for Transportation Safety, Ministry of Education, Wuhan, Hubei, China

Jiangping Zhou
Department of Urban Planning and Design, Faculty of Architecture, The University of Hong Kong (HKU), Pok Fu Lam, Hong Kong SAR, China

CHAPTER ONE

Global synthesis of transport and land use planning

Xinyu Jason Cao[a,*], Chuan Ding[b], and Jiawen Yang[c]
[a]Humphrey School of Public Affairs, University of Minnesota Twin Cities, Minneapolis, MN, United States
[b]School of Transportation Science and Engineering, National Engineering Laboratory for Comprehensive Transportation Big Data Application Technology, Beihang University, Beijing, China
[c]School of City Planning and Design, Peking University Shenzhen Graduate School, Shenzhen, GD, China
[*]Corresponding author: e-mail address: cao@umn.edu

Contents

Abstract

Many countries in the world have started to pursue for low-carbon transportation. Built environment interventions and transportation programs have become prevailing strategies for reducing greenhouse gas emissions. As one of the seminal series on "Advances in Transport Policy and Planning," this book synthesizes the knowledge of land use and transport planning and their integration worldwide. We grouped the chapters in this book into three parts. Part I focuses on the impacts of land use and transportation programs on travel behavior. Part II elaborates on the movements of planning effort for urbanity and associated implications for transportation. Part III highlights research and practices pertinent to integrated transport and land use planning, particularly transit-oriented development. These chapters will help guide the development of research and practices in this field for years to come.

Keywords: Literature review, Sustainable transportation, Integration, coordination, TOD

Urban sprawl and auto dependence are notorious for their contribution to greenhouse gas (GHG) emissions and climate change. The development history of many developed countries shows that auto dependence and urban sprawl reinforce each other in the two-way circle. Auto-oriented transportation policies make private vehicles the dominant mode of transport. The underpriced driving leads to excessive auto use beyond the socially optimal level and stimulates low-density and sprawling development. In turn, the automobile-centered accessibility associated with urban sprawl makes

Advances in Transport Policy and Planning, Volume 9
ISSN 2543-0009
https://doi.org/10.1016/bs.atpp.2021.10.003

driving more of a necessity than a choice (Levinson and Krizek, 2018). Although urban planners and transportation engineers worldwide have deployed various strategies to address auto dependence, their effectiveness is limited because of the lack of coordinated efforts in transport and land use planning (Boarnet, 2010). At the same time, many developing countries have been undergoing unprecedented industrialization and urbanization. They seem to be repeating the same path as developed countries have done. The rapid growth in disposable income and urban population results in the proliferation of private vehicles and expansion of human settlements to urban fringes (Cervero, 2013), coupled with large-block development and relatively poor accessibility.

Different countries employ different approaches to mitigating transportation-related GHG emissions, largely due to their differences in development stages, land use and transportation patterns, and institutional contexts. Compact city and multifunctional land use are prevalent strategies in European countries to combating urban sprawl and its transportation impacts while smart growth and New Urbanism play a key role in the United States (Dieleman and Wegener, 2004). On the other hand, countries in the global south have faced many unique challenges (such as informal development and institutional fragmentation) during their rapid urbanization and often have had inadequate capacity to address the issues (Cervero, 2013). As Cervero (2013, p. 7) pointed out, "whatever progress [developed countries] make in reducing greenhouse gas emissions (GHG) and fuel consumption will be quickly eclipsed if rapidly growing countries like India, China, and Brazil continue to mimic American-style patterns of suburbanization, car ownership, and travel."

During the past decade, some initiatives in transport and land use planning have emerged. For example, several American cities (such as Buffalo, NY, Minneapolis and St. Paul, MN) have abandoned minimum parking requirements, a "radical" movement in the excessively automobile-centered country; the city of Minneapolis also abolished the single family housing zoning. In China, as many cities are initiating or expanding metro transit lines, transit-oriented development (TOD) has become a dominant tool for the development in transit catchment areas. The development potential associated with metro transit also incentivizes city governments to pursue for the deployment of metro transit (Yang et al., 2016). Furthermore, the recently implemented transition from master planning to spatial territory planning requires more thorough coordination of land development and various infrastructure sectors, including transportation. Despite the challenges, these new initiatives are likely to affect land use and transportation systems in the long term.

As many countries in the world aim for carbon-neutral transportation in the near future, integrated transport and land use planning becomes essential to accomplishing the ambitious goals. This book synthesizes the knowledge of land use and transport planning worldwide. The contributors include scholars from five continents: Asia, Australia, Europe, North American, and South America. The chapters include literature review and synthesis of state of research and state of practice on various issues in transport and land use. Based on the theme of the chapters in this book, they are grouped into three parts. Chapters "Smart growth and travel behavior: A synthesis with a focus on the United States" by Tian, "Mass transit investments and land use in Latin America and the Caribbean: A review of recent developments and research findings" by Erik Vergel-Tovar, "Residential self-selection in the relationship between the built environment and travel behavior: A literature review and research agenda" by Wee and Cao emphasize the impacts of land use and transportation programs on travel behavior; Chapters "Compact urban development in Norway: Spatial changes, underlying policies and travel impacts" by Næss, "The shifting coalition for land-use and transport policy reform in the United States" by Levine, "Linking off-street parking to local transport and resilience policies" by King highlight prominent movements of progressive planning for urbanity and associated implications for transportation; Chapters "Pathway toward integrated transportation-land use planning in China" by Yang and Yang, "Advances in integrated land use transport modeling" by Zhong et al., "Transit oriented development: A bibliometric analysis of research" by Shatu et al., "Corridor transit oriented development: Concept, practice, and research needs" by Zhang, "Big and/or open data and transit-served area research" by Zhou focus on the integration of transport and land use planning. The reminder of this chapter offers a brief overview of these chapters.

1. Part I: Impacts on travel behavior

In the 1990s, smart growth has emerged as an important growth management model to counter the sprawling-type development and it has been instrumental to policy-making in the United States during the past few decades (Chapin, 2012). In Chapter "Smart growth and travel behavior: A synthesis with a focus on the United States," Guang Tian scrutinizes the influences of smart growth policies and strategies on travel behavior. His review emphasizes five strategies, including compact development, mixed-use development, park and open space, urban growth boundary, and TOD. He concludes that mixed-used developments can capture about a quarter of individuals' trips, reducing the average trip distance, and that about a quarter of external trips are by alternative modes of transport. Attractive and accessible parks and open spaces are also conducive to walking and biking. Furthermore, TOD can reduce auto travel demand by half. Overall, his review substantiates the effects of most smart growth policies and strategies in curbing auto use and promoting walking, biking, and transit.

During the past three decades, mass transit systems, including metro transit, light rail transit, bus rapid transit, and cable car, have proliferated under the context of rapid and informal urbanization in Latin America and the Caribbean (LAC). However, the English literature has limited knowledge of how the systems affect land development and people's travel. In Chapter "Mass transit investments and land use in Latin America and the Caribbean: A review of recent developments and research findings," C. Erik Vergel-Tover surveys refereed research papers, graduate students' theses and dissertation, and research reports written in English, Spanish, and Portuguese. He focuses on two traditional questions in the field of transport and land use: the effects of transit investments on land development and property values and the effects on travel behavior. His review offers mixed evidence for the former effects. Although TOD promotes ridership, many low-income residents have poor access to mass transit infrastructure and informal transit plays a critical role in meeting their daily travel needs. Furthermore, his review suggests that the integration between transport and land use planning "is more important now than it has ever been."

Residential self-selection has been a critical issue in the debate over the relationship between the built environment and travel behavior. Previous studies often show that built environment variables are associated with travel behavior but they fall short of substantiating the causal connection. For instance, people who like walking may selectively live in a pedestrian-friendly neighborhood and walk more to fulfill their travel preference. In this case, it is the preference rather than the neighborhood that causes the behavior. In Chapter "Residential self-selection in the relationship between the built environment and travel behavior: A literature review and research agenda," van Wee and Cao offer an overview of the recent development in the area of residential self-selection. They also call for innovative research from the following perspectives: disentangling the changing attitudes, conducting qualitative studies, addressing multiple causal structures, extending the empirical focus, and emphasizing policy relevance in future research.

2. Part II: Movements toward planning for urbanity

Many urban areas in Nordic countries have experienced sizeable population densification during the past decades. In Chapter "Compact urban development in Norway: Spatial changes, underlying policies and travel impacts," Petter Næss elaborates on the conditions, strategies, and instruments that facilitate compact urban development in Norway. Specifically, Norwegian natural context and the existing built environment, demographic and economic context, cultural context, and political conditions offer a favorable environment for policy shift from sprawl development to urban densification. Several policy instruments (including farmland preservation, greenbelt, and land use and transportation coordination) have been devised to promote sustainable land use. Norwegian Cities also implement sustainable transport policies and land use strategies (such as transit improvement, transportation pricing, urban containment, and TOD). Næss also offers ample empirical evidence to substantiate that compact development reduces vehicular travel and associated energy use. Overall, the Norwegian policy shift in the past three decades offers a best practice for planners to promote sustainable land use and transport planning.

Since the 2000s, a pro-housing coalition has emerged in the United States to improve housing affordability, mitigate greenhouse gas emissions, and address social injustice. In Chapter "The shifting coalition for land-use and transport policy reform in the United States," Jonathan Levine discusses its similarities to and divergences from earlier coalitions including anti-growth, pro-growth, and social justice, its broad society goals, and different views within the pro-housing coalition. The coalition has endorsed a variety of land use planning reforms pertinent to single family zoning, minimum lot sizes, and minimum parking requirements. These reforms enhance density and accessibility and the competitiveness of alternative modes of transport and thence have the potential to promote sustainable multimodal transportation systems.

Free and oversupplied parking is a chronic issue in the land use and transport system. Municipal governments often impose minimum parking requirements on different land uses to prevent parking spillover into surrounding neighborhood (Shoup, 2011). As a local transport policy, parking is also a land use issue because it occupies a substantial share of urban lands and shapes the distribution of other land uses. In Chapter "Linking off-street parking to local transport and resilience policies," David King elaborates on the negative consequences of required parking: more driving, less affordable housing, density decline, and the lower performance of TOD. By contrast, paid parking and parking cash out can help mitigate the demand for parking and the reliance on automobiles. Given the evolving landscape of transportation systems, King calls for planning practices and future research on parking reform and emerging technologies, the deployment of shared parking, and parking planning for climate resilience.

3. Part III: Transport and land use integration

Because transportation and land use influence each other (Giuliano and Agarwal, 2017), achieving the goals of sustainable transportation requires the coordination of land use and transport planning and policies. In Chapter "Pathway toward integrated transportation-land use planning in China," Yang and Yang emphasize integrated transport and land use planning (ITLUP) in China and present the case of Shenzhen as a pioneer practice. They first review ITLUP practices worldwide from the perspectives of governance arrangement, coordination mechanism, and implementation tools. Then they discuss the challenges of ITLUP in China because of its unique characteristics. Finally they elaborate on the ITLUP practice of Shenzhen from the perspectives of land management, multimodal transportation integration, and integration between land use and transportation during four periods. As a result of deliberation and coordinated effort, TOD has become a hallmark in Shenzhen. Although it is not a new concept (Renne and Appleyard, 2019), the Shenzhen government paves the way for the development of this ITLUP tool within the institutional context of China. The exemplary application of TOD in Shenzhen has influenced transportation and land use development in many other Chinese cities.

Likewise, forecasting the effects of land use and transport policies requires integrated land use and transport models (ILUTMs). In Chapter "Advances in integrated land use transport modeling," Zhong et al. compare the features of traditional four step travel demand forecasting models and ILTUMs and highlight the uniqueness of ILTUMs. They also review the history, development, and recent trends of these models, and present the challenges associated with model development and application. Note that ILTUMs are not widely used by planning agencies because of their sophisticated model specification. Future research should make the models friendly to planners and capable for policy analysis.

As one of the most adopted ITLUP tool, TOD has been increasingly studied by scholars worldwide. Shatu et al. conduct a bibliometric analysis of TOD research. In Chapter "Transit oriented development: A bibliometric analysis of research," they offer an overview of TOD research in the English literature during the past three decades (1993–2020). Through a co-occurrence analysis of keywords, they show that previous TOD studies emphasize four key themes of research: design and outcomes, broader policy priorities and goals, planning, and analysis method. The bibliometric coupling analysis shows five additional themes: accessibility and typology, design and travel behavior outcome, economic effects, social impacts, and contextual effects. They also identify the most productive and influential scholars, document sources (journals), and countries.

Although individual TODs produce transportation and development benefits, a coordinated network of TODs along the transit corridor is expected to bring about synergistic effects. In Chapter "Corridor transit oriented development: Concept, practice, and research needs," Ming Zhang presents three examples of corridor TOD on three continents. Using the concept of travel shed, he discusses how to define corridor TOD. Then he summarizes how scholars employ the typological approach and performance-based optimization to plan and analyze corridor TOD. He also shows that corridor TOD offers many opportunities for researchers to address policy questions, by highlighting three research needs: the network effect on transit performance and multimodal complementarity, coordinated development at the corridor level, and housing affordability.

In Chapter "Big and/or open data and transit-served area research," Jiangping Zhou elaborates on how to use big and open data to define transit service areas, evaluate their TOD characteristics, and assess their performance, no matter whether they are at the nodal or corridor level. He first reviews how previous studies employ traditional data to address these issues and then uses recent research to show that big and open data offer great potential to improve the understanding. Finally, he proposes a few areas for future research: the establishment of big and open data inventory, pilot studies to show the significance of big and open data, and the integration of big and open data with traditional data and qualitative data.

References

Boarnet, M.G., 2010. Planning, climate change, and transportation: thoughts on policy analysis. Trans. Res. Part A: Policy Pract. 44, 587–595.

Cervero, R., 2013. Linking urban transport and land use in developing countries. J. Transp. Land Use 6, 7–24.

Chapin, T.S., 2012. From growth controls, to comprehensive planning, to smart growth: Planning's emerging fourth wave. J. Am. Plann. Assoc. 78, 5–15.

Dieleman, F., Wegener, M., 2004. Compact City and urban sprawl. Built Environ. 30, 308–323.

Giuliano, G., Agarwal, A., 2017. Land use impacts of transportation investments. In: Giuliano, G., Hanson, S. (Eds.), The Geography of Urban Transportation, fourth ed. The Guilford Press, New York, NY, pp. 218–246.

Levinson, D.M., Krizek, K.J., 2018. Metropolitan Transport and Land Use: Planning for Place and Plexus, Second ed. Routledge, New York.

Renne, J.L., Appleyard, B., 2019. Twenty-five years in the making: TOD as a new name for an enduring concept. J. Plan. Educ. Res. 39, 402–408.

Shoup, D.C., 2011. The High Cost of Free Parking. Planners Press, American Planning Association, Chicago.

Yang, J., Chen, J., Le, X., Zhang, Q., 2016. Density-oriented versus development-oriented transit investment: decoding metro station location selection in Shenzhen. Transp. Policy 51, 93–102.

CHAPTER TWO

Smart growth and travel behavior—A synthesis with a focus on the United States

Guang Tian*
Department of Planning and Urban Studies, University of New Orleans, New Orleans, LA, United States
*Corresponding author: e-mail address: gtian@uno.edu

Contents

Abstract

The contemporary society faces many challenges such as climate change, loss of natural recourses, pollutions, traffic congestion, obesity, and inequality. They are associated with sprawling land use developments that have been the dominant pattern in the United States and across the globe for several decades. On the contrary, smart growth promotes compact development, infill development or redevelopment in existing neighborhoods, mixed-use development, high accessibility supported by multimodal transportation options, and open spaces and the natural environment. Smart growth has significant impacts on people's travel behavior. Empirical studies from the United States and other countries showed that adopting the smart growth principles on land use patterns and transportation could reduce vehicle miles traveled (VMT) and auto dependency through shorter travel distance and mode shifts. With compact

Advances in Transport Policy and Planning, Volume 9
ISSN 2543-0009
https://doi.org/10.1016/bs.atpp.2021.02.005

and mixed-use developments, destinations are closer to origins and each other, thus travel distances are shorter. With developments toward well-connected streets with multimodal transportation services, walking, cycling, and taking transit become viable options. The mode choice starts to shift from dominantly driving to these alternative modes. Despite the transportation and other benefits that it has, smart growth faces many challenges in practice, such as consumer preferences, mixed information, lack of tools. With the intensification of climate change and other crises we are facing today, it becomes urgent to overcome these challenges to implement smart growth principles more widely across the globe.

Keywords: Smart growth, Built environment, D-variables, Mixed-use development, Travel behavior, VMT, Walking and cycling, Transit

1. Introduction

Today, our society faces many challenges, such as climate change, loss of natural recourses, pollutions, traffic congestion, obesity, inequality, etc. Some of them are associated with how human beings build cities (for example, develop lands, build transportation infrastructure, etc.) and interact with the natural environment. Several decades after World War II, urban sprawl has become the dominant development pattern in the United States and across the globe due to consumer preferences, cheap lands, regulations, etc. (Ewing and Hamidi, 2015). Many farmlands and forests were turned into large-scale, single-use, and low-density suburbs. Accordingly, automobile became the dominant transportation mean. This type of urban development and high auto dependency contribute to the aforementioned challenges.

Under this context, smart growth was proposed in recent decades (Chapin, 2012). It becomes more and more popular among researchers, planners, developers, and policy makers as an anti-sprawling strategy. Smart growth promotes high density and mixed-use developments with well-connected streets and various transportation options (such as, walking, biking, and transit). It can help our society deal with some of the challenges we are facing now. For instance, smart growth promotes compact, high density, and infill developments, which can reduce the consumption of land and preserve the natural environment. Smart growth promotes street connectivity, walkability, and transit usage, which can reduce auto dependency, emissions, and traffic congestion. Smart growth promotes diverse housing choices and affordable housing, which can help relive inequality and housing crisis.

Everything about smart growth sounds wonderful and promising as it was proposed for. However, there are voices like "why we discuss it more than we do it" (Downs, 2005, p. 367). Some critiques of smart growth include that the market prefers sprawl than smart growth, smart growth hurts the economy, or smart growth reduces affordability (Litman, 2018). There is also a limited understanding of consumers' attitudes toward the type of living style smart growth promotes (Tian et al., 2015).

This chapter will review the current literature mainly in, but not limited to, the United States with the aim to provide readers some insights into the following questions on smart growth:

- What is smart growth? (What are its main characteristics? How is it different from urban sprawling?)
- What are the benefits of smart growth, with a focus on the relationship between smart growth and travel behavior?
- What are the criticism and challenges that smart growth is facing?

2. What is smart growth?

2.1 Definition of smart growth

There is no consensus on the definition of smart growth. Different researchers and professional communities have their own definitions of what smart growth is. Here are a few examples from different organizations:

> *Smart Growth America:* "Smart growth is an approach to development that encourages a mix of building types and uses, diverse housing and transportation options, development within existing neighborhoods, and community engagement."
>
> ***Smart Growth America (2020)***
>
> *United States Environmental Protection Agency:* "Smart growth covers a range of development and conservation strategies that help protect our health and natural environment and make our communities more attractive, economically stronger, and more socially diverse."
>
> ***EPA (2020)***
>
> *American Planning Association:* "[Smart growth] supports choice and opportunity by promoting efficient and sustainable land development, incorporates redevelopment patterns that optimize prior infrastructure investments, and consumes less land that is otherwise available for agriculture, open space, natural systems, and rural lifestyles."
>
> ***American Planning Association (2020)***

No matter how it is defined, smart growth often includes features that are not sprawling. The main characteristics of sprawl include: "(1) leapfrog or scattered development, (2) commercial strip development, or (3) large expanses of low-density or single-use development (as in sprawling bedroom communities)" (Ewing, 1997, p. 108), and (4) "any development pattern characterized by poor accessibility, or lack of functional open space" (Ewing and Hamidi, 2015, p. 413). On the contrary, smart growth often includes these features: compact development, infill development or redevelopment in existing neighborhoods, mixed-use development, high accessibility supported by multimodal transportation options, and open spaces and the natural environment.

2.2 Principles of smart growth

With different definitions of smart growth, researchers and organizations also have different principles of smart growth:
- American Planning Association lists 16 principles (American Planning Association, 2020);
- United States Environment Protection Agency and Smart Growth Network list the same 10 principles (EPA, 2020; Smart Growth Network, 2006);
- Downs (2005) lists six common principles and adds three additional principles;
- Smart Growth America lists 10 principles (Smart Growth America, 2020);
- Urban Land Institute lists 10 principles (Corrigan, 2004).

A summary of these principles and their main features are shown in Table 1. These principles cover from the built environment (land use, transportation, and housing) and the natural environment to the process of planning, policy, law and regulation. Downs (2005) also added one more principle of using impact fees to cover public costs of new developments instead of paid by the community in general.

2.3 Strategies and policies of smart growth

Various strategies and polices guide developments toward smart growth. Some of them are overlapped with each other, but with emphasis on different dimensions. Of all those strategies and policies, here are a few most common ones that may have more direct or indirect effects on people's travel behaviors.

Compact development—emphasizes on overall patterns.

> "[A] development pattern with spatial contiguity, strong centers, mixed land uses, medium to high densities, good accessibility, and permanent open spaces."
>
> ***Ewing and Hamidi (2015), p. 414)***

Table 1 Summary of key principles of smart growth from professional communities (American Planning Association, 2020; Corrigan, 2004; EPA, 2020; Smart Growth America, 2020).

Principles	Main features
Mixed uses	Put different uses (houses, offices, restaurants, shops, schools, etc.) next to each other (in a same building, block, or development)
Compactness/density	Raise density, build centers, infill development within and revitalize existing communities, create growth boundary to limit outward extension
Transportation	Create walkable communities and multimodal transportation system: high-quality public transportation, safe and convenient biking and walking infrastructure, and well-connected and -maintained streets
Housing	Provide diverse housing types and choices, including affordable housing
Natural environment	Identify and sustain parks, open space, farmland, natural beauty, and critical environmental areas
Sense of place	Preserve communities' characters, faster distinctive and attractive communities
Transparency and engagement	Make transparent and collective decisions, engage citizens, communities and stakeholders in all aspects of the planning process and at every level of government
Regulation and zoning	Adopt more diverse regulations and policies to make it easy to do the right thing

Mixed-used development (MXD)—emphasizes on land uses.

> "A mixed-use development or district consists of two or more land uses between which trips can be made using local streets, without having to use major streets. The uses may include residential, retail, office, and/or entertainment. There may be walk trips between the uses."
>
> ***Tian et al. (2020), p. 3)***

Urban growth boundary—emphasizes on growth control.

> "Under Oregon law, each of the state's cities and metropolitan areas has created an urban growth boundary around its perimeter – a land use planning line to control urban expansion onto farm and forest lands."
>
> ***Metro (2020)***

Transit-oriented development (TOD)—adds the transportation element to an MXD.

> "TODs are widely defined as compact, mixed-use developments with high-quality walking environments near transit facilities."
>
> ***Ewing et al. (2017), p. 70)***

Complete streets—emphasizes on street design.

> "Complete Streets are streets designed and operated to enable safe use and support mobility for all users. Those include people of all ages and abilities, regardless of whether they are travelling as drivers, pedestrians, bicyclists, or public transportation riders."
>
> ***U.S. Department of Transportation (2020)***

2.4 Impacts and benefits of smart growth

Many studies show the negative outcomes of sprawl: high vehicle miles traveled (VMT) and associated traffic congestion and safety, air pollution, energy consumption, and greenhouse gas (GHG) emissions; physical inactivity and obesity; high infrastructure and public service costs; central city and downtown decline; housing and transportation affordability; loss of the natural environment (Ewing and Hamidi, 2015; Hamidi and Ewing, 2015).

As an alternative development pattern, smart growth carries potential benefits in opposition to the negative consequences of sprawl: reducing VMT and associated externalities; improving public health while promoting walking, cycling, and other physical activities; lowering infrastructure and public service costs by shared fiscal responsibility; promoting community and activity centers with compact and infill developments; reducing overall housing plus transportation costs; promoting parks and green infrastructure and preserving natural recourses and environment. More importantly, smart growth promotes choices for all, instead of the same value for everyone. It provides housing and transportation choices and access to opportunities for everyone.

Smart growth is a different way of developing lands and building cities, it has significant impacts on transportation. The following of this chapter will focus on impacts of smart growth on people's travel behaviors.

3. Smart growth and travel behavior

The ways in which smart growth affects travel can be measured in the two methods proposed by Cervero (2006): post-processing and direct modeling. Not every component of smart growth can be directly measured or drawn connections with travel behavior and travel choices. This review limits the strategies of smart growth to the following ones: built environmental D-variables, mixed-use development, park and open space, urban growth boundary, transit-oriented development, and others.

3.1 Compact development (built environmental D-variables)

The first three principles of smart growth emphasize on the built environment of land use patterns, transportation system and physical infrastructure. They are well known as compact development and measured by the five D-variables in the literature (Ewing and Cervero, 2001, 2010): population and employment *d*ensity, land use *d*iversity, street *d*esign, *d*estination accessibility, and *d*istance to transit. The relationship between these built environmental variables and travel behavior are one of the most studied areas in transportation planning (Stevens et al., 2019). Hundreds of empirical studies and a dozen of literature reviews on this topic have been done in the last couple decades. In fact, there are enough empirical studies that make it possible to conduct meta-analyses. Probably, the most famous one is Ewing and Cervero's, 2010 meta-analysis. Ewing and Cervero (2010) calculated the weighted average elasticities of VMT, transit use, and walking with respect to each of these built environmental variables. An elasticity is the ratio of the percent change in one variable associated with the percent change in another variable. It is unit-free, thus one of the most widely used measures of effect size. From a practice standpoint, it is very useful for practitioners to quantify transportation outcomes of a project or policy.

Following Ewing and Cervero's methodology, Stevens (2017) conducted a meta-regression on VMT, Yang et al. (2019) conducted a meta-analysis on cycling, and Aston et al. (2020) conducted a meta-analysis on transit use. No meta-analysis has been found on walking since Ewing and Cervero's. There are a couple recent systematic literature review about the built environment effects on walking and cycling (Smith et al., 2017; Wang et al., 2016). All of these meta-analyses and literature reviews included empirical studies from the United States and across the world. The findings of these studies are summarized in Table 2 and the following texts.

For built environment effects on VMT, both Ewing and Cervero's and Stevens' studies found that VMT had a negative elasticity with respect to D-variables in most cases. Although they did not agree on the interpretations of the results and some other technical issues (Ewing and Cervero, 2017; Stevens, 2017), the differences between their numbers are actually smaller than their disagreements, as shown in Table 2. Their main disagreement

Table 2 Elasticities of VMT, walking, cycling, and transit use with respect to D-variables based on meta-analyses.

		VMT		Walking	Cycling	Transit use	
		Ewing and Cervero (2010)	Stevens (2017)	Ewing and Cervero (2010)	Yang et al. (2019)[a]	Ewing and Cervero (2010)	Aston et al. (2020)
Density	Household/ population density	−0.04	−0.22	0.07	<0.01	0.07	0.10
	Job density	0.00	−0.07	0.04	–	0.01	0.08
	Commercial floor area ratio	–	–	0.07	–	–	–
	Commercial density	–	–	–	–	–	0.15
Diversity	Land use mix (entropy index)	−0.09	0.11	0.15	0.09	0.12	0.26
	Jobs-housing balance	−0.02	0.00	0.19	–	–	0.16
	Distance to a store	–	–	0.25	–	–	–
Design	Intersection/street density	−0.12	−0.14	0.39	–	0.23	–
	% 4-way intersections	−0.12	−0.06	−0.06	–	0.29	–
	Connectivity	–	–	–	0.08	–	0.17
	Availability of cycling facilities	–	–	–	0.07	–	–
	Cycling safety design features	–	–	–	0.04	–	–

Destination accessibility	Job accessibility by auto	−0.20	−0.20	–	–	–	–
	Job accessibility by transit	−0.05	0.00	–	–	–	–
	Distance to downtown	−0.22	−0.63	–	–	–	–
	Job within 1 mile	–	–	0.15	–	–	–
	Local access	–	–	–	–	–	0.06
Distance to transit	Distance to nearest transit stop	−0.05	−0.05	0.15	–	0.29	–

[a]Cycling for transportation purposes, which was defined as the use of bicycles to travel from one place to another.

is whether these numbers are considered large or small (which could be subjective), not the numbers themselves. Nevertheless, except for the land use entropy index, a majority of their numbers have the same negative sign. That means the VMT decreases when the built environment is oriented toward smart growth—high density, mixed uses, well-connected streets with multimodal transportation.

For built environment effects on walking, Ewing and Cervero's study found that walking had a positive elasticity with respect to most of the D-variables, except for the percentage of four-way intersections. The elasticities with respect to variables of diversity and design tend to be larger than variables of density and others. Two recent literature review studies (Smith et al., 2017; Wang et al., 2016) confirmed that these relationships were consistent.

For built environment effects on cycling, Yang et al. conducted a meta-analysis based on 39 empirical studies published between 2007 and 2017. They found that one diversity variable (land use mix) and three design variables (street connectivity, the presence of cycling paths and facilities, and cycling safety features) were the most important D-variables to promote cycling for transportation purposes.

For built environment effects on transit use, both Ewing and Cervero's and Aston et al.'s studies found that transit use had a positive elasticity with respect to some D-variables. Although not all of their D-variables were overlapped, they found that a variety of variables such as density, diversity, design, and distance to transit could increase transit uses. In addition, Aston et al. found the effects of some additional built environmental variables, including local access or walkability and pedestrian and cycle amenities.

To summarize, the smart growth principles on land use patterns and transportation, measured by D-variables, can reduce VMT (auto dependency) through shorter travel distance and mode shifts. With developments toward compact, high density, and mixed uses, destinations are closer to origins and each other, thus travel distances are shorter. With developments toward well-connected streets with multimodal transportation facilities and services, more travel choices are available. Walking, cycling, and taking transit become options. The mode choice starts to shift from dominantly driving to other modes (walking, biking, transit, etc.).

3.2 Mixed-use development

As one of the iconic characteristics of smart growth, MXD is always recommended as a smart growth strategy to reduce traffic impacts. Mixed-use strategy emphasizes on putting different uses (such as residential, retail, office, entertainment, etc.) together or closer to each other. It can happen either vertically (within buildings) or horizontally (among blocks) or both. Theoretically, the transportation benefits of MXDs are obvious. By putting different destinations within a certain area, trips can be chained up with one auto or transit trip plus multiple short walking trips. The average trip distance will be shorter and there will be not only vehicle trips.

However, it is challenging to actually quantify the traffic impacts of MXDs. In practice, the estimation of trip generation for different land uses is dominated by Institute of Transportation Engineers' (ITE) *Trip Generation Manual* (Institute of Transportation Engineers, 2017). When coming to MXD, ITE's method has many issues (Currans, 2017; Gruyter, 2019; Tian et al., 2020), such as outdated data, small sample size, suburb contexts, etc. Fortunately, a few empirical studies have investigated the traffic impacts of MXDs independently, besides being exanimated as one of the D-variables—land use diversity.

Zhang et al. (2009) and Pang (2014) studied 42 MXDs in Austin, Texas. Their main findings include: MXDs captured 40% more trips internally than non-MXDs; residents of MXDs generated 0.2 more home-based-work trips and 0.3 fewer non-home-based-other trips; trips within MXDs were 1.9 miles shorter for home-based-work trips, 0.65 mile longer for home-based-non-work trips, and 1.2 miles shorter for non-home-based-work trips; there were more zero- or one-car households in MXDs than non-MXDs.

Schneider et al. (2013) examined the transportation impacts of 30 smart-growth areas in California. The smart-growth areas were selected based on the definition of "places where many common activities (e.g., workplaces, parks, coffee shops, stores, other homes) are located within a convenient walking distance of where many people live and work" (Schneider et al., 2012, p. 1). They found that the actual peak-hour vehicle trips of these smart-growth areas were fewer than a half of ITE's numbers. Although the total person trips at these locations were close to the numbers from ITE, a large proportion of these person trips were generated by walking, cycling, or transit. Specifically, 27% of person trips were generated by walking, 3% by cycling, and 21% by transit at the smart-growth locations.

Ewing et al. (2011) developed a methodology to quantify the internal capture rate of MXDs (the trips that are captured within the MXD). Following the same methodology, Tian et al. (2020) looked at 622 MXDs from 31 metropolitan areas across the United States. They found that MXDs could capture as high as 47.1% trips internally, of which 94.4% could be walking trips. On average, MXDs captured 23.3% trip internally, of which 69.4% were walking trips. Even for the trips that were generated externally (entering or leaving MXDs), 26.5% of them were walking, biking or transit trips (12.9% walking, 2.3% biking, and 11.3% transit).

In sum, the main impacts of MXDs on transportation are capturing trips internally and generating higher share of non-auto trips. MXDs may generate the same amount of or even more total trips as single-use developments or non-MXDs. However, a significant share of these trips can be captured internally and a significant share of these trips can be done by walking, biking or taking transit.

3.3 Park and open space

Smart growth always emphasizes the importance of parks and the preservation of open and green spaces and other natural areas. Empirical studies showed that the existence of park and open spaces within developments had many benefits including encouraging more walking and cycling. Most of these studies come from public health field, of which the interest is in the relationship between parks and physical activities (walking and cycling are considered as physical activities). Studies found that large, attractive, and easily accessible parks and open spaces were associated with high level of walking (Billie et al., 2005; Schipperijn et al., 2017; Smith et al., 2017; Zhang et al., 2020). More interestingly, Tao et al. (2020) explored the nonlinear relationship between the built environment and active travel in the Twin Cities. They found that distance to park was the most important variable to people's daily active travel. When the nearest park was beyond 0.2 mile, the level of active travel decreased significantly.

Besides, studies examined the effects of parks on walking or biking for transportation purpose. Focusing on transit users' mode choice in Atlanta (GA), Boston (MA), and Portland (OR) of the United States, Park et al. (2019) found that people were more likely to walk or take transit to access a transit station when the station had a park nearby.

By reviewing 39 empirical studies from 2007 to 2017, Yang et al. (2019) found that there was emerging evidence for the relationship between commuting cycling behavior and availability of green spaces and strong evidence for the relationship between general cycling behavior and availability of green spaces. The elasticity of cycling for general purpose with respect to availability of green spaces is 0.27, which means 1% increase in availability of green spaces is associated with a 0.27% increase in cycling time.

To sum, not only the existence of parks and open spaces matters for people to or not to walk or cycle (either for recreational purpose or for transportation purpose), but also the size, attractiveness and accessibility of parks and open spaces matter to the intensity of people's walking and cycling.

3.4 Urban growth boundary

Urban growth boundary has been adopted worldwide as a policy to control growth and grow smarter. The first urban growth boundary in the United States was adopted back to 1950s. Since then, hundreds of cities and counties and a couple states (Oregon, Washington) have mandated urban growth boundary. Perhaps Portland, Oregon is the iconic metropolis of the urban growth boundary policy, which was approved in 1980. Since then, several decades have passed. What effects has the urban growth boundary policy had on the residents' travel behaviors in Portland?

The author has not found direct evidence of urban growth boundary to reduce auto dependency from any empirical studies in the current literature. Jun (2004, 2008) studied the smart growth policies of Portland. The author did not find a clear relationship between urban growth boundary and reduced auto dependency, while other smart growth strategies (mixed land uses, public transit services, etc.) were associated with less driving alone. In a simulation study, Azaria et al. (2013) found that urban growth boundary could potentially reduce VMT per person by as much as 25% over 40 years.

3.5 Transit-oriented development (TOD)

Peter Calthorpe proposed the concept of TOD in 1993 (Calthorpe, 1993). Since then, TOD has been applied and studied worldwide as another iconic strategy toward smart growth. The literature on TOD is rich with an exponential growth in citations over the past decades (28 citations in 2000, 184 in 2010, and 1515 in 2018) (Renne and Appleyard, 2019). Another chapter in this book focuses on this topic. In order to avoid duplication, this chapter did not conduct a complete review on TOD and its transportation impacts. Instead, it only presents findings of a series of studies done by the author of this chapter and his colleagues (Ewing et al., 2017, 2019; Tian et al., 2017) to give the readers a quick overview.

By studying six TODs across the United States, Ewing et al. (2019) found that TODs could reduce vehicle trip generation relative to ITE's guideline from 30.2% to 65.3% and peak parking demand relative to actual parking supply from 16% to 48.8%. Even at one transit-adjacent development (TAD, a large-scale mixed-use development adjacent to a commuting-rail station) studied, they found the vehicle trip generation was 25.3% less than ITE's guideline and the peak parking demand was 58.8% less than the actual parking supply.

3.6 Other strategies

Creating centers is another principle of smart growth. Although monocentric development was the dominant development pattern for decades in the United States and is still the case for many small and medium metropolitan areas, polycentric developments are promoted in some large metropolitan areas because of their transportation benefits. Park et al. (2020) identified 589 centers in 28 metropolitan areas in the United States and studied travel behaviors of the households living these centers. They found that households living centers drove 5.2 miles less per day than households living outside centers. Households living centers also made 0.21 more walking trip per day than their counterparts outside centers. In addition, they found travel tours (sequences of trips that starts and ends at home) related to centers comprised more walking, cycling, or transit trips than travel tours outside centers.

Complete street is also a strategy of smart growth, which has been applied in many cities aiming to create safe streets for all users. Although the author did not find sufficient empirical studies that directly investigate the impact of complete street on safety and travel choices, there are studies on the relationship between certain elements of complete street and travel behaviors (Buehler and Pucher, 2012; Lyons et al., 2020; MacLeod et al., 2018; Marshall and Ferenchak, 2019; Yang et al., 2019). Together, these studies presented evidence that pedestrians and cyclists oriented street elements and design (such as protected intersections, protected and separated bike lanes, and other walking and cycling facilities and safety features) were associated with lower severe accident rates and safer street environment, as well as higher walking and cycling activities.

4. Challenges to smart growth

Despite the transportation related effects and other benefits that it has, smart growth faces criticism and challenges. There are studies arguing that smart growth creates negative impacts, while its benefits are modest. For instance, Echenique et al. (2012) conducted a simulation study to compare the costs and benefits of compact against sprawling urban forms in England. They concluded that "[s]mart growth principles should not unquestioningly promote increasing levels of compaction on the basis of reducing energy consumption without also considering its potential negative consequences. In many cases, the potential socioeconomic consequences of less housing choice, crowding, and congestion may outweigh its very modest CO2 reduction benefits" (Echenique et al., 2012, p. 136). Of course, this single simulating study has many issues and drew its own criticism. While it cannot overturn numerous empirical studies that show the benefits of smart growth, it does signal that there is not no doubt about smart growth.

Other arguments that induce doubt about smart growth include consumer preferences of single-family houses and auto dependent sprawling suburbs, cost of living, congestion, etc. (Litman, 2018). As Gordon and Richardson (1997) argued, low-density suburbs were dominantly preferred by residents and suburbanization could reduce traffic congestion by shifting traffic from urban cores to less congested suburban roads. Based on an estimation of an 8% elasticity of driving with respect to density, Duranton and Turner (2018) argued that smart growth was not cost effective to reduce driving and related traffic congestion or emissions.

However, the literature also shows studies that counter these arguments. Consumer preferences can vary, especially across different life cycle cohorts. Tian et al. (2015) studied residents' housing preferences toward smart growth in the Salt Lake City metropolitan area of Utah. They found that residents in different life cycles have different preferences. While young families with children favor single-family homes, young adults without children like to live close to work and elderlies prefer a mix of housing types. In term of cost of living, Hamidi and Ewing (2015) found that although the housing cost was higher in compact metropolitan areas than sprawling ones, the transportation cost was lower and the combined cost of housing plus transportation was lower in compact areas than sprawling areas. By studying 157 urbanized areas in the United States, Ewing et al. (2018) found neither sprawl nor compact development can reduce traffic congestion.

While the previous section shows rich literature on this topic, it is a challenging task to quantify the effect of smart growth on travel behavior. The effect could be overestimated or underestimated, if the residential self-selection issue was not properly handled (Cao and Chatman, 2016). The geographic and urban context where a study was conducted may also play a role. As Aston et al. (2020) pointed out, significantly more studies outside of the United States have been done in the recent decade and showed that the increasing geographical diversity was acting to change the effects at the indicator level. Even when similar results were found, scholars may interpret the results very differently, which then could present confusing pictures to practitioners.

Indeed, as Downs stated, "[s]mart Growth is much more talked about than actually carried out in practice" (Downs, 2005, p. 367). Smart growth faces many challenges in practice. Not only is there lack of tools that can be applied directly to measure the benefits of smart growth at smaller scales (like project level) by developers or local municipalities, but also may some benefits of smart growth not be observable by only applying certain principles of smart growth or in a short period of time.

5. Conclusion

The message is clear in the literature. No matter what definition is used, smart growth has strong effects on travel behavior, at the least in the United States urban context. With the built environmental D-variables (measuring the smart growth principles on land use patterns and transportation) go up (except distance to downtown, which is the reverse direction), VMT goes down and walking, cycling and transit use go up. More specifically, among the smart growth strategies, MXDs can capture trips as much as 23.3% on average internally and generate non-auto trips as much as 26.5% on average externally. Parks and open spaces are important for people to walk or cycle and the size, attractiveness and accessibility of parks and open spaces matter to how much people walk or cycle. TODs generate about half or less vehicle trips and peak parking demands than their suburban counterparts. Smart growth reduces VMT and facilities walking, cycling, and the usage of public transportation.

At the same time, smart growth has not been widely implemented in practice as it should be or is expected. It faces many challenges and obstacles. With the intensification of climate change and other crises we are facing today, it becomes urgent to overcome these challenges and obstacles to implement smart growth principles more widely in the United States and across the globe. More research and studies are needed to be conducted outside the United States to diversify the urban contexts, clear up doubts about smart growth, accurately quantify the benefits of smart growth, and develop tools that can be used directly in practice at smaller scales (like project level) to promote smart growth.

References

American Planning Association, 2020. APA Policy Guide on Smart Growth. Retrieved from, American Planning Association. November 1. https://www.planning.org/policy/guides/adopted/smartgrowth.htm.

Aston, L., Currie, G., Delbosc, A., Kamruzzaman, M., Teller, D., 2020. Exploring built environment impacts on transit use—an updated meta-analysis. Transp. Rev. 41 (1), 73–96.

Azaria, D.E., Troy, A., Hy, L.B., Ventriss, C., Voigt, B., 2013. Modeling the effects of an urban growth boundary on vehicle travel in a small metropolitan area. Environ. Plann. B. Plann. Des. 40 (5), 846–864.

Billie, G.-C., Broomhall, M.H., Knuiman, M., Collins, C., Douglas, K., Ng, K., Donovan, R.J., 2005. Increasing walking: how important is distance to, attractiveness, and size of public open space? Am. J. Prev. Med. 28 (2), 169–176.

Buehler, R., Pucher, J., 2012. Cycling to work in 90 large American cities: new evidence on the role of bike paths and lanes. Transportation 39 (2), 409–432.

Calthorpe, P., 1993. The Next American Metropolis: Ecology, Community, and the American Dream. Princeton Architectural Press, New York.

Cao, X., Chatman, D., 2016. How will smart growth land-use policies affect travel? A theoretical discussion on the importance of residential sorting. Environ. Plann. B. Plann. Des. 43 (1), 58–73.

Cervero, R., 2006. Alternative approaches to modeling the travel demand impacts of smart growth. J. Am. Plann. Assoc. 72 (3), 285–295.

Chapin, T.S., 2012. Introduction: from growth controls, to comprehensive planning, to smart growth: planning's emerging fourth wave. J. Am. Plann. Assoc. 78 (1), 5–15.

Corrigan, M.B., 2004. Ten Principles for Smart Growth on the Suburban Fringe. ULI–the Urban Land Institute, Washington, D.C.

Currans, K.M., 2017. Issues in trip generation methods for transportation impact estimation of land use development: a review and discussion of the state-of-the-art approaches. J. Plan. Lit. 32 (4), 335–345.

Downs, A., 2005. Smart growth: why we discuss it more than we do it. J. Am. Plann. Assoc. 71 (4), 367–378.

Duranton, G., Turner, M.A., 2018. Urban form and driving: evidence from US cities. J. Urban Econ. 108, 170–191.

Echenique, M.H., Hargreaves, A.J., Mitchell, G., Namdeo, A., 2012. Growing cities sustainably: does urban form really matter? J. Am. Plann. Assoc. 78 (2), 121–137.

EPA, 2020. Smart Growth. Retrieved from, EPA. Novermber 1. https://www.epa.gov/smartgrowth/about-smart-growth.

Ewing, R., 1997. Is Los Angeles-style sprawl desirable? J. Am. Plann. Assoc. 63 (1), 107–126.

Ewing, R., Cervero, R., 2001. Travel and the built environment: a synthesis. Transp. Res. Rec. 1780, 87–114.

Ewing, R., Cervero, R., 2010. Travel and the built environment: a meta-analysis. J. Am. Plann. Assoc. 76 (3), 265–294.

Ewing, R., Cervero, R., 2017. "Does compact development make people drive less?" The answer is yes. J. Am. Plann. Assoc. 83 (1), 19–25.

Ewing, R., Hamidi, S., 2015. Compactness versus sprawl: a review of recent evidence from the United States. J. Plan. Lit. 30 (4), 413–432.

Ewing, R., Greenwald, M., Zhang, M., Walters, J., Feldman, M., Cervero, R., … Thomas, J., 2011. Traffic generated by mixed-use developments—six-region study using consistent built environmental measures. J. Urban Plann. Dev. 137 (3), 248–261.

Ewing, R., Tian, G., Lyons, T., Terzano, K., 2017. Trip and parking generation at transit-oriented developments: five US case studies. Landsc. Urban Plan. 160, 69–78.

Ewing, R., Tian, G., Lyons, T., 2018. Does compact development increase or reduce traffic congestion? Cities 72, 94–101.

Ewing, R., Tian, G., Park, K., Sabouri, S., Stinger, P., Proffitt, D., 2019. Comparative case studies: trip and parking generation at Orenco Station TOD, Portland Region and Station Park TAD, Salt Lake City Region. Cities 87, 48–59.

Gordon, P., Richardson, H.W., 1997. Are compact cities a desirable planning goal? J. Am. Plann. Assoc. 63 (1), 95–106.

Gruyter, C.D., 2019. Multimodal trip generation from land use developments: international synthesis and future directions. Transp. Res. Rec. 2673 (3), 136–152.

Hamidi, S., Ewing, R., 2015. Is sprawl affordable for Americans? Exploring the association between housing and transportation affordability and urban sprawl. Transp. Res. Rec. 2500 (1), 75–79.

Institute of Transportation Engineers, 2017. Trip Generation Manual, tenth ed. ITE, Washington, D.C.

Jun, M.-J., 2004. The effects of Portland's urban growth boundary on urban development patterns and commuting. Urban Stud. 41 (7), 1333–1348.

Jun, M.-J., 2008. Are Portland's smart growth policies related to reduced automobile dependence? J. Plan. Educ. Res. 28, 100–107.

Litman, T., 2018. Evaluating Criticism of Smart Growth. Victoria Transport Policy Institute, Victoria, BC.

Lyons, T., Choi, D.-A., Park, K., Ameli, S.H., 2020. Safety and nonoptimal usage of a protected intersection for bicycling and walking: a before-and-after case study in Salt Lake City, Utah. Sustainability 12 (21), 9195.

MacLeod, K.E., Sanders, R.L., Griffin, A., Cooper, J.F., Ragland, D.R., 2018. Latent analysis of complete streets and traffic safety along an urban corridor. J. Transp. Health 8, 15–29.

Marshall, W.E., Ferenchak, N.N., 2019. Why cities with high bicycling rates are safer for all road users. J. Transp. Health 13, 285–301.

Metro, 2020. Urban Growth Boundary. Retrieved from, Metro. Novermber 1. https://www.oregonmetro.gov/urban-growth-boundary.

Pang, H., 2014. Mixed Land Use and Travel Behavior: A Case Study for Incorporating Land Use Patterns Into Travel Demand Models. The University of Texas at Austin, Austin, TX.

Park, K., Choi, D.-A., Tian, G., Ewing, R., 2019. Not parking lots but parks: a joint association of parks and transit stations with travel behavior. Int. J. Environ. Res. Public Health 16 (4), 547.

Park, K., Ewing, R., Sabouri, S., Choi, D.-A., Hamidi, S., Tian, G., 2020. Guidelines for a polycentric region to reduce vehicle use and increase walking and transit use. J. Am. Plann. Assoc. 86 (2), 236–249.

Renne, J.L., Appleyard, B., 2019. Twenty-five years in the making: TOD as a new name for an enduring concept. J. Plan. Educ. Res. 39 (4), 402–408.

Schipperijn, J., Cerin, E., Adams, M.A., Reis, R., Smith, G., Cain, K., et al., 2017. Access to parks and physical activity: an eight country comparison. Urban For. Urban Green. 27, 253–263.

Schneider, R., Shafizadeh, K., Sperry, B., Bochner, B., Handy, S., 2012. California Smart-Growth Trip Generation Rates Study, Appendix E: Data Collection Methodology and Results. Retrieved from, University of California, Davis. http://downloads.ice.ucdavis.edu/ultrans/smartgrowthtripgen/Appendix_E_Data_Collection_Method.pdf.

Schneider, R., Shafizadeh, K., Sperry, B.R., Handy, S.L., 2013. Methodology to gather multimodal trip generation data in smart-growth areas. Transp. Res. Rec. 2354 (1), 68–85.

Smart Growth Network, 2006. This is Smart Growth. Retrieved from https://www.epa.gov/sites/production/files/2014-04/documents/this-is-smart-growth.pdf.

Smart Growth America, 2020. What is Smart Growth? Retrieved from, Smart Growth America. November 1. https://smartgrowthamerica.org/our-vision/what-is-smart-growth/.

Smith, M.J., MacMillan, A., Field, A., Baas, P., Mackie, H., 2017. Systematic literature review of built environment effects on physical activity and active transport–an update and new findings on health equity. Int. J. Behav. Nutr. Phys. Act. 14 (1), 158.

Stevens, M.R., 2017. Does compact development make people drive less? J. Am. Plann. Assoc. 83 (1), 7–18.

Stevens, M.R., Park, K., Tian, G., Kim, K., Ewing, R., 2019. Why do some articles in planning journals get cited more than others? J. Plan. Educ. Res. 0739456X19827083.

Tao, T., Wu, X., Cao, J., Fan, Y., Das, K., Ramaswami, A., 2020. Exploring the nonlinear relationship between the built environment and active travel in the twin cities. J. Plan. Educ. Res. 0739456X20915765.

Tian, G., Ewing, R., Greene, W., 2015. Desire for smart growth: a survey of residential preferences in the Salt Lake region of Utah. Hous. Policy Debate 25 (3), 446–462.

Tian, G., Ewing, R., Weinberger, R., Shively, K., Stinger, P., Hamidi, S., 2017. Trip and parking generation at transit-oriented developments: a case study of Redmond TOD, Seattle region. Transportation 44, 1235–1254.

Tian, G., Park, K., Ewing, R., Watten, M., Walters, J., 2020. Traffic generated by mixed-use developments—a follow-up 31-region study. Transp. Res. Part D: Transp. Environ. 78 (2020), 102205.

U.S. Department of Transportation, 2020. Complete Streets. Retrieved from, U.S. Department of Transportation. Novermber 11. https://www.transportation.gov/mission/health/complete-streets.

Wang, Y., Chau, C.K., Ng, W.Y., Leung, T.M., 2016. A review on the effects of physical built environment attributes on enhancing walking and cycling activity levels within residential neighborhoods. Cities 50, 1–15.

Yang, Y., Wu, X., Zhou, P., Gou, Z., Lu, Y., 2019. Towards a cycling-friendly city: an updated review of the associations between built environment and cycling behaviors (2007–2017). J. Transp. Health 14, 100613.

Zhang, M., Kone, A., Tooley, S., Ramphul, R., 2009. Trip Internalization and Mixed-Use Development: A Case Study of Austin Texas. Southwest Region University Transportation Center (US), Austin, TX.

Zhang, X., Melbourne, S., Sarkar, C., Chiaradia, A., Webster, C., 2020. Effects of green space on walking: does size, shape and density matter? Urban Stud. 57 (16), 3402–3420. 0042098020902739.

CHAPTER THREE

Sustainable transit and land use in Latin America and the Caribbean: A review of recent developments and research findings

C. Erik Vergel-Tovar*
Department of Architecture, School of Architecture and Design, Universidad de los Andes, Bogotá, Colombia
*Corresponding author: e-mail address: c.vergel@uniandes.edu.co

Contents

Advances in Transport Policy and Planning, Volume 9
ISSN 2543-0009
https://doi.org/10.1016/bs.atpp.2021.05.001

Abstract

Several cities in Latin America and the Caribbean (LAC) are currently developing or expanding metro systems or improving and consolidating Bus Rapid Transit (BRT) networks. More recently, some cities have begun to implement cable car systems as mass transit solutions for urban peripheries. This chapter presents a comprehensive literature review of research into the implementation of these mass transit systems and examines the coordination between transport systems and land use in the LAC region. It provides a systematic examination of theoretical approaches, methodologies, and research findings in the literature, with a focus on the implications of mass transit investments and land-use planning for accessibility and travel behavior. The literature on the relationship between mass transit investments and the urban fabric in this region is still growing and the current research emphasizes exploring the impacts of transport and mobility improvements on cities and the influence of urban form on travel behavior. The empirical evidence on these relationships in this region remains mixed.

Keywords: Accessibility, Transport, Land use, Travel behavior, Latin America

1. Introduction

Mass transit systems in Latin America and the Caribbean (LAC) have evolved rapidly over the past three decades. The implementation of metro systems has increased significantly since the 1990s, and a number of expansion projects are in the pipeline, with several cities planning to add rail lines to their systems. Light rail transit (LRT) systems are less common, existing in just eight cities by 2020. On the other hand, Bus Rapid Transit (BRT) networks began to proliferate throughout the region in the early years of the 21st Century, inspired by the experiences of Curitiba (Brazil), Quito (Ecuador), and Bogotá (Colombia). More recently, some cities have begun to innovate, designing and implementing cable car systems as mass transit solutions, especially for informal settlements in mountainous or hilly areas where public space is at a premium. The development and implementation of these mass transit systems have encouraged a large number of scholars to conduct research from a range of different perspectives.

The LAC region has experience a rapid urbanization over a short period. The percentage of the population living in towns and cities has risen from 40% in the 1950s to 70% in the 1990s. The rapid urbanization left little room for the implementation of planning measures capable of anticipating transportation demand, infrastructure provision and transit supply (UN-HABITAT, 2012). LAC cities initially displayed a monocentric spatial structure, but they have recently been influenced by the dynamics of polycentric urban growth (UN-HABITAT, 2013). The rapid urbanization also led to significant differences between the income levels and location of urban dwellers, resulting in the emergence of overcrowded downtown areas. Authorities struggled to provide adequate mass transit planning responses to this rapid urban growth. Inadequate and inappropriate road infrastructure and high levels of automobile use are linked to disparities in the jobs-housing balance, in particular for the urban poor (Cervero, 2013).

The study of the transport and land use connection in the LAC region is based on theories about the urban spatial structure and the bid rent theory (Alonso, 1964; Muth, 1969), but recent studies explore additional issues such as accessibility and equity. Using the urban spatial structure framework in studies of mass transit investments and land use in the LAC region, scholars test hypotheses about the influence of accessibility benefits on land and property values. These studies also examine the influence of mass transit investments on spatial and land use patterns, concentration of activities, and the development of transport and land use models aiming to predict changes in the spatial structure (Lau and Kam, 2005; Rodrigue, 2020). Emerging research focuses on the relationships between mass transit investments and equity issues, mostly accessibility for low-income groups. The observed positive associations between mass transit investments and land values lead to concerns of the access to land and housing of low-income groups. Pro poor mobilization of land value increments through innovative value capture mechanisms and citizenship participation through planning tools influence the scholarly work of equity issues in the LAC region (Irazábal, 2008; Smolka, 2013). In terms of mobility and access for disadvantaged groups, transportation scholars are actively developing the research agenda by linking transport studies with human geography and urban sociology theories of exclusion (Hine and Kamruzzaman, 2020) and by exploring the implications of transport decision-making on equity outcomes (Jones and Lucas, 2012).

This chapter provides a comprehensive literature review of studies that explore two aspects of the connections between transport and land use. First, it describes analyses of the urban impacts of mass transit systems, focusing on land development and property values. Second, it describes studies that investigate the influence of urban form on travel behavior associated with mass transit investments. The review covers research written in English, Spanish and Portuguese. It includes published academic articles, masters and doctoral dissertations, and studies produced by multilateral organizations.

The chapter comprises six sections. Section 2 describes the evolution of four types of mass transit systems in the LAC region: metro, LRT, BRT and cable cars. Section 3 provides a review of the literature on the urban impacts of mass transit systems. Section 4 includes a literature review of studies looking at the influence of mass transit and urban form on travel behavior. Section 5 discusses research findings and the methods used in the literature and describes opportunities for new studies in the LAC region. Section 6 offers an overview of general research trends in the field and identifies areas for further research.

2. Recent developments in mass transit investment in Latin America and the Caribbean

Recent years have seen a boom in mass transit investments in the LAC region, mostly in the form of the resurgence of metro systems, the consolidation of the BRT networks, the emergence of LRT projects and the promotion of cable cars as an innovative transport solution. During the 20th Century, 13 LAC cities in six countries (Argentina, Brazil, Chile, Colombia, Puerto Rico, and Venezuela) have designed and developed metro systems, while 29 cities have implemented BRT networks (BRTDATA.ORG, 2020). In the same period only one LRT system was built, in Mexico City (UrbanRail.Net, 2004). To date, the 21st Century has witnessed a rapid evolution of mass transit investments in the LAC region, with nine cities implementing new metro systems or expanding existing metro networks, seven cities implementing LRT projects, 147 cities inaugurating new BRT networks, and eight cities innovating with cable cars as mass transit solutions. The remainder of this section describes the evolution of these four types of mass transit system in the LAC region.

2.1 Metro systems

Metro systems are part of the urban rail network that provide commuter services as part of the transit network in metropolitan areas. Metro systems are expensive infrastructure projects that require both capital investment and local capacity. Metro systems are characterized by rail-based vehicle technology, with scheduled services and fixed stations (underground, ground level and elevated infrastructure). They are considered to be one of the transit systems with the highest passenger-carrying capacity. They travel at relatively high speeds, their frequency is reliable and they are comfortable (Pulido et al., 2018). Metro systems also provide high levels of accessibility within their areas of influence linked to economic dynamics such as access to employment, concentration of activities and more intense land use around stations. They constitute an important part of the infrastructure for intra-urban economic development in the form of manufacturing, trade and services (Mitric, 1997).

Fig. 1 shows the locations of 22 metro systems implemented in the LAC region. The first city to implement a metro system, which entered into operation in 1913, was Buenos Aires (Argentina). The system is known as the *Subte* because its 54 km of track runs entirely underground (that is, it is *subterranean*). The first metro line in Mexico City (Mexico) was completed before the end of the 1960s. This metro system is the longest in the region, at 176.8 km. In Sao Paulo (Brazil), the metro system opened in the 1970s. The system currently has five lines, which connect with seven suburban commuter rail lines. Santiago de Chile (Chile) and Rio de Janeiro (Brazil) implemented their first metro lines in the 1970s. In the 1980s Caracas (Venezuela), Recife, Portoalegre and Belo Horizonte (all in Brazil), and Guadalajara (Mexico) joined the group. During the 1990s, Monterrey (Mexico), Medellín (Colombia) and San Juan (Puerto Rico) also inaugurated metro systems. Over the past 20 years, the LAC region has witnessed new metro systems in nine cities, including Brasilia, Fortaleza and Salvador in Brazil, Valparaíso in Chile, Maracaibo in Venezuela, Santo Domingo in the Dominican Republic, Lima in Peru, Panama City in Panama, and Quito in Ecuador.

2.2 LRT systems

According to Cervero (1984), LRT systems use rail infrastructure and fixed stations, consist of electrically powered trains running along exclusive lanes or shared rights of way and travel at lower speeds than metro systems. LRT systems have their origins in streetcars, trolley cars, and tramways, have dedicated rights of way at surface level, are powered by electrical connectors and operate using single- *or* multi-car vehicles. Currently, there are eight LRT systems in the LAC region, as shown in Fig. 2.

The evolution of LRT systems in the LAC region shows a recent growth of this type of systems. Mexico City implemented an LRT in 1986 known as *Tren Ligero de la Ciudad de Mexico* as part of its public transport network, with an initial line of 13.04 km including 18 stations. The system was expanded at the end of the 1980s and beginning of the 1990s, and after 2000, the terminal station Xochimilco was relocated due to capacity constraints. After Mexico

Fig. 1 Cities in Latin America and the Caribbean with metro systems. *Source: Author based on ArcGIS, 2020. Cities. Retrieved from: https://hub.arcgis.com/; ArcGIS, 2020. Latin America and the Caribbean Countries. Retrieved from: https://hub.arcgis.com/; METROBITS.org, 2004. World Metro Database. Retrieved 01/12/20, 2020, from http://micro.com/metro/about.html; UrbanRail.Net, 2004. Americas: Metro Rail, Subway & Light Rail Systems. Retrieved 12/01/20, 2020, from http://www.urbanrail.net/am/america.htm.*

City, the cities of Recife (Brazil) and Mendoza (Argentina) implemented LRT systems in 2012, followed by Santos (Brazil) and Medellin (Colombia) in 2015. Fortaleza (Brazil) opened an LRT system in 2017, and Cuenca (Ecuador) opened its LRT system in 2020.

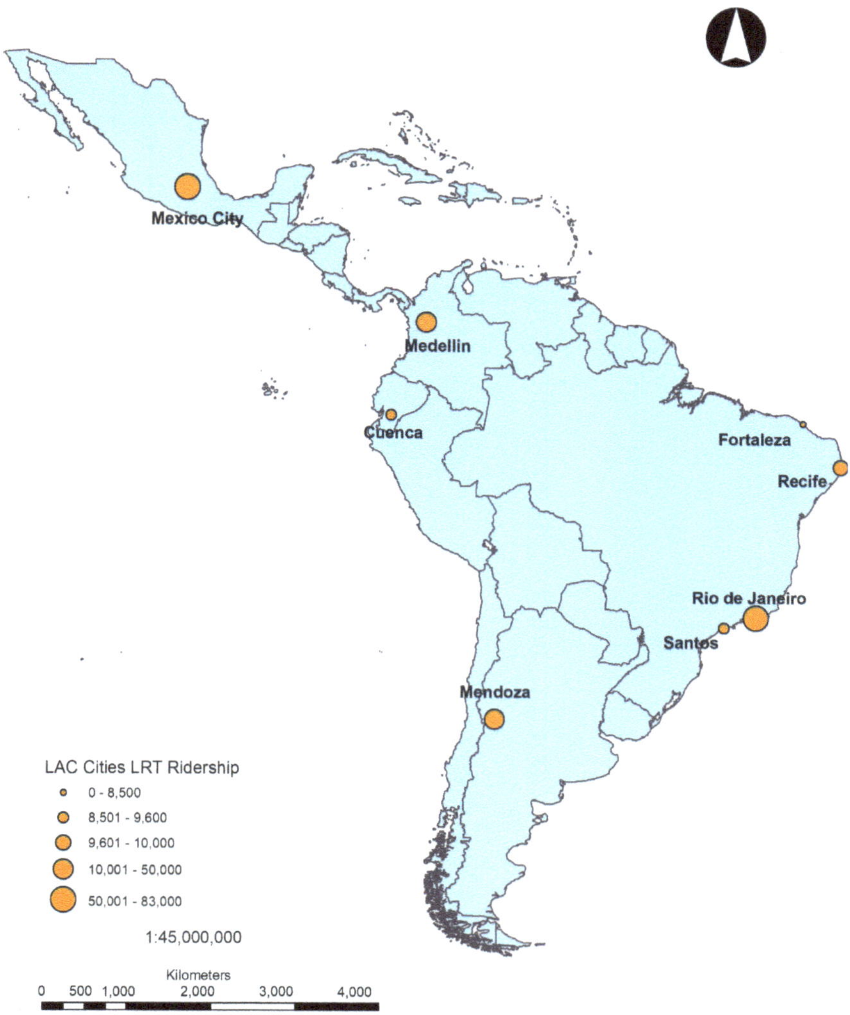

Fig. 2 Cities in Latin America and the Caribbean with light rail transit systems. *Source: Author based on ArcGIS, 2020. Cities. Retrieved from: https://hub.arcgis.com/; ArcGIS, 2020. Latin America and the Caribbean Countries. Retrieved from: https://hub.arcgis.com/; UrbanRail.Net, 2004. Americas: Metro Rail, Subway & Light Rail Systems. Retrieved 12/01/20, 2020, from http://www.urbanrail.net/am/america.htm.*

2.3 BRT systems

BRT networks provide cost-effective mass transportation combining fixed stops, high capacity bus vehicles, exclusive lanes to reduce travel times, and high frequency services. They are intended to provide intelligent transportation systems with a recognizable identity or brand (Levinson et al., 2003), a

Fig. 3 Cities in Latin America and the Caribbean with BRT networks. *Source: Author (ArcGIS, 2020. Cities. Retrieved from: https://hub.arcgis.com/; ArcGIS, 2020. Latin America and the Caribbean Countries. Retrieved from: https://hub.arcgis.com/; BRTDATA.ORG, 2020. Global BRT Data. Retrieved 10/20/2020, from https://brtdata.org/location/latin_america).*

marketing strategy and a clear customer service approach (Wright, 2011). Currently, 57 BRT networks operate in the LAC region (see Fig. 3).

As illustrated in Fig. 4, LAC countries have been designing and implementing BRT systems since the 1970s. During the 1970s, Lima implemented segregated bus lanes running along the central part of the city's widest

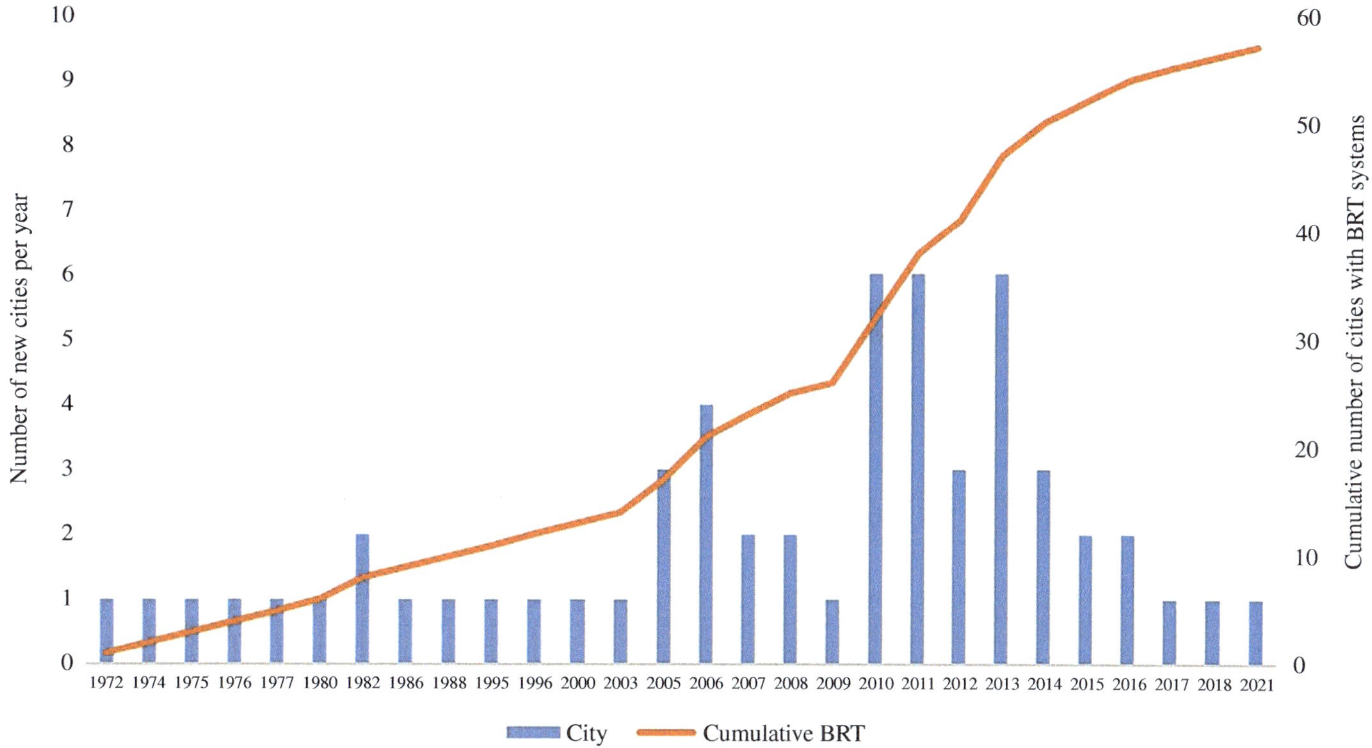

Fig. 4 BRT networks in Latin America and the Caribbean over time. *Source: Author (BRTDATA.ORG, 2020. Global BRT Data. Retrieved 10/20/2020, from https://brtdata.org/location/latin_america).*

thoroughfare *Avenida Paseo de la República* creating what is known as the Via *Expresa*. The latter connects Lima's downtown area around the *Juana Alarco* Park and *Paseo de los Héroes Navales* to the *Barranco* district in the south of the city (Sánchez León et al., 1978).

There are two tipping points in the evolution of BRT networks in the region. First, the Brazilian city of Curitiba implemented a BRT network as an innovative mass transit solution that followed urban development axes, allowing the city to concentrate population centers along planned corridors. This innovative approach, integrating land use and transportation planning, is what made Curitiba a transit metropolis (Cervero, 1998). Second, two major cities in the region—Quito and Bogotá—have implemented large-scale segregated bus lane systems based on the Curitiba experience (Mejía-Dugand et al., 2013). Quito's system significantly improved access to the Historic Center—a UNESCO World Heritage Site—by way of the electric BRT network known as *Trolebús*, opened in 1995. In 2000, Bogotá developed a BRT (the *TransMilenio*) system with innovations such as exclusive dual lanes at stops in order to increase passenger capacity (Vergel-Tovar, 2016). Since the implementation of the *TransMilenio*, 44 cities in the region have implemented or initiated development of this type of mass transit system, including Santa Cruz de la Sierra (Bolivia), whose service was slated to become operational in February 2021 (Fig. 4).

2.4 Cable cars

Cable cars are an innovative urban transportation system that is used to address the transportation demands of populations settled in urban peripheries characterized by informal urban growth, high density and poor infrastructural and service provision. They tend to be located in mountainous or hilly areas where it is difficult to provide ground transportation services (Economist, 2017; Hidalgo and Velásquez, 2015). Cable cars use electrically propelled steel cables to transport suspended cabins (gondolas). They travel between fixed stations located at different elevations (Canon et al., 2017). Since the opening of the first cable car line in Medellín in 2004, seven other cities in the LAC region have built similar systems (Yañez-Pagans et al., 2019). Fig. 5 shows the nine LAC cities where cable car systems currently operate (the great metropolitan area of Mexico City includes the *Cablebus* and the Cable Car in Ecatepec).

Medellín pioneered the design and implementation of mass transit cable car systems. In 2004, the city implemented a line known as *Línea K*, linking

Fig. 5 Cities in Latin America and the Caribbean with cable car systems. *Source: Author (ArcGIS, 2020. Cities. Retrieved from: https://hub.arcgis.com/; ArcGIS, 2020. Latin America and the Caribbean Countries. Retrieved from: https://hub.arcgis.com/; Yañez-Pagans, P., Martinez, D., Mitnik, O.A., Scholl, L., Vazquez, A., 2019. Urban transport systems in Latin America and the Caribbean: lessons and challenges. Lat. Am. Econ. Rev. 28 (1), 15. doi:10.1186/s40503-019-0079-z).*

the Acevedo Metro Station and the Santo Domingo Public Library at the top of the mountainside on which informal settlements developed as part of the *Comuna nororiental*. Since 2004, the city has expanded its transit network with additional cable car lines (Heinrichs and Bernet, 2014). In 2010,

Caracas inaugurated its own cable car system, as a response to the transportation needs of residents in informal settlements, who, thus far, had only limited access to the city's principal activity nodes. At the same time, the city of Manizales (Colombia) began the implementation of a network of Cable Cars as a mass transit solution.

Following implementation in Medellín and Caracas, cable car systems spread rapidly throughout the region. In 2011, Rio de Janeiro implemented an ambitious cable car system intended to improve accessibility for the residents of one of the city's largest informal settlements, the *Complexo Alemão*. However, the system ceased operations in 2016 due to financial constraints (Globo, 2016). Mérida (Venezuela) implemented a cable car system in 2012 as part of the *Trolmerida* mass transit system connecting the city center and the San Jacinto area. In 2014, La Paz (Bolivia) constructed the largest network of cable cars in the LAC region known as *Mi Teleférico*, with three lines in the first phase: the red line, 2.4 km long, the yellow line (3.9 km) and the green line (3.7 km). The network was expanded to include two more lines (blue, 4.7 km long, and orange, 2.6 km) (Garsous et al., 2019).

Two cities in Colombia and one city in Mexico were next. Cali implemented its cable car system in 2015, improving access for informal settlements along hilly areas that have traditionally lacked access to the formal transit supply. Ecatepec in Greater Mexico City (Mexico) implemented its system in 2016, while Bogotá did so in 2018. The system is known as *TransMicable* and is located in the south of the city, providing access to informal settlements in hilly areas where informal transit services provided transportation along with a couple of feeder routes belonging to the BRT system (Villar-Uribe, 2021). The most recent Cable Car in the region began commercial operations in 2021 in Mexico City with the name "*Cablebus*." The "Cablebus" network includes two lines, Line 1 opened at the beginning of 2021 and it is expected that Line 2 starts commercial operations in the second half of 2021 (Network, 2021).

3. The relationship between mass transit investments with land use, economic development and social changes

This section provides a literature review of research into the effects of mass transit investments on the urban fabric. It summarizes research findings of both quantitative and qualitative analyses for the region. Fig. 6 shows the associations between keywords of the literature review. At the end of this section is Table 1 with a summary of the literature review.

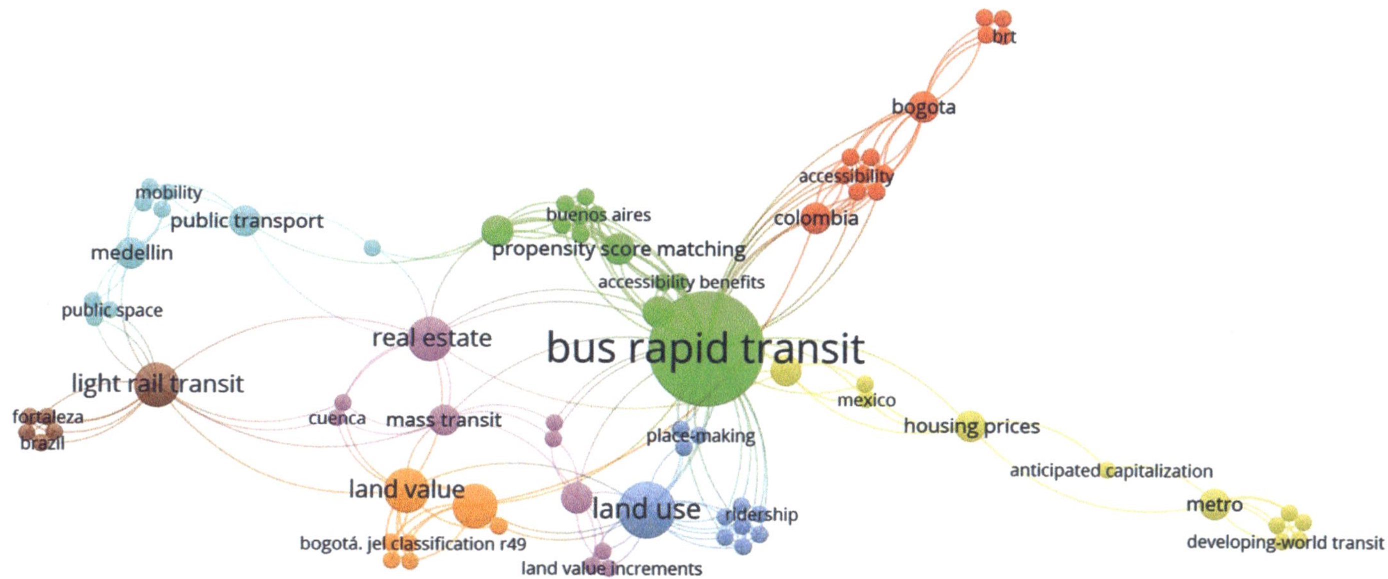

Fig. 6 Network of keywords and associations, literature review: the effects of mass transit investments on land use, economic development and social changes. *Source: Own elaboration with VOSViewer (2021).*

Table 1 Literature review, the relationship between mass transit investments with land use, economic development and social changes: A review of research findings.

City, Country	Year	Authors	Title	Research design and methods	Main findings
Metro systems and land use, economic development and social changes					
Santiago de Chile, Chile	2008	Agostini, C. and G. Palmucci	The Anticipated Capitalisation Effect of a New Metro Line on Housing Prices	Hedonic price model Capitalization effects, log models	After the announcement of the new metro line (2000 and 2004): increments in average apartment prices by 4.2% and 7.9%. With the location of stations identified: increments in average apartment prices by 3.1% and 5.5%, with variations according to distance to metro stations
Mexico City, Mexico	2014	Guerra, E.	Mexico City's suburban land use and transit connection: the effects of the Line B Metro expansion	Before and after statistical analysis of changes based on household travel surveys	Density increased around stations, but findings suggest few or no effect on commercial land uses in downtown areas
Santiago de Chile, Chile	2016	Asahi, K.	Better Urban Transport Improves Labour Market Outcomes: Evidence from a Subway Expansion in Chile	Fixed effects models	The study found a positive association between employment rates (increments by 3.1% for each kilometers closer to the network) and distance to the subway network

Sao Paulo, Brazil	2018	Costa, A. B.	Transportation and urban development in São Paulo: exploring how transportation has shaped and still shapes the city	Differences-in-differences econometric method	Transit and urban development in already consolidated areas: findings suggest that for each 1% increase in the transit network an average increase of 0.26% in building density is expected. Transit and urban development in non-consolidated areas: findings suggest that each five minutes closer to transit, in terms of walking distance, an increase of 40% in the number of new apartment units is expected
Buenos Aires, Argentina	2019	Rosanovich, S. A. and A. P. Di Giovambattista	Spatial analysis and non-lineal effects of proximity to the subway network on housing prices in Buenos Aires	Non-linear hedonic price models	The study found non-linear effects of the subway network on housing prices per square meter with changes of −5% within 200 meters but changes of 3.6% between 200 and 600 meters in relation to the distance to subway stations
Sao Paulo, Brazil	2021	Sandroni, P.	Textos Empiricos V: Infraestrutura de transportes e impactos sobre os preços dos terrenos do entorno: um estudo exploratório em São Paulo	Before and after data analysis land parcel values Line 4 metro system (Butantã Station)	Four development projects evaluated with before and after data: projects that applied density bonus tools (payment for additional floor area ratio (FAR) using the *outorga onerosa* tool) suggest significant increments in appraisal values after the opening of the *Butantã* metro station
Light-rail transit LRT systems and land use, economic development and social changes					
Fortaleza, Brazil	2017	Freitas, C. F. S.	Undoing the right to the city: World Cup investments and informal settlements in Fortaleza, Brazil	Qualitative data analysis, field work visits and participant observation	LRT design and implementation issues regarding road section requirements, resettlement of households, and land acquisition issues as part of the construction process

Continued

Table 1 Literature review, the relationship between mass transit investments with land use, economic development and social changes: A review of research findings.—cont'd

City, Country	Year	Authors	Title	Research design and methods	Main findings
Cuenca, Ecuador	2018	Hermida, C., D. Moreno, et al.	Impact on the value of rental and purchase values for residential and commercial properties, related to distance from the axis of the tram system in Cuenca, Ecuador	Hedonic pricing model	Housing rents (asking prices): increments in housing rents by 0.29% for each 1% of distance further away from the system. Commercial uses (asking prices): reduction in commercial rents by 0.20% for each 1% of distance further away from the system
Medellin, Colombia	2019	Gutiérrez Torres, K.	Public space: transformation and urban cohesion. The case of the light-rail transit Ayacucho in Medellin	Fieldwork observation, qualitative data analysis, spatial data analysis	Increase of real estate dynamics and land use changes within the influence area of the light rail transit system *Ayacucho*, and creation of new public spaces. Significant change in building typologies (from one and two story structures to high-rise residential building and commercial developments)
Bus Rapid Transit BRT systems and land use, economic development and social changes					
Bogota, Colombia	2004	Rodriguez DA, Targa F	Value of accessibility to Bogota's bus rapid transit system	Hedonic price model Spatial autocorrelation	Multifamily residential properties (asking prices, 494 observations): increments from 6.8% to 9.3% for every 5 min of time closer to BRT stations
Bogota, Colombia	2007	Perdomo JA, Mendieta JC, Mendoza CA, Baquero AF.	Study of the Effect of the TransMilenio Mass Transit Project on the Value of Properties in Bogotá, Colombia	Propensity score matching	Residential uses (304 observations) and commercial uses (40 observations): increments of 22% for properties with access to the BRT

Bogota, Colombia	2009	Rodriguez DA, Mojica CH.	Capitalization of BRT network expansions effects into prices of non-expansion areas	Difference-in-difference (before and after) hedonic model	Properties (asking prices): higher asking prices between 13% and 14% in areas served by the first phase of the BRT system in comparison with control areas (without access to the BRT)
Bogota, Colombia	2010	Munoz-Raskin R.	Walking Accessibility to Bus Rapid Transit in Latin America: Does It Affect Property Values? The Case of Bogota, Colombia	Econometric hedonic analysis	New properties (value premiums): properties in close proximity to feeder lines with value premiums of 8.7% in comparison to properties located at 5–10 min walking distance to the system
Ecatepec, Mexico	2012	Flores Dewey	The Value of a Promise: Housing Price Impacts of Plans to Build Mass Transit in Ecatepec, Mexico	Hedonic price model	No evidence regarding the effects of the announcement of the BRT line on property values
Bogota, Colombia	2013	Bocarejo, J. P., I. Portilla, et al.	Impact of Transmilenio on density, land use, and land value in Bogotá	Difference in difference	Population density (2001–2008): differences of 1437 inhabitants/km^2 and 1715 inhabitants/km^2 between treatment and control groups. Built-up area (2001–2008): areas served by the BRT (treatment) showed higher housing built-up area changes (3700 m^2) in relation to the control group (without access to BRT), but higher changes on commercial and office built-up area in the control group

Continued

Table 1 Literature review, the relationship between mass transit investments with land use, economic development and social changes: A review of research findings.—cont'd

City, Country	Year	Authors	Title	Research design and methods	Main findings
Mexico City, Mexico	2013	Velandia, D.	The Impact of Bus Rapid Transit System on Land Prices in Mexico City	Quasi-experimental approach (region-block as the geographic unit of analysis)	BRT Line 1: increments of approximately 15% in land values. BRT Line 2: no evidence of changes on land values due to BRT investments (this finding might be related to the time taken to assess the effect)
Bogota, Colombia	2014	Cervero, R. and D. Dai	BRT TOD: Leveraging transit oriented development with bus rapid transit investments	Log-linear regression equation	Changes on FAR (2004–2010): increments of 5% (phase one and three corridors); increments of 7% (phase two corridors). Higher building activity in areas served by BRT terminals (urban peripheries)
Bogota, Colombia Quito, Ecuador	2016	Vergel-Tovar, C. E.	Examining the reciprocal relationship between bus rapid transit and the built environment in Latin America	Quasi-experimental research design, difference-in-difference methods with propensity scores, and qualitative data analysis	Bogota built-up area (BRT corridors phase one 2000–2013 in relation to controls): densification with increments on built-up area along (Av. Caracas: 4.8% in 2000 and 1.8% in 2013; Autonorte: 7.2% in 2000 and 3.1% in 2013) Bogota land uses (BRT corridors phase one 2000-2013 in relation to controls): predicted probabilities for residential land uses decreasing from 75% to 59%; and predicted probabilities for commercial land uses increasing from 1% to 35%.Quito (new developments): increments from 25% to 45% along Ecovía corridor and increments from 23% to 24% along Corredor Central Norte

Bogota, Colombia Quito, Ecuador	2016	Rodriguez, D. A., Vergel-Tovar, E., and Camargo, W. F	Land development impacts of BRT in a sample of stops in Quito and Bogotá	Quasi-experimental research design to examine quantitatively changes in land development. Regression analysis with treatment and control corridors	Bogotá (square meters treatment and control areas 2001–2010): percentage change of square meters from new developments of 56% (Suba) and 35% (Humedal Cordoba) around BRT stations. Bogotá (building permits treatment and control areas 2001–2010): building permits approved per hectare from 0.74 to 2.29 around BRT stations.Quito: increments on building price of 3% (*Corredor Norte*), 5% (*Trolebus*) and a reduction of 2.5% (*Ecovia*), with increments for single-family housing units of 9.4% (*Corredor Norte*)
Barranquilla, Colombia	2017	Garza, N.	Transport infrastructure and the spatial dynamics of real estate markets	Before and after data analysis	Analysis of the BRT system in Barranquilla (Colombia). Effects on land prices at the initial stage of the BRT, with negative or no effects in the stages close to completion
Bogotá, Pereira, Cali, Barranquilla and Bucaramanga	2019	Vergel-Tovar, C. E. and W. Camargo	Urban development impacts of bus rapid transit in Colombia: challenges and opportunities	Before and after data analysis	Results suggest that BRT terminals had the most significant impacts on land development after the implementation of the BRT systems in the five cities analyzed
Buenos Aires, Argentina	2020	D'Elia, V. V., M. C. Grand, et al.	Bus rapid transit and property values in Buenos Aires: Combined spatial hedonic pricing and propensity score techniques	Spatial hedonic pricing, propensity scores	Property values (672, 569, 490 and 497 observations in different models): the study did not find statistically significant impacts of the BRT system on property values. Local conditions and sample size might explain the non-statistically significant impacts (study area is a commuting area with an already consolidated urban development environment)

Continued

Table 1 Literature review, the relationship between mass transit investments with land use, economic development and social changes: A review of research findings.—cont'd

City, Country	Year	Authors	Title	Research design and methods	Main findings
Bogotá, Colombia	2021	Guzman, L. A., H. D. Enríquez, et al.	BRT system in Bogotá and urban effects: More residential land premiums?	Coarsened Exact Matching (CEM)	The study found positive effects of the BRT on land values in low-income areas, but the analysis did not find significant effects on medium and high-income areas (negative in some cases)
Cable Cars and land use, economic development and social changes					
Medellin, Colombia	2011	Brand, P., and Dávila, J. D.	Mobility innovation at the urban margins: Medellín's Metrocable	Available data analysis	Key role of public sector comprehensive interventions (infrastructure provision, slum/urban upgrading) to maximize the benefits of cable cars for low-income groups
Medellin, Colombia	2012	Cerdá, M., Morenoff, J. D., Hansen, B. B., Tessari Hicks, K. J., Duque, L. F., Restrepo, A., and Diez-Roux, A. V.	Reducing violence by transforming neighborhoods: a natural experiment in Medellín, Colombia	Propensity score matching, before and after data analysis (treatment and control groups)	Neighborhood analysis: homicide rate was higher by 66% in intervention areas than in control areas, but violence rates decreased 75% more in intervention areas than in control areas

3.1 The effects of metro systems

Agostini and Palmucci (2008) examined the changes in apartment values in anticipation of the expansion of the metro system in the Greater Santiago Area (Chile) between 2000 and 2004. They found that average apartment prices increased between 4.2% and 7.9% following the announcement of the new line and then increased between 3.1% and 5.5% when the locations of the new metro stations were made public. The anticipatory capitalization effects varied by the distance of properties from the closest metro station. The expansion of the metro system in Mexico City also provided an opportunity to determine the effects of a metro system on urban form. A statistical analysis using before and after data found that the expansion of Line B was positively associated with increased density around stations (Guerra, 2014); however, this study found few or no effects on downtown commercial development. Asahi (2016) examined the effects of the expansion of the subway system in Santiago de Chile on employment, finding positive associations between job density and proximity to the subway network.

Costa (2018) analyzed the effects of the expansion of the metro system and commuter rail infrastructure on urban form in Sao Paulo, finding a higher concentration of jobs in close proximity to the transportation network and a 40% price increase for new real estate development units. An ex-post spatial analysis exploring the effects of subway stations on housing prices in Buenos Aires found nonlinear associations between prices per square meter and distance from stations, with negative association of −5% (from 0 to 200m) and positive association of 3.6% (between 200 and 600m). It also found heterogeneity between the impacts of subway lines, differentiated by housing attributes, such as the presence of amenities (e.g., gym or pool facilities) within housing developments (Rosanovich and Di Giovambattista, 2019). The implementation of Line 4 of Sao Paulo's metro system provided an opportunity to study its effects on land values. A before and after data analysis of the effects of the Butantã Station (metro system line 4 in Sao Paulo) on changes in property value suggested that proximity to the new station was associated with significant increases in property prices (Sandroni, 2021). The positive association could be attributable to development incentives, such as density bonuses for increased floor area ratio (FAR) via the application of the *outorga onerosa* urban management instrument.

3.2 The effects of LRT systems

A limited number of studies have used quantitative or qualitative approaches to examine the effects of LRT systems. Whatever the approach is, the

Fig. 7 Light-rail transit LRT system in Cuenca Ecuador. *Source: Fernandez de Cordova, N., Pauta Pesantez, A., 2020. Picture LRT System in the Historic Center in Cuenca, Ecuador.*

challenge lies in how to address the transformation of the built environment caused by the changes to the road section required by this type of mass transit system. This aspect becomes even more controversial when the plans involve the development of an LRT in historic city centers, such as the city of Cuenca in Ecuador (Fig. 7), another UNESCO World Heritage site (ICOMOS, 2014). Research on the effects of the construction phase of the Cuenca LRT on property rental and purchase prices suggests mixed results. Hermida et al. (2018) developed a hedonic pricing model and found that residential rental prices fall with proximity to the LRT corridor, while commercial rental prices increase. The study found no changes in sale prices of properties intended for commercial and residential use (Hermida et al., 2018).

Recent LRT projects in Brazil and Colombia offer researchers opportunities to examine urban impacts qualitatively. Freitas (2017) examined the social impacts of resettlement dynamics caused by transportation investments in Fortaleza, associated with an ambitious agenda to build a range of infrastructure projects including LRT systems in the context of the Soccer World Cup. The Fortaleza LRT project brought about several social management challenges as construction was planned for sections of the city characterized by informal settlements, which required land purchases to enable changes to be made to the road section and the relocation of households. There were also compensation issues related to the precarious tenure of many of the people affected by the construction work (Freitas, 2017). Similar issues emerged during the design and construction of the LRT project known as *Tranvía de Ayacucho*, in Medellin (Gutiérrez Torres, 2019). This LRT system provides access to the downtown area of Medellin at the San Antonio transportation hub of the elevated metro system. The study of the impacts of the LRT system looked at the effects on highly consolidated blocks of one and two-story buildings in downtown Medellin (Gutiérrez Torres, 2019). This study found land acquisition issues emerged, associated with the construction of LRT stations and the clearing of space for turning points. The study found that a significant number of new building types has been constructed close to the LRT stations, consolidating a real estate dynamic that suggests the system led to accessibility benefits.

3.3 The effects of BRT systems

Most of the studies examining the influence of BRT networks on property values, urban development, density and changes in the built environment focus on Bogotá (Fig. 8). The pioneer study, conducted in 2004, focused on the accessibility benefits of the *TransMilenio* system on property values, finding an increase of between 6.8% and 9.3% in property values for every 5 min reduction in travel time to a BRT station (Rodriguez and Targa, 2004). Another study found that property prices increased 22% with access to the BRT network (Perdomo et al., 2007). In 2009, an analysis of the opening of the second phase of the BRT system in Bogota showed that asking prices increased between 13% and 14% for properties served by *Transmilenio* (phase one) when compared with control groups (properties without access to the BRT system). The study also found similar premiums for properties within 500 m of the BRT network and those located between 500 m and 1 km from any part of the mass transit infrastructure (Rodríguez and Mojica, 2009). *TransMilenio* feeder routes also had positive effects on property values, research suggesting premiums of 8.7% for properties with immediate access to feeder routes, compared to those located within 5–10 min walking distance (Munoz Raskin, 2010). A 2013 study of Bogotá's *TransMilenio* system suggested that the areas it served experienced densification, especially in the urban periphery (Bocarejo et al., 2013). Research into changes to Bogotá's built-up areas suggests that rents for multifamily housing units closer to the BRT network were higher per square

Fig. 8 BRT system in Bogotá, Colombia. *Source: Vergel-Tovar, C.E., 2019. Picture BRT Bogotá, Colombia.*

meter than for housing units located further away (Cervero and Dai, 2014). A recent study on the impacts of the BRT system on land values in Bogota found mixed outcomes, showing that the system in Bogota appears to have positive effects on land values for low-income areas but no effects on medium and high-income areas, and even some negative effects associated with externalities of the system such as noise (Guzman et al., 2021).

An anticipatory planning study of the potential effects of the Ecatepec BRT in Mexico suggested that the announcement of the mass transit project had no effect at all on property values (Flores Dewey, 2012). However, research into the opening of two lines of the BRT network in Mexico City found a certain positive effect on land prices. In particular, Line 1 was associated with a 15% increase in land prices, although no similar effect was found for Line 2 (Velandia, 2013). The study of the BRT network in the Colombian city of Barranquilla (Garza, 2017) found that land prices increased when construction activities started but that the effects on land prices were negative or null when the inauguration date was approaching. The system took several years to build and this was probably a significant contributor to the finding. D'Elia et al. (2020) examined the recent implementation of the BRT network in Buenos Aires to gauge its effects on property values. The study used spatial hedonic pricing models and propensity scores, concluding that the BRT had non-statistically significant impacts on property prices. The BRT corridor serves an already consolidated area that attracts several trips to downtown Buenos Aires, principally benefitting transit users commuting to the area of study.

A comparative study examining the urban development impacts of the Bogotá and Quito BRT networks produced mixed results. In Bogotá, areas served by BRT stations had higher concentrations of development in terms of square meters built, and approved development licenses. In Quito, building prices increased along the *Corredor Norte* (3%) and the *Trolebús* corridor (5%), but fell along the *Ecovía* corridor (2.5%). However, prices of single-family housing units along *Corredor Norte* increased by 9.4% (Rodriguez et al., 2016). A more detailed study of Bogotá and Quito (Vergel-Tovar, 2016) found minimal effects for built-up areas and mixed results for land use changes (residential and commercial) in areas served by the BRT network in Bogotá. The study also found effects along the *Ecovía* corridor in Quito and minimal effects for the consolidated *Trolebús* and *Corredor Central Norte* corridors in Quito. The qualitative data analysis identified five emerging themes that might explaining the difficulties coordinating transport and land use in Bogotá and Quito.

Another comparative study (Vergel-Tovar and Camargo, 2019) that used secondary sources to explore the land development impacts of BRT networks in five Colombian cities (Bogotá, Pereira, Cali, Barranquilla, and Bucaramanga) had mixed results. Especially in the periphery, most areas served by BRT terminals experienced significant changes in terms of new development. Private sector responses occurred in all areas, with commercial and housing developments built in close proximity to the BRT terminals, which were sometimes initiated prior to the BRT investment itself, in anticipation of the implementation of the mass transit system. The authors of this study considered these impacts to be *missed opportunities* for TOD, given that the land developments in question were characterized by private sector responses, in the absence of urban management tools designed to capture land value increments.

3.4 The effects of cable car systems

The cable car system in Medellin (Fig. 9) was the subject of a comprehensive study examining the socioeconomic and physical conditions of areas served by this type of transit system. The authors suggested that the public sector should intervene further to improve infrastructure, facilities and urban upgrading in order to maximize benefits for low-income groups (Brand and Dávila, 2011).

Fig. 9 Cable Car system in Medellín, Colombia. *Source: Vergel-Tovar, C.E., 2021. Picture Cable Car Medellín, Colombia.*

Cerdá et al. (2012) examined the influence of the *MetroCable* on social cohesion and changes in criminality indicators. It employed a natural experiment to analyze the influence of the transit system on reduced violence levels in neighborhoods, concluding that the homicide rate fell by 66% in the treatment groups (neighborhoods with access to *MetroCable* compared to control groups). Another study confirms the reduction by 41% of the number of homicides, between 2004 and 2006, in the influenced area of the Cable Car in Medellin, and a reduction by 49% between 2004 and 2012, in comparison to the reduction of crime in the city (Canavire-Bacarreza et al., 2016). These results suggest that investment in cable cars, alongside improvements in infrastructure in peripheral informal neighborhoods, is linked to reduced levels of violence. As cable cars are a recent urban transit innovation in the LAC region research is incipient, and what does exist focuses on the role they play in saving travel time and increasing access to jobs.

4. The relationship between mass transit investments and urban form with travel behavior

This section provides an overview of recent studies focusing on mass transit provision, accessibility, urban form and travel behavior. In the LAC region, there are a limited number of studies on the relationships between urban form and travel behavior associated with mass transit systems. Some explore the influence of built environment attributes on mass transit ridership. Others examine issues related to accessibility for low-income groups and changes in travel patterns resulting from mass transit investments. Most of the research reviewed in this section focuses on Metro systems and BRT networks, as the more recent implementation of LRT systems has yet to produce evidence to the literature. The section also includes a few studies on cable car systems. Fig. 10 shows the associations of the literature review by keywords. Although BRT is still predominant, emerging studies are looking at Cable Cars, while equity is taking a more dominant role in recent studies. At the end of this section is Table 2 with a summary of the literature review.

4.1 Metro systems and BRT networks

Studies analyzing the influence of metro systems on travel behavior are to a great extent lacking in LAC-related literature. Guerra et al. (2018) focused on a full range of transit services. They examined travel patterns of residents of Mexico's 100 largest urban centers and found that in denser environments with better transit supply, commuters are less likely to drive. The study of the expansion of the Line B of the Metro system in Mexico City also provides insights regarding changes on travel, this study was cited in Section 3 as well. Based on statistical analysis of household travel surveys, this study found that residents served by the expansion of the Line B are more likely to travel by Metro (Guerra, 2014).

Direct demand studies regarding BRT systems suggest a significant influence of urban form on mass transit ridership. Estupiñán and Rodríguez (2008) conducted statistical analyses to determine the influence of specific local accessibility attributes on station boarding in Bogotá. The study found that pedestrian-oriented environments with barriers to automobile use are supportive of the BRT network in terms of ridership levels. Direct ridership models conducted with built environment data collected in the vicinity of BRT stations in seven cities in Latin America provide insights regarding the influence of urban form on travel in the region. Vergel-Tovar and Rodriguez (2018) found positive associations between BRT ridership and built environment factors that describe compact urban forms involving multifamily residential developments mixed with commercial uses and the presence of institutional buildings and public facilities. The study also found that

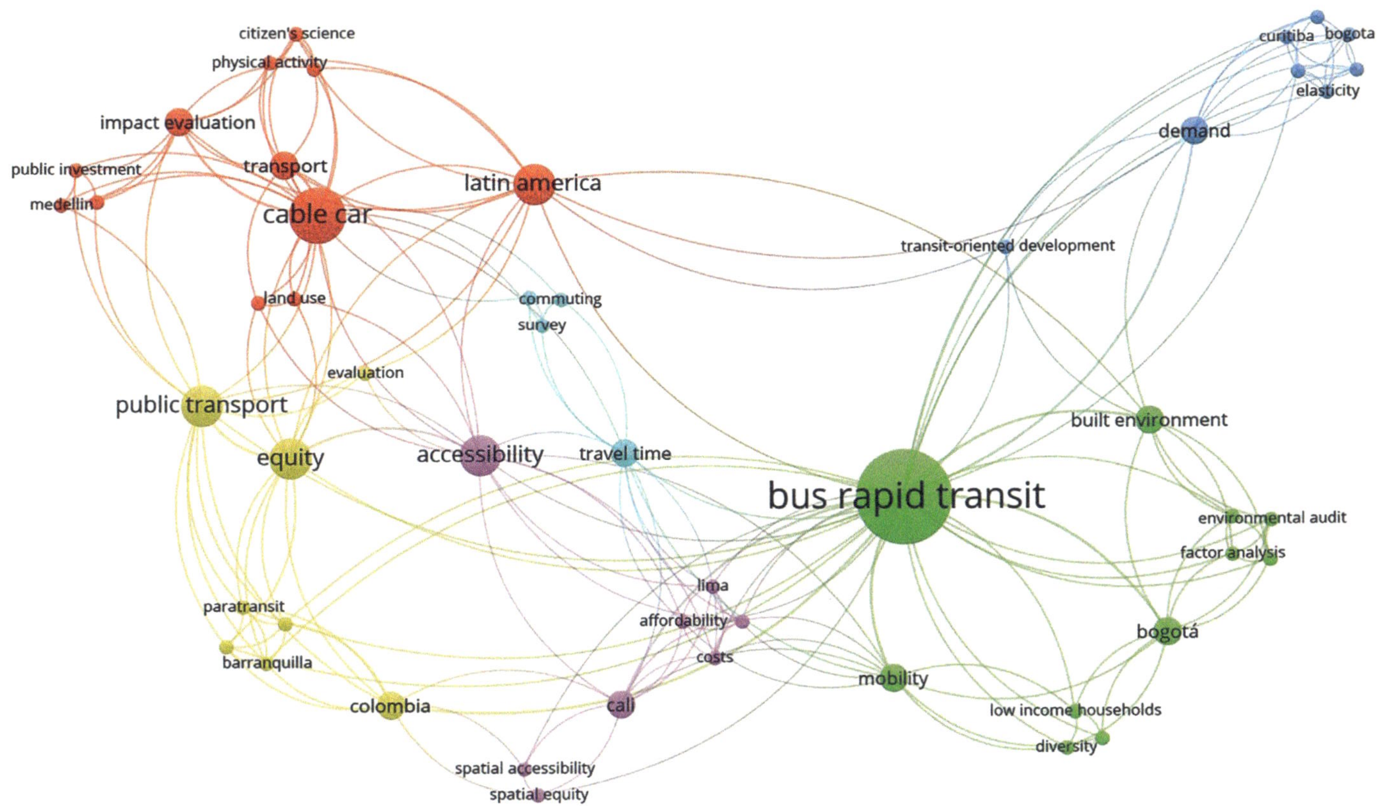

Fig. 10 Network of keywords and associations, literature review: mass transit investments, urban form and travel behavior studies. *Source: Own elaboration with VOSViewer (2021).*

Table 2 Literature Review, the relationship between mass transit investments with urban form and travel behavior: A review of research findings.

City, Country	Year	Authors	Title	Research design and methods	Main findings
Metro and BRT					
Bogota, Colombia	2008	Estupiñán, N. and D. A. Rodríguez	The relationship between urban form and station boardings for Bogota's BRT	Two-stage least square regression, exploratory factor analysis	Built environment attributes such as support for walking and barriers to car use close to BRT stations are associated with higher ridership levels
Cali, Colombia	2012	Delmelle, E. C. and I. Casas	Evaluating the spatial equity of bus rapid transit-based accessibility patterns in a developing country: The case of Cali, Colombia	Spatial data analysis	The study found gaps in the coverage of the BRT system for high-income and low-income groups, but the BRT system serves better middle-income areas
Mexico City, Mexico	2014	Guerra, E.	Mexico City's suburban land use and transit connection: The effects of the Line B Metro expansion	Statistical models (binomial logit, OLS, Tobit and Poisson regression) with household travel surveys data	Expansion new metro line: residents in areas served by the network expansion are more likely to use the metro system
Cali, Colombia Lima, Peru	2016	Scholl, L., C. P. Bouillon, et al.	Urban Transport and Poverty: Mobility and Accessibility Effects of IDB-supported BRT Systems in Cali and Lima	Mixed-methods	BRT coverage: the study found gaps in the coverage area of the BRT system, especially for low-income groups. Access to the BRT system in some areas is possible via informal transit services, mostly in Lima

Continued

Table 2 Literature Review, the relationship between mass transit investments with urban form and travel behavior: A review of research findings.—cont'd

City, Country	Year	Authors	Title	Research design and methods	Main findings
Bogota, Colombia	2017	Combs, T. S.	Examining changes in travel patterns among lower wealth households after BRT investment in Bogotá, Colombia	Difference-in-differences research design	The study found that the BRT system had no substantial or significant impact in the ability for low-income households to meet their regular travel needs
Mexico's 100 largest urban areas, Mexico	2018	Guerra, E., C. Caudillo, et al.	Urban form, transit supply, and travel behavior in Latin America: Evidence from Mexico's 100 largest urban areas	Statistical analysis (households survey)	Built environment attributes and transit: residents in areas with higher densities and residents in areas better served by transit services (all forms of transit) are less likely to drive (commuting trips)
Bogota, Curitiba, Sao Paulo, Goainia, Quito, Guayaquil, Ciudad de Guatemala	2018	Vergel-Tovar, C. E. and D. A. Rodriguez	The ridership performance of the built environment for BRT systems: Evidence from Latin America	Direct ridership models, factor analysis, cluster analysis	BRT ridership and built environment factors: built environment factor measuring compactness with presence of multifamily residential uses were positively associated with ridership; built environment factor measuring presence of public and institutional land uses along the corridor were positively associated with BRT ridership. BRT station typologies: BRT stations with a mixture of land use, presence of institutional uses and public facilities were positively associated with ridership (mostly BRT terminals and stations with high quality pedestrian-friendly environments)

Curitiba, Bogota, and Quito	2019	Vergel-Tovar, C. E.	Is density enough? Population density and bus rapid transit ridership demand in Curitiba, Quito and Bogota	Log-linear regression models, direct demand models	Positive association between population density and BRT ridership in Curitiba with an elasticity of 0.26, positive association between population density and BRT ridership in Bogota with an elasticity of 0.25 (BRT Terminals)
Barranquilla, Colombia	2020	Santana Palacios, M., A. Cochran, et al.	Bus rapid transit arrives in Barranquilla, Colombia: Understanding a changing landscape through residents' travel experiences	Semi-structured interviews with BRT users	Travel experience of BRT users: the study found differences in the travel experience for users getting access to trunk corridors and those getting access via feeder routes. Those users getting access via feeder routes experienced long walking distances and higher waiting times
São Paulo, Rio de Janeiro, Curitiba and Recife, Brazil	2020	Boisjoly, G., B. Serra, et al.	Accessibility measurements in São Paulo, Rio de Janeiro, Curitiba and Recife, Brazil	Spatial data analysis: accessibility to jobs and mass transit	Four metropolitan areas analysis: the study found that lower-income households are in disadvantaged in terms of access to public transport services
Cable Cars					
Medellin, Colombia	2014	Bocarejo, J. P., Portilla, I. J., Velásquez, J. M., Cruz, M. N., Peña, A., and Oviedo, D. R.	An innovative transit system and its impact on low income users: the case of the Metrocable in Medellín	Difference-in-difference models	Access to employment centers, travel times and costs: residents of areas served by the Cable Car double their access to the number of opportunities that can be reached through the system. The study found small changes on travel times reduction and cost savings for residents served by the Cable Car

Continued

Table 2 Literature Review, the relationship between mass transit investments with urban form and travel behavior: A review of research findings.—cont'd

City, Country	Year	Authors	Title	Research design and methods	Main findings
Medellin, Colombia	2016	Canavire-Bacarreza, G. Duque, J. C. Urrego, J. A.	Moving citizens and deterring criminals: Innovation in public transport facilities	Spatial difference-in-difference, spatial analytical level using max-p modeling	Crime reduction: the study found that the number of homicides in the area served by the Cable Car decreased by 41% (2004–2006) and by 49% (2004 and 2012) more in comparison to the general crime reduction in the city
La Paz, Bolivia	2018	Garsous, G., Suárez-Alemán, A., and Serebrisky, T.	Cable cars in urban transport: Travel time savings from La Paz-El Alto (Bolivia)	Statistical analysis comparing commuting travel times of using cable cars (treatment group) over other transport modes (control group)	Travel times: the study found that the Cable Car reduced by an average of 22% the commuting times in comparison to other transportation modes
Bogota, Colombia	2020	Sarmiento, O. L., et. Al.	Urban Transformations and Health: Methods for TrUST—a Natural Experiment Evaluating the Impacts of a Mass Transit Cable Car in Bogotá, Colombia	Quasi-experimental study using a mixed-methods approach	Base line: this study developed a comprehensive approach to study the impacts of the Cable Car TransMicable on environmental and social determinants related to health outcomes, physical activity and perceptions of residents living in proximity to the system through a quasi-experimental design with a control group

BRT stations with public facilities and institutional land uses are positively associated with BRT ridership, especially in the case of BRT terminals. A similar study exploring associations between population density and BRT ridership in Curitiba, Quito and Bogotá found elasticities of 0.26 in Curitiba and 0.25 in Bogotá, only for BRT terminals (Vergel-Tovar, 2019a).

Recent studies are looking at accessibility issues for low-income groups in relation to mass transit investments. The study of the BRT system in Bogota found no clear relationship between BRT investments and significant changes in travel patterns for low-income households, especially in urban peripheries where access to the system is provided by feeder routes (Combs, 2017). In particular, there is no relationship between the BRT network and tour frequency or travel purpose for low-income residents. Research on Cali and Lima has examined accessibility issues associated with the implementation of BRT networks. In the case of Cali, one study found that the BRT network provides better access for middle-income groups than for their high- or low-income counterparts (Delmelle and Casas, 2012). A comparative study of Cali and Lima found that it is not easy to extend BRT networks to urban peripheries that are principally inhabited by low-income groups. The study also found that, because of gaps in coverage of the BRT networks in both cities—and especially in Lima—low-income residents tend to access the BRT network using informal transit services (Scholl et al., 2016). A recent multi-city study examining accessibility to jobs and mass transit in São Paulo, Rio de Janeiro, Curitiba and Recife, in Brazil, found that lower-income households face difficulties in accessing job opportunity areas with the current supply of mass transit services (Boisjoly et al., 2020). The study of travel experiences of BRT users in Barranquilla also suggest that residents served by the system find advantages in reduction of travel times but with strong differences in time savings for those who access the system with feeder routes. The travel experience is less attractive for BRT users who need to walk more and experience higher waiting times, especially those users taking feeder routes (Santana Palacios et al., 2020).

4.2 Cable car systems

This section focuses on research examining changes in travel times, access to job opportunity areas and crime rates. Several studies examine the improvements in mobility indicators for residents located in the areas now served by cable cars. A study of the cable car connecting *El Alto and La Paz* (Bolivia) found a reduction of 22% in travel time equivalent to a daily reduction of 9 min for residents with access to the transit system compared to control groups (Garsous et al., 2019). Bocarejo et al. (2014) found that access to employment opportunities and urban services was doubled for users of the *Acevedo-Santo Domingo Savio* line of Medellin's *MetroCable*, compared to control groups. More recently, a quasi-experimental study about the Metrocable in Bogotá identified health benefits for the residents served by the Cable Car system (Sarmiento et al., 2020).

5. Discussion

This section provides a general discussion of the issues presented in this chapter, providing a summary of the research findings and methods used in the studies included in the literature review.

5.1 Mass transit investment, land use and economic development: Research methods and findings

In general, different research methods are used to examine different transit modes. In studies of metro systems the following methods are used: hedonic price models, before and after data analysis (survey and land price data), fixed effects models, and difference-in-difference models. Studies of LRT systems use mixed-methods, again including hedonic pricing models, qualitative analysis with participant observation, fieldwork visits and spatial data analysis. Quantitative approaches dominate the literature on BRT networks. Studies use hedonic price models, propensity score matching techniques, difference-in-difference models, quasi-experimental research design with treatment and control areas, before and after and spatial data analyses, and matching techniques. Several studies also employ qualitative analysis to further explain quantitative results.

Research findings for the LAC region vary significantly by mass transit mode. To date, no studies have explored urban development impacts of cable cars in the region. Studies on the impacts of metro systems are limited. Given that several cities are working toward implementing metro systems, we might expect the number of studies in the region to grow in the future but, for the moment, only the cases of Santiago de Chile, Mexico City, Sao Paulo and Buenos Aires have been examined. Results suggest that metro systems have heterogeneous impacts on the urban fabric. In some cases, the initial announcement of plans to expand these systems appears to affect housing prices and land values, while in others they have no discernible impact.

However, all the studies confirm that metro systems have a positive effect on housing prices and land values, especially when measuring accessibility benefits in terms of distance to metro stations. Research on Sao Paulo suggests that certain land use planning tools, such as density bonus, may open the door for further research examining the mechanisms of value capture, an important financing instrument.

Metro systems are being implemented in the region at a vertiginous rate with new metro systems and expansions appearing in Lima, Fortaleza, Panama, Salvador de Bahia, Quito and Bogotá. Panama City implemented its system in 2014 with underground and elevated infrastructure, with stations like *San Miguelito* in Panama highlighting the challenges of providing infrastructure for active mobility (pedestrians and bike users) that is integrated with elevated infrastructure at the intersection of two mass transit system lines (Fig. 11). Lima (Peru) and Bogotá (Colombia) are also expanding and designing elevated metro infrastructure. Certainly, all these recent projects provide an opportunity to study the impacts of new metro systems on the urban fabric as well as testing hypotheses based on previous studies conducted in cities like Buenos Aires, Santiago, and Sao Paulo.

Findings for LRT systems suggest the complexity involved in the insertion of these mass transit systems in the urban fabric, including land

Fig. 11 *San Miguelito* Metro Station, Panama City, Panama. *Source: Uribe, A., 2020. Picture San Miguelito Metro Station. Panama City, Panama.*

acquisition issues and resettlements dynamics caused in particular by the requirement to change road sections in already consolidated urban areas. Studies examining property prices suggest that the incentives provided by this kind of corridor are greater for commercial uses, while real estate dynamics also suggest that land use development is intensifying because of accrued accessibility benefits. Qualitative studies suggest that increases in the area of available public space are associated with land acquisition processes that affect residents of resettlement or relocation projects, leading to compensation issues concerning land values and appraisals. Considering the complexity of implementing LRT projects in terms of the potential transformation of road sections, especially near the stations and at some intersections, future studies should employ multiple methods for in-depth exploration of the impacts of these systems on land development and travel behavior.

Although few studies examine the impacts of LRT systems on the urban fabric in the region, the increasing prevalence of this type of mass transit systems will surely promote further research, which will, in turn, be required to anticipate their potential effects, especially in conservation areas such as historic city centers and to identify opportunities to implement value capture mechanisms. Before and after studies will provide insights into property values and land use changes due to accessibility benefits created by the systems. It would be useful for future studies on the effects of this system to focus on land use changes and opportunities for promoting transit-oriented features around the stations in line with heritage preservation measures. The implementation of LRT systems connecting downtown areas in Latin America with urban peripheries and expansion areas also constitute an opportunity to test hypotheses regarding urban impacts by comparing different sections along the mass transit infrastructure.

Results for BRT networks also suggest heterogeneous impacts. The review conducted in this chapter confirms that BRT has the potential of land developments, but in line with (Stokenberga, 2014), there presence of BRT is a necessary factor but not the only one needed to promote a more intense land use and development and increments in land values. There are premiums associated with proximity to stations because of the accessibility benefits provided by BRT networks. Some studies suggest that premiums on property and land values fluctuate spatially, implying that BRT networks have heterogeneous impacts in which other attributes of the built environment influence the relationship. To date, there is no evidence to suggest that the announcement of plans to construct BRT lines affects property and land values. In line with (Zhang and Yen, 2020) meta-analysis, there is also a gap in the LAC region regarding studies of BRT systems impacts on land and property values over time. This review confirms that there is still no evidence that suggest anticipatory effects of BRT systems on land and property values. As mentioned previously in a BRT systems literature review conducted by Deng and Nelson (2011) there is still little research in the LAC region on built-up areas and land use. The findings obtained to date, suggest that, as in the case of LRT, commercial uses are positively associated with proximity to stations, but that there are fewer residential uses near LRT corridors after the implementation of the mass transit system, principally because of the negative externalities associated with the operation of these systems. BRT impacts on the density and expansion of built-up areas are also more intense within the influence area of terminals, mostly located in urban peripheries.

5.2 Mass transit investments, urban form and travel behavior: Research methods and findings

Quantitative research methods dominate the studies examining the influence of urban form on travel in the context of mass transit investments. Methods include two-stage least square regression with exploratory factor analysis, spatial data analysis, mixed-methods (survey data and interviews) and difference-in-difference methods. Other studies used statistical analysis of survey data, direct ridership models with factor and cluster analysis, log-linear regression models (elasticities), propensity score matching, before and after data analysis (treatment and control groups), combined with qualitative analysis.

Research findings for metro systems and BRT networks suggest that the built environment plays an important role in explaining travel behavior and thus its relevance to mass transit. Studies suggest that high-quality pedestrian environments with mixed land uses support transit. However, they also highlight the challenges associated with improving access to mass transit for low-income groups, who tend to be located in urban peripheries and use other means of transport such as informal transit to access to mass transit systems. The analysis of distribution and modal split of commuting changes when metro systems serves residents shows a reduction in private vehicle use, especially in urban areas with a higher concentration of jobs. Findings regarding the role of the built environment on transit use suggest that compact urban forms with multifamily uses combined with institutional land uses support the ridership levels of mass transit.

Studies on the impacts of cable cars on the urban fabric are still incipient; however, mixed methods approaches applied in Medellin suggest that these mass transit investments require different techniques to capture their effects on complex urban environments. A number of studies suggest that cable cars are changing the current panorama while others examining the influence of cable cars on travel times, access to jobs, and crime issues suggest that this innovation is leading to new hypotheses for future research projects. The literature shows that the most significant impact is associated with the reduction of travel times for residents served by cable cars and that local residents also gained greater access to job centers. The implementation of cable cars in urban peripheries is also associated with lower crime rates, and changes associated with the implementation of other policies such as the development of public facilities and social programs in the intervention areas.

However, mass transit systems still face the challenge of interacting with informal transit services, especially in urban peripheries. Although areas with urban forms characterized by higher densities and better transit supply revealed that commuters are less likely to drive, further research is required to understand the implications of the coexistence of mass transit systems and informal transport services in the LAC region. Existing studies examining improved access to public transport services, including mass transit, suggest that lower-income groups remain at a disadvantage in terms of access to jobs and core activity nodes.

6. Conclusions and further research

Coordination between transport and land use is a desirable outcome, bearing in mind the rapid urban growth experienced by LAC cities in recent decades, which has transformed the region into one of the most urbanized in the world. Given that a number of LAC cities have implemented mass transit systems in already urbanized areas, an interesting debate has emerged concerning the challenge of ensuring integrated transit and land use planning. The implementation of mass transit systems in already urbanized areas along consolidated urban environments is intended to respond to current transportation demands. At the same time, the implementation of these systems in areas where new developments may take place require the application of land management tools to guarantee the integration between transport and land use planning. The literature review in this chapter suggests that this coordination is more important now than it has ever been. Understanding and anticipating the effects of mass transit on the urban fabric will provide key inputs to promote sustainable urban development in the region. Examining the factors that explain travel behavior associated with urban form features and mass transit investments can also help to design cities with sustainable mobility at all levels.

The literature review regarding the transportation and land use connection in LAC suggests that impacts of mass transit investments on the urban fabric are heterogeneous. Although mass transit investments have positive effects on land and property values, these impacts are not homogenous across space. This suggests that value capture mechanisms might be difficult to apply without urban management instruments associated with accessibility benefits brought about by mass transit investments. The appreciation of housing prices given by accessibility benefits constitute another challenge in LAC, as low-income groups usually access land and housing in urban peripheries, making it even more difficult for them to improve their mobility and accessibility. Few studies have explored the relationship between mass transit investments and land use changes, with some insights regarding effects on land developments and influence on more compact urban forms. Future studies examining land use changes are required, and the expansion of new rail-based and BRT projects in the region will certainly provide new opportunities to explore this relationship further.

The associations between mass transit investments, urban form, and travel behavior also highlight the difficulties for mass transit infrastructure to improve access for low-income groups. The high levels of informality in the LAC region in terms of urban growth, access to land and housing and the informal economy render the study of travel behavior issues even more challenging. Although some studies suggest that transit-oriented development features such as mixed land uses, high-quality pedestrian environments, and proximity between commercial, residential and institutional land uses support ridership levels of mass transit systems, there is still a significant share of the transport demand, which is captured by informal transit. This issue is also associated with the fact that mass transit infrastructure is built far from low-income neighborhoods. As mentioned above, cable cars are changing this and future studies on associations between this innovative transit solution, urban form, and travel behavior will provide additional insights.

Future research in the LAC region may seize the opportunity of current efforts to implement mass transit projects in large cities. Although cities are moving rapidly to this front, research on the influence of these investments on the urban fabric and the analysis of travel behavior issues are not keeping pace. First, lack of data is one of the most important barriers to developing more research into the coordination between transport and land use in the region. It is important to promote the culture of producing reliable and open data sources on the urban spatial structure of cities and even more important to make sure that databases capture information relating to the periods before and after mass transit investments. Second, timing is another challenge, considering that transportation investments are expensive and that planning stages are therefore usually shorter in comparison to those required for land use planning processes. Causality becomes the next step in the process following several research projects analyzing the effects using cross sectional data analysis.

Third, the analysis of social and environmental impacts constitutes a challenge that requires mixed-methods approaches, promoting more quasi-experimental research designs, and qualitative methods with fieldwork observation. Mixed methods approaches clearly suggest an interesting path to follow in order to gain in-depth understanding of the transport and land use connection in the LAC region. Emerging studies are incorporating qualitative data analysis to further examine the impacts, especially from a social and environmental perspective. These approaches provide additional insights regarding mass transit impacts and more importantly, some unintended consequences of transport and mobility infrastructure projects, especially those related to the potential displacement of low-income groups further away from main activity nodes.

Fourth, the increasing interest in the transport and land use connection in the LAC region by donors constitutes an opportunity to develop more studies with a comprehensive approach. Multilateral organizations are currently promoting a culture of research and encouraging studies examining the potential impacts of mass transit investments. Scholars are exploring the implementation of research methods and techniques that have already been used in other regions, as well as associated issues such as potential gentrification dynamics and relocation of communities within the influence area of mass transit investments. Mixed-methods research projects can certainly provide key inputs that help identify new variables for quantitative research methods and suggest ways of managing the potential unintended consequences of mass transit investments in terms of equity.

Fifth, it is important to develop more studies on value capture and land use issues, including the relationship with the location of affordable housing. Accessibility and affordability issues are clearly important in the transport and land use connection in the region, especially in terms of understanding sustainable urban development from a comprehensive approach. In terms of travel behavior issues, most of the emerging literature is related to Metro, BRT and Cable Cars, with studies mostly focused at the system level, and thus is expected that in the near future new studies will focus on the individual level studies.

Finally, further research will be needed to understand the connection between transport systems and land use, in order to compare research findings with those for other regions. The urban spatial structure of cities in the LAC region requires innovative approaches to better understand the influence of informal urban growth dynamics on the transport and land use connection. Sustainable urban development relies heavily on sustainable transport. Recent research in the LAC region suggests the importance of equity in guaranteeing access to all urban residents and spreading the benefits of accessibility widely in urban areas.

Acknowledgments

The author gratefully acknowledges the support of Universidad de los Andes for this work. He would also like to thank Martin Silva for his support in creating the ArcGIS maps for this chapter; Carla Hermida, Nicole Fernández De Córdova and Andres Pauta Pesántez for the picture of Cuenca, Ecuador; and Alvaro Uribe for the picture of Panama City (Panama). The author would like to express his thanks to Professor Jason Cao for his kind invitation to take part in this publication. Last but not least, the author would like to express his gratitude to Tiziana Laudato for the multiple reviews of this manuscript.

References

Agostini, C., Palmucci, G., 2008. Capitalización anticipada del metro de Santiago en el precio de las viviendas. El Trimestre Económico 2 (298), 403–431.

Alonso, W., 1964. Location and Land Use; Toward a General Theory of Land Rent. Harvard University Press, Cambridge. 1964.

Asahi, K., 2016. Better Urban Transport Improves Labour Market Outcomes: Evidence from a Subway Expansion in Chile. Available at SSRN 2781807, https://doi.org/10.2139/ssrn.2781807.

Bocarejo, J.P., Portilla, I., Pérez, M.A., 2013. Impact of transmilenio on density, land use, and land value in Bogotá. Res. Transp. Econ. 40 (1), 78–86. https://doi.org/10.1016/j.retrec.2012.06.030.

Bocarejo, J.P., Portilla, I.J., Velásquez, J.M., Cruz, M.N., Peña, A., Oviedo, D.R., 2014. An innovative transit system and its impact on low income users: the case of the Metrocable in Medellín. J. Transp. Geogr. 39, 49–61.

Boisjoly, G., Serra, B., Oliveira, G.T., El-Geneidy, A., 2020. Accessibility measurements in São Paulo, Rio de Janeiro, Curitiba and Recife, Brazil. J. Transp. Geogr. 82, 102551. https://doi.org/10.1016/j.jtrangeo.2019.102551.

Brand, P., Dávila, J.D., 2011. Mobility innovation at the urban margins: Medellín's Metrocables. City 15 (6), 647–661.
BRTDATA.ORG, 2020. Global BRT Data. Retrieved 10/20/2020, from https://brtdata.org/location/latin_america.
Canavire-Bacarreza, G., Duque, J.C., et al., 2016. Moving Citizens and Deterring Criminals: Innovation in Public Transport Facilities. CAF Development Bank Of Latinamerica.
Canon, L., Jia, W., Darido, G., 2017. Innovation in the Air: Using Cable Cars for Urban Transport. Retrieved from World Bank Blogs website https://blogs.worldbank.org/transport/innovation-air-using-cable-cars-urban-transport.
Cerdá, M., Morenoff, J.D., Hansen, B.B., Tessari Hicks, K.J., Duque, L.F., Restrepo, A., Diez-Roux, A.V., 2012. Reducing violence by transforming neighborhoods: a natural experiment in Medellín, Colombia. Am. J. Epidemiol. 175 (10), 1045–1053.
Cervero, R., 1984. Journal report: light rail transit and urban development. J. Am. Plann. Assoc. 50 (2), 133–147. https://doi.org/10.1080/01944368408977170.
Cervero, 1998. The Transit Metropolis: A Global Inquiry. Island Press, Washington, D.C.
Cervero, R., 2013. Linking urban transport and land use in developing countries. J. Transp. Land Use 6 (1), 7–24.
Cervero, R., Dai, D., 2014. BRT TOD: leveraging transit oriented development with bus rapid transit investments. Transp. Policy 36, 127–138. https://doi.org/10.1016/j.tranpol.2014.08.001.
Combs, T.S., 2017. Examining changes in travel patterns among lower wealth households after BRT investment in Bogotá, Colombia. J. Transp. Geogr. 60, 11–20. https://doi.org/10.1016/j.jtrangeo.2017.02.004.
Costa, A.B., 2018. Transportation and Urban Development in São Paulo: Exploring How Transportation has Shaped and Still Shapes the City. Advisor, Prof. Dr. Ciro Biderman. Escola de Administração de Empresas de São Paulo. Fundação Getúlio Vargas, São Paulo. Retrieved from https://bibliotecadigital.fgv.br/dspace/bitstream/handle/10438/25695/DoctoralDissertation_AdrianoBorgesCosta.pdf.
D'Elia, V.V., Grand, M.C., León, S., 2020. Bus rapid transit and property values in Buenos Aires: combined spatial hedonic pricing and propensity score techniques. Res. Transp. Econ. 80, 100814. https://doi.org/10.1016/j.retrec.2020.100814.
Delmelle, E.C., Casas, I., 2012. Evaluating the spatial equity of bus rapid transit-based accessibility patterns in a developing country: the case of Cali, Colombia. Transp. Policy 20, 36–46. https://doi.org/10.1016/j.tranpol.2011.12.001.
Deng, T., Nelson, J.D., 2011. Recent developments in bus rapid transit: a review of the literature. Transplant. Rev. 31 (1), 69–96. https://doi.org/10.1080/01441647.2010.492455.
Economist, 2017. Subways in the Sky: Why Latin America is Seeing a Cable-Car Boom. The Economist. Retrieved from https://www.economist.com/the-americas/2017/10/26/why-latin-america-is-seeing-a-cable-car-boom.
Estupiñán, N., Rodríguez, D.A., 2008. The relationship between urban form and station boardings for Bogota's BRT. Transp. Res. A Policy Pract. 42 (2), 296–306. https://doi.org/10.1016/j.tra.2007.10.006.
Flores Dewey, O., 2012. The Value of a Promise: Housing Price Impacts of Plans to Build Mass Transit in Ecatepec, Mexico Working Paper. Lincoln Institute of Land Policy.
Freitas, C.F.S., 2017. Undoing the right to the city: world cup investments and informal settlements in Fortaleza, Brazil. J. Urban Aff. 39 (7), 953–969. https://doi.org/10.1080/07352166.2017.1328974.
Garsous, G., Suárez-Alemán, A., Serebrisky, T., 2019. Cable cars in urban transport: travel time savings from La Paz-El Alto (Bolivia). Transp. Policy 0967-070X. 75, 171–182. https://doi.org/10.1016/j.tranpol.2017.05.005.

Garza, N., 2017. Transport infrastructure and the spatial dynamics of real estate markets. In: Paper Presented at the International Symposium: Transportation Innovations and Urban Land in Latin America, Berkeley, CA.

Globo, 2016. Teleférico do Alemão, no Rio, é fechado por falta de pagamento. Globo. Retrieved from http://g1.globo.com/rio-de-janeiro/noticia/2016/10/teleferico-do-alemao-no-rio-e-fechado-por-falta-de-pagamento.html.

Guerra, E., 2014. Mexico City's suburban land use and transit connection: the effects of the line B metro expansion. Transp. Policy 32, 105–114. https://doi.org/10.1016/j.tranpol.2013.12.011.

Guerra, E., Caudillo, C., Monkkonen, P., Montejano, J., 2018. Urban form, transit supply, and travel behavior in Latin America: evidence from Mexico's 100 largest urban areas. Transp. Policy 69, 98–105. https://doi.org/10.1016/j.tranpol.2018.06.001.

Gutiérrez Torres, K., 2019. Espacio público: transformación y cohesión urbana. El caso del tranvía de Ayacucho en Medellín. (Master). Universidad Nacional de Colombia, Sede Medellín, Medellín. Retrieved from https://repositorio.unal.edu.co/handle/unal/77576?show=full.

Guzman, L.A., Enríquez, H.D., Hessel, P., 2021. BRT system in Bogotá and urban effects: more residential land premiums? Res. Transp. Econ., 101039. https://doi.org/10.1016/j.retrec.2021.101039.

Heinrichs, D., Bernet, J.S., 2014. Public transport and accessibility in informal settlements: aerial cable cars in Medellín, Colombia. Transp. Res. Proc. 4 (1), 55–67.

Hermida, C., Moreno, D., Pacheco, D., Tonón, L., Cortés, A., 2018. Impacto en el valor de ventas y arriendos de inmuebles con uso residencial y comercial, provocado por la implementación de un sistema tranviario en la ciudad de Cuenca, Ecuador. Revista 180 42, 1–13. https://doi.org/10.32995/rev180.Num-42.(2018).art-576.

Hidalgo, D., Velásquez, J.M., 2015. Cables Aéreos: Una solución de movilidad para zonas marginadas. Blog Ciudades Sostenibles. División de Vivienda y Desarrollo Urbano (HUD). Retrieved from https://blogs.iadb.org/ciudades-sostenibles/es/cables-aereos/.

Hine, J., Kamruzzaman, M., 2020. Transport and social exclusion. In: International Encyclopedia of Human Geography. Elsevier, pp. 429–434.

ICOMOS, 2014. Report on the ICOMOS Advisory Mission to Historic Centre of Santa Ana de los Rios de Cuenca (C 863) 18th to 21st August 2014. International Council on Monuments and Sites ICOMOS.

Irazábal, C.e., 2008. Ordinary Places, Extraordinary Events: Citizenship, Democracy and Public Space in Latin America. Routledge, London, New York.

Jones, P., Lucas, K., 2012. The social consequences of transport decision-making: clarifying concepts, synthesising knowledge and assessing implications. J. Transp. Geogr. 21, 4–16. https://doi.org/10.1016/j.jtrangeo.2012.01.012.

Lau, K.H., Kam, B.H., 2005. A cellular automata model for urban land-use simulation. Environ. Plann. B. Plann. Des. 32 (2), 247–263.

Levinson, H., Zimmerman, S., Clinger, J., Rutherford, S., Smith, R., Cracknell, J., Soberman, R., 2003. Bus rapid transit volume 1: case studies in bus rapid transit. In: Transit Cooperative Research Program TCRP Report. vol. 1. Transportation Research Board TRB, Washington DC.

Mejía-Dugand, S., Hjelm, O., Baas, L., Ríos, R.A., 2013. Lessons from the spread of bus rapid transit in Latin America. J. Clean. Prod. 50, 82–90. https://doi.org/10.1016/j.jclepro.2012.11.028.

Mitric, S., 1997. Approaching Metros as Potential Development Projects (W. A. U. D. D. Transportation, Trans.) Working Paper. The World Bank, Washington DC.

Munoz Raskin, R., 2010. Walking accessibility to bus rapid transit: does it affect property values? The case of Bogota, Colombia. Transp. Policy 17 (2), 72–84. https://doi.org/10.1016/j.tranpol.2009.11.002.

Muth, R.F., 1969. Cities and Housing; The Spatial Pattern of Urban Residential Land Use. University of Chicago Press, Chicago (1969).
Network, L., 2021. Ciudad de México estrena su primer metrocable. Retrieved from https://la.network/ciudad-de-mexico-estrena-su-primer-metrocable/.
Perdomo, J., Mendoza, C., Mendieta, J.C., Baquero, A., 2007. Study of the Effect of the TransMilenio Mass Transit Project on the Value of Properties in Bogotá, Colombia Working Paper. Lincoln Institute of Land Policy, Cambridge, MA.
Pulido, D., Darido, G., Munoz-Raskin, R., Moody, J., 2018. The Urban Rail Development Handbook. International Bank for Reconstruction and Development/The World Bank, Washington DC.
Rodrigue, J.-P., 2020. The Geography of Transport Systems. Routledge.
Rodriguez, D., Targa, F., 2004. Value of accessibility to Bogota's bus rapid transit system. Transplant. Rev. 24 (5), 587–610. https://doi.org/10.1080/0144164042000196000.
Rodríguez, D.A., Mojica, C.H., 2009. Capitalization of BRT network expansions effects into prices of non-expansion areas. Transp. Res. A Policy Pract. 43 (5), 560–571.
Rodriguez, D.A., Vergel-Tovar, E., Camargo, W.F., 2016. Land development impacts of BRT in a sample of stops in Quito and Bogotá. Transp. Policy 51, 4–14. https://doi.org/10.1016/j.tranpol.2015.10.002.
Rosanovich, S.A., Di Giovambattista, A.P., 2019. Inversión pública y plusvalías urbanas. Análisis espacial y efectos no lineales de la proximidad de la red de subterráneos sobre los precios de la vivienda en Buenos Aires. Rev. Transp. Territ. 20, 307–337.
Sánchez León, A., Calderon Cockburn, J., Guerrero, L., 1978. Paradero final?: el transporte público en Lima metropolitana. Centro de Estudios y Promoción del Desarrollo, Lima, Perú.
Sandroni, P., 2021. Textos Empíricos V. In: Sandroni, P. (Ed.), Concentração da terra urbana, captura de mais valias e especulação: Outorga onerosa e CEPACS na cidade de São Paulo—Ensaios teóricos, empíricos e ficcionais. Paulo Sandroni, p. 230. São Paulo, Brasil.
Santana Palacios, M., Cochran, A., Bell, C., Hernández Jiménez, U., Leshner, E., Trejo Morales, F., Chatman, D.G., 2020. Bus rapid transit arrives in Barranquilla, Colombia: understanding a changing landscape through residents' travel experiences. Travel Behav. Soc. 21, 131–139. https://doi.org/10.1016/j.tbs.2020.06.003.
Sarmiento, O.L., Higuera-Mendieta, D., et al., 2020. Urban Transformations and Health: Methods for TrUST—a Natural Experiment Evaluating the Impacts of a Mass Transit Cable Car in Bogotá, Colombia. Front. Public Health 8, 64.
Scholl, L., Bouillon, C.P., Oviedo, D., Corsetto, L., Jansson, M., 2016. Urban Transport and Poverty: Mobility and Accessibility Effects of IDB-Supported BRT Systems in Cali and Lima. Inter-American Development Bank.
Smolka, 2013. La urbanización latinoamericana y el argumento por la recuperación de plusvalías. In: Implementación de la Recuperación de Plusvalías en América Latina. Lincoln Institute of Land Policy, Cambridge.
Stokenberga, A., 2014. Does bus rapid transit influence urban land development and property values: a review of the literature. Transplant. Rev. 34 (3), 276–296. https://doi.org/10.1080/01441647.2014.902404.
UN-HABITAT, 2012. State of Latin American and Caribbean Cities. United Nations Human Settlements Programme (UN-Habitat), Nairobi, Kenya, p. 194.
UN-HABITAT, 2013. Planning and Design for Sustainable Urban Mobility: Global Report on Human Settlements 2013. United Nations Human Settlements Programme (UN-Habitat), Nairobi, Kenya, p. 348.
UrbanRail.Net, 2004. Americas: Metro Rail, Subway & Light Rail Systems. Retrieved 12/01/20, 2020, from http://www.urbanrail.net/am/america.htm.

Velandia Naranjo, D.J., 2013. The Impact of Bus Rapid Transit System on Land Prices in Mexico City. Working Paper, Lincoln Institute of Land Policy.

Vergel-Tovar, C.E., 2016. Examining the Reciprocal Relationship Between Bus Rapid Transit and the Built Environment in Latin America (Ph.D. Doctoral Dissertation). University of North Carolina at Chapel Hill, Chapel Hill, North Carolina, United States. Retrieved from https://cdr.lib.unc.edu/concern/dissertations/rr171x488.

Vergel-Tovar, C.E., 2019a. ¿Es la densidad suficiente? Análisis de la relación entre la densidad poblacional y la demanda de pasajeros en los sistemas de transporte público masivo tipo BRT (Bus Rapid Transit) en Curitiba, Quito y Bogotá. Medio Ambient. Urban. 90 (1), 1–22.

Vergel-Tovar, C.E., Camargo, W., 2019. Urban development impacts of bus rapid transit in Colombia: challenges and opportunities. In: Developing Bus Rapid Transit. Edward Elgar Publishing.

Vergel-Tovar, C.E., Rodriguez, D.A., 2018. The ridership performance of the built environment for BRT systems: evidence from Latin America. J. Transp. Geogr. 73, 172–184. https://doi.org/10.1016/j.jtrangeo.2018.06.018.

Villar-Uribe, J.R., 2021. Modernización del transporte público en la periferia urbana:¿ el fin del transporte informal? Caso de estudio: sistema de cable aéreo Transmicable en la localidad de Ciudad Bolívar, Bogotá-Colombia. Rev. Bras. Gest. Urbana 13 (4), 1–18. https://doi.org/10.1590/2175-3369.013.e20190367.

Wright, L., 2011. Bus rapid transit: a review of recent advances. In: Dimitriou, H.T., Gakenheimer, R.A. (Eds.), Urban Transport in the Developing World: A Handbook of Policy and Practice. Edward Elgar, Cheltenham, UK; Northhampton, MA.

Yañez-Pagans, P., Martinez, D., Mitnik, O.A., Scholl, L., Vazquez, A., 2019. Urban transport systems in Latin America and the Caribbean: lessons and challenges. Lat. Am. Econ. Rev. 28 (1), 15. https://doi.org/10.1186/s40503-019-0079-z.

Zhang, M., Yen, B.T.H., 2020. The impact of bus rapid transit (BRT) on land and property values: a meta-analysis. Land Use Policy 96, 104684. https://doi.org/10.1016/j.landusepol.2020.104684.

CHAPTER FOUR

Residential self-selection in the relationship between the built environment and travel behavior: A literature review and research agenda

Bert van Wee[a,*] **and Xinyu Jason Cao**[b]

[a]Faculty of Technology, Policy and Management, Delft University of Technology, Delft, The Netherlands
[b]Humphrey School of Public Affairs, University of Minnesota Twin Cities, Minneapolis, MN, United States
*Corresponding author: e-mail address: g.p.vanwee@tudelft.nl

Contents

Abstract

This chapter gives an overview of the current debates on residential self-selection and presents a related research agenda. Here, we define residential self-selection as "the tendency of people to choose residential locations based on their travel abilities, needs and preferences." Debates relate to theory/causalities (including the role of attitudes), research methods, empirical findings (including the magnitude of the importance of residential self-selection for the influence of the built environment on travel behavior and the dominance of OECD (Organization for Economic Co-operation and Development) countries), and the implications for planning. The main contribution is

Advances in Transport Policy and Planning, Volume 9
ISSN 2543-0009
https://doi.org/10.1016/bs.atpp.2020.08.004

in translating the current debates into a research agenda. Challenging avenues for future research are partly inspired by these debates, and include changing attitudes, qualitative research, multiple causal structures, extending the scope to other areas than residential areas, the existence of threshold values for the strength of preferences to be important for residential self-selection, the role of perceived accessibility, non-OECD countries, and planning implications.

Keywords: Land use, Residential choice, Travel choice, Selection bias, Attitudes, Causality

1. Introduction

Following Mokhtarian and Cao (2008, p. 205), residential self-selectin (RSS) refers to the tendency that people intentionally choose residential locations to meet their travel needs and preferences. For example, a person preferring to travel by train chooses a residential location close to a railway station. RSS studies assume that households can choose their residential location given their scarce financial resources. The level to which this is possible strongly varies geographically, because of varying housing market conditions for both owners and renters. Furthermore, it may be constrained by the availability of mobility instruments. For example, individuals who have no vehicles may have to live in the areas with transit services.

RSS generally results from socio-economic and demographic characteristics and attitudinal factors (Mokhtarian and Cao, 2008). Because almost all studies on the connection between the built environment (BE) and travel behavior control for the former, this chapter emphasizes attitude-induced RSS. The attitudinal factors mainly apply to travel and/or accessibility/residential preferences. In case of travel, the most common focus is on preferences for specific modes or travel behavior attitudes in general; in case of accessibility, researchers study attitudes toward having destination options nearby. People can self-select their place of residence for other reason than travel-related attitudes, such as preferences for specific environmental characteristics of neighborhoods. But only few studies have looked into this option to self-select, examples being Nijland et al. (2007) studying noise-related RSS, and Hamersma et al. (2017) studying environmental-quality related RSS. James et al. (2015) show that people can also self-select based on health-related characteristics, such as body mass index. We limit this chapter to travel attitudes and accessibility related RSS. Furthermore, we limit the chapter to RSS, and not to other forms of self-selection. As Van Wee (2009) argues, people can self-select in other respects, such as the place to work.

In addition RSS studies often emphasize the importance of addressing RSS because it does influence the impact of the BE on travel behavior. BE policies have often been advocated because of their potential role in reducing the negative impacts of travel behavior on the environment. So a better understanding of the impact of the BE on travel behavior needs to explicitly include the role of RSS in this impact. This better understanding is not only of interest scientifically because it informs us the causal relationship between the BE and travel behavior, but also for policy and planning: it makes clear how large the impact of BE policies on travel behavior is, after correcting for RSS. The pros and cons of options for BE policies depend on the impacts of these options on travel behavior and related externalities (noise, pollution, CO_2 emissions, road safety, etc.), and on possibilities for people to live in areas they prefer, both because of accessibility and travel options, but also because of preferences for the BE in general (livability, attractiveness). Because BE changes generally have long term impacts, it is very important that policy makers and planners are well informed about the implications of policy and planning options.

RSS has become a hot topic in the literature on the impact of the BE on travel behavior. A search on November 122,019 in SCOPUS on "residential self-selection" and "residential sorting" resulted in 167 hits and all but one papers were published since 2005. Sixteen of these papers were cited more than 100 times, and 24 papers were published in 2019 (including two papers formally published in 2020), showing that the research topic is very timely. Already as early as 2008 and 2009, two reviews of the RSS literature were published: one about methodologies (Mokhtarian and Cao, 2008), and one on empirical findings (Cao et al., 2009). The latter paper included 38 empirical studies, which showed how rapidly the literature had evolved.

Despite the high number of RSS papers, the debate on methodologies, findings, and implications is very lively, as expressed by a special issue in the *Journal of Transport and Land Use* (Cao, 2014). As discussed in Section 2, although earlier literature focuses on the question of RSS exists at all, and the extent to which it influences the impact of the BE on travel behavior, more recent literature discusses causal mechanism, dynamics in attitudes, more advanced research methodologies, and implications for policy and planning. Empirical research carried out so far is almost exclusively quantitative research (Næss, 2019). Summarizing the literature up till now, there is a general consensus on the existence of the phenomenon of RSS, and the facts that RSS influences the quantitative impacts of BE variables on travel behavior variables. In addition, there is a general agreement on the preferred method to study quantitatively the magnitude of RSS, as well as the impact of RSS, via the BE, on travel behavior: longitudinal (panel based) studies. This contradicts the often cross-sectional studies published in the past 15 years. Nevertheless, Section 2 shows several topics are still open for debate, including causalities, methods, findings, and implications.

Because of uncertainty about the contribution of RSS in explaining the impact of the BE on travel behavior, as well as about the potential implications for policy, it is of paramount importance for both researchers and practitioners to better understand the phenomenon of RSS. The uncertainty mainly relates to the varying quantitative effects of BE variables on travel behavior indicators, such as mode choice and vehicle miles traveled (van Herick and Mokhtarian, 2020), and also on residential choice. Changes in travel behavior and residential choice do influence the environment and accessibility levels, and because of the uncertainties in residential choice and travel behavior, these influences are also uncertain. To the best of our knowledge, a comprehensive overview of current debates, linked to a research agenda, is lacking. Consequently, this chapter aims to contribute to this debate by (1) presenting an overview of the current debates, and (2) discussing avenues for future research in the area of RSS. The emphasis is on theoretical and methodological issues, not so much on the implications.

It is worth noting that Guan et al. (2020), a recent review, emphasizes the interaction between the BE and attitudes on travel behavior, the causal structure among RSS, the BE, and travel behavior, and measurement issues of BE variables and attitudes. Our literature study has a different structure and different focuses. It is conducted in a less traditional way (see Van Wee and Banister (2016) for the more general methodology of doing literature reviews). This chapter is more a discussion paper aiming to present a research agenda based on current debates, instead of a full fledge literature review paper on RSS. We searched for papers in SCOPUS using the string ("residential self-selection" OR "residential sorting"). We used SCOPUS because it is more inclusive than Web of Science (WoS). We realized that WoS includes more older papers. However, because the literature on RSS is quite recent, this feature of WoS is not important. Because we are interested in the current debates, we sorted based on date and started selecting the most recent papers. If still actual debates refer back to older papers, we included these older papers. This explains why the focus is mainly on papers published since 2014. After reading papers published between

2014 and (November 12) 2019, we experienced a saturation in the debate topics. Therefore, we aim to include all debates since Cao et al. (2009) but results reveal that papers published since 2014 probably cover all dominant topics that are still open for debate. The recommendations originate from analytical thinking and exchange of ideas between the authors of this chapter.

Section 2 summarizes dominant debates since Cao et al. (2009), followed by Section 3 presenting a research agenda.

2. The evolution of debates

This section summarizes the evolution of dominant debates during the past decade, mainly since 2014, without having the ambition to give a full overview of the debates. Science is all about theory, methods, and empirical knowledge, and debates first of all relate to these topics. A next debate concentrates around the implications of findings, and finally we discuss some specific other topics.

2.1 Theory/causality

A first debate focuses on the causal structure of attitudes (including travel attitudes and residential preferences), residential choice, and travel behavior. Cao et al. (2009) propose several alternative conceptualizations. For example, attitudes can be an antecedent for residential choice and travel behavior, but they can also be an intervening factor, so that causality runs from travel behavior via attitudes to residential choice, or vice versa. Attitudes can modify the influence of the BE, as shown by the studies on residential dissonance and travel behavior (Cao, 2015; De Vos et al., 2018; Kamruzzaman et al., 2013; Phani Kumar et al., 2018). Heinen et al. (2018) further add to those conceptualizations and reflect on the methodological implications.

Relationships among attitudes, residential choice, and travel behavior can be unidirectional (in both directions between any two of the three blocks) or bi-directional. Assuming only three (clusters of) variables, attitudes, residential choice, and travel behavior, in theory there are three relationships, and each can be unidirectional (in each direction), bi-directional, or absent, resulting in $3 \times 4 = 12$ conceptualizations. Some scholars also argue that RSS should be studied in the context of mobility biographies or using a life-oriented approach (Scheiner, 2014; Zhang, 2014; Zhao and Zhang, 2018). If other (clusters of) variables are included, such as socio-economic and demographic variables, characteristics of the transport system or the land use system, life events, and other life domains, the number of theoretically possible conceptualizations increases rapidly. So far it is not fully clear which conceptualizations are more likely in general or in a specific case.

An important discussion with respect to causality relates to the static or dynamic nature of attitudes. A quite common assumption is that attitudes are stable, an assumption that has often been made in the context of the Theory of Planned Behavior (Ajzen, 1991), and if so, there is no "incoming arrow" to "attitudes" in causal models. But this does not have to be the case (De Vos et al., 2018; Gim, 2013): attitudes can change in general. Especially, they can be influenced by the BE, referred to as "environmental determinism" by Ewing et al. (2015) or "residential determination" by Lin et al. (2017). This topic has recently gained more attention in the literature (e.g., Farinloye et al., 2019; Kroesen, 2019; Van de Coevering et al., 2018; Wang and Lin, 2019), but it is still not well understood.

2.2 Methods

A second cluster of debates concentrates on the methods. Previous studies employ various approaches to identify and address RSS, including direct questioning, statistical control, instrument variables, sample selection models, propensity score matching, joint models, and longitudinal design (Cao et al., 2009; Mokhtarian and Cao, 2008). After reviewing the approaches, they conclude that longitudinal Structural Equation Models are the ideal methodology, one category being natural experiments (e.g., Boarnet et al., 2005; Zhang et al., 2017), and the other being panel studies on movers. Since then, several studies have applied the approach to analyze panel or quasi-longitudinal data of movers in the context of RSS (Cao and Ermagun, 2017; Wang and Lin, 2019). However, Heinen et al. (2018) argue that such studies still do not overcome all methodological issues of competitor methodologies, and suggest—as explained above—additional conceptualizations and "repeating analyses with and without individuals who relocated during the study, and with and without statistical controls for residential relocation" (p. 393). But such studies are not easy to conduct, because of problems in finding adequate data collection options, and because such studies are often data intensive (if attitudes are measured in an advanced way) and can result in high level (and selective) non-response.

Note that the debates on causalities and methods are related: the lack of understanding of causality is partly the result of a lack in longitudinal studies (Van de Coevering et al., 2018).

2.3 Empirical findings

A third debate focuses on the magnitude of the importance of RSS for travel behavior in general, as well as relative to the stand-alone impact of the BE on travel behavior (Mokhtarian and van Herick, 2016). Some studies find only few impacts, whereas other studies find the impact of RSS to strongly downplay the (independent) role of the BE (van Herick and Mokhtarian, 2020). In particular, they conclude, based on a review of 39 studies (and including 56 models) published before 2016, that of the total influence of the BE in these models 36–100% can be attributed to the BE itself. The variation partly comes from travel behavior outcomes being used (such as travel distance vs. travel time, cars vs. transit) (Cao and Fan, 2012). In theory RSS can occur based on travel attitudes and preferences in multiple ways. Mode choice is the most dominant travel behavior indicator, followed by vehicle miles traveled, whereas travel times, travel frequencies, and time of day choices are mentioned less frequently.

A quite common finding is that RSS is most important for people who prefer to travel by non-motorized transportation such as active travel, transit, and train (e.g., Ettema and Nieuwenhuis, 2017; Wolday et al., 2019). This is likely because the degree of RSS is influenced by "the supply of development alternative to conventional suburban neighborhoods" (Wolday et al., 2019, p. 88). Furthermore, if people self-select for travel-related reasons, this can be due to attitudes toward modes, but also because they do not like to travel at all, as shown by De Vos and Witlox (2016). The importance of RSS can also depend on the population of interest. Disadvantaged people and individuals in certain life courses can be more or less responsive to RSS than the general population (Cheng et al., 2019; Humphreys and Ahern, 2019). To conclude: the relative importance of RSS remains quite unclear.

A next empirical debate follows from the country focus: most studies on RSS focus on cities and regions in OECD countries, and there is much less evidence about the importance of RSS for the debate of the BE and travel behavior in other countries. Even within OECD countries, the importance of RSS varies. The effect of RSS appears stronger in the North America than in Europe (Gim, 2012; Næss, 2009; Wolday et al., 2019), probably because the latter is more transit friendly and less sprawling than the former. Furthermore, Wang and Lin (2014) argue that the RSS phenomenon could be different in China because of the limited residential and travel choices and Chinese's unique preferences for land use and transportation system. Since then, we have seen a growing number of studies on China. For example, Cao and Yang (2017) explore RSS in Guangzhou, China, and indeed find RSS to also play a role in that city; Zhang et al. (2017) use a natural experiment to account for RSS effect on auto ownership and fuel consumption in Beijing. Studies from other non-OECD countries are limited, the Iranian study of Etminani-Ghasrodashti and Ardeshiri (2016) and the Vietnam study of Tran et al. (2016) being exceptions.

2.4 Implications

A next debate focuses on the implications of RSS for planning, see, for example, Næss (2014) and an associated commentary (Van Wee and Boarnet, 2014) in the aforementioned special issue (Cao, 2014). If the impact of the BE on travel behavior is partly due to RSS, the independent impact of the BE on travel behavior is likely to be overestimated, although underestimations are also possible (see Cao and Chatman, 2016; Kroesen and Chorus, 2018). On the other hand, Næss (2009, 2014) and Levine (1999) argue that the phenomenon of RSS itself shows that the BE has an impact on travel behavior. If people have preferences for specific modes and residential areas, they should be provided with the "right" environment, to allow them to travel by, for example, public transport or active modes, and to reduce travel by personal vehicles (Zhang and Zhang, 2018). Providing the "right" BE reduces residential dissonance (see, for example, De Vos et al., 2012; Frank et al., 2007; Huang et al., 2016). Linking this to the discussion on causal structures (see above), in this case the BE is an enabler for travel preferences.

Chatman (2014) argues that an accurate estimation of the BE effect on travel behavior by controlling for RSS may not be conducive to predicting the effect of certain land use and transportation policies. It depends on how people with certain attitudes respond to the changes in the BE. Furthermore, he contends that the research of land use and travel behavior should consider housing supply and market demand. A promise underlying the argument that enabling RSS may amplify the BE effect on travel behavior is that developments alternative to suburban neighborhoods are undersupplied (Cao and Chatman, 2016). However, whether there is an undersupply of the alternative development is debatable (Cao, 2008; Levine and Inam, 2004).

2.5 Specific topics

Although most debates concentrate on the topics as discussed above, a few more debates, often discussed in one or a few papers but important to the RSS issue, have emerged. One debate focuses on the questions of "who decides with respect to residential choices," at least as far as related to RSS. It is generally assumed that the respondents being surveyed make such a decision, but Guan and Wang (2019) argue that such decisions are made at the household level. In particular, they find that husbands' attitudes are more important to residential choice whereas wives' attitudes have a larger effect on commuting distance in China. The discussion on this topic is still in its infancy.

It is also interesting to know how the size of a metropolitan area affects the degree of RSS. Most studies use the data from large metropolitan areas and find the prevalence of RSS. However, many medium and small metropolitan areas may not have large variations in the BE and do not experience severe traffic congestion. Therefore, there may be fewer motivations for RSS. Wolday et al. (2019) find that RSS is more pronounced in the larger Oslo metropolitan area than in the smaller Stavanger region, where transit supply is limited, even in central business districts. Moreover, in three small cities in Norway, travel-related attitudes have hardly any effect on car driving distance (Wolday, 2018). In rural Sichuan, China, travel attitudes have few effects on travel behavior and carbon emissions (Ao et al., 2019).

A next topic is travel satisfaction and the link with RSS. Ye and Titheridge (2017) explain that travel satisfaction can influence travel attitudes, which links this topic to the reverse causality debate. Cao and Ettema (2014) find that RSS has an important influence on satisfaction with travel and conclude that deploying rail transit will improve individuals' travel satisfaction, especially those who prefer transit. De Vos et al. (2016) find that travel satisfaction differs between people living in urban vs. suburban areas (and between consonants and dissonants). The link between RSS and travel satisfaction is also relevant for the RSS debate, because the expected utility at the time of making a decision, such as a residential move, does not have to match the experienced utility.

3. A research agenda

This section is limited to recommendations for future research that are not already extensively discussed in the literature. We therefore do, for example, not discuss the importance of longitudinal studies. The rationale for selecting the topics varies between the topics. Putting "changing attitudes" on the agenda directly follows from the importance of attitudes as discussed above. The plea for qualitative studies is a reaction to the quantitative focus of almost all research done in this area, whereas we still poorly understand the motivations and mechanisms for people to self-select in specific neighborhoods or neighborhood types. The topic of causal structures follows from the fact that previous research is inconclusive with respect to the causal structures linking RSS, travel behavior, and BE variables. The topics discussed under the umbrella of "extending the empirical focus" result from overviewing the literature published until now, and analytical thinking. Recommending research on the link with planners and policy makers originates from the fact that the RSS debate is generally put in a context of the relevance or not of implementing BE concepts to influence travel behavior.

3.1 Changing attitudes

In line with others, such as Bruns and Matthes (2019), we recommend more research into the area of attitude changes, both in general as well as with respect to those initiated by the BE. Due to the exposure to a new residential environment and travel options, people might change their attitudes (Kroesen, 2019; Kroesen and Chorus, 2018), but attitudes can also change for other reasons, such as changing environmental awareness. If attitudes change due to the BE, the impact of the BE on travel behavior might be underestimated compared to results derived assuming attitudes to be constant (see for further discussion Chatman, 2009, Kroesen and Chorus, 2018, and Næss, 2014), making it a very relevant topic for understanding the impact of the BE on travel behavior. The process of attitude change is still poorly understood (Van Wee et al., 2019). Longitudinal studies might reveal attitude changes, but if these changes are not explicitly included, the role attitudes play in models might depend on the moment of measuring attitudes in these studies. Moreover, attitude change can influence results of cross-sectional studies. For example, if attitudes change after a move, measuring attitudes after that move do not reflect the attitudes at the moment the decision for the residential choice was made (Guan et al., 2020).

Attitudes changes are relevant for causal structures: BE impacts on attitudes can explicitly be modeled. Latent class transition models (see Van de Coevering et al., 2018) can reveal groups of people that change attitudes over time. In other words, such models allow researchers to assess changes in attitudes based on unknown characteristics of the persons or households, and these attitude changes can next be included in models linking RSS, the BE and travel behavior.

3.2 Qualitative studies

In line with some scholars (e.g., Bruns and Matthes, 2019; Farinloye et al., 2019; Næss, 2015), we recommend to take a step back from the many quantitative studies, and do some qualitative research, like in-depth interviews or focus group meetings. As topics to study we see several avenues. First of all qualitative studies allow researchers to better understand the motivations of people to self-select or not (at least because of travel/accessibility preferences and attitudes, maybe also for other reasons). Researchers can explicitly ask if and how travel-related attitudes played a role in people's residential choice. Secondly such research can study the role of restrictions to be able to choose the preferred residential location, housing market restrictions and financial restrictions being two important candidate types of restrictions. Thirdly such research could focus on the inclusion of people who make the decisions (individual, individual and partner), and secondary players who influence their decisions (children living with their parents or not (anymore), other family, members and even employers—note that some employers force people, like nurses, to live not too far from the working location.[a] Fourthly such research could explore changes in attitudes, as discussed above. When and how did people's attitudes change, which factors played a role, to what extent did the BE play a role, were some factors related or not?

A fifth topic is the spatial scale at which people self-select. People can decide to self-select, but the question is: at which spatial scale? They might

[a] This, for examples applies to many nurses in the Netherlands—they should live close to work to be able to be at work within a short time period. The current Minister of Housing argued that for that reason nurses should be given priority in the allocation of social housing in Amsterdam—see https://www.nursing.nl/verpleegkundigen-moeten-voorrang-krijgen-op-sociale-huurwoningen/

self-select in a specific neighborhood (type) but also more specifically in a smaller part of a neighborhood. For example, if they want shops to be nearby because they prefer to walk to shops, not the full neighborhood might be the level to self-select, but only a part of it, the part near shops. But it could also be that they self-select at the level of the city as a whole. They might, for example, prefer to live somewhere in a medium sized city without specific preferences for locations within that city. We expect the spatial scale of RSS to be strongly correlated to the motivations to self-select. If people primarily self-select based on a commuting mode choice preference for rail, they probably search for a dwelling at a reasonable distance from a station. But if they self-select because they prefer to walk or cycle to destinations like shops, medical and other services, restaurants etc., they probably select specific neighborhoods. Then the answers to this question can help policymakers identify appropriate geographical scales for planning interventions.

Wolday et al. (2019) is an example of qualitative research in the area of RSS. They find that although all interviewees value good accessibility, suburbanites appreciate the supportive environment for children and affordability more than accessibility. This study shows the interplay of travel-related motivations, housing and financial restrictions, and secondary household members in residential location decisions.

Despite the inherent limitations of qualitative research, especially with respect to representativeness, forms of bias, and resulting in qualitative outcomes only, such research could be an important step, and the limitations could at least partly be addressed in follow-up quantitative research. The strong focus on quantitative research so far is understandable because of the link with the debate of the BE and travel behavior: RSS can help quantify the independent effect of the BE, an important component of travel demand forecasting models. But we argue that the RSS mechanisms at the individual or household level are still poorly understood, and deserve more attention. The results of qualitative analyses can be used either to formulate hypotheses tested by quantitative studies, or to explain the underlying reasons for the observed relationships between the BE and travel behavior in quantitative studies (e.g., Wolday et al., 2018).

3.3 Multiple causal structures

In line with the discussion on causalities, we argue that there is not one "best" causal structure, but there could be multiple. The reasons is the heterogeneity between people and households—see Cao and Chatman (2016), Jarass and Scheiner (2018), and Kim and Mokhtarian (2018). The challenge then is to find out which causal structure applies to which people or households. Methods to study this heterogeneity and the causal structures that apply to link the BE, RSS, travel behavior, attitudes and socio-demographic variables first should have data for at least two moments in time to allow for the exploration of causalities. In addition they should be able to identify (groups of) people for which different causalities apply. One option is Latent Class Transition Modeling. Classes then related to the causal structures that apply. Kim and Mokhtarian (2018) also discuss the strengths of Latent Class models (LCM) for RSS research, but do not link the discussion to the existence of multiple causal structures.

3.4 Extending the empirical focus

A first topic in this category is travel behavior at other places than in the residential area, to the best of our knowledge an almost completely overlooked topic. For example, people who start walking or cycling more in their residential area might also walk or cycle more as a form of egress transport, from a station to their workplace. They might even decide to travel by train (as opposed to driving) because of the increased perceived attractiveness of egress travel (walk or cycle as opposed to bus, tram or metro). Or at a holiday destination they could also adapt their travel mode to what they are used, and they might even chose for other holiday destinations because of the preferences for travel and options available at the destinations. Researchers could, for example, match residential neighborhoods and travel behavior that originates at the neighborhoods and figure out the extent to which RSS translates into the behavior outside of the neighborhoods.

Next we highlight the potential threshold effect of RSS, referring to the fact that preferences or attitudes should have a certain minimum level of importance to play a role in residential choice (Galster, 2018). A qualitative analysis shows that although both urban residents and suburbanites appreciate transit accessibility and proximity to facilities, RSS will be limited to only those who have strong preferences for these attributes (Wolday et al., 2019). This makes sense because households often face various constraints in residential location choice and are unable to exercise their travel-related preferences. However, it is unclear how strong these preferences should be to make people self-select them based on these preferences? Overall, we need to examine the non-linear and synergistic effects of RSS and the BE on travel behavior. Gradient boosting decision trees is a candidate analysis approach (Ding et al., 2018).

Furthermore, the debate on RSS can be linked to the debate on perceived accessibility—for travel behavior, experienced constraints for activity participation and appreciation of levels of accessibility, perceived accessibility is what matters, e.g., expressed as perceptions of travel times (or generalized transport costs) to relevant destinations—see, for example, Lättman et al. (2016), Lättman et al. (2018), and Liu et al. (2018). Accessibility research generally studies measured levels of accessibility, based on characteristics of the land use and the transport system, and sometimes on characteristics and restrictions/constraints of people and availability of services (e.g., opening hours of kindergartens). Linking accessibility to RSS, it is important to realize that what matters for RSS are perceived levels of accessibility (by available and preferred transport modes), and secondly, changed attitudes because of the exposure to a new or changed BE can influence the perceptions of accessibility. A more general question is how to handle the relationship between objective-measured BE characteristics and their subjective measures. Previous studies often include both of them in a single-equation model, by treating them exchangeable and overlooking their intrinsic connections (e.g., Handy et al., 2006; Spears et al., 2013). However, environmental psychology suggests that subjective BE characteristics should mediate the corresponding objective characteristics and travel behavior (Ma and Cao, 2017; Ma et al., 2014; Mehrabian and Russell, 1974).

Finally, we emphasize the importance of geographical context. As argued above, most studies on RSS focus on OECD countries, or China, leaving many options to study the relationship among RSS, the BE, and travel behavior in other countries and regions. And even within the OECD (between and within countries) or China, a lot of heterogeneity could influence study results. Candidate factors for this heterogeneity could be the availability of high quality infrastructure for active modes, the social status of specific transport modes and the importance of this status for attitudes and choices, housing market characteristics and the level of freedom to make a residential choice, and (perceived) restrictions to mode choice likely due to perceived social safety of women in some countries and times of day or the fact that until recently women were not allowed to drive a car in Saudi Arabia. For example, the options to self-select one's residence depends on the availability of houses within the budget to rent or buy, at the neighborhoods or neighborhood types preferred. Availability of neighborhood types and house types depend on (past) land use policies, and (the absence of) regulations with respect to the housing market. Both land use policies and such regulations vary widely across the globe. Not only are RSS studies in other than mainstream countries recommended, so are cross-country and cross-culture comparisons because these can help validate the generalizability of the findings of RSS studies. Because experiences in OECD countries cannot a priori be transferred to developing countries, research in these countries is very important. Many of these countries face rapid population growth and increasing shares of the population living in urban areas. Consequently they are currently developing their land use and transportation system, and early interventions to facilitate RSS can help achieve the goal of sustainable transportation (Cervero, 2013).

3.5 Implications

In line with the debate for planning as discussed above, we recommend more research into the importance of findings for planners and policy makers in general but also into options to strengthen the impact of the BE on travel behavior. Moreover, an important topic is to study how to reach planners so that they are aware of the relevance of RSS studies, and how to translate the findings in such a way that planners can include the findings in their planning activities.

4. Concluding remarks

In this chapter, we show several avenues for future research. Not all topics are of equal importance. Departing from the fact that, as explained in the introduction, a better understanding of the impact of the BE on travel behavior needs to explicitly include the role of RSS in this impact. We think that three topics are most important. The first one is the qualitative studies as suggested above, and the second topic is studies exploring which causal structures apply to which persons or households (probably via the latent class models). Thirdly, and as a specific case of the second topic, a better understanding of if, how and for whom attitude changes apply, deserves more attention, especially because if attitudes changes due to a changing BE, the impact of the BE could be underestimated, not overestimated, as often argued in the RSS debate. Especially longitudinal studies that include (changing) attitudes seem promising.

Our chapter does not only aim to be relevant for researchers, but also for practice. If researchers are better able to quantitatively estimate the effects of candidate BE policies, planners and policy makers can be better informed about the travel behavior, residential choice, and other policy relevant effects (accessibility, environment) of such policies. In addition, providing information (documents, videos, …) about best practices with respect to BE policies could be helpful to bring BE policies under the attention of planners and policy makers. Such information could show the BE changes and their impacts on residential choice, travel behavior and policy relevant effects, plus the mechanisms explaining such impacts (such as direct travel behavior changes, but also attitude changes after relocations).

To conclude: now that for about a decade and a half, RSS has been studied and debated frequently, it is time for a next generation of studies.

References

Ajzen, I., 1991. The theory of planned behaviour. Organ. Behav. Hum. Decis. Process. 50, 179–211.

Ao, Y., Yang, D., Chen, C., Wang, Y., 2019. Effects of rural built environment on travel-related CO_2 emissions considering travel attitudes. Transp. Res. Part D: Transp. Environ. 73, 187–204.

Boarnet, M.G., Anderson, C.L., Day, K., McMillan, T., Alfonzo, M., 2005. Evaluation of the California Safe Routes to School legislation—urban form changes and children's active transportation to school. Am. J. Prev. Med. 28, 134–140.

Bruns, A., Matthes, G., 2019. Moving into and within cities—interactions of residential change and the travel behavior and implications for integrated land use and transport planning strategies. Travel Behav. Soc. 17, 46–61.

Cao, X., 2008. Is alternative development undersupplied? Examination of residential preferences and choices of northern California movers. Transp. Res. Rec. 2077, 97–105.

Cao, J., 2014. Residential self-selection in the relationship between the built environment and travel behavior: introduction to the special issue. J. Transp. Land Use 7, 1–3.

Cao, X., 2015. Heterogeneous effects of neighborhood type on commute mode choice: an exploration of residential dissonance in the Twin Cities. J. Transp. Geogr. 48, 188–196.

Cao, X., Chatman, D., 2016. How will smart growth land-use policies affect travel? A theoretical discussion on the importance of residential sorting. Environ. Plann. B. Plann. Des. 43, 58–73.

Cao, X., Ermagun, A., 2017. The influences of the Hiawatha LRT on changes in travel behavior: a retrospective study on movers. Urban Stud. 54, 2504–2520.

Cao, X., Ettema, D., 2014. Satisfaction with travel and residential self-selection: how do preferences moderate the impact of the Hiawatha light rail line? J. Transp. Land Use 7, 93–108.

Cao, X., Fan, Y., 2012. Exploring the influences of density on travel behavior using propensity score matching. Environ. Plann. B. Plann. Des. 39, 459–470.

Cao, X., Yang, W., 2017. Examining the effects of the built environment and residential self-selection on commuting trips and the related CO_2 emissions: an empirical study in Guangzhou, China. Transp. Res. Part D: Transp. Environ. 52B, 480–494.

Cao, X., Mokhtarian, P.L., Handy, S.L., 2009. Examining the impacts of residential self-selection on travel behaviour: a focus on empirical findings. Transp. Rev. 29, 359–395.

Cervero, R., 2013. Linking urban transport and land use in developing countries. J. Transp. Land Use 6, 7–24.
Chatman, D.G., 2009. Residential choice, the built environment, and nonwork travel: evidence using new data and methods. Environ. Plan A 41, 1072–1089.
Chatman, D.G., 2014. Estimating the effect of land use and transportation planning on travel patterns: three problems in controlling for residential self-selection. J. Transp. Land Use 7, 47–56.
Cheng, L., De Vos, J., Shi, K., Yang, M., Chen, X., Witlox, F., 2019. Do residential location effects on travel behavior differ between the elderly and younger adults? Transp. Res. Part D: Transp. Environ. 73, 367–380.
De Vos, J., Witlox, F., 2016. Do people live in urban neighbourhoods because they do not like to travel? Analysing an alternative residential self-selection hypothesis. Travel Behav. Soc. 4, 29–39.
De Vos, J., Derudder, B., Van Acker, V., Witlox, F., 2012. Reducing car use: changing attitudes or relocating? The influence of residential dissonance on travel behavior. J. Transp. Geogr. 22, 1–9.
De Vos, J., Mokhtarian, P.L., Schwanen, T., Van Acker, V., Witlox, F., 2016. Travel mode choice and travel satisfaction: bridging the gap between decision utility and experienced utility. Transportation 43, 771–796.
De Vos, J., Ettema, D., Witlox, F., 2018. Changing travel behaviour and attitudes following a residential relocation. J. Transp. Geogr. 73, 131–147.
Ding, C., Cao, X., Wang, Y., 2018. Synergistic effects of the built environment and commuting programs on commute mode choice. Transp. Res. A Policy Pract. 118, 104–118.
Etminani-Ghasrodashti, R., Ardeshiri, M., 2016. The impacts of built environment on home-based work and non-work trips: an empirical study from Iran. Transp. Res. A Policy Pract. 85, 196–207.
Ettema, D., Nieuwenhuis, R., 2017. Residential self-selection and travel behaviour: what are the effects of attitudes, reasons for location choice and the built environment? J. Transp. Geogr. 59, 146–155.
Ewing, R., Hamidi, S., Grace, J.B., 2015. Compact development and VMT—environmental determinism, self-selection, or some of both? Environ. Plann. B. Plann. Des. 43, 737–755.
Farinloye, T., Mogaji, E., Aririguzoh, S., Kieu, T.A., 2019. Qualitatively exploring the effect of change in the residential environment on travel behaviour. Travel Behav. Soc. 17, 26–35.
Frank, L.D., Saelens, B.E., Powell, K.E., Chapman, J.E., 2007. Stepping towards causation: do built environments or neighborhood and travel preferences explain physical activity, driving, and obesity? Soc. Sci. Med. 65, 1898–1914.
Galster, G.C., 2018. Nonlinear and threshold effects related to neighborhood: implications for planning and policy. J. Plan. Lit. 33, 492–508.
Gim, T.-H.T., 2012. A meta-analysis of the relationship between density and travel behavior. Transportation 39, 491–519.
Gim, T.-H.T., 2013. Testing the reciprocal relationship between attitudes and land use in relation to trip frequencies: a nonrecursive model. Int. Reg. Sci. Rev. 39, 203–227.
Guan, X., Wang, D., 2019. Residential self-selection in the built environment-travel behavior connection: whose self-selection? Transp. Res. Part D: Transp. Environ. 67, 16–32.
Guan, X., Wang, D., Jason Cao, X., 2020. The role of residential self-selection in land use-travel research: a review of recent findings. Transp. Rev. 40, 267–287.
Hamersma, M., Heinen, E., Tillema, T., Arts, J., 2017. New highway development in the Netherlands: a residents' perspective. Transp. Res. Part D: Transp. Environ. 51, 326–339.

Handy, S., Cao, X., Mokhtarian, P.L., 2006. Self-selection in the relationship between the built environment and walking: empirical evidence from Northern California. J. Am. Plann. Assoc. 72, 55–74.
Heinen, E., Wee, B.V., Panter, J., Mackett, R., Ogilvie, D., 2018. Residential self-selection in quasi-experimental and natural experimental studies: an extended conceptualization of the relationship between the built environment and travel behavior. J. Transp. Land Use 11 (1), 939–959.
Huang, X., Cao, X., Cao, X., Yin, J., 2016. How does the propensity of living near rail transit moderate the influence of rail transit on transit trip frequency in Xi'an? J. Transp. Geogr. 54, 194–204.
Humphreys, J., Ahern, A., 2019. Is travel based residential self-selection a significant influence in modal choice and household location decisions? Transp. Policy 75, 150–160.
James, P., Hart, J.E., Arcaya, M.C., Feskanich, D., Laden, F., Subramanian, S.V., 2015. Neighborhood self-selection: the role of pre-move health factors on the built and socioeconomic environment. Int. J. Environ. Res. Public Health 12, 12489–12504.
Jarass, J., Scheiner, J., 2018. Residential self-selection and travel mode use in a new inner-city development neighbourhood in Berlin. J. Transp. Geogr. 70, 68–77.
Kamruzzaman, M., Baker, D., Washington, S., Turrell, G., 2013. Residential dissonance and mode choice. J. Transp. Geogr. 33, 12–28.
Kim, S.H., Mokhtarian, P.L., 2018. Taste heterogeneity as an alternative form of endogeneity bias: investigating the attitude-moderated effects of built environment and socio-demographics on vehicle ownership using latent class modeling. Transp. Res. A Policy Pract. 116, 130–150.
Kroesen, M., 2019. Residential self-selection and the reverse causation hypothesis: assessing the endogeneity of stated reasons for residential choice. Travel Behav. Soc. 16, 108–117.
Kroesen, M., Chorus, C., 2018. The role of general and specific attitudes in predicting travel behavior—a fatal dilemma? Travel Behav. Soc. 10, 33–41.
Lättman, K., Friman, M., Olsson, L.E., 2016. Perceived accessibility of public transport as a potential indicator of social inclusion. Soc. Incl. 4 (3), 36–45. Transport Policy and Social Inclusion 10.17645/si.v4i3.481.
Lättman, K., Olsson, L.E., Friman, M., 2018. A new approach to accessibility—examining perceived accessibility in contrast to objectively measured accessibility in daily travel. Res. Transp. Econ. 69, 501–511.
Levine, J., 1999. Access to choice. Access 14, 16–19.
Levine, J., Inam, A., 2004. The market for transportation-land use integration: do developers want smarter growth than regulations allow? Transportation 31, 409–427.
Lin, T., Wang, D., Guan, X., 2017. The built environment, travel attitude, and travel behavior: residential self-selection or residential determination? J. Transp. Geogr. 65, 111–122.
Liu, C., Susilo, Y.O., Dharmowijoyo, D.B.E., 2018. Investigating intra-household interactions between individuals' time and space constraints. J. Transp. Geogr. 73, 108–119.
Ma, L., Cao, J., 2017. How perceptions mediate the effects of the built environment on travel behavior? Transportation 46, 175–197.
Ma, L., Dill, J., Mohr, C., 2014. The objective versus the perceived environment: what matters for bicycling? Transportation 41, 1135–1152.
Mehrabian, A., Russell, J., 1974. An Approach to Environmental Psychology. MIT Press, Cambridge.
Mokhtarian, P.L., Cao, X., 2008. Examining the impacts of residential self-selection on travel behavior: a focus on methodologies. Transp. Res. B Methodol. 42, 204–228.
Mokhtarian, P.L., van Herick, D., 2016. Viewpoint: quantifying residential self-selection effects: a review of methods and findings from applications of propensity score and sample selection approaches. J. Transp. Land Use 9 (1), 7–26.

Næss, P., 2009. Residential self-selection and appropriate control variables in land use: travel studies. Transp. Rev. 29, 293–324.
Næss, P., 2014. Tempest in a teapot: the exaggerated problem of transport-related residential self-selection as a source of error in empirical studies. J. Transp. Land Use 7 (3), 57–79.
Næss, P., 2015. Built environment, causality and travel. Transp. Rev. 35, 275–291.
Næss, P., 2019. Meta-analyses of built environment effects on travel: no new platinum standard. J. Plan. Educ. Res. 0739456X19856425.
Nijland, H.A., Hartemink, S., van Kamp, I., van Wee, B., 2007. The influence of sensitivity for road traffic noise on residential location: does it trigger a process of spatial selection? J. Acoust. Soc. Am. 122, 1595–1601.
Phani Kumar, P., Ravi Sekhar, C., Parida, M., 2018. Residential dissonance in TOD neighborhoods. J. Transp. Geogr. 72, 166–177.
Scheiner, J., 2014. Residential self-selection in travel behavior: towards an integration into mobility biographies. J. Transp. Land Use 7 (3), 15–28.
Spears, S., Houston, D., Boarnet, M.G., 2013. Illuminating the unseen in transit use: a framework for examining the effect of attitudes and perceptions on travel behavior. Transp. Res. A Policy Pract. 58, 40–53.
Tran, M.T., Zhang, J., Chikaraishi, M., Fujiwara, A., 2016. A joint analysis of residential location, work location and commuting mode choices in Hanoi, Vietnam. J. Transp. Geogr. 54, 181–193.
Van de Coevering, P., Maat, K., van Wee, B., 2018. Residential self-selection, reverse causality and residential dissonance. A latent class transition model of interactions between the built environment, travel attitudes and travel behavior. Transp. Res. A Policy Pract. 118, 466–479.
van Herick, D., Mokhtarian, P.L., 2020. How much does the method matter? An empirical comparison of ways to quantify the influence of residential self-selection. Travel Behav. Soc. 18, 68–82.
Van Wee, B., 2009. Self-selection: a key to a better understanding of location choices, travel behaviour and transport externalities? Transp. Rev. 29, 279–292.
Van Wee, B., Banister, D., 2016. How to write a literature review paper? Transp. Rev. 36, 278–288.
Van Wee, B.V., Boarnet, M., 2014. Reaction to the paper Tempest in a Teapot: the exaggerated problem of transport-related residential self-selection as a source of error in empirical studies. J. Transp. Land Use 7 (3), 81–86.
Van Wee, B., De Vos, J., Maat, K., 2019. Impacts of the built environment and travel behaviour on attitudes: theories underpinning the reverse causality hypothesis. J. Transp. Geogr. 80, 102540.
Wang, D., Lin, T., 2014. Residential self-selection, built environment and travel behavior in the Chinese context. J. Transp. Land Use 7, 5–14.
Wang, D., Lin, T., 2019. Built environment, travel behavior, and residential self-selection: a study based on panel data from Beijing, China. Transportation 46, 51–74.
Wolday, F., 2018. Built environment and car driving distance in a small city context. J. Transp. Land Use 11 (1), 747–767.
Wolday, F., Cao, J., Næss, P., 2018. Examining factors that keep residents with high transit preference away from transit-rich zones and associated behavior outcomes. J. Transp. Geogr. 66, 224–234.
Wolday, F., Næss, P., Cao, X., 2019. Travel-based residential self-selection: a qualitatively improved understanding from Norway. Cities 87, 87–102.
Ye, R., Titheridge, H., 2017. Satisfaction with the commute: the role of travel mode choice, built environment and attitudes. Transp. Res. Part D: Transp. Environ. 52, 535–547.
Zhang, J., 2014. Revisiting residential self-selection issues: a life-oriented approach. J. Transp. Land Use 7, 29–45.

Zhang, M., Zhang, W., 2018. When context meets self-selection: the built environment–travel connection revisited. J. Plan. Educ. Res. 40 (3), 304–319.
Zhang, Y., Zheng, S., Sun, C., Wang, R., 2017. Does subway proximity discourage automobility? Evidence from Beijing. Transp. Res. Part D: Transp. Environ. 52, 506–517.
Zhao, P., Zhang, Y., 2018. Travel behaviour and life course: examining changes in car use after residential relocation in Beijing. J. Transp. Geogr. 73, 41–53.

CHAPTER FIVE

Compact urban development in Norway: Spatial changes, underlying policies and travel impacts

Petter Næss*
Professor of Planning in Urban Regions, Norwegian University of Life Sciences, Department of Urban and Regional Planning, Ås, Norway
*Corresponding author: e-mail address: petter.nass@nmbu.no

Contents

Abstract

This chapter discusses the compact city policy pursued in Norway over the last decades, discusses conditions for its implementation and assesses its merits in terms of promoting sustainable urban mobility. Nearly all the largest Norwegian cities have increased their population density over the past two decades, and in some cities, such as Oslo and Trondheim, the density increase has been substantial. Several physical, demographic, economic, cultural and political conditions have facilitated Norway's urban densification, but a pronounced change in planners' attitudes has doubtlessly also played an important role, resulting in a hegemonic discourse since the turn of the millennium, centered on the compact city. National policies and planning guidelines have supported the compact urban development. Norway's urban containment policies have saved land and reduced the amount of car travel, both by reducing trip distances, facilitating better transit provision, and as an enabling condition for urban road toll schemes.

Keywords: Urban densification, Conditions, Policies, Travel impacts, Norway

Advances in Transport Policy and Planning, Volume 9
ISSN 2543-0009
https://doi.org/10.1016/bs.atpp.2021.02.003

1. Introduction

The purpose of this chapter is to provide an overview of the particularly strong urban densification that has occurred in Norwegian cities over the last decades, its underlying policies and its travel behavioral impacts. In many European countries, the compact city has attained hegemonic status as a sustainable urban form, not the least in Norway (Andersen and Røe, 2016; Jenks et al., 1996). A compact urban development can provide accessibility to facilities through proximity instead of by means of a high mobility by car, thus combining important environmental and social aspects of sustainability. Suburbanites tend to travel more often by car and drive longer distances than inner-city dwellers do, with clear differences in energy use for transportation and related emissions as a result. Car commuting is also often considerably lower among employees at inner-city than suburban workplaces (Næss, 2012). Compared to urban sprawl, densification is also favorable for the protection of natural landscapes, arable land and biodiversity, particularly when channeled to "brownfield" sites. Moreover, apartment buildings and other "compact" housing types require, other things being equal, less energy for space heating and cooling per square meter than detached single family houses (Høyer and Holden, 2001) and less material for the construction of the buildings and connecting infrastructure (Burchell et al., 1998).

The following presentation is based mainly on official statistics and published research articles and reports, but also includes some new analyses made specifically for the present chapter. By showing how a high degree of urban containment, amid rapid population growth in the largest cities, has been possible in an affluent country such as Norway, the chapter offers a "best practice" example for planners, policy-makers and environmentalists in other cities and metropolitan areas. Moreover, by providing an updated review of research findings from Norway and other Nordic countries on travel behavioral impacts of built environment characteristics, the chapter offers an opportunity to judge the extent to which Norway's compact development over recent decades has actually reduced car driving in urban areas, compared to more sprawling urban development.

This chapter is organized as follows. In Section 2, the spatial development of the largest Norwegian cities will be described and briefly compared with urban development in other Nordic countries and in Europe at large. Section 3 includes a discussion of strategies, instruments and conditions that have enabled the strong degree of densification in Norwegian cities. Section 4 gives an overview of research findings from Nordic studies over the last 15 years, with estimates of the impacts of residential location, workplace location and (based on a few older studies) overall urban population density and concentration. Some brief concluding remarks round off the chapter in Section 5.

2. Spatial urban development

2.1 The European context

In Europe, urban densification has been promoted as a favorable model for urban development at least since three decades ago, when the Commission of European Communities (1990) pointed at the Compact City as a sustainable urban form. However, the implementation of urban containment policies has varied between different parts of Europe, and some scholars have claimed urban containment to be contrary to the economic and cultural trends of modern, affluent societies. The British geographer Breheny (1995) considered decentralization as the inevitable outcome of the expressed location preferences of people and firms. Writing from an American context, Bruegmann (2008) claimed that virtually the entire history of modern cities is the history of the spreading outward of urban activity at ever lower densities, where every period of economic growth has allowed a new group of people to move out. In a similar vein, Sieverts (1999) characterized new development in German urban regions as typically taking place in the areas between the cities, and not within or immediately adjacent to the cities. As late as in 2006, the European Environmental Agency considered urban sprawl as a common phenomenon throughout Europe (EEA, 2006).

However, actual urban development in European countries has been much more nuanced than predicted by debaters such as Breheny, Bruegmann and Siewerts. Although population densities were reduced between 1980 and 1990 in a number of large European cities (Newman and Kenworthy, 1999) reurbanization trends have gradually become more pronounced in some European countries. Between 1990 and 2015, although urban spatial development was dominated by outward expansion in Eastern European countries, urban densification and intra-metropolitan concentration became more pronounced in the rest of Europe, particularly in Northern Europe (Fig. 1). In cities all over Europe, some densification has taken place within parts of the existing urbanized areas, but in most countries densification has been combined with outward expansion, where the latter has dominated in Eastern Europe while densification has become increasingly dominant in the Nordic countries.

Among the Nordic countries, densification became a strong trend already in the 1990s in the largest Norwegian and Swedish cities and in

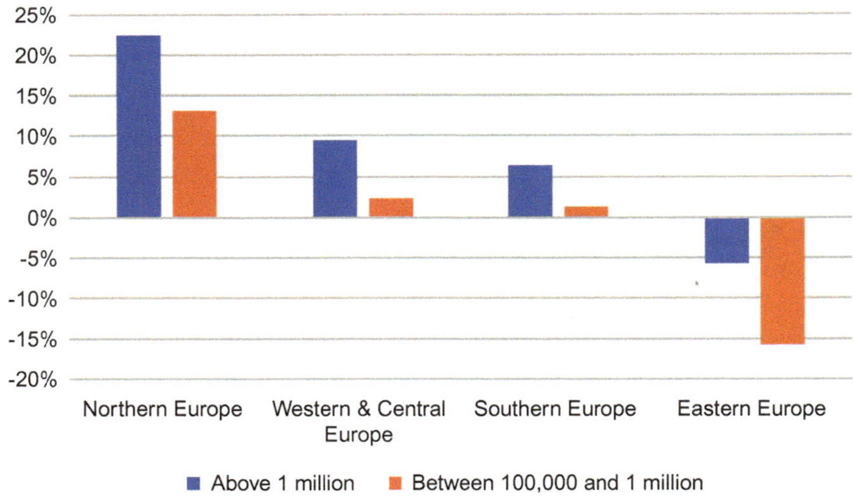

Fig. 1 Changes in urban population density from 1990 to 2015 in urban regions with main cities of different population sizes and in different parts of the EU/EFTA area. *Based on Eurostat, 2020a. Database—Eurostat. https://ec.europa.eu/eurostat/web/transport/data/database (accessed September 2020); Eurostat, 2020b. NUTS—Nomenclature of Territorial Units for Statistics. https://ec.europa.eu/eurostat/web/nuts/background (accessed August 2020); Eurostat, 2020c. Population Change—Demographic Balance and Crude Rates at National Level. https://appsso.eurostat.ec.europa.eu/nui/show.do?dataset=demo_gind&lang=en (accessed July 2020).*

Danish cities a decade or two later. In Finland and Iceland, densification has mainly been evident during the last decade. Fig. 2 shows how the capital cities of Norway and Finland both followed trajectories of declining population density until the late 1980s, when Oslo started a process of strong density increase whereas Helsinki's density reached its lowest level in 2005 and did not start a clear upward trend until 2010.

2.2 The 15 largest Norwegian cities

In the following, we will take a closer look at population density development in the 15 largest Norwegian cities. "City" is here defined as the continuous urbanized area regardless of any municipal or other territorial borders, corresponding to what is sometimes referred to as the morphological city. Fig. 3 shows the location and population size of these 15 cities, as well as 5 cities in Denmark and Iceland (see Section 4).

During the past two decades, 13 of the 15 largest Norwegian cities have increased their population density. At an aggregate scale (i.e., on average,

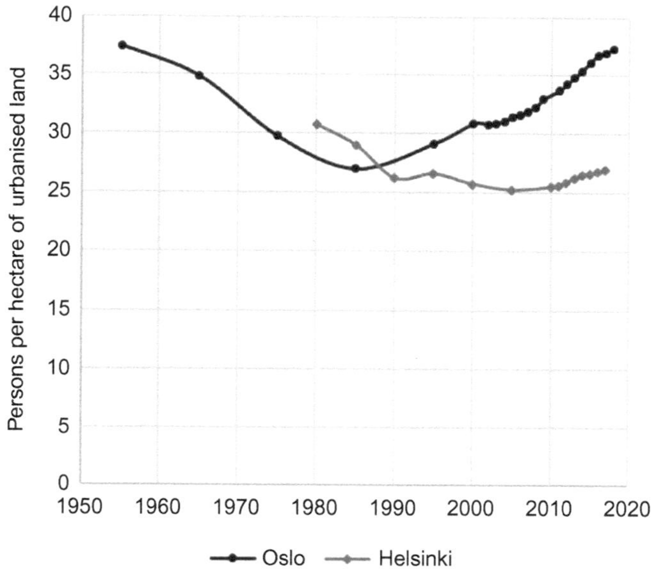

Fig. 2 Changes in population density within the morphological cities of Helsinki and Oslo between 1955 and 2018. *Based on Engebretsen, 1993. Arealbruk i tettsteder 1955–1992. TØI Report 177/1993. Institute of Transport Economics, Oslo; Riksrevisjonen, 2007. Riksrevisjonens undersøkelse av bærekraftig arealplanlegging og arealdisponering i Norge (Dokument nr. 3:11 (2006–2007)). Norwegian National Auditing Office, Oslo; Statistics Norway, 2019. Areal og befolkning i tettsteder, etter tettsted, tid og statistikkvariabel. Statistics Norway, Oslo/ Kongsvinger. https://www.ssb.no/statistikkbanken (accessed March 3, 2019); YKR, 2019. Finnish Monitoring System of Spatial Structure and Urban Form. Finnish Environment Institute (SYKE) and Statistics Finland, Helsinki. Reprinted from Tiitu, M., Næss, P., Ristimäki, M., 2020. The urban density in two Nordic capitals—comparing the development of Oslo and Helsinki metropolitan regions. Eur. Plan. Stud. https://doi.org/10.1080/09654313.2020. 1817865.*

weighted by the population size of each city), the population density of the 15 cities increased by 14.8%. While the total urbanized land of the 15 cities increased by 12.6% between 2000 and 2020, the population increased by 29.6%. Fig. 4 shows how the population density of each city has developed since 2000.[a] The highest percentage increase (22.5%) occurred in Oslo, where the population density within the continuous urban area increased from 31.3 persons per hectare in 2000 to 38.4 in 2020. The density increase

[a] Statistics Norway changed their urban area demarcation criteria in 2013. In the present study, the population densities prior to 2013 have been corrected by changing the population density figures by the percentage of difference between the 2013 and 2012 measurements, adjusted for the estimated real population density change from 2012 to 2013. The latter was estimated based on the mean annual changes from 2009 to 2012 and from 2013 to 2016.

Fig. 3 Nordic cities and metropolitan areas where population density changes (red dots) and/or built environment impacts on travel (blue circles) referred to in this chapter have been investigated. Population size within the continuous urban area of each city (the morphological city) is shown in parentheses. (1) Tromsø, NO (41,000), (2) Bodø, NO (42,000), (3) Trondheim, NO (189,000), (4) Ålesund, NO (54,000), (5) Bergen, NO (260,000), (6) Oslo, NO (1,036,000), (7) Drammen, NO (109,000), (8) Moss, NO (47,000), (9) Haugesund, NO (45,000), (10) Tønsberg, NO (53,000), (11) Sandefjord, NO (45,000), (12) Fredrikstad/Sarpsborg, NO (116,000), (13) Stavanger/Sandnes, NO (228,000), (14) Porsgrunn/Skien, NO (94,000), (15) Kristiansand, NO (65,000), (16) Frederikshavn, DK (23,000), (17) Aalborg, DK (117,000), (18) Copenhagen, DK (1,268,000), (19) Reykjavik, IS (218,000), and (20) Helsinki, FI (1,191,000).

was also high in Trondheim, Norway's fourth largest city, with a population density in 2020 16.7% higher than that in 2000. There is a tendency of higher density increase in the largest cities ($P = 0.068$), but this trend is not very consistent. For example, the city with the lowest population size in 2020 (Tromsø) has the second-highest calculated density increase (21.3). The case of Tromsø is, however, a bit special, since the 2013 change in Statistics Norway's urban area demarcation criteria (cf. note 1) resulted in the exclusion of two large suburban districts. If these two districts, which include 40% of the population of the city according to the pre-2013 demarcation, had been included, the density increase of Tromsø would probably have been more moderate, since most of the densification has taken place within the post-2013 urban area demarcation.

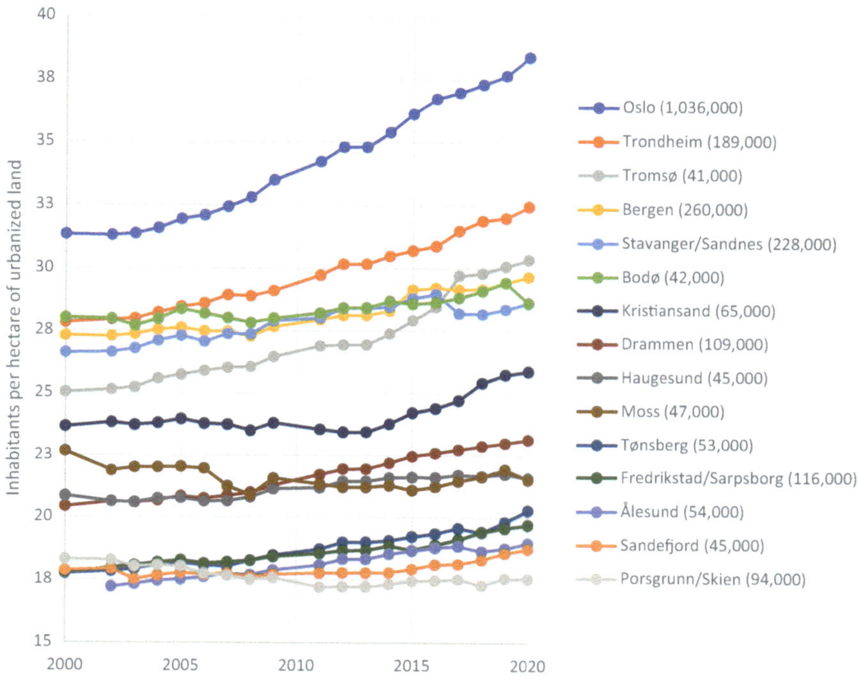

Fig. 4 Density development 2000–20 in the 15 most populated Norwegian cities. Densities are calculated as the number of inhabitants per hectare within the continuous urban area of each city (the morphological city). Population size of each city is shown in parentheses. *Based on Statistics Norway, 2020. Areal og befolkning i tettsteder, etter tettsted, tid og statistikkvariabel. Statistics Norway, Oslo/Kongsvinger. https://www.ssb.no/statistikkbanken (accessed November 15, 2020).*

On average for all the cities, the density increase was somewhat stronger in the second than in the first decade of the 20-year period. This has partly to do with the population growth, which was moderate in some cities in the first years after the turn of the millennium. Without population growth, there is not much scope for population density increase unless existing built-up areas at the urban fringe are demolished and converted to non-urban land. Such demolition has occurred very rarely, if at all, in the 15 cities during the 20-year period.

The cities of Porsgrunn/Skien and Moss deviate from the general pattern as their density has decreased by 4.3% and 5.1%, respectively, over the last 20 years. In Porsgrunn/Skien, a conurbation of two previously separate industrial cities grown into one continuous urban area, the urbanized land increased by 8.4% over the years 2000–08, with only 3.5% population growth. This city had at the outset a low population density, and the physical potential for densification was thus large. However, the city has until recently located a considerable part of new development to "greenfield" areas on the urban fringe, possibly as a result of local cultural and political conditions. In Moss, another previously important industrial city, the reduction in the calculated population density occurred in 2007 when the city expanded into a neighboring, less dense urban settlement that was then included within the urban area demarcation. Over the following 13 years, there was a slight density increase (1.2%), but Moss still comes out as one of the cities with the lowest degrees of densification. In both Porsgrunn/Skien and Moss, parts of the former industrial areas have become the locations of other types of jobs, but with lower job densities than typical for the trades that have moved into the old industrial areas. These examples might indicate that cities with moderate population growth and where large industrial sites have become vacant due to closure are less prone to undergo a strong densification process. On the other hand, the industrial "twin city" of Fredrikstad/Sarpsborg has undergone considerable densification over the 20-year period, with 10.8% higher population density in 2020 than 20 years earlier. To an even greater extent this is the case for Drammen, also a former industrial city, which has increased its population density by 13.3% over the period.

As indicated above in the example of Tromsø, densification has taken place in the inner parts of the cities rather than in the suburbs, for example on centrally located, derelict or abandoned industrial sites or harbor and dock areas that have become obsolete due to relocation of shipping activities. This is, for example, the case in Trondheim and Drammen, where former industrial and harbor areas close to the city center have been transformed into areas for restaurants, cultural arenas as well as dwellings. To an even greater extent, such transformations have occurred in Oslo.

2.3 Other Nordic cities

Besides Norway, urban densification has been most prominent in Sweden over recent decades. A downward trend in urban population densities was turned in the 1990s, and since the turn of the millennium, densities have increased considerably (Statistics Sweden, 2020). Among the largest Swedish cities, the capital city Stockholm increased its population density by 19.5% over the first two decades of the present century, increasing from 32.3 inhabitants per hectare in 2000, 36.0 in 2010, to 38.6 in 2019. Densification was also strong in Malmö, Sweden's third-largest city but the densest of all Swedish cities. In Malmö, the population density increased from 35.8 inhabitants per hectare in 2000 via 36.5 in 2010 and with a very strong increase in the last decade, reaching 41.8 persons per hectare in 2019. For the whole period 2000–19, this implies a density increase of 16.5%. Density development was less clear in Sweden's second-largest city, Gothenburg, with an overall density increase of 2.3% from 2000 to 2019, but with density increase in the first decade (up from 25.1 to 27.0 inhabitants per hectare) but reduction in the last 9 years (down to 25.7 in 2019). The latter reduction was mainly due to expansion of the city into an existing, low-density suburb, which then became included within the urban area demarcation.

As indicated by Fig. 2, urban densities have only recently started to rise in Finland. This is largely also the case in Denmark, where urban densification took off later than in Norway and Sweden. Available statistics on urban densities in Denmark only cover the period 2017–20 (Statistics Denmark, 2020). Over these 3 years, the population density of the morphological city of Copenhagen increased by 2.8% (up from 47.2 to 48.5 persons per hectare). Copenhagen stands out from other Danish cities with more than twice as high population density as in the third and fourth largest cities, Odense (22.8 persons/ha) and Aalborg (23.3 persons/ha). The highest density increase from 2017 to 2020 among the larger Danish cities occurred in Aarhus (4.0%, up from 27.4 to 28.5 persons/ha).

Statistics for density development in Iceland are only available from the Nomenclature for Territorial Units for Statistics (NUTS) database, and this information may not be as reliable as the figures from the national statistical bureaus of the Nordic countries. According to NUTS statistics, the population density of the morphological city of Reykjavik increased by 14% from 2000 to 2015 (European Commission's Joint Research Center, 2016).

2.4 A close-up on the Oslo region

As evident from Figs. 2 and 4, Oslo has been a forerunner in urban containment and has undergone a particularly strong population density increase

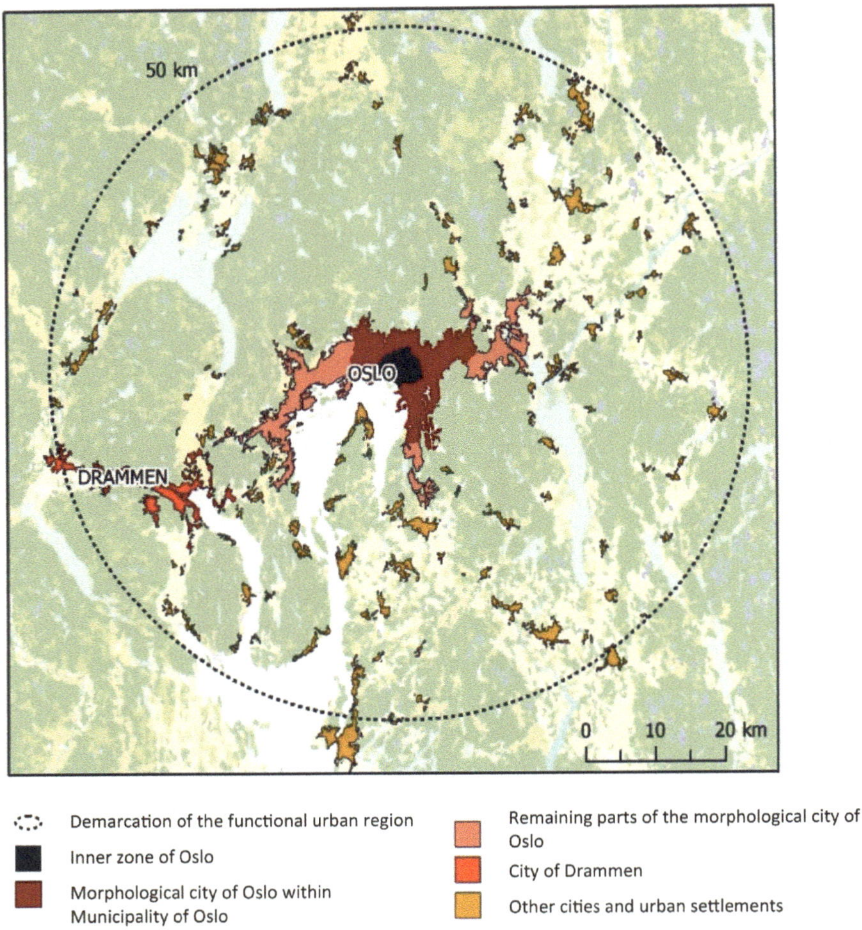

Fig. 5 Demarcations of the functional urban region, different parts of the morphological city of Oslo, and other cities and urban settlements within the functional urban region of Oslo. *Reprinted from Tiitu, M., Næss, P., Ristimäki, M., 2020. The urban density in two Nordic capitals—comparing the development of Oslo and Helsinki metropolitan regions. Eur. Plan. Stud. https://doi.org/10.1080/09654313.2020.1817865.*

over the last decades. Fig. 5 shows the functional urban region of Oslo, defined as the area within a 50 km radius from the city center of Oslo, and the urbanized areas within this region. This demarcation of the region was chosen based on information from previous studies of commuting in the

Oslo region (Engebretsen and Gjerdåker, 2012; Jukvam, 2002).[b] In addition to Oslo (population: 1,036,000), Drammen (population: 109,000) is a relatively large city within this region. On the map, the urban area of Oslo has been divided into three parts: The inner zone, consisting of the six most central administrative districts of Oslo municipality (black); the outer zone of the municipality of Oslo, consisting of the nine remaining administrative districts (dark red); and the part of the morphological city stretching into nine neighboring municipalities (light red). Drammen is shown in medium-red and other urban settlements in orange.

Within the 50 km radius circle, the total population increased by 33% from 1.14 million to 1.53 million over the period 2000–20. The urban settlement population increased by 35% from 1.07 million in 2000 to 1.47 million in 2020. In addition, there is a rural population of around 60,000 in the region; this population decreased slightly by 3% over the period. The greatest part of new housing construction in the region during the period has taken place as densification, reflected in an overall increase in population density for all urban settlements in the region by 18% from a weighted average of 25.1 to 29.6 inhabitants per hectare. Among the 113 urban settlements within the defined functional urban region, 29 smaller and mostly peripheral urban settlements still reduced their population density during this 20-year period. These urban settlements represented 6% of the regional population in 2020. All the remaining urban settlements increased their population density.

Fig. 6 shows how the population densities of different parts of the morphological city of Oslo have developed over the period 2000–20 and how the inhabitants' average distance to the city center of Oslo has developed over the period. As mentioned above, the morphological city of Oslo has

[b] Among three societal processes mentioned by Onsager and Selstad (2004) as important for the generation of regions (interaction, identification and institutionalizing), our demarcation is based on the first aspect. Regional demarcation criteria based on identification (e.g. name, culture, dialect, feeling of belonging, local patriotism) or institutionalizing (political, economic and cultural institutions) are thus disregarded. Moreover, within the criterion of interaction the demarcation is also simplified, as it disregards kinds of interaction other than commuting (such as non-work-based interaction, or ecological interactions) (Davoudi, 2008). The demarcation may also somewhat underestimate the actual size of the commuting hinterland of Oslo to the north and north-east while overestimating its size somewhat in the southeastern and southwestern direction (cf. Engebretsen and Gjerdåker, 2012, 40). Despite these shortcomings, I still consider the 50 km radius-based definition as useful for the purpose of the present chapter.

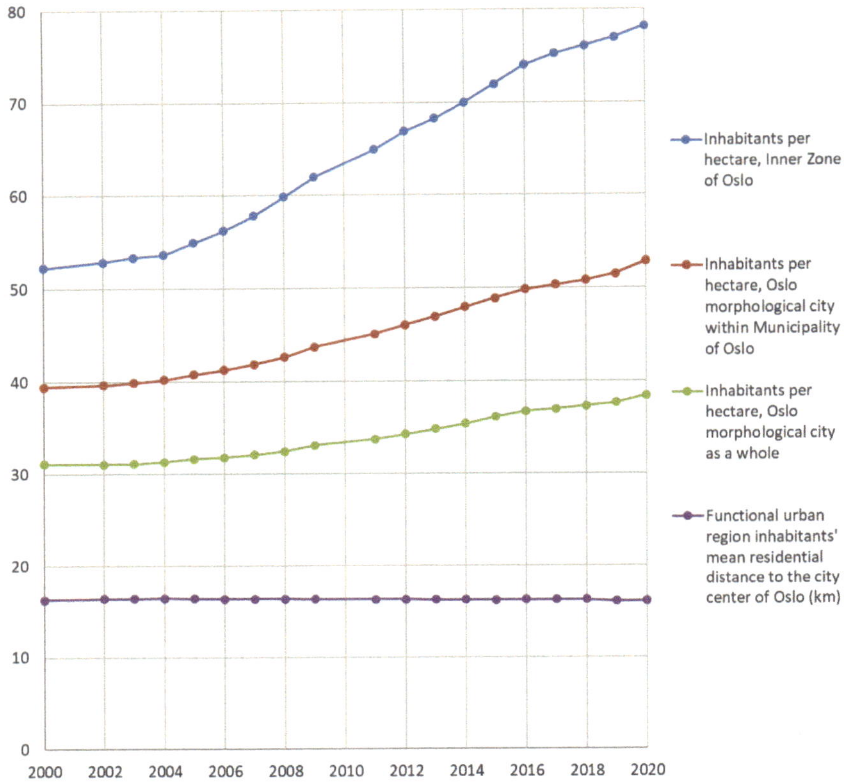

Fig. 6 Changes in population densities within different parts of the morphological city of Oslo and changes in the functional urban region inhabitants' mean distance to the city center of Oslo over the period 2000–20. The functional urban region is defined as the area within a 50 km radius from the city center of Oslo. *Based on Statistics Norway, 2020. Areal og befolkning i tettsteder, etter tettsted, tid og statistikkvariabel. Statistics Norway, Oslo/Kongsvinger. https://www.ssb.no/statistikkbanken (accessed November 15, 2020); Municipality of Oslo, 2020. Folkemengde, ti soner—Antall. Municipality of Oslo, Statistikkbanken, Oslo. http://statistikkbanken.oslo.kommune.no/webview/ (accessed November 2020).*

undergone substantial densification over recent decades. From 2000 to 2020, the population density increased from 31.1 to 38.4 persons per hectare. While the population increased by 34% over the period, the size of the urbanized area increased by only 9%.

The increase was particularly strong in the last 12 years of the period, with population density increasing by 0.47 persons per hectare annually over the years 2008–20, compared to 0.18 annually from 2000 to 2008. This strong population density increase must be seen in the light of the rapid population growth that Oslo experienced during the period 2008–20 (from

856,900 to 1,036,100 inhabitants). Without the high population growth rate, the strong population density increase would not have possible, regardless of any strategy for compact urban development.

The increase in population density has been particularly strong in Oslo's "Inner zone," which increased its population from 152,000 to 228,000 from 2000 to 2020. Since the spatial extension of the urbanized land in this zone remained constant, this implies a population density increase of 50% over the 20-year period, reaching 78 persons per hectare. The medium-central and outer parts of the morphological city increased their population density as well. In the part of the morphological city belonging to the municipality of Oslo but outside its Inner Zone, the population density increased by 25% (from 36.4 to 45.6 persons per hectare). For the municipality of Oslo as a whole, the urban population density increase was 34%. Within the parts of the morphological city situated outside the municipality of Oslo, the population density increase was 17% (from 21.2 to 24.9 persons per hectare).

Apart from Oslo, the functional region includes one other urban settlement of more than 100,000 inhabitants: Drammen, with its center at a distance (as the crow flies) of 36 km from the city center of Oslo. A considerable part of the new development over the period 2000–20 in Drammen took place as densification, but there was also some outward urban expansion. The increase in population density from 2000 to 2020 was 14%. Most of this increase occurred over the last half of the period. The average population density of the urban settlements outside Oslo and Drammen was 16.2 persons per hectare in 2000 and increased to 18.1 persons per hectare in 2020, i.e., a growth of 12%. This is clearly lower than the regional average of 18%.

Despite the considerable population growth, there is hardly any tendency of decentralization of the population from the inner to the outer parts of the region. Such decentralization has sometimes been advocated in order to reduce the pressure for development in Oslo and the surrounding municipalities. The functional urban region as we have defined includes 111 urban settlements apart from the morphological cities of Oslo and Drammen. These urban settlements have a total population of 325,000 (ranging from 215 to 21,600), which makes up 21% of the population within the 50-km-radius functional urban region. The population of these settlements increased by 54% from 2000 to 2020, which is considerably higher than the average for the functional region as a whole (35%) and represents a decentralization tendency counteracting the centralizing effect of the strong densification and population growth in Oslo. These two decentralizing and centralizing tendencies almost outweigh each other, resulting in a nearly constant average distance to the city center of Oslo for the overall population of the functional urban region (16.19 km in 2000 and 15.99 km in 2020). Within the morphological city of Oslo there was a slight concentration of the population, in contrast to the decades before the turn of the millennium. While the population growth of the morphological city took place on average 20 km from the city center during the years 1980–89, this distance was on average only 8 km over the period 2005–20 (Statistics Norway, 2020; Strand et al., 2013). As a result, the mean residential distance to the city center among all inhabitants of the morphological city decreased by 2.5% over the period.

3. Conditions, strategies and instruments promoting densification

Several circumstances have contributed to the strong densification that most of the largest Norwegian cities have undergone over the last two decades (Næss et al., 2011a,b; Tiitu et al., 2020). Table 1 summarizes some of the most important factors.

3.1 Influential background conditions

In addition to policy instruments promoting compact urban development (see below), several spatial, cultural and political conditions have facilitated urban densification.

Extensive suburban development after World War II had resulted in rather low densities of Norwegian cities and urban regions by the 1980s. The reserves of plots where urban densification could easily take place were thus relatively large, making up a considerable potential for densification. In addition, areas vacant for urban transformation increased from the 1980s and onward as manufacturing industries moved abroad as a result of globalization processes. These traits are typical for cities not only in Norway but also in many parts of Europe. In addition, the rocky terrain surrounding many Norwegian cities has counteracted spatial expansion of the city, which would require costly terrain leveling works unless the expansion could instead take place on farmland. However, farmland is a very scarce resource in Norway, and increased awareness about Norway's vulnerability to blockages in the international food supply system has resulted in gradually more strict policies against farmland conversion.

Strong economic growth and high in-migration to the largest Norwegian cities (largely from abroad, but also from rural regions), combined with higher birth surplus due to increased average life span, have contributed to a high pace of development. Combined with a relatively low density at the outset, strong economic growth since the 1990s, and strong protection of surrounding areas

Table 1 Strategies, instruments and conditions supportive of urban densification in Norwegian cities.

Influential conditions Barriers and risks	Influence of natural context and existing built environment	• Surrounding rocky terrain making urban expansion costly • Farmland a scarce resource • Moderate urban density at the outset • Vacant sites due to deindustrialization
	Influence of demographic and economic context	• High population growth, economic growth and pace of development
	Influence of cultural context	• "Cafe culture" and urban living gaining in popularity • Strong tradition of skiing and walking in surrounding forests providing popular support for urban containment
	Influence of political conditions on planning and decision-making	• Quite high acceptance of public land use control and state-level policy instruments • Moderate inter-municipal competition
Instruments and strategies	Key land use policy instruments promoting sustainability	• Strong greenbelt policy in the largest cities • National policy provisions on coordinated land use and transport planning • Restrictive national policy on farmland conversion
	Dominant conception of sustainable land use strategies	• Urban containment, inner-city densification • Polycentric development at public transport nodes
	Dominant conception of sustainable transport strategies	• Public transport improvement, road tunnel building to lead traffic away from city centers and housing • Transportation pricing

against urban expansion, this has facilitated a high pace of development within existing urban area demarcations and hence a rapid increase in urban population densities.

Residential preferences have changed—a trend observed in Norwegian cities (Saglie, 1998; Støa and Aune, 2003) as well as internationally. In particular, an increasing interest among the population for "urban culture" and "café life" has been observed (Di Marino et al., 2020; Hellevik, 1996; Sjaastad et al., 2007). This rising popularity for urban living has especially been pronounced among young people and middle-age inhabitants whose children have moved away from home. In addition, the increasingly multicultural population of the larger cities, especially Oslo, has arguably contributed to increase the share of the population preferring other types of housing than the detached single-family house (Ruud et al., 2013). Although the middle class previously largely preferred to live in the suburbs, the "new" middle class is more prone to prefer to live in the central parts of the city (Lees et al., 2008). Increased attractiveness of inner-city living has driven housing prices upward, most dramatically in Oslo but substantially also in other large cities. This has entailed considerable gentrification of residential neighborhoods close to city centers. In some cities, densification has required renewed investments in technical and social infrastructure in the inner city. This has, in turn, made inner-city living and job locations more attractive, leading to a higher population base, facilitating further infrastructure improvements. Thus, it has been a self-amplifying process.

The strong outdoor recreation interests result in protecting cities' surrounding "marka" areas against urban expansion. Norway has a longstanding and strong outdoor recreation culture emphasizing cross-country skiing and walking. Although the tradition of making a trip on foot or skiing in the forests each weekend, which was very strong in the decades up to the 1980s, has weakened somewhat, there is still solid popular support of protecting the natural areas adjacent to the cities for their outdoor recreational opportunities.

Norway has for a long time been one of the OECD countries with the highest confidence in national government, and among the Nordic countries Norway is on top in this regard (OECD, 2016). Norwegians' trust in national government also manifests itself in a quite high acceptance of public land use control and state-level policy instruments. Moreover, compared to many other European countries (for example, France and Italy), Norwegian municipalities usually cover a relatively large area. For many of the largest Norwegian cities (including Bergen and Trondheim), the entire morphological city is contained within one municipality. Oslo, where the morphological city includes areas in 10 municipalities, and Stavanger/Sandnes (four municipalities) are in this sense atypical. The competition in regions where the functional city is divided between many municipalities is a well-known phenomenon in urban theory and political economy literature (e.g., Logan and Molotch, 1996). Although a study among planners and policy-makers some years ago showed a widespread wish for improved regional coordination of spatial development in the Oslo metropolitan area, competition between different municipalities for investments and taxpayers had influenced land use development to a lesser degree in the Oslo than in the Copenhagen metropolitan area (Næss et al., 2011b). The Norwegian Planning and Building Act provides possibilities for higher-level authorities to influence municipalities' land use development through, among others, county plans and national-government policy guidelines. Although these plans and guidelines are not legally binding, they are politically important and provide the formal basis for objections from counties and state authorities to raise objections against municipal proposals violating the county plans and national guidelines (see below).

3.2 Instruments and strategies

Like in most European countries, the Norwegian planning system gives the authority over land use to the municipalities, although conditionally (see below). The Norwegian Planning and Building Act and its predecessor, the Building Act, have since 1965 provided legal instruments for municipalities to forbid the construction of non-agricultural buildings and technical installations on land set aside in the municipal master plan for non-development. Since 1985, such prohibition against conversion into construction sites applies automatically for all parts of the municipality that are not set aside in the master land use plan for construction purposes.[c] This provides municipalities with an important instrument to control urban sprawl. Particularly in the largest cities, strong greenbelt policies have been pursued to protect surrounding forests and other natural areas as outdoor recreation areas for the urban population. In Norway as well as in other Nordic countries except Denmark, the traditional Right to roam (also called the right of access) has since 1957 been incorporated in the Outdoor Recreation Act. It gives the public the right to walking, skiing, jogging,

[c] In addition, intra-urban green areas as well as green areas at the urban fringe can be protected through more detail-scale zoning plans.

swimming and most other forms of non-motorized movement on non-cultivated land. This right ensures that everybody gets to experience nature, even on larger privately owned areas. The right covers most shores, bogs, forests and mountains and is an important precondition for the solid popular support of greenbelt policies in Norwegian urban regions.

The municipal authority over land-use planning is only a conditional authority. If municipal plan proposals are at odds with important national or regional interests, state sectoral agency, the county governor (who is the central-state representative at the regional level) or the politically elected county council can raise formal objections. Such objections are often raised pursuant to central government policy guidelines adopted by the government by authority of the Planning and Building Act. The plan will then have to be finally adopted by the ministry responsible for planning, currently the Ministry of Local Government and Modernization. One important policy guideline is on coordinated residential, land use and transport planning,[d] adopted in 2014 as a slight revision of a similar central government policy guideline enacted already in 1993. These policy guidelines put pressure on the municipalities to cover their need for development within existing urban area demarcations instead of through outward urban expansion. Particularly in the years 1993–2013, the sanctioning possibilities provided by these guidelines had an important disciplining effect as well as providing a formal base for the national government to stop sprawling municipal land use proposals. Although the conservative-liberalist national government in force since 2013 has put pressure on regional state authorities to raise fewer objections and has itself changed to a more liberal practice when deciding on objections by against municipal plans (Strand and Næss, 2017), the central government policy guidelines still play an important role in supporting compact urban development. Moreover, since 2012, a large parliamentary majority has adopted the goal of zero growth in private car traffic in the 10 largest Norwegian urban regions. With expected population growth, the goal implies substantial per capita reduction in car driving over the next decades. The zero-growth objective has been included in National Transport Plans adopted since 2013 and in regional land use and transport plans of affected urban regions. Allocation of state funding for infrastructure development and transit operation in these regions depends on, among others, the municipalities' progress in following up the zero-growth goal.

[d] https://www.regjeringen.no/no/dokumenter/Statlige-planretningslinjer-for-samordnet-bolig–areal--og-transportplanlegging/id2001539/.

At the same time, the Norwegian government has in recent years emphasized polycentric development as a strategy for reducing pressure on the larger cities (Ministry of Transport, 2013). Key to this strategy is compact development around main railroad and metro nodes. This is reflected, among others, in the regional plan for Oslo and the neighboring Akershus county, where better balance between workplaces in Oslo and in regional cities in Akershus is promoted to achieve better directional balance and utilization of the transport system. The plan also argues that polycentric development could shorten travel distances (Municipality of Oslo/County of Akershus, 2015). This resonates with a widespread belief that employees at suburban workplaces would on average enjoy shorter commuting distances than those of centrally located jobsites but, as will be shown in Section 4, this belief is at odds with research findings.

Norway has also since 1975 had a rather restrictive national policy on farmland conversion, introduced for national preparedness reasons because farmland is a scarce resource in Norway, covering only 3% of the national territory. This policy was somewhat relaxed in 1993 but was stepwise tightened again in 2004 and 2016 with a current objective of keeping the annual conversion of farmland below one third of the level in 2004 (Ministry of Food and Agriculture, 2016)—a goal that has been met since 2017 (Skog, 2020).

Particularly in the Oslo region, planning authorities have also placed strong emphasis on protecting forests and other natural areas surrounding the cities (often termed the "marka" area of each city) as outdoor recreation areas for the urban population. In its 1949 municipal master plan, the municipality of Oslo established a "black line," beyond which no urban expansion should take place. Although the master plans are mandatorily revised each fourth year, Oslo municipality's "marka border" has remained almost unchanged since the 1976 master plan.[e] Similarly, a "red line" around the "marka areas" of Trondheim has effectively protected the surrounding forests and bogs against urban development since the 1970s, except one residential area developed in the northeastern part of the surrounding forests in the 1980s.

The urban containment policies that most of the larger Norwegian cities have pursued reflect the strong status of the compact city as an ideal among

[e] Following a national directive, "marka borders" were also established since 1986 in the other municipalities of Oslo metropolitan area. In addition, the Marka forest areas of the Oslo region were protected in 2009 by a national law, making it even more difficult for municipalities to expand their urban areas beyond the "marka border."

Norwegian urban planners. In 2002, Hoftun (2002) stated that the compact city had obtained hegemonic status within the Norwegian profession of spatial planners as a model for sustainable urban development. During the last decades, the increasingly prevailing understanding among participants in the Norwegian land-use-planning discourse has been that densification rather than sprawl is preferable, because it can both save valuable land and reduce car travel (Andersen and Røe, 2016; Hanssen et al., 2015; Næss et al., 2011a). According to Hoftun, strong discourse coalitions have been formed around the storylines of "save land" and "transportation," making it difficult for strategies placing less emphasis on these issues to gain foothold among planners and policy-makers.

Particularly in the Oslo Metropolitan Area, the discourses supporting compact city development have converged into a doctrine (Faludi and van der Valk, 1994) or hegemonic discourse (Hajer, 1995) for urban development. In the municipality of Oslo, supporters of urban containment, motivated mostly by the desire to protect the Marka forest areas surrounding the city, made their voices heard during the decades following World War II but did not get the upper hand until the 1980s (Næss, 1981; TOBIAS, 1998). The transportation impacts of outward urban expansion became an additional argument against sprawl in the 1990s. Planners in Oslo's neighboring municipalities also became more and more oriented toward densification. Similar processes of discourse formation have taken place in most other Norwegian urban regions and also in smaller towns. This is evident from a recent study of attitudes to measures in urban development (Moberg, 2021), where the opinions of planners, bureaucrats and politicians mostly from small towns in 2020 have been compared with the opinions of a similar sample of respondents in 1991 (Næss, 1993a). According to this study, the support of construction of detached single-family houses decreased from 52% of the respondents in 1991 to 35% in 2020. Conversely, the proportion supporting construction of apartment buildings and other forms of concentrated housing increased from 53% in 1991 to 78% in 2020. The respondents were also more supportive in 2020 than in 1991 of concentrated urban development in general and densification in existing residential areas, although the rates of change were smaller than for housing types and parking capacity. Reflecting the reduced role of manufacturing industries in Norway as well as in many other European countries, the share of respondents who support establishing new spacious industrial sites has diminished considerably (down from 67% to 48%) (Moberg, 2021).

The attitudes among planners, bureaucrats and politicians to measures within urban transport policy have also become more supportive to environmentally friendly mobility since 1991. The support of improved public transit was overwhelmingly high already in 1991 (93%, increasing to 95% in 2020). The important changes are in the willingness to establish restrictions on car driving. There has been a substantial reduction in the support of increased parking capacity (down from 44% to 31%) and a corresponding strong increase in the support of reduced road and parking capacity (up from 55% to 74%). There has also been a strong increase in the support of local road taxes (road pricing, toll cordons, etc.), up from 41% to 59%, and in 2020, 63% of the respondents were in favor of increased parking fees.[f] In 1991, respondents were strongly (81%) in favor of building bypass roads leading traffic away from, e.g., downtown areas and residential neighborhoods. Especially in Oslo but also in other cities, such bypass roads were often built as tunnels, thus facilitating urban regeneration along previous surface-level urban highways. However, in 2020 the support of new bypass road construction was reduced to 58%, possibly reflecting increased costs due to new safety regulations as well as some saturation effect in the wake of the quite massive bypass road construction over the last decades (Moberg, 2021).

Like in 1991, planners and bureaucrats were more oriented than politicians toward dense housing types, concentrated development and limitation of parking capacity in 2020, and this difference has increased since 1991. For some dimensions in urban spatial development, there has also been an increased political polarization along the left-right axis. The support of concentrated urban development and reduced road and parking capacity was clearly stronger among politicians on the left than on the right wing in 1991, but this difference has become more evident in 2020. While the support of these strategies has increased among left-wing politicians, those belonging to the right-wing parties have become more negative (Moberg, 2021).

4. Travel behavioral impacts of Norway's urban densification

There has for several decades been a widespread understanding among participants of the Norwegian land use planning discourse that densification rather than sprawl is preferable in order to reduce car travel.

[f] The question about parking fees was not asked in 1991.

This understanding is also reflected as a key premise in most cities' land use plans and in governmental White Papers on the topic. Counterclaims to the state-of-art knowledge have been expressed by a minority of debaters, but they have not created any widespread doubt about the validity of the pro-density claim (Næss et al., 2011a). One important reason for the widespread confidence in urban densification as a means to promote sustainable mobility may be the fact that a large number of empirical studies on the influences of built environment characteristics have been carried out in Norwegian and other Nordic urban areas.

Nordic cities and metropolitan areas have been the study areas of forerunning research combining qualitative and quantitative methods to identify, in as plausible way as possible, causal impacts of built environment characteristics on travel behavior (Næss, 2015a, b, 2020). As mentioned in the previous section, national and regional policies and plans in the Nordic countries can, to some extent, influence the pattern of development in regions where the functional city covers more than one municipality. This may be one of the explanations why Nordic studies have focused to a greater extent on built environment characteristics at a city-wide or metropolitan scale, rather than following the "D-variable" agenda (Cervero and Kockelman, 1997; Ewing and Cervero, 2010) that has sometimes led to a myopic focus on the neighborhood scale, especially in the USA (see Boarnet and Crane, 2001; Handy, 2018). Distinct from this, most Nordic studies have taken the *location* of neighborhoods relative to downtown and other relevant centers within the urban structure into account when estimating the effects of neighborhood-scale characteristics such as local-area density, land use diversity or street design.

The Nordic studies have found the following spatial characteristics to be the most important ones[g] for maintaining accessibility while reducing transportation volumes and promoting environmentally friendly modes of travel:

- High population density for the city as a whole (the continuous urbanized area, i.e., the morphological city)
- Residential location close to the main center of the city/the metropolitan area
- Location of specialized, labor-intensive or visitor-intensive jobs close to the main center of the city/the metropolitan area.

[g] Based on the elasticities, the standardized regression coefficients and/or the proportion of variance attributable to the spatial characteristics in question.

Tables 2–4 summarizes results found in Nordic studies of impacts of overall urban density and population concentration (Table 2), residential location (Table 3) and workplace location (Table 4). The studies of impacts of the overall urban population density are few and date back to the 1990s, and their dependent variable is energy use for transportation, without any decomposition into effects on transportation distances and modes. The studies of residential and workplace location do, however, include a number of recent studies as well as some from the 1990s, and they show effects in term of travel distances as well as modes. The direct effects of neighborhood-scale densities are generally smaller than those of the above-mentioned metropolitan-scale and city-scale characteristics. However, for the overall population density of a city to be high and the average distances of dwellings and jobs to the city center to be low, each neighborhood must also have a sufficiently high density.

The findings in Table 2 about the impacts of overall urban density are in line with international studies, including Keyes (1976) and Newman and

Table 2 Nordic studies published since 1993 on effects of overall urban population density and concentration on annual energy use per capita for transportation.

Geographical case	Reference	Methods	Built environment variable	Elasticity	*P*-value
22 Nordic cities/towns	Næss et al. (1996)	Cross-sectional quantitative based on gasoline and diesel sales and electricity for transit	Urban area per capita	0.292	0.032
67 Swedish cities/towns	Næss (1993b)	Cross-sectional quantitative based on gasoline and diesel sales and electricity for transit	Urban area per capita	0.410	0.000
22 Nordic cities/towns	Næss et al. (1996)	Cross-sectional quantitative based on gasoline and diesel sales and electricity for transit	Degree of decentralized pattern of residence within the urban area	0.612	0.027

Table 3 Nordic studies published since 2005 on effects of residential distance to the center of the main city of the metropolitan area on travel distance by car.

Geographical case	Reference	Study area population	Methods	Travel behavior variable	Elasticity	*P*-value
Copenhagen metropolitan area (DK)	Næss (2005)	1.8 mill.	Quantitative and qualitative; cross-sectional with some retrospectively longitudinal	Travel distance by car on weekdays, including intra- and outside-metropolitan travel	0.270	0.000
Copenhagen morphological city (DK)	Næss (2015b)	1.3 mill.	Quantitative and qualitative; cross-sectional	Weekly traveling distance by car or motorbike	0.37	0.001
Oslo metropolitan area (NO)	Næss et al. (2017)	1.2 mill.	Qualitative and quantitative; cross-sectional and retrospectively longitudinal	Weekly car driving distance including intra- and outside-metropolitan travel	0.287	0.000
Oslo metropolitan area (NO)	Næss et al. (2019a)	1.2 mill.	Qualitative and quantitative; cross-sectional and retrospectively longitudinal	Weekly intra-metropolitan distance traveled by car	0.823	0.000
Oslo morphological city (NO)	Engebretsen et al. (2018)	1.0 mill.	Cross-sectional quantitative	Daily car driving distance	0.238	0.000
Bergen morphological city (NO)	Engebretsen et al. (2018)	0.25 mill.	Cross-sectional quantitative	Daily car driving distance	0.390	0.000

Reykjavik metropolitan area (IS)	Næss et al. (2021)	0.23 mill.	Qualitative and quantitative; cross-sectional and retrospectively longitudinal	Weekly car driving distance including intra- and outside-metropolitan travel	0.330	0.000
Stavanger metropolitan area (NO)	Næss et al. (2017)	0.3 mill.	Qualitative and quantitative; cross-sectional and retrospectively longitudinal	Weekly car driving distance including intra- and outside-metropolitan travel	0.259	0.000
Stavanger metropolitan area (NO)	Næss et al. (2019a)	0.3 mill.	Qualitative and quantitative; cross-sectional and retrospectively longitudinal	Weekly intra-metropolitan distance traveled by car	0.525	0.000
Stavanger/ Sandnes morphological city (NO)	Engebretsen et al. (2018)	0.21 mill.	Cross-sectional quantitative	Daily car driving distance	0.256	0.000
Trondheim morphological city (NO)	Engebretsen et al. (2018)	0.18 mill	Cross-sectional quantitative	Daily car driving distance	0.365	0.000
Frederikshavn municipality (DK)	Næss and Jensen (2000, 2004)	0.035 mill	Cross-sectional quantitative and qualitative	Weekly car driving distance including intra- and outside-municipality travel	0.329	0.000
Kongsvinger morphological city (NO)	Wolday (2018)	0.012 mill.	Cross-sectional quantitative	Car driving distance	0.265	0.001

Table 4 Nordic studies published since 2005 on effects of workplace distance to the center of the main city of the metropolitan area on commuting travel mode (upper part) and commuting distance (lower part).

Geographical case	References	Study area population	Methods	Travel behavior variable	Elasticity	*P*-value
Copenhagen metropolitan area (DK)	Næss (2007)	1.8 mill.	Qualitative and cross-sectional quantitative	Proportion of commuting trips by car during investigated period	Positive; elasticity not calculated	0.069
Oslo metropolitan area (NO)	Næss et al. (2019a)	1.2 mill.	Qualitative and cross-sectional quantitative	Likelihood of being a regular car commuter	Positive; elasticity not calculated	0.000
Oslo metropolitan area (NO)	Næss et al. (2019b) and Wolday et al. (2019)	1.2 mill.	Qualitative and quantitative; cross-sectional and retrospectively longitudinal	Likelihood of being a regular car commuter	0.519	0.000
Oslo morphological city (NO)	Engebretsen et al. (2018)	1.0 mill.	Cross-sectional quantitative	Likelihood of commuting by car	Positive; elasticity not calculated	0.000
Bergen morphological city (NO)	Engebretsen et al. (2018)	0.25 mill.	Cross-sectional quantitative	Likelihood of commuting by car	Positive; elasticity not calculated	0.000
Stavanger metropolitan area (NO)	Næss et al. (2019a)	0.3 mill.	Qualitative and quantitative; cross-sectional and retrospectively longitudinal	Likelihood of being a regular car commuter	Positive; elasticity not calculated	0.002
Stavanger/Sandnes morphological city (NO)	Engebretsen et al. (2018)	0.21 mill.	Cross-sectional quantitative	Likelihood of commuting by car	Positive; elasticity not calculated	0.026

Trondheim morphological city (NO)	Engebretsen et al. (2018)	0.18 mill	Cross-sectional quantitative	Likelihood of commuting by car	Slightly pos.; elasticity not calculated	0.212
Copenhagen metropolitan area (DK)	Næss (2007)	1.8 mill.	Qualitative and cross-sectional quantitative	Commuting distance	Slightly neg.; elasticity not calculated	0.228
Oslo metropolitan area (NO)	Næss et al. (2019a)	1.2 mill.	Qualitative and cross-sectional quantitative	Commuting distance	0.140	0.000
Oslo metropolitan area (NO)	Næss et al. (2019b) and Wolday et al. (2019)	1.2 mill.	Qualitative and quantitative; cross-sectional and retrospectively longitudinal	Commuting distance	0.136	0.003
Oslo morphological city (NO)	Engebretsen et al. (2018)	1.0 mill.	Cross-sectional quantitative	Commuting distance	0.406	0.000
Stavanger metropolitan area (NO)	Næss et al. (2019a)	1.2 mill.	Qualitative and cross-sectional quantitative	Commuting distance	0.183	0.000
Stavanger/Sandnes morphological city (NO)	Engebretsen et al. (2018)	0,22 mill.	Cross-sectional quantitative	Commuting distance	0.500	0.000
Bergen morphological city (NO)	Engebretsen et al. (2018)	0.25 mill.	Cross-sectional quantitative	Commuting distance	0.425	0.000
Trondheim morphological city (NO)	Engebretsen et al. (2018)	0.18 mill	Cross-sectional quantitative	Commuting distance	0.582	0.000

Kenworthy (1989, 1999). The effect of the degree of decentralized pattern of residence within the urban area reflects the same mechanism as the effects of residential distance to the city center shown in Table 3. The latter studies show very converging results, although the elasticities between the distance from the dwelling to the city center and car travel vary, depending on, among others, city context (e.g., population size; monocentric vs polycentric) and whether travel distance by car is measured as intra-metropolitan travel or also includes travel outside the metropolitan area. The findings in Table 3 are in line with a host of international studies (including Ewing and Cervero, 2010; Headicar, 2000; Milakis et al., 2008, 2015; Mogridge, 1985; Næss, 2010; Newman and Kenworthy, 1989; Zegras, 2010; Zhou and Kockelman, 2008) as well as Nordic studies where effect estimates have not been translated into elasticities (Czepkiewicz et al., 2018; Elldér, 2014; Hartoft-Nielsen, 2001a; Martamo, 1995; Næss et al., 1995). Residential location close to the city center has also been found to contribute to reduced car ownership in two of the largest Norwegian metropolitan areas, the Oslo and Stavanger regions (Cao et al., 2019).

The effects of workplace location are generally stronger on modal split than on commuting distances, as can be seen in Table 4. Except from the study of Trondheim (Engebretsen et al., 2018) at the bottom of the table, all studies show strong impacts on the proportions of car commuting. The effect found in the Copenhagen study (Næss, 2007; upper row of Table 4) has a rather weak *P*-value, but this must be seen in the light of the low number of respondents of this workplace analysis (travel diary participants, a sub-set of the much larger number of respondents included in most of the Copenhagen study referred to in Table 3 (Næss, 2005)). The small and uncertain effect found in the Trondheim study must be seen in the light that only the *direct* effect of workplace location is reported. A very strong effect of density in the local area of the workplace was found in the same study. Since local-area densities are heavily influenced by neighborhoods' distance to the city center (Alonso, 1964), there is thus a strong indirect effect of workplace location via local-area density. Such indirect effects also exist for the other studies shown in Tables 3 and 4. However, only direct effects are shown in the tables. The tendency of higher shares of car commuting to suburban workplaces is in line with older Nordic studies (Hanssen, 1995; Hartoft-Nielsen, 2001b; Monsen, 1983; Næss and Sandberg, 1996; Strømmen, 2001) as well as a number of studies from other parts of the world, including Cervero and Landis (1992), Schwanen et al. (2001), Yang (2005), Aguiléra et al. (2009), Aguiléra and Voisin (2014), Hu and Schneider (2017) and Vale et al. (2018).

Apart from the Copenhagen study (Næss, 2005), all the studies in Table 4 show tendencies of somewhat shorter commuting distances to workplaces located close to the city center. This, too, is in line with older studies in the Nordic countries (Hartoft-Nielsen, 2001b; Martamo, 1995; Næss and Sandberg, 1996; Strømmen, 2001) as well as in a wider international scope (Cervero and Landis, 1992; Schwanen et al., 2001; Yang, 2005).

As mentioned above, the Nordic studies mostly show stronger effects of city- or metropolitan-scale built environment characteristics (such as residential and workplace distance to the city center) than of local neighborhood characteristics. Space only allows illustrating this for studies in two metropolitan areas, those of Oslo and Stavanger (Table 5).

Table 5 Effects of residential location and local built environment characteristics[a] on different aspects of travel behavior among respondents from Oslo and Stavanger, controlled for demographic, socioeconomic and residential preference variables.

Aspect of travel behavior	Weekly distance traveled by car for commuting and seven non-work purposes		Car share of distance traveled for commuting and seven non-work purposes		Walk/bike share of distance traveled for commuting and seven non-work purposes	
Metropolitan area	Oslo $N=991$	Stavanger $N=667$	Oslo $N=956$	Stavanger $N=648$	Oslo $N=958$	Stavanger $N=653$
Distance to the main city center (km)	4.72 ***0.401*** (0.000)	4.39 ***0.324*** (0.000)	0.0087 ***0.234*** (0.000)	0.0095 ***0.175*** (0.000)	−0.0069 ***−0.255*** (0.000)	−0.0093 ***−0.192*** (0.000)
Distance to the closest second-order center (km)	1.35 ***0.058*** (0.063)	4.92 ***0.282*** (0.000)	n.s.	n.s.	−0.0047 ***−0.087*** (0.009)	n.s.
Distance to the closest local center (km)	n.s.	n.s.	n.s.	n.s.	0.0056 ***0.058*** (0.096)	n.s.
Inhabitants per hectare within the 1 km^2 grid square of the dwelling	n.s.	−0.475 ***−0.072*** (0.064)	−0.0010 ***−0.112*** (0.001)	−0.0024 ***−0.092*** (0.018)	0.0017 ***0.253*** (0.000)	0.0022 ***0.092*** (0.026)

[a]n.s. refers to not significant at the 0.1 level. The effects are controlled for demographic, socioeconomic and residential preference variables.
Unstandardized and standardized (in bold italics) regression coefficients, levels of significance (*P*-values) in parentheses.
Modified from Næss, P., Strand, A., Wolday, F., Stefansdottir, H., 2019a. Residential location, commuting and non-work travel in two urban areas of different size and with different center structures. Prog. Plan. 128, 1–36.

As mentioned above, most of the Nordic studies since have combined statistical analyses with in-depth qualitative interviews. The purpose of the latter has been to identify the rationales (Næss and Jensen, 2005) influencing interviewees' choices of activity participation, activity locations and travel modes, and how built environment characteristics, in combination with these rationales and time-geographical constraints (Hägerstrand, 1970), influence travel behavior. Based on one of these studies (Næss et al., 2021), Tables 6 and 7 show rationales for activity location choice (Table 6) and travel mode choice rationales (Table 7) and their implications for geographical differences in trip distances and travel modes, respectively. The rationales found among the interviewees of this study are very similar to those found in other studies in the Nordic countries as well as in Portugal and China (Næss, 2005, 2013, 2015c; Næss et al., 2018, 2019a,b).

Most of the rationales contribute, to a greater or lesser extent, to longer trip distances and higher predilection to car travel among suburbanites than among inner-city residents. A similar study of rationales related to commuting, focusing on relationships between workplace location and travel modes for journeys to work, shows similarly that most of the rationales encourage employees at suburban workplaces to commute by car while those working at centrally located workplaces are encouraged to commute by transit (Næss et al., 2019a,b).

The compact urban development in Norwegian cities and the improved transit provision and transportation pricing facilitated by the densification have exerted substantial influence on travel behavior. Compact and concentrated urban development reduces not only car driving distances and the modal share of car travel, but also car ownership (Zegras, 2010; Ding et al., 2018; Cao et al., 2019). Although some scholars (e.g., Boarnet and Crane, 2001) have postulated that the shorter trip distances in compact cities would increase trip frequencies, empirical results from the Nordic countries show only small such effects, if any at all (Næss, 2006). In a Nordic context, residential location also does not seem to affect overall travel time much, although weak but counteracting tendencies have been found when considering weekend and weekday travel separately (Næss, 2006). For workplace location, a tendency of shorter travel time to suburban jobs has still been found (Wolday et al., 2019), reflecting the more congested conditions in the central parts of metropolitan areas.

The impacts of urban containment on travel distances and mode choice have been strong enough to outweigh counteracting trends such as a steadily increasing affluence level, which could otherwise be expected to induce

Table 6 Rationales for activity location choice and their implications for geographical differences in trip distances, compared to the trip distances of persons with "average" residential location.

Rationales for location of activities	Encourages trip distances among inner-city residents to become	Encourages trip distances among residents living close to suburban centers to become	Encourages trip distances among residents living at non-central locations to become
Main rationales, applying to commuting as well as non-work trips			
Choosing the "best facility"			
Generally	Shorter	Somewhat longer	Considerably longer
Workplace/ place of education	Considerably shorter	Longer	Considerably longer
Non-work facilities	Shorter	Somewhat shorter	Longer
Minimizing the friction of distance			
Generally	Shorter	Shorter	Longer
Accessibility by car	Longer	Somewhat shorter	Somewhat longer
Accessibility by non-motorized modes	Considerably shorter	Shorter	Longer
Less important rationales, applying mainly to non-wok trips			
Social contacts	Shorter	Somewhat shorter	Longer
Variety-seeking	Somewhat shorter	Slightly shorter	Somewhat longer
Place attachment	Ambiguous effect	Ambiguous effect	Ambiguous effect
Urban atmosphere	Somewhat shorter	Somewhat longer	Longer

From Næss, P., Stefansdottir, H., Peters, S., Czepkiewicz, M., Heinonen, J., 2021. Residential Location and Travel in a Car-Oriented City. Paper under review.

more travel by car. Based on available traffic count data for the years 2009–18 (Norwegian Public Roads Administration, 2020), there was virtually no increase in total road traffic within the morphological city of Oslo over these years. While there was a traffic increase for heavy vehicles, the

Table 7 Travel mode choice rationales and their implications for geographical differences in travel modes, compared to the trip distances of persons with "average" residential location.

Rationales for travel mode choice	Travel modes encouraged for inner-city residents	Travel modes encouraged for residents living close to suburban centers	Travel modes encouraged for residents living at non-central locations
Main rationales			
Time-saving	Non-motorized (local trips) and car (longer trips)	Car	Car
Convenience and comfort	Non-motorized (local trips) and car (longer trips)	Car	Car
Physical exercise	Non-motorized for many trips	Non-motorized for some trips	Non-motorized for a few trips
Frustration aversion	Non-motorized	Car	Car
Secondary, less important rationales			
Ingrained habits	Depending on background, but most often car	Depending on background, but most often car	Car
Economic expenses	Transit and non-motorized	Transit and non-motorized	Transit and non-motorized
Safety	Motorized	Motorized	Motorized
Social contact	All modes	All modes	All modes
Caretaking	Most often car	Most often car	Most often car
Environmental concerns	Non-motorized and transit	Non-motorized and transit	Non-motorized and transit

From Næss, P., Stefansdottir, H., Peters, S., Czepkiewicz, M., Heinonen, J., 2021. Residential Location and Travel in a Car-Oriented City. Paper under review.

traffic volume of light vehicles decreased slightly (by approximately 1%) over this period. Since the population increased by 14% over this period, this indicates a per capita reduction in car traffic by 15% over these 9 years. Similarly, in Trondheim, total traffic across the cordons for which data are available increased by 2.5% from 2009 to 2018 and light vehicle traffic by 1%. With 15% population growth over the same years, this indicates a similar (14%) per capita reduction in car traffic over the 9-year period as in Oslo. Traffic counts from Bergen and Stavanger indicate stagnated overall traffic growth and reduced car traffic per capita in these cities as well (Norwegian Public Roads Administration, 2020). There may of course be several reasons for the reduced per capita traffic, but the compact spatial development that Norwegian larger cities have undergone has clearly played an important role.

As an illustrative example, we have calculated the differentials in car driving distance and overall transportation energy compared to the actual situation if Oslo had continued its sprawling urban development of the decades prior to 1985 (cf. Fig. 2) over the period until 2020. If urban area per capita had increased linearly at the same pace from 1985 to 2020 as it did 1965–1985, the population density of the morphological city of Oslo would then have dropped to 20 persons per hectare (i.e., to the same level as the present density of the New York/Newark urbanized area, USA) instead of its actual increase to 38.4 persons per hectare in 2020. Moreover, population growth would have taken place on average 20 km from the city center of Oslo instead of 8 km as observed over the years 2005–20. Among the whole morphological city population in 2020, the mean residential would then have been 11.1 km instead of 8.1 km. Given the elasticities shown in Tables 2 and 3, per capita energy use for transportation would have been 20% higher if the population density had continued to decrease until 2020 like it did 1965–85 instead of starting to increase at it actually did from the late 1980s. Moreover, if the inhabitants' mean residential distance to the city center had increased since 2000 like it did 1980–90, inhabitants' mean intra-metropolitan travel distance by car would have been nearly 20% longer than the actual figure.

5. Concluding remarks

Most of the largest Norwegian cities have changed their urban developmental patterns from sprawl in the post-World War 2 period until around 1990 to a strong densification trend in the present century. Over the past two decades, 13 of the 15 most populated Norwegian cities have increased their population density, and for some of the cities, such as Oslo and Trondheim, the density increase has been substantial (22.5% and 17%, respectively) over this 20-year period. Similar trends have been observed in Sweden, and more lately also in Denmark, Finland and Iceland.

Several physical, demographic, economic, cultural and political conditions have facilitated Norwegian cities' U-turn from sprawl to urban densification as the dominant trend in recent decades. Norwegians' strong tradition for outdoor recreation in forests and other natural areas has provided strong popular support greenbelt policies, and Norway's scarcity of farmland has motivated restrictions on farmland conversion. There has also been high awareness among Norwegian planners and politicians about travel behavioral impacts of urban spatial development, and since 2012 an ambitious goal of zero growth in car traffic in the 10 largest urban regions has been in included in national-government white papers and transport plans.

The urban containment policies have saved land and reduced the amount of car travel. Needless to say, considerable uncertainty pertains to hypothetical calculations like the ones presented at the end of Section 5. Nevertheless, these examples as well as the observed traffic development in Norwegian cities show that affluent and growing cities can influence their trajectory of traffic development substantially through land use planning. The compact urban development is probably also an important enabling condition for the road toll schemes established in several of the largest Norwegian cities. With continued sprawl like in the years before 1990, economic measures to reduce car driving would be politically difficult to implement, since it would be very inconvenient and time-consuming for many people to reach their destinations by other travel modes than the private car.

While the travel behavioral impacts of urban containment have been quite extensively researched in the Nordic countries, more studies are needed on the impacts of compact city development on perceived housing quality, neighborhood satisfaction, housing affordability and gentrification/displacement of low-income groups. There is also a need for studies of conditions enhancing or counteracting compact city development in cities where the density is at the outset higher than in cities of the Nordic countries, and the various social impacts of such urban development in these contexts.

References

Aguiléra, A., Voisin, M., 2014. Urban form, commuting patterns and CO2 emissions: what differences between the municipality's residents and its jobs? Transp. Res. A 69, 243–251.

Aguiléra, A., Wenglenski, S., Proulhac, L., 2009. Employment suburbanization, reverse commuting and travel behavior by residents of the central city in the Paris metropolitan area. Transp. Res. A 43 (7), 685–691.

Alonso, W., 1964. Location and Land Use. Harvard University Press, Cambridge, MA.

Andersen, B., Røe, P.G., 2016. The social context and politics of large scale urban architecture: investigating the design of Barcode, Oslo. Eur. Urban Reg. Stud. 24 (3), 304–317.

Boarnet, M.G., Crane, R., 2001. Travel by Design. Oxford University Press, Oxford.

Breheny, 1995. The compact city and transport energy consumption. Trans. Inst. Br. Geogr. 20 (1), 81–101.

Bruegmann, 2008. Point: Sprawl and accessibility. J. Transp. Land Use 1 (1), 5–11.

Burchell, R.W., Shad, N.A., Listokin, D., Phillips, H., Downs, A., Seskin, S., Davis, J.S., Moore, T., Helton, D., Gall, M., 1998. The Costs of Sprawl—Revisited. National Academy Press, Washington, DC.

Cao, X.J., Næss, P., Wolday, F., 2019. Examining the effects of the built environment on auto ownership in two Norwegian urban regions. Transp. Res. D 67, 464–474.

Cervero, R., Kockelman, K., 1997. Travel demand and the 3Ds: density, diversity, and design. Transp. Res. Part D: Transp. Environ. 2 (3), 199–219.

Cervero, R., Landis, J., 1992. Suburbanization of jobs and the journey to work: a submarket analysis of commuting in the San Francisco Bay area. J. Adv. Transp. 26, 275–297.

Commission of European Communities, 1990. Green paper on the urban environment. Office for the Official Publications of the European Communities, Luxembourg.

Czepkiewicz, M., Ottelin, J., Ala-Mantila, S., Heinonen, J., Hasanzadeh, K., Kyttä, M., 2018. Urban structural and socioeconomic effects on local, national and international travel patterns and greenhouse gas emissions of young adults. J. Transp. Geogr. 68, 130–141.

Davoudi, S., 2008. Conceptions of the city region: a critical review. Proc. Inst. Civ. Eng. Urban Des. Plan. 161 (2), 51–60.

Di Marino, M., Akhavan, M., Mariotti, I., Chavoshi, S.H., 2020. New working spaces in the age of digital transformation: location factors and implications for planning in two cities of Oslo and Milan. In: Presentation at the 5th RGCS Virtual Symposium "Collaborative Practices, Workspaces and Communities in the Wake of the Covid-19 Crisis", December 14–15, 2020.

Ding, C., Wang, Y., Tang, T., Mishra, S., Liu, C., 2018. Joint analysis of the spatial impacts of built environment on car ownership and travel mode choice. Transp. Res. D 60, 28–40.

EEA, 2006. Urban Sprawl in Europe: The Ignored Challenge. European Environmental Agency, Copenhagen.

Elldér, E., 2014. Residential location and daily travel distances: the influence of trip purpose. J. Transp. Geogr. 34, 121–130.

Engebretsen, Ø., Gjerdåker, A., 2012. Potensial for regionforstørring. TØI report 1208/2012. Institute of Transport Economics, Oslo.

Engebretsen, Ø., Næss, P., Strand, A., 2018. Residential location, workplace location and car driving in four Norwegian cities. Eur. Plan. Stud. 26 (10), 2036–2057.

European Commission's Joint Research Center, 2016. Global Human Settlement Population Grid. Accessed February 2020 from https://ghsl.jrc.ec.europa.eu/ghs_pop.php.

Ewing, R., Cervero, R., 2010. Travel and the built environment: a meta-analysis. J. Am. Plan. Assoc. 76 (3), 265–294.

Faludi, A., van der Valk, A., 1994. Rule and Order: Dutch Planning Doctrine in the 20th Century. Klüver, Dordrecht.

Hägerstrand, T., 1970. What about people in regional science? Pap. Reg. Sci. 24, 7–24.

Hajer, M.A., 1995. The Politics of Environmental Discourse—Ecological Modernisation and the Policy Process. Oxford University Press, Oxford.
Handy, S., Spring 2018. Enough With the "D's" Already—Let's Get Back to "A". 2018 Transfers, pp. 1–3.
Hanssen, J.U., 1995. Transportation impacts of office relocation: a case study from Oslo. J. Transp. Geogr. 3, 247–256.
Hanssen, G.S., Hofstad, H., Saglie, I.-L. (Eds.), 2015. Kompakt byutvikling—muligheter og utfordringer. Universitetsforlaget, Oslo.
Hartoft-Nielsen, P., 2001a. Boliglokalisering og transportadfærd. Danish Forest and Landscape Research Institute, Hørsholm.
Hartoft-Nielsen, P., 2001b. Arbejdspladslokalisering og transportadfærd. Danish Forest and Landscape Research Institute, Hørsholm.
Headicar, P., 2000. The exploding city region: should it, can it, be reversed? In: Williams, K., Burton, E., Jenks, M. (Eds.), Achieving Sustainable Urban Form. Spon, London, pp. 160–173.
Hellevik, O., 1996. Nordmenn og det gode liv. Universitetsforlaget, Oslo.
Hoftun, S., 2002. The Emergence of a Sustainable Urban Form: A Study of the Different Factors Influencing What Is Considered the Best Strategy for Urban Sustainability in Norway. M.Sc. dissertation, University of Oslo/Aalborg University, Oslo/Aalborg.
Høyer, K.G., Holden, E., 2001. Housing as basis for sustainable consumption. Int. J. Sustain. Dev. 4 (1), 48–58.
Hu, L., Schneider, R.J., 2017. Different ways to get to the same workplace: how does workplace location relate to commuting by different income groups? Transp. Policy 59, 106–115.
Jenks, M., Burton, E., Williams, K. (Eds.), 1996. The Compact City: A Sustainable Urban Form? E. and F. N. Spon, London.
Jukvam, D., 2002. Inndeling i bo- og arbeidsmarkedsregioner. Rapport 2002:20. Norwegian Institute for Urban and Regional Research, Oslo.
Keyes, D.L., 1976. Energy and land use: an instrument of US conservation policy? Energy Policy 4, 225–236.
Lees, L., Wyly, E., Slater, T., 2008. Gentrification. Routledge, London and New York.
Logan, J., Molotch, H.L., 1996. The city as a growth machine. In: Campbell, S., Fainstein, S. (Eds.), Readings in Urban Theory. Blackwell, Malden, MA, pp. 291–337.
Martamo, R., 1995. Työssäkäyntietäisyydet Suomessa (Distance Between Workplace and Residence in Finland). Miljöministeriet, Markanvändingsavdelningen.
Milakis, D., Vlastos, T., Barbopoplos, N., 2008. Relationships between urban form and travel behaviour in Athens, Greece. A comparison with western European and North American results. Eur. J. Transp. Infrastruct. Res. 8, 201–215.
Milakis, D., Cervero, R., van Wee, B., 2015. Stay local or go regional? Urban form effects on vehicle use at different spatial scales: a theoretical concept and its application to the San Francisco Bay Area. J. Transp. Land Use 8 (2), 59–86.
Ministry of Food and Agriculture, 2016. Meld. St. 11 (2016–2017), Endring og utvikling: En fremtidsrettet jordbruksproduksjon. Ministry of Food and Agriculture, Oslo.
Ministry of Transport, 2013. National Transport Plan 2014-2023 (White paper no. 26 [2012-2013]). Ministry of Transport, Oslo.
Moberg, K.R., 2021. Environmentally Friendly Urban Development: Changes in Decision-Makers' Attitudes, Problem Perceptions and Policy Preferences Over Three Decades. forthcoming. Draft paper under review.
Mogridge, M.H.J., 1985. Transport, land use and energy interaction. Urban Stud. 22, 481–492.
Monsen, G., 1983. Bedriftsflytting—endring i arbeidsreise og energiforbruk. Cand. polit. dissertation, University of Oslo, Oslo.

Municipality of Oslo/County of Akershus, 2015. Regional Plan for Land Use and Transport. Accessed January 2016 from https://www.akershus.no/ansvarsomrader/samferdsel/samferdselsplanlegging/regional-planfor-areal-og-transport-i-oslo-og-akershus/.
Næss, P., 1981. Boligbygging i Marka? Oslo og Omland Friluftsråd, Oslo.
Næss, P., 1993a. Can urban development be made environmentally sound? J. Environ. Plan. Manag. 36 (3), 309–333.
Næss, P., 1993b. Transportation energy in Swedish towns and regions. Scand. Hous. & Plann. Res. 10 (4), 187–206.
Næss, P., 2005. Residential location affects travel behavior—but how and why? The case of Copenhagen metropolitan area. Prog. Plan. 63 (2), 167–257.
Næss, P., 2006. Accessibility, activity participation and location of activities. Exploring the links between residential location and travel behavior. Urban Stud. 43 (3), 627–652.
Næss, P., 2007. The impacts of job and household decentralization on commuting distances and travel modes: experiences from the Copenhagen region and other Nordic urban areas. Informationen zur Raumentwicklung. Bundesinstitut für Bau-, Stadt- und Raumforschung, Bonn., 149–168. Heft 2/3.2007.
Næss, P., 2010. Residential location, travel and energy use: the case of Hangzhou metropolitan area. J. Transp. Land Use 3 (3), 27–59.
Næss, P., 2012. Urban form and travel behavior: experience from a Nordic context. J. Transp. Land Use 5 (2), 21–45.
Næss, P., 2013. Residential location, transport rationales and daily-life travel behavior: the case of Hangzhou metropolitan area, China. Prog. Plan. 79 (1), 1–50.
Næss, P., 2015a. Built environment, causality and travel. Transp. Rev. 35 (3), 275–291.
Næss, P., 2015b. The explanatory qualitative-quantitative method. In: Pinho, P., Silva, C. (Eds.), Mobility Patterns and Urban Structure. Ashgate, Farnham, pp. 101–120.
Næss, P., 2015c. Residential location and travel behavior. In: Pinho, P., Silva, C. (Eds.), Mobility Patterns and Urban Structure. Ashgate, Farnham, pp. 151–186.
Næss, P., 2020. Validating explanatory qualitative research: enhancing the interpretation of interviews in urban planning and transportation research. Appl. Mobil. 5 (2), 186–205.
Næss, P., Jensen, O.B., 2000. Boliglokalisering og transport i Frederikshavn. ISP Publications No. 256, Aalborg University, Aalborg.
Næss, P., Jensen, O.B., 2004. Urban structure matters, even in a small town. J. Environ. Plan. Manag. 47 (1), 35–56.
Næss, P., Jensen, O.B., 2005. Bilringene og cykelnavet. Boliglokalisering, bilafhængighed og transportadfærd i Hovedstadsområdet. Aalborg University Press, Aalborg.
Næss, P., Sandberg, S.L., 1996. Workplace location, modal split and energy use for commuting trips. Urban Stud. 33 (3), 557–580.
Næss, P., Røe, P.G., Larsen, S.L., 1995. Travelling distances, modal split and transportation energy in thirty residential areas in Oslo. J. Environ. Plan. Manag. 38 (3), 349–370.
Næss, P., Sandberg, S.L., Røe, P.G., 1996. Energy use for transportation in 22 Nordic towns. Scand. Hous. & Plann. Res. 13 (2), 79–97.
Næss, P., Næss, T., Strand, A., 2011a. Oslo's farewell to urban sprawl. Eur. Plan. Stud. 19 (1), 113–139.
Næss, P., Strand, A., Næss, T., Nicolaisen, M., 2011b. On their road to sustainability? The challenge of sustainable mobility in urban planning and development in two Scandinavian capital regions. Town Plan. Rev. 82 (3), 287–317.
Næss, P., Cao, X., Strand, A., 2017. Which D's are the important ones? The effects of built environment characteristics on driving distance in Oslo and Stavanger. J. Transp. Land Use 10 (1), 945–964.
Næss, P., Peters, S., Stefansdottir, H., Strand, A., 2018. Causality, not just correlation: residential location, transport rationales and travel behavior across metropolitan contexts. J. Transp. Geogr. 69, 181–195.

Næss, P., Strand, A., Wolday, F., Stefansdottir, H., 2019a. Residential location, commuting and non-work travel in two urban areas of different size and with different center structures. Prog. Plan. 128, 1–36.
Næss, P., Tønnesen, A., Wolday, F., 2019b. How and why does intra-metropolitan workplace location affect car commuting? Sustainability 11, 1196.
Næss, P., Stefansdottir, H., Peters, S., Czepkiewicz, M., Heinonen, J., 2021. Residential Location and Travel in a Car-Oriented City. Paper under review.
Newman, P.W.G., Kenworthy, J.R., 1989. Cities and Automobile Dependence. Gower Publications, Aldershot.
Newman, P.W.G., Kenworthy, J.R., 1999. Sustainability and Cities: Overcoming Automobile Dependence. Island Press, Washington DC and Covelo, California.
Norwegian Public Roads Administration, 2020. Trafikkregistreringer. Accessed November 2020 from https://www.vegvesen.no/fag/trafikk/trafikkdata/trafikkregistreringer.
OECD, 2016. Trust in Government. Accessed November 2020 from https://www.oecd-ilibrary.org/docserver/gov_glance-2017-76-en.pdf?expires=1605890791&id=id&accname=guest&checksum=EF2604D17C48BB351E3C92FE10C97C7A.
Onsager, K., Selstad, T. (Eds.), 2004. Regioner i utakt. Tapir akademisk forlag, Trondheim.
Ruud, M.E., Barlindhaug, R., Nørve, S., 2013. Fremtidige boligbehov. NIBR-rapport 2012:25. Norwegian Institute for Urban and RegionalResearch, Oslo.
Saglie, I.-L., 1998. Density and Town Planning. Implementation of a Densification Policy. Doctoral thesis, Oslo School of Architecture, Oslo.
Schwanen, T., Dieleman, F.M., Diest, M., 2001. Travel behaviour in Dutch monocentric and policentric urban systems. J. Transp. Geogr. 9, 173–186.
Sieverts, 1999. Zwischenstadt: Zwischen Ort und Welt, Raum und Zeit, Stadt und Land. Birkhäuser.
Sjaastad, M., Hansen, T., Medby, P., 2007. Bokvalitet i by og etterspurte bebyggelsestyper. SINTEF-Byggforsks skriftserie 10–2007. SINTEF-Byggforsk, Oslo.
Skog, K.L., 2020. The Institutional Capability for Farmland Preservation in Land Use Planning. Ph.D. thesis, Norwegian University of Life Sciences, Ås.
Statistics Denmark, 2020. Folketal 1. januar efter folketal, areal og befolkningstæthed, byområder og landdistrikter og tid. Accessed November 19, 2020. https://www.statistikbanken.dk/statbank5a/default.asp?w=1280.
Statistics Norway, 2020. Areal og befolkning i tettsteder, etter tettsted, tid og statistikkvariabel. Statistics Norway, Oslo/Kongsvinger. Accessed November 15, 2020. https://www.ssb.no/statistikkbanken.
Statistics Sweden, 2020. Folkmängd och landareal i tätorter, per tätort. Accessed November 13, 2020. http://www.statistikdatabasen.scb.se/pxweb/sv/ssd/START__MI__MI0810__MI0810A/LandarealTatortN/.
Støa, E., Aune, M., 2003. Byboliger, boligkvalitet og bærekraft—urbane boligkulturer sett i lys av ressursbruk og miljøadferd. SINTEF, Trondheim.
Strand, A., Næss, P., 2017. Local self-determination, process-focus and subordination of environmental concerns. J. Environ. Policy Plan. 19, 156–167.
Strand, A., Engebretsen, Ø., Kwong, C.K., Isberg, L., Christiansen, P., 2013. Transportkonsekvenser av ulike utbyggingsalternativer i Regional plan for areal og transport i Oslo og Akershus. TØI rapport 1267/2013. Institute of Transport Economics, Oslo.
Strømmen, K., 2001. Rett virksomhet på rett sted—om virksomheters transportskapende egenskaper. Doctoral dissertation, Norwegian University of Technology and Science, Trondheim.
Tiitu, M., Næss, P., Ristimäki, M., 2020. The urban density in two Nordic capitals—comparing the development of Oslo and Helsinki metropolitan regions. Eur. Plan. Stud. https://doi.org/10.1080/09654313.2020.1817865.

TOBIAS, 1998. Information Magazine From the Municipal Archives of Oslo, No. 3. Accessed June 2020 from https://www.oslo.kommune.no/OBA/tobias/pdf_arkiv/Tob1998-3.PDF.

Vale, D., Pereira, M., Viana, C.M., 2018. Different destination, different commuting pattern? Analyzing the influence of the campus location on commuting. J. Transp. Land Use 11 (1), 1–18.

Wolday, F., 2018. Built environment and car driving distance in a small city context. J. Transp. Land Use 11 (1), 747–767.

Wolday, F., Næss, P., Tønnesen, A., 2019. Workplace location, polycentricism and car commuting. J. Transp. Land Use 12 (1), 785–810.

Yang, J., 2005. Commuting impacts of spatial decentralization: a comparison of Atlanta and Boston. J. Reg. Anal. Policy 35, 69–78.

Zegras, C., 2010. The built environment and motor vehicle ownership and use: evidence from Santiago de Chile. Urban Stud. 47, 1793.

Zhou, B., Kockelman, K., 2008. Self-selection in home choice: use of treatment effects in evaluating the relationship between the built environment and travel behavior. Transp. Res. Rec. 2077, 54–61.

CHAPTER SIX

The shifting coalition for land-use and transport policy reform in the United States

Jonathan Levine*
Taubman College of Architecture and Urban Planning, The University of Michigan, Ann Arbor, MI, United States
*Corresponding author: e-mail address: jnthnlvn@umich.edu

Contents

Abstract

Municipal planning and politics in the United States has seen the emergence of a "pro-housing" coalition, alongside the traditional pro-growth, anti-growth, and social-justice coalitions that have traditionally dominated the municipal scene. The coalition seeks liberalization of rules, from parking regulations to single-family zoning, that have constrained housing development in accessible areas, pushing it to more remote locales. The policies that this coalition has supported have distinct transportation implications, including promotion of accessibility and transportation and land-use choice.

Keywords: Land-use planning, Zoning, Parking, Housing, Accessibility

Advances in Transport Policy and Planning, Volume 9
ISSN 2543-0009
https://doi.org/10.1016/bs.atpp.2021.02.004

1. Introduction

The game of urban land-use planning is a three-part affair within which municipal *anti-growth*, *pro-growth*, and *social-justice* coalitions compete (and occasionally collaborate), wrote Berke et al. in 2006 (Berke et al., 2006) (p. 22). In the anti-growth corner are neighborhood associations representing homeowner interests, who seek to limit development densities and defend the character—whether quasi-rural, historic, or simply exclusive—of their residential environments (Fischel, 2001). Within this anti-growth coalition, homeowners are frequently allied with environmental groups concerned about the threat that development can pose to the ecological integrity of the landscape (Monkkonen, 2016). The pro-growth coalition, earlier referred to as the "growth machine," (Molotch, 1976) consists of firms and institutions that stand to profit monetarily from growth: developers, landowners, building-industry interests, downtown and suburban businesses, and chambers of commerce. The social advocacy coalition of low-income and minority populations and progressive activists strive for a more equitable distribution of material and environmental resources in cities and regions and focus on issues of affordable housing, environmental injustice, tenant protection, and access to economic opportunity.

Since the publication of Berke et al. (2006), a realignment has yielded a fourth urban coalition: a loose and shifting pro-housing[a] alliance of renters, progressives, and libertarians who hold that exclusionary land-use policies in urban and suburban areas exacerbate housing unaffordability and racial segregation and increase long-distance commuting and greenhouse-gas emissions. Rather than being viewed as antithetical to equity, affordability, and environment, ample housing development is seen as necessary toward progress in those goals. The coalition has gone under various names: YIMBY (yes in my backyard); Neighbors for More Neighbors; and as place-specific organizations such as Portland for Everyone, Citizens' Housing & Planning Association (Boston), Greater Greater Washington (DC), Open New York, Desegregate Connecticut, and Evolve Austin. The coalition draws on longstanding planning ideas including smart growth, opposition to exclusionary zoning, parking-policy reform, complete streets, and job-housing balance. The pro-housing coalition has at times made common cause with the pro-growth coalition but does not primarily constitute of profit-seeking

[a] I use the term "pro-housing" to align with the terms of Berke et al. (2006): anti-growth, pro-growth, and social-justice.

firms, but individual citizens who are homeowners or renters; the latter group is a visible element of the coalition that stands to benefit directly from alleviation of local housing shortages. Pro-housing interests spurred a number of regulatory reforms, notably the 2019 elimination of single-family zoning in Minneapolis and larger cities in Oregon. Similar reforms were set in motion in 2021 by the city councils of Sacramento and the U.S. birthplace of single-family zoning, Berkeley (The Upzoning Wave Finally Catches Up to California, 2021). In all these cases, elimination of single-family zoning meant permitting certain types of multi-unit buildings formerly excluded from the single-family zone, rather than mandating multifamily development.

While the coalition centers around housing provision, its policies have notable implications for transportation. First is the issue of transportation and land-use choice. American land-use planning has had the effect of reducing the range of choice of for households who would seek, for some combination of preference and affordability considerations, to live in high-accessibility walkable, bikeable, and transit-supportive neighborhoods (Levine, 2006). Reforms advanced by the pro-housing coalition are oriented toward removing obstacles to this choice where it had previously been constrained. Second, where zoning and other land-use regulatory restrictions limit the population that can be accommodated in high-accessibility areas, they force growth in more remote and lower-accessibility areas, degrading metropolitan pedestrian, cycling, transit, and even auto accessibility, and therefore the service that the transportation system offers. Conversely, easing population-restricting regulations in urban, inner-suburban, and transit-adjacent areas can increase metropolitan accessibility. These reforms would be facilitated by a shift in transportation planning, and the transportation aspects of land-use planning, from a mobility to an accessibility basis (Levine et al., 2019). Finally, reductions in obstacles to housing supplies in high-accessibility areas have potential implications for operational transportation considerations, such as mode share for transit, cycling, and walking, the burden of parking provision, vehicle-kilometers traveled, street design, and transportation's externalities, notably greenhouse gases.

In this chapter, I outline ideas common to the pro-housing coalition, together with internal controversies and their implications for vital municipal alliances. I then argue that the planning "game" described by Berke et al. (2006), when expanded to all four coalitions, is also an apt structuring of municipal electoral politics in many U.S. cities and towns. Finally, I describe major families of policy reform that fit under the "pro-housing" label and how these ideas have played out in selected jurisdictions.

2. Animating ideas of the pro-housing coalition

The pro-housing coalition is, in many ways, the polar opposite of the anti-growth coalition. Even one of its monikers, "YIMBY," originated as term signifying an antithetical relationship. The term "NIMBY" (not in my backyard), from the mid-1970s through much of the 1990s, referred largely to mobilization against specific locally unwanted land uses such as power plants, waste-disposal sites, group homes, or homeless shelters, as opposed to a generalized opposition to housing development that is denser than its surroundings (Brion, 1987; Mark, 2019; Matheny and Williams, 1985; Takahashi, 1997). As a consequence, early use of "YIMBY" as NIMBY's antithesis focused on the specific problem of siting locally unwanted but regionally necessary land uses (Lake, 1993). By the end of the century, the NIMBY term had expanded to incorporate opposition to housing development (e.g., Pendall, 1999), a shift that ensured that "YIMBY" would, on short order, come to signify a pro-housing stance linking increased housing supplies, including market-rate housing, to desirable outcomes pertaining to affordability and environmental performance (Bell, 2002; Nozzi, 2003). The Maine State Housing Authority was an early adopter of this flavor of pro-housing message, launching an advertising campaign in 2001 featuring photographs of what, two decades hence, would come to be known as essential workers with captions that remained surprisingly up-to-date such as "she can teach your kids calculus, but she can't be your neighbor" and "she can save your life, but she can't be your neighbor" (Bell, 2002; Maine State Housing Authority, 2020).

The message blossomed into a full-fledged movement with activism in the San Francisco Bay Area starting around 2014 (Dougherty, 2020). Citizen involvement in municipal land-use decisions was, and remains, focused on a homeowning class that is whiter, wealthier, and more educated than the population as a whole. This population frequently uses its political clout to thwart, delay, or constrain housing development, particularly that which is proposed near single-family homes but deviates from this form in density or expected race or social class of future occupants (Einstein et al., 2019). While activism against exclusionary zoning had begun decades earlier (Davidoff and Gold, 1970; Whittemore, 2020), a core idea of the emerging movement was to develop renters' awareness of their personal stake in land-use decisions as a tool to overcome a traditional localist bias in U.S. land-use planning. Homeowners who saw themselves as harmed by nearby potential development tended to be aware of proposals—sometimes via required official notification—and keenly alert to the stakes involved. Moreover, they tended to be direct constituents of the municipal politicians empowered with the land-use regulatory decisions. By contrast, future beneficiaries of proposed housing, whether potential residents or simply those for whom loosened constraints on housing supply promised to ease shortages and unaffordability, were rarely aware of their stakes in individual land-use decisions and might not even be alerted to the presence of such decisions on the agenda. Moreover, they would frequently hail from jurisdictions other than the one facing the regulatory question, rendering them non-constituents to the relevant decision makers.

Pro-housing activism sought to overcome these systemic obstacles by fostering an awareness among renters of their interest in sometimes-remote decisions; an urban resident might weigh in during public hearings, for example, on a decision to allow dense, transit-adjacent housing in a suburb several towns over from their home municipality. Frequently, the resultant clashes took on a generational cast, with millennials priced out of home ownership arguing against baby boomers who had been in their homes for decades whose home values had increased rapidly with housing scarcity born in part of the exclusionary regulations they continued to defend (Shaw, 2020a).

2.1 The pro-housing coalition and societal goals

Despite the obvious economic self-interest of the renter class, the animating ideas of the movement pertained to primarily broader societal goals, including racial justice. Increased national consciousness on the legacy and persistence of institutional racism led to a reconsideration of the role of zoning in the establishment and perpetuation of extreme residential segregation in the United States. This was aided by publication of the influential *The Color of Law* (Rothstein, 2017), which demonstrated the many ways, from tax policy to affordable-housing decisions to state-sanctioned violence, that U.S. racial segregation is fundamentally a governmental product, as opposed being simply the autonomous outcome of market decisions fueled by individual preferences and prejudices. Notable among this list was zoning in general, and single-family zoning in particular: racial segregation was among both the intent and effects of this particular regulatory tool. Viewed through this lens, while explicit arguments for single-family zoning may have shifted from promotion of race and class segregation to those based in neighborhood character and infrastructure capacity, the difference was of little consequence, since such exclusion was woven into the United States's fabric of institutional racism.

Closely related was the societal goal of housing affordability (as distinct from the narrow self-interest of activist renters in high-priced metropolitan regions). The connection between exclusionary land regulations and housing scarcity had been made decades earlier (Frieden, 1979). The scarcity was in large part a product of a homeowner-environmentalist alliance, which Frieden criticized both for its malleability and the inconsistency of its environmentalism: "Sierra Club chapters, for example, have opposed some suburban housing on the grounds that it would generate unnecessary long-distance commuting; have opposed other housing near suburban job centers on the grounds that it should be located closer to the central cities; and have opposed new housing near the central cities on the grounds that it would use up open space there" (Frieden, 1979, 9). In the intervening decades, housing affordability had become top concern in larger metropolitan areas around the country, particularly in the West and Northeast (Collinson, 2011; Myers and Park, 2019). Limitations on growth in centrally located areas inevitably constrained supply and drove prices up (Been et al., 2019). The process pushed households into more remote locales where housing might be more affordable but where added transportation costs ate up much of, or even negated, the savings (Center for Neighborhood Technology, 2020).

The concern about added transportation costs extended beyond the monetary. Individual travelers pushed into areas demanding heavy car use bore costs in time and lifestyle interference. External costs were particularly significant, notably those related to car emissions, a dominant factor in the significantly larger per capita carbon footprint in suburban (and especially exurban) areas compared to cities (Jones and Kammen, 2014). Stringent land-use regulations in urban and close-in suburban areas tend to limit the number of people who could reside in these relatively low-carbon zones, pushing them into higher-carbon areas. Policy reform, within this formulation does not amount to compelling or even incentivizing people to live closer in and at higher densities in order to solve transportation-related problems, but rather changing regulations to allow more of those choices to be made (Levine, 2006).

The argument that facilitating those choices is a pro-environmental move challenges the longstanding union between environmentalists and homeowners motivated to preserve the exclusive character of their surroundings, as described by Frieden (1979): "...opponents [of home-building] have been active for a long time, resisting new housing because they were afraid of what it would do to their property taxes or to the social makeup of their neighborhoods. But they never enjoyed as much success before as they have since they learned how to team up with environmentalists" (Frieden, 1979, 119). Opposing housing development in high-accessibility areas may have reduced environmental impacts these specific areas, or more broadly, environmental impacts *per hectare*. But this opposition, paradoxically, increased environmental impacts per capita as it pushed households into residence in zones in which their emissions would predictably be higher. And since population growth in a metropolitan region proceeded independently of the land-use regulations of individual municipalities, "slow-growth" policies amounted in practice to policies for more dispersed growth, with its attendant environmental impacts.

2.2 Internal controversies and potential alliances

Common to all elements of the coalition was an orientation toward land-use regulatory reform to remove obstacles to housing development in areas close to transit, employment, and other destinations. Beyond that agreement, at least two distinct wings of the coalition were evident. Libertarian-leaning "market urbanists" tended to prioritize relaxation of barriers to market-rate housing development over below-market-rate housing provision via inclusionary zoning, negotiated agreements, or public subsidy. Tenant protections were controversial, and rent control was an anathema to some in this group. Housing supply was the surest route toward affordability, and techniques that threated to limit supply could have perverse consequences, a position that frequently put market urbanists at odds with activists concerned about gentrification and displacement (Axel-Lute, 2019; Shaw, 2018). By contrast, the progressive wing of the pro-housing coalition took an "all of the above" position, highlighting expansion of housing supplies of all types and placing great importance on development of below-market-rate affordable housing and tenant protections (Dougherty, 2020; Shaw, 2020a).

The split has significant implications for potential alliances, with the progressives better poised than libertarian-leaning market urbanists to form alliances with the social-justice coalition. Despite potential natural affinity between the social-justice coalition and the progressive wing of the pro-housing coalition, such alliances were rare, with divisions emerging along several dimensions. First, an approach based on confronting homeowners and municipal politicians can conflict with the needs of non-profit housing developers, who often see their task as constructing or acquiring and preserving housing without alienating municipal constituencies (Axel-Lute, 2019). Second, and more fundamental are differences in views regarding market-rate housing and displacement of lower-income populations. Progressive elements of pro-housing coalition tend to see broadly shared benefits for increases in market-rate housing supply through a rapidly operating "migration chain" whereby new construction, even when targeted at the high end of the market, triggers a series of relocations that, within a couple of years, reaches to households below the median income for the area (Mast, 2019). By contrast, much of the social-justice coalition see greater potential for new housing to displace existing lower-income residents (Agnotti and Morse, 2016). Third, where members of the pro-housing coalition saw potential for market-driven easing of housing shortages, many progressives saw planning for the express purpose of making land more expensive (Stein, 2019).

A notable effort to bridge these gaps was launched in 2019 with the California-based "3Ps" Coalition (housing production, preservation, and protection) of private and non-profit developers, foundations, policy groups, elected officials, business, labor, and social-justice organizations (3Ps Housing Plan, 2019; Shaw, 2019). Eschewing the tenets of the libertarian wing of the YIMBY movement, the coalition endorsed legislation in both regulatory liberalization and tenant protection, including bills regulating rent gouging, allowing accessory dwelling units, streamline affordable-housing approval, mandating eviction notification, expanding density-based affordability bonuses, reducing parking requirements, identifying up-zoning opportunities, and facilitating broadly based, small-scale densification, or "gentle density" (Toderian, 2010). The coalition succeeded in applying political leverage that would not have been available to the less-connected tenant-advocacy groups in isolation, and was instrumental in some statewide legislative successes.

3. The camps of U.S. municipal electoral politics

The rise of the pro-housing coalition in planning processes is mirrored by its emergence as a player in municipal electoral politics. Across many cities and towns in the United States, local politics is an interplay among the four poles of pro-growth, pro-housing, social-justice, and anti-growth constituencies. Not all four elements are evident in every locale, and the lines between the camps are frequently blurred. But in many cases, this four-part structure matches local politics more closely than the traditional conservative-liberal or Republican-Democratic divides. This can be seen, for example, in the prevalence of anti-housing-development sentiment in liberal jurisdictions, as well as in Republican rhetoric during the 2020 elections (Adler, 2020; Einstein et al., 2019:13; Nall and Marble, 2020), or Democrats and Republicans working at the federal level on YIMBY-styled proposals (as reported favorably by the libertarian Reason magazine) (Britschgi, 2019). In general, voters' views of desirable policies toward development are more a function of their generation and tenancy status (homeowner vs non-homeowner) than of their partisan affiliation.

For example, in New York City, the pro-housing group "Open New York" advocated a slate of candidates for the first time in 2020, supporting candidates who promoted upzoning, legalizing accessory dwelling units, and equitable zoning changes. Open New York pursued housing-supply expansion in middle-to-upper income neighborhoods, avoiding projects in lower-income and gentrifying areas in order to minimize worries about displacement. This stance enabled coalitions with some progressives, and some of Open New York's candidates were similarly endorsed by the left-leaning Working Families Party. By contrast, there were no overlapping City Council endorsements between Open New York and the Democratic Socialists of America, who opposed "rezonings that simply encourage gentrification and unlock development value for private landlords" (Campanile, 2020; Chadha, 2020).

On the other side of the country, San Diego exhibited Republican-based "YIMBY" politics, as reported by City News Service (Walsh, 2019): "[Republican Kevin] Faulconer declared himself the city's first 'YIMBY' mayor during his State of the City address in January and has since proposed policies like eliminating building height limits, authorizing unlimited housing density and eliminating parking requirements for new housing developments built near transit, an ordinance the council approved 8-1 in March." Over the previous decade, it had largely been Democrats who had championed restrictive land-use policies, at least in the context of single-family neighborhoods (Burnett, 2019).

Attitudes toward growth constitute the principal cleavage in a range of places, including college towns and high-tech commuting magnets. For example, municipal politics in Ann Arbor, Michigan revolve around two factions, which function as virtual political parties notwithstanding the fact that both are composed nearly entirely of Democrats. The overarching disagreement between the faction centers on development policy, with one side tending to welcome compact development in town, and the other more resistant (Firke and Levine, 2020). Elections in November 2019 in Cambridge, Massachusetts and Boulder, Colorado centered on development issues, with pro-housing slates prevailing in both cities (Shaw, 2020c). Austin, Texas politics are structured similarly, with progressive candidates on one side highlighting their championing of housing development incorporating market-rate and affordable units (Casar, 2020) and being described as friends to and advocates for "more housing and more walkable development" (Vote Tracker, 2020). On the other side, candidates champion their fight for neighborhoods, opposition to development agreements and upzonings (Alter, 2020) and their "struggle against provisions that greatly expand density" in their part of the city (Clifton, 2019).

The structure of municipal representation may be relevant to electoral outcomes. Citywide elections, e.g., for mayor, can be more amenable to pro-housing candidates than district or ward elections, e.g., for city council representative. The breadth of the citywide constituency can facilitate coalition building among pro-housing forces, while in district elections, narrower constituencies and property-protection concerns can dominate, leading sometimes to situations in which pro-housing mayors clash with more anti-growth city councils (Randy Shaw, interviewed in Sisson, 2019).

4. Versions of the reform

The pro-housing coalition has supported a range of land-use policy reforms across diverse U.S. cities. This section presents a structure for understanding these reforms, focusing on those that have two characteristics: first, they represent liberalization of restrictive land-use regulatory rules with the purpose or effect of lowering impediments to housing development; and second, they apply throughout a jurisdiction, as opposed to, for example, upzonings of individual neighborhoods. The intent is to describe broad families of such reforms rather than provide a complete catalog of municipal actions and cities implementing them.

4.1 Elimination of single-family zoning

The importance of single-family-zoning elimination stems from several sources, notably the dominance of single-family living in U.S. About 2010, 63.3% of Americans lived in detached single-family homes, compared to 34.7% of residents of the European Union (Hirt, 2014). Because of the land intensiveness of single-family living, this number understates the dominance of the single-family zone in the U.S. metropolitan landscape. For example, single-family zoning accounts for 75% of residential land in Los Angeles, 84% in Charlotte, and 94% in San Jose (Badger and Bui, 2019). Those numbers pertain to the cities alone; when entire metropolitan regions are included, those numbers would increase. For example in greater Boston, 70% of municipalities zone least 80% of their entire land area for single-family housing (Wegmann, 2020). The large share of territory devoted to the single-family zone implies that even modest changes to its regulatory regime can have a significant effect on housing supply.

Yet this dominance has rendered the single-family zone remarkably resistant to reform. The physical pattern engendered by single-family zoning—detached, single-family living—remains the salient feature of the US residential landscape, and in fact the American single-family zone is particularly exclusionary even relative to parallel zones of other countries (Hirt, 2014). This adds up to extraordinary electoral power for the single-family homeowner, particularly at the municipal level, and this constituency uses its electoral clout to guard its prerogatives zealously. The provocatively titled "The Egregious Invalidity of the Exclusive Single-Familiy Zone" (Babcock, 1983) received little traction, and that zone was described over two decades later as nearly "forever" based on the a power of its residents within the U.S.'s decentralized approach to land-use regulation (Levine, 2006). And yet by the publication of articles with titles like "It's Time to End Single-Family Zoning" (Manville et al., 2020) and "Death to Single-Family Zoning…and New Life to the Missing Middle" (Wegmann, 2020), the single-family zoning had been eliminated in two major U.S. jurisdictions, with an additional one on track for such elimination in the subsequent year.

"Missing Middle" here refers to "missing middle housing," a framework, frequently invoked in debates over land-use policy, that argues for the reform of U.S. zoning laws to allow a range of housing types including duplexes, cottage courts, townhouses, and stacked triplexes that traditionally fleshed out the housing stock between detached single-family houses and midrise developments (Parolek, 2020). Prior to the broad diffusion of exclusive single-family zoning, these housing types were ubiquitous in U.S. cities and helped households match their housing choices with their needs and pocketbooks. They offered surprisingly high densities without overwhelming their lower-density surroundings. A great value of the missing-middle framework is that, as opposed to standard zoning, which amounts to an exclusion of that which is disallowed, missing-middle analyses and associated form-based codes constitute an affirmative prescription of housing types that can be provided, an attribute that can both improve urban design and assuage nervous neighbors. Transportation considerations figure prominently in the argument for missing-middle housing, including generating sufficient population density for public transportation, supporting pedestrian-oriented commercial areas within walking distance of people's homes, reducing households' transportation expenses, and reducing the need for parking (Parolek, 2020: 15, 47, 55).

These reforms alter an institution that had been widespread since the early 20th century (Fischel, 2004). Single-family zoning's century-long history meant that much of the territory regulated in this fashion is in highly accessible close-in urban and suburban neighborhoods. Where similar areas in cities worldwide might evolve to higher density forms with changed economic conditions, single-family zoning thwarted that evolutionary process, forcing more affordable-housing forms into more remote locales (Levine, 2006). Elimination of single-family zoning can thus enable multi-family construction in particularly high-priority locations.

The rigid exclusion of anything other than single-family detached structures from so much metropolitan territory has origins at least in part in racial and class-based exclusion, making its reform an especially urgent priority for the planning field as it confronts its role in fostering segregation. After the U.S. Supreme Court found explicitly racial zoning to be unconstitutional in Buchanan v. Warley (1917), cities developed land-use regulatory techniques that would pass constitutional muster while still segregating by class, race, or both. Single-family zoning featured prominently among these. This was the case, for example, in St. Louis, where single-family neighborhoods with racially exclusive covenants were zoned in 1919 "first residential" for exclusive single-family use (Rothstein, 2017). It was explicit in the legal writing of the time. For example, Progressive-era legal scholar Ernst Freund, while regretting racial discrimination, developed a legal rationale for single-family zoning to bolster segregation. He uses the term "social conditions" as a euphemism for whites' desires for residential segregation:

As illustrating [social conditions], however, regrettable prejudice may be, the coming of colored people into a district readily occurs to one [i.e., a white person] who lives on the South Side of Chicago. Even if were not for the position taken by the United States Supreme Court, a legal color line would probably be impossible in Northern states; and generally speaking any attempt to give official recognition to social differences would be utterly futile, partly because it would be repudiated by public sentiment, partly because it would be impossible to find an appropriate legal form (Freund, 1929:146–7).

Explicit racial exclusion would thus not work. What would, then be the "appropriate legal form" to achieve this perhaps "regrettable" goal? Regulating strictly for nuisance, which would demand proof of unreasonable interference with safety, health, or morals, would not be up to the task. On the other hand, regulation of amenity, which is always in the eye of the beholder, would be on shaky legal ground. The solution lay, for Freund, in *conformity*, or the principle that zoning could regulate to promote consistency between changes in the built environment and what was already found there. This would allow greater regulation than a nuisance standard, but would not be subject to the legal challenges that regulatory enforcement of beauty or amenity would be. Single-family zoning had found its legal theory.

While such explicitness about racial segregation as a goal would wane, in part because of the legal vulnerabilities such rhetoric could engender, discriminatory intent remained over the decades, with racially explicit language being used to promote exclusion of denser development at least into the 1970s (Rothstein, 2017).

4.1.1 Minneapolis' elimination of single-family zoning

Largely informed by the history of single-family zoning's role in racial exclusion—and its own location in one of the most segregated urban counties in the United States (Cortright, 2020)—Minneapolis began in 2010 a planning process, Minneapolis 2040, that came to be strongly shaped by the 2013 election, which yielded several new progressive members of City Council. Through coalitions with racial-justice advocates, affordable-housing proponents, and the AARP, supporters on Council succeeded in eliminating the single-family zone by 2019 (Trickey, 2019). In the process, municipal planners cultivated extensive public engagement over 2 years and 200 meetings, with particular outreach to underrepresented communities. While elimination of single-family zoning was controversial, political divisions appeared less between Republicans and Democrats than between older and younger people, with the latter much more favorably inclined to the reforms (McCormick, 2020). The initial proposal was to allow up to a fourplex throughout the former single zone in the city; this was later reduced to a maximum of three units as a compromise. Importantly, the elimination of single-family zoning was paired with inclusionary zoning, affordable-housing expansion, and tenant protections (Mogush and Worthington, 2020).

The practical implication was that undeveloped or redeveloping lots within the formerly single-family zone could be built with up to three units as a by-right proposal. The same principle applied to the division of existing structures. Single-family zoning had previously restricted development to people who could afford single-family homes on the site, with many of those being very large homes on small lots. In all cases, the multi-unit structures would need to fit within the same envelope that had formerly contained single-family construction (Minneapolis 2040, 2021). That is, the reform did not alter previous height or floor-area ratio limitations or setback requirements from streets and lot lines. This adherence to previous limits meant that that the reform would be inadequate to the task of legalizing the full range of "missing middle" housing types but would be more acceptable to residents of formerly single-family zones seeking stability in their neighborhoods' basic built forms.

Elimination of the single-family zone as part of the Minneapolis 2040 plan was closely associated with supportive transportation policies. The plan's complete-streets policy creates a hierarchy of street uses, with the pedestrian offered highest priority, followed by the cyclist and transit user, and the driver accorded the lowest priority Other supportive transportation policies adopted as part of the plan include travel-demand management, incentivizing shared mobility options, and maximizing vehicle occupancy (Minneapolis 2040, 2021).

4.1.2 State of Oregon's elimination of single-family zoning

The State of Oregon has a long tradition of state-level requirements limiting municipal planning prerogative. These include the Oregon Transportation Planning Rule (which requires allowance of transit-oriented development), and SB 100, which established urban growth boundaries around all incorporated cities and urbanized unincorporated areas (Seltzer, 2015). This tradition facilitated the passage of House Bill 2001 in 2019, making the State of Oregon the first to take action against single-family zoning at the state level.

Oregon's plan resembled Minneapolis' in that the reform mandated no change in the envelope of height limitations and setback requirements that municipalities had previously imposed on development within their single-family zones. But in contrast to the Minneapolis plan, which applied uniformly across the jurisdiction, Oregon graduated the requirements with the size of the urban area. Outside of the Portland Metro boundary, the new requirements kicked in at a city population of 10,000. For cities between 10,000 and 25,000 in population, state law mandated that duplexes be allowed "on each lot or parcel zoned for residential use that allows for the development of detached single family dwellings," thus removing these cities' ability to exclude duplexes throughout their single-family and many other residential zones. "Large cities" faced a greater limitation on their regulatory prerogative. These included all cities with a population of over 25,000, all cities with in the Portland Metro boundary with a population of more than 1000, and unincorporated areas within the Portland Metro boundary that are served by sufficient urban services, including sanitary sewers, water, fire protection, parks, open space, recreation, streets, roads, and mass transit (OregonLaws.org, 2020). These large cities were required to allow duplexes, triplexes, quadplexes, cottage clusters, and townhouses in residentially zoned areas that allow for single-family dwellings. In acknowledgement of the transportation/land-use connection, the bill also provided funds for planning assistance to help local governments develop plans in areas where infrastructure was inadequate to the increased residential densities the law contemplated (Department of Land Conservation and Development, 2019).

The Oregon law explicitly adopted language of "missing middle" housing Like those of Minneapolis, Oregon's reforms will enable some forms of missing-middle housing, but remaining regulations on lot sizes, setbacks, lot coverage, or parking will constrain others. Nevertheless, the political achievement of statewide repeal of single-family zoning can hardly be overstated. Notably, the measure passed both houses of the Oregon legislature on bipartisan basis; for example, in the Oregon Senate, 72% of Democrats and 50% of Republicans voting supported the bill (Oregon State Legislature, 2019) in a session that was otherwise marked with partisan rancor (The Oregonian, 2019). As of this writing, the Oregon law, like the Minneapolis repeal, is too recent to be assessed for impacts on housing affordability, environmental performance, or racial integration. But in combination, reforms in Minneapolis and Oregon demonstrate both the political feasibility of challenges to single-family zoning and the breadth of the potential coalitions behind these reforms.

4.1.3 "Deeper affordability": Portland, Oregon

Anticipating (and spurring) Oregon's reforms, the City of Portland revised its zoning code, eliminating single-family zoning a year before the enactment of statewide legislation. In addition, in 2020, Portland went further with reforms granting citywide bonuses and other concessions to buildings in which at least half the units are affordable. In combination, these two reforms went farther than any other city in legalizing a full range of missing-middle housing types. Like the Oregon reforms, Portland's action allowed up to quadplexes throughout residential zones and on any lot in the city. By 2020, the city had legalized up to six residential units per lot for buildings in which at least half the units were affordable to households earning up to 60% of the area median income (City of Portland, 2020). Reforms of parking requirements for multifamily buildings, and elimination of such requirements where affordability criteria are met, furthered design flexibility. The city did not constrain multifamily homes to the previous building envelope, instead gearing floor-area-ratio limits to the number of units in a building: duplexes were allowed to be somewhat larger than single-family houses for a given lot size, and triplexes and quadplexes could be larger still (City of Portland, 2019). Gearing the allowable floor-area ratio to the number of units in a building was designed to enhance the feasibility of multifamily development compared to the common redevelopment of small lots for very large and pricey single-family homes.

Portland's reforms were backed by a broad coalition including members of the traditional pro-growth coalition (Think Real Estate, Business for a Better Portland) and social-justice coalition (Sunrise PDX, Anti-Displacement PDX), in addition to pro-housing advocates (Sightline Institute, Portland:Neighbors Welcome). This pro-housing initiative had notable support from transportation-advocacy organizations (Oregon Walks, Portlanders for Parking Reform), environmental groups (Oregon Environmental Council, Urban Greenspaces Institute), and the AARP (formerly the American Association of Retired Persons), an important partner in a number of pro-housing initiatives (Portland: Neighbors Welcome, 2020).

4.2 Single-family zoning reforms conditioned on affordability

For other jurisdictions, however, complete elimination of single-family zoning remained, at the time of this writing, a bridge too far. Ambitious proposals had surfaced in Virginia, Nebraska, and California without success. A notable effort, spearheaded by California State Senator Scott Wiener, was largely structured around public-transport availability and accessibility more broadly. It would have required municipalities to allow construction of 45–55 ft in height within a half mile of rail or ferry stations, lifted dwelling-unit limitations within in areas that are job-rich or with one-quarter of a mile of a bus stop, and allowed fourplexes in residential zones throughout the state. After an initial failed attempt, the bill returned with significant modifications oriented toward promotion of affordability and discouragement of displacement of low-income residents, including inclusionary zoning requirements for projects of 11 units or more, affordability-based density bonuses, and a phasing plan whereby sensitive communities would not be upzoned immediately but would be delayed for 5 years pending the conclusion of community-based processes to determine how to implement the changes (California Legislative Information, 2019). Despite the affordability-oriented modifications, which were oriented in part toward building coalitions with social-justice advocates, the bill failed in the California Senate on an 18–15 vote.

Yet the affordability dimension would prove key to other, more limited reforms. Proposals to reform zoning requirements for construction that is 100% affordable are more limited in scope than the far-reaching reforms enacted in Minneapolis and Oregon (and much more so than the even more ambitious reforms contemplated in the Wiener bill). But linking relaxation of single-family zoning with 100%-affordability requirements presented a natural platform for alliance between the pro-housing and social-justice coalitions and ensured a tight and visible coupling between the regulatory-reform and housing-affordability agendas.

4.2.1 100%-affordable-housing zoning overlay: Cambridge, Massachusetts

The City of Cambridge, Massachusetts is unusual in the U.S. context in that only 7% of its parcels are zoned for single-family homes exclusively. This meant that the reforms pioneered in Minneapolis and Oregon would have little impact if translated to the Cambridge context. Moreover, lot-size and floor-area ratio requirements in these zones would have constituted additional binding constraints to multifamily development; simply allowing multifamily homes within the previous building envelope would not have led significant increases in Cambridge's zoned housing capacity. For this reason, alteration to the building's envelope would be necessary for the overlay zone to have effect (Affordable Housing Overlay Reality, 2020). Cambridge's approaches was effectively to eliminate single-family zoning, but only for buildings with 100% affordable units. The enacted reform shifted regulations for affordable housing in all neighborhoods, but the change depended on the base zoning of the district. Significant alterations for qualified affordable development included raising building heights: from under 40 to 45 ft, from 40 to 50 ft to 65 ft, and from above 50 to 80 ft. Where floor-area ratio limits were 1.0, they were doubled to 2.0 for qualified construction, and minimum lot-area requirements per dwelling unit were eliminated (City of Cambridge, 2020).

The reforms emerged from a public planning process entitled "Envision Cambridge," the mobility section of which acknowledges the role of land-use-policy adjustments to support sustainable transportation choices (City of Cambridge, 2018:20). Political mobilization was led in part by the pro-housing group "A Better Cambridge," which advocates increasing housing supplies by allowing higher densities, particularly near public transit. The organization's mission statement that "increasing housing, creating more affordable housing, and enhancing tenant protections are critical to ensuring more people can live here and stay here" is an example of a platform amenable to a coalition of pro-housing and social-justice activists (A Better Cambridge, 2020). The zoning overlay that was enacted succeeded in part because of political mobilization on behalf of pro-housing candidates, who in 2019 achieved the council supermajority the proposal would need to pass (Eisner, 2020). The measure quickly had ripple effects, increasing interest in similar legislation in nearby Somerville, Newton, and potentially, Boston (Shaw, 2020b).

4.2.2 "Affordability unlocked": Austin, Texas

Like Cambridge, Austin Texas enacted an affordability-based program that effectively repealed single-family zoning for buildings that met affordability requirements. In Austin, the criteria included guaranteed 40-year affordability for at least half the units in building, and in the case of rental housing, tenant protections. Qualifying buildings could include up to six dwelling units per lot in single-family zones and receive development waivers pertaining to height, floor-area ratio, parking requirements, setbacks and others. Buildings with at least 75% of units affordable could include up to six units in single-family zones; thus five- and sixplexes with four and five affordable units, respectively, would qualify. Developments that met more stringent requirements, including location within one-quarter mile of a major transit corridor, were allowed higher limits, including a 50% height bonus and up to eight dwelling units per building (City of Austin, n.d.). Response in the rapidly growing Austin market was quick. Within a year of the program's initiation, 2700 housing units, 2300 of them affordable, were certified as qualified development proposals under the program. At least 650 of these units would not have been developable but for the existence of the program (Brey, 2020). Affordability in the Austin program was geared to households ranging from 30% to 80% of median family income (City of Austin, n.d.).

4.3 Elimination of parking requirements

Zoning reform that eliminates parking requirements throughout a jurisdiction is not as obvious a pro-housing move as the policies above, which directly allow the construction of more housing on a lot. But the high cost of parking provision means that bundling minimum parking requirements with housing significantly raises the costs of a home (Shoup, 2011). Construction prices in 2018 per above-ground spot ranged from $23,000 in Phoenix to $38,000 in Los Angeles and $46,000 in Honolulu. Below-ground parking was even pricier: $36,000, $59,000, and $74,000 per spot in the three cities, respectively (Rider Levett Bucknall, 2018; Shoup, 2018). These costs are construction costs only and do not include land, operations, or maintenance. Parking requirements, which are ostensibly a measure to accommodate auto traffic, end up reducing population and housing densities (Manville et al., 2013) Parking requirements would be of little consequence to housing prices if they did not constitute binding constraints, that is, if even in the absence of the requirements, developers would provide at least as much parking on their own. This condition does not hold generally, and residential requirements in fact lead developers to provide more parking than they would have otherwise (Gabbe et al., 2020a). In many circumstances, parking requirements thus constitute an impediment to housing affordability and a constraint on production.

Elimination of parking requirements does not mean elimination of parking. Rather, it amounts to allowing developers, rather than planners, to determine desirable parking levels. In principle, profit maximization would lead developers to expand parking until the point that the marginal revenue from the last spot provided (presumably recoupable as housing rents or sales prices) equals the spot's marginal cost. Whether developers behave in such an economically rational fashion is not known, but a common outcome in the face of zero parking regulations was to provide some parking but less than had previously been required (Gabbe et al., 2020b).

Cities that eliminated parking requirements citywide as of this writing include Buffalo (2016), Hartford (2017), San Francisco (2018), Minneapolis (2018), Edmonton (2020), and for residential properties,

Berkeley (2021) (Andersen, 2021; Gosselin, 2017; Hess, 2017; Ramey, 2020; Schmitt, 2018; Wylie, 2018). Some smaller locales have followed suit, and numerous others have selectively reduced or eliminated requirements in some areas of the city (Strong Towns, 2019).

4.4 Reducing minimum lot sizes

Notable among the reforms described above is the short time span within which all occurred: they were all enacted within the 5 years from 2016 to 2021. Unlike these changes, a much earlier pro-housing reform has had time to bear fruit and has been meticulously studied. While the City of Houston, Texas is renowned in the planning world for its lack of formal zoning, it has virtually all other layers of conventional land-use regulation, including a subdivision code, which controls minimum lot sizes (Lewyn, 2004). Within the Interstate 610 freeway loop, an area of approximately 14 by 18 km in central Houston, the city dropped minimum required lot sizes from 5000 square feet—the standard in postwar U.S. suburbs—to 3500 square feet or to 1400 square feet if certain other conditions were met. The impetus for the change appeared to be a confluence of market-driven developer interest and support from planning staff and commissioners, based on a mix of housing and transportation considerations, including pedestrian friendliness, sidewalk-oriented commercial development, and more urbanist parking designs (Kapur, 2004:10053). The change was eased politically by provisions that protected homeowners who might otherwise have opposed this reform from its effects. The first of these protections is the extensive system of municipally enforced deed restrictions in Houston, which would continue to govern the land it controlled even after lot-size minima were reduced. The second was an opt-out mechanism, termed "Special Minimum Lot Size," by which residents of a block or area could petition for a larger minimum block size that those specified in the ordinance. In combination, these two mechanisms served to blunt what might otherwise have been anti-growth opposition to the reform (Gray and Millsap, 2020).

The 1998 reform predated the emergence of the pro-housing coalition in the form described in this chapter but appeared to spur close-in housing production markedly, facilitating the development of over 25,000 units that would previously not have been developable. Buildings enabled by the reform tended to be developed in relatively affluent neighborhoods, suggesting that market-driven gentrification and displacement were not occurring as a consequence of the process. On the other hand, the land-use reforms did not do much to revitalize low-income areas (Gray and Millsap, 2020).

The presence of Houston on the list of housing reformist cities amounts, in a sense, to a physical embodiment of independence of the pro-housing agenda from traditional right-left politics. Where Portland had long been the darling of liberal planners, Houston's unique approach to land-use regulation had been admired by libertarians (Siegan, 1972). While the reforms and the coalitions on which they were based differed between the two cities, the idea that exclusionary regulations impede housing development where it is most needed was an obvious common thread running through both municipal reforms.

5. The land-use/transportation connection

While the reforms discussed in this chapter were primarily based in land-use-regulatory policy, the transportation dimensions of the policies were explicit in both the stated intent of the policies and the language of the advocacy coalitions that supported them. Transportation-related motivations for the reforms included goals in enhancing cycling, walking, transit, and street design, and in reducing long-distance commuting. In the case of the State Oregon, there was explicit recognition that infrastructure limitations, including those based in transportation, may demand additional plans lest they become a constraint on densification. And many of the reforms dealt explicitly with parking, a service at the juncture of the transportation and land-use systems.

Moreover, by facilitating housing development in urban and inner-ring suburban areas, the reforms created potential for accessibility gains. While greater population density can sometimes slow automotive traffic, the proximity benefits of density tend to outweigh any automobility disadvantages, leading to a positive relationship between metropolitan densities and accessibility by car (Levine et al., 2012). This positive relationship holds even more strongly in the case of transit accessibility. Yet U.S. land-use planning practices grounded in highway level of service, such as traffic-impact analysis, can limit these accessibility gains by excluding or constraining development that threatens to exacerbate congestion beyond targeted limits. These limits on accessibility gains would be eased with a shift from mobility to accessibility as the organizing principle of transportation planning and the transportation aspects of land-use planning (Levine et al., 2019).

For example, project-level assessments of traffic impact, which center on automobility, could be reformed to gauge accessibility impacts instead. Such analyses would incorporate any congestion-exacerbating effect of development but would analyze it in conjunction with the proximity benefits that the new development offers its residents (Levine et al., 2017).

The emergence of the pro-housing coalition in U.S. planning and municipal politics, together with its advocated reforms, provide rich opportunities for land-use and transport research. Once sufficient post-implementation experience has accrued, policies may be evaluated for impacts including housing production and affordability, accessibility, and auto use. Locales where the reforms unleash a high level of housing production may hold lessons for those in which development impacts are more muted. And as successful experience accumulates, research should be able to shed light on the processes of reform itself, including the perennially vexing problem of changing antiquated policies that are exacerbating, rather than ameliorating, societal and environmental problems.

6. Conclusion

The "Twilight of Single-Family Zoning" (Ziegler and Edward, 1982) has been forecast for decades, and few would expect a rapid fade to night illuminated by the bright stars of expanded housing choice. But the rapidly occurring land-use regulatory reforms enacted between 2016 and 2021 suggested that the political landscape for planning in U.S. cities and towns began to shift. Longstanding central elements of U.S. land-use planning such as single-family zoning and parking minima started falling in rapid succession. A pro-housing coalition took its place beside traditional pro-growth, anti-growth, and social-justice coalitions, which previously formed the triad of the land-use planning game, with potentially far-reaching implications for the practice of transport and land-use planning. Despite its expansion and generational appeal, however, the pro-housing coalition was rarely powerful enough to push through reforms on its own. Instead, success tended to come through compromise and joint efforts with the social-justice coalition, the pro-growth coalition, or both.

This potential three-party coalition places pro-housing activists at the political center and can be politically transformative, as evidenced in Portland's "deeper affordability" reform process. Coalition building toward one side tends to limit opportunities on the other, however. Where development interests tend to welcome regulatory liberalization and the opportunity it affords to expand housing supplies, they are frequently hostile to requirements pertaining to subsidized housing and tenant protection, core tenets of the social-justice coalition. The pro-housing coalition can serve important roles when it seeks to inform potential coalition partners about both the necessity and the insufficiency of market-driven housing-supply expansions in solving what has emerged as dire housing shortages in many U.S. metropolitan areas.

Despite conflicting ideologies and goals, there were indicators of a broadly based pro-housing coalition across the political spectrum. Where municipal officials had zealously guarded local prerogative, mayors of Oakland, Sacramento, and San Jose expressed support for ending single-family zoning (Gimme Shelter: The California Housing Crisis Podcast, 2019). Economist William Fishchel of Dartmouth, long a sympathetic analyst of local government and homeowner behavior in the land-use regulatory realm (Fischel, 2001, 2015) called eliminating single-family zoning a "momentous idea" of which he heartily approved (McCormick, 2020). Similar reforms were advocated by Clovis Honoré, President of the San Diego NAACP (National Association for the Advancement of Colored People): "If you think your single-family community should not have apartment dwellers, you have to ask yourself why. And especially if you know and understand that you exist in a single-family community because your government deliberately segregated and discriminated against people, is that something you want to continue? Is that something you buy into and support?" (KUSI News, 2019) Writing in libertarian Reason magazine, Steven Greenhut offers that "abolishing single-family zoning expands freedom and choice" (Greenhut, 2020). Notwithstanding remaining differences, the ideological transcendence of the view that exclusionary regulations harmed the affordability, equity, and sustainability of U.S. metropolitan areas suggests the viability of directions of reforms that had been virtually inconceivable for decades.

References

3Ps Housing Plan, 2019. https://www.3pshousingplan.org. (accessed 12/26/2020).

A Better Cambridge, 2020. https://www.abettercambridge.org/about. (accessed 1/4/2021).

Adler, B., October 29, 2020. No, Democrats Won't 'Destroy' the Suburbs. But They Will Remake Them. Washington Post. https://www.washingtonpost.com/outlook/no-democrats-wont-destroy-the-suburbs-but-they-will-remake-them/2020/10/29/ea8c42a2-195c-11eb-82db-60b15c874105_story.html. (accessed 1/2/2021).

Affordable Housing Overlay Reality, 2020. https://www.ahoreality.org/articles/eliminating-single-family-zoning-isnt-enough. (accessed 12/30/2020).

Agnotti, T., Morse, S., 2016. Zoned Out! Race, Displacement, and City Planning in New York City. Terreform, New York.
Alter, A., 2020. Re-Elect Alison Alter. https://www.alisonalter.com/managing-growth. (accessed 12/29/2020).
Andersen, T., January 27, 2021. Berkeley Flips Script on Minimum Parking Requirements for Residential Developers. San Francisco Business Times. https://www.bizjournals.com/sanfrancisco/news/2021/01/27/berkeley-no-parking-minimums-for-developments.html. (accessed 1/28/2021).
Axel-Lute, M., 2019. YIMBYs: Friend, Foe, or Chaos Agent? Shelterforce. February 19 https://shelterforce.org/2019/02/19/yimbys-friend-foe-or-chaos-agent/. (accessed 1/2/2021).
Babcock, R.F., 1983. The egregious invalidity of the exclusive single-family zone. Land Use Law & Zoning Digest 35 (7), 4–8.
Badger, E., Bui, Q., June 18, 2019. Cities Start to Question an American Ideal: A House With a Yard on Every Lot. New York Times. https://www.nytimes.com/interactive/2019/06/18/upshot/cities-across-america-question-single-family-zoning.html. (accessed 1/5/2021).
Been, V., Ellen, I.G., O'Regan, K., 2019. Supply skepticism: housing supply and affordability. Hous. Policy Debate 29 (1), 25–40.
Bell, C.A., 2002. Workforce housing: the new economic imperative. Fannie Mae Foundation, Hous. Facts Find. 4 (2), 3–7. https://www.innovations.harvard.edu/housing-facts-findings-vol-4-no-2. (accessed 1/5/2021).
Berke, P.R., Godschalk, D.R., Kaiser, E.J., Rodriguez, D.A., 2006. Framing the Land Use Planning Process. Urban Land Use Planning, 5th. University of Illinois Press, Urbana and Chicago, p. 22.
Brey, J., September 22, 2020. Waiving Regulations for Affordable Housing Shows Results in Austin. Next City. https://nextcity.org/daily/entry/waiving-regulations-for-affordable-housing-shows-results-in-austin. (accessed 12/31/2020).
Brion, D.J., 1987. Essay on Lulu, Nimby, and the problem of distributive justice. Boston Coll. Environ. Aff. Law Rev. 15, 437.
Britschgi, C., June 26, 2019. The YIMBY Movement has Made it to D.C. Republicans are Leading the Way. Reason. https://reason.com/2019/06/26/the-yimby-movement-has-made-it-to-d-c-republicans-are-leading-the-way/. (accessed 12/28/2020).
Buchanan v. Warley, 1917. 245 U.S. 60.
Burnett, C.M., 2019. Parties as an organizational force on nonpartisan city councils. Party Polit. 25 (4), 594–608.
California Legislative Information, 2019. SB-50 Planning and Zoning: Housing Development: Streamlined Approval: Incentives. https://leginfo.legislature.ca.gov/faces/billCompareClient.xhtml?bill_id=201920200SB50&showamends=false. (accessed 12/30/2020).
Campanile, C., November 14, 2020. Democratic Socialists Endorse 6 Candidates in Bid to Run NYC Council. New York Post. https://nypost.com/2020/11/14/democratic-socialists-endorse-6-candidates-for-nyc-council/. (accessed 1/4/2021).
Casar, G., 2020. Austin City Council, District 4. https://www.casarforcouncil.com/. (accessed 12/29/2020).
Center for Neighborhood Technology, 2020. https://htaindex.cnt.org/. (accessed 12/21/2020).
Chadha, J., December 17, 2020. Group Pushing for More Housing Backs a Slate of Council Candidates. Politico New York. https://www.politico.com/states/new-york/city-hall/story/2020/12/17/group-pushing-for-more-housing-backs-a-slate-of-council-candidates-1347663.

City of Austin, n.d. Affordability Unlocked Development Bonus Program, https://www.austintexas.gov/department/affordability-unlocked-development-bonus-program (accessed 2/13/2021).
City of Cambridge, 2018. Community Development Department. Envision Cambridge Executive Summary. http://envision.cambridgema.gov/wp-content/uploads/2019/01/2019-01-22-Envision-Cambridge-Exec-Summary-Web-Pages.pdf. (accessed 1/26/2021).
City of Cambridge, 2020. City Council Meeting of October 5. https://cambridgema.iqm2.com/Citizens/FileOpen.aspx?Type=1&ID=2303&Inline=True. (accessed 12/20/2020).
City of Portland, July 2019. Residential Infill Project Summary, Revised Proposed Draft. https://www.portland.gov/sites/default/files/2019-07/2019_february_rip_revised_proposed_draft.pdf. (accessed 1/5/2021).
City of Portland, July 20, 2020. City Council Approves All Six Residential Infill Project Amendment Packages. https://www.portland.gov/bps/rip/news/2020/7/20/city-council-approves-all-six-residential-infill-project-amendment-packages. (accessed 12/31/2020).
Clifton, J., December 26, 2019. Tovo Reflects on a Year of Challenge and Success. Austin Monitor. https://www.austinmonitor.com/stories/2019/12/tovo-reflects-on-a-year-of-challenge-and-success/. (accessed 12/29/2020).
Collinson, R., 2011. Rental Housing Affordability Dynamics, 1990—2009. Cityscape, pp. 71–103.
Cortright, J., August 17, 2020. America's Least (and most) Segregated Cities. City Commentary. https://cityobservatory.org/most_segregated/. (accessed 1/2/2021).
Davidoff, P., Gold, N.N., 1970. Exclusionary zoning. Yale Rev. Law Soc. Action 1, 56.
Department of Land Conservation and Development, November 6, 2019. Key Elements of House Bill 2001 (Middle Housing). https://www.oregon.gov/lcd/UP/Documents/HB2001TechnicalOverview.pdf. (accessed 12/29/2020).
Dougherty, C., 2020. Golden Gates: Fighting for Housing in America. Penguin Publishing Group.
Einstein, K.L., et al., 2019. Neighborhood Defenders: Participatory Politics and America's Housing Crisis. Cambridge University Press.
Eisner, D., October 1, 2020. The Historical Affordable Housing Overlay is About to Pass. How Did it Overcome So Many Obstacles? A Better Cambridge. https://www.abettercambridge.org/the_historic_affordable_housing_overlay_is_about_to_pass_how_did_it_overcome_so_many_obstacles. (accessed 12/30/2020).
Firke, S., Levine, J., August 2020. Factions of Ann Arbor and the August 4 Election. Washtenaw Jewish News, p. 6. https://washtenawjewishnews.org/PDFs/WJN-08-20-web.pdf. (accessed 12/28/2020).
Fischel, W.A., 2001. The Homevoter Hypothesis: How Home Values Influence Local Government Taxation, School Finance, and Land-Use Policies. Harvard University Press.
Fischel, W.A., 2004. An economic history of zoning and a cure for its exclusionary effects. Urban Stud. 41 (2), 317–340.
Fischel, W.A., 2015. Zoning Rules! The Economics of Land Use Regulation. Lincoln Institute of Land Policy.
Freund, E., 1929. Some inadequately discussed problems of the law of city planning and zoning. Ill. Law Rev. 24, 135.
Frieden, B.J., 1979. The Environmental Protection Hustle. MIT Press, Cambridge, MA.
Gabbe, C.J., Pierce, G., Clowers, G., 2020a. Parking policy: The effects of residential minimum parking requirements in Seattle. Land Use Policy 91.
Gabbe, C.J., Pierce, G., Clowers, G., Fall 2020. How Developers Respond to Parking Reform: Reducing Minimum Parking Requirements can Help Alleviate Urban Housing Crises.

Transfers. https://transfersmagazine.org/magazine-article/how-developers-respond-to-parking-reform/?mc_cid=226327184d&mc_eid=5983f4a60f. (accessed 1/1/2021).
Gimme Shelter: The California Housing Crisis Podcast, 2019. Mayors-Only Panel (and Liam), With Libby Schaaf, Sam Liccardo, Darrell Steinberg and Michael Tubbs. https://soundcloud.com/matt-levin-4/mayors-only-panel-and-liam-with-libby-schaaf-sam-liccardo-darrell-steinberg-and-michael-tubbs. (accessed 1/5/2021).
Gosselin, K.R., December 20, 2017. Development, Business Expansion Could Follow New Hartford Parking Regulations. Hartford Courant. https://www.courant.com/real-estate/property-line/hc-biz-hartford-parking-minimums-lifted-citywide-20171219-story.html. (accessed 1/1/2021).
Gray, M.N., Millsap, A.A., 2020. Subdividing the unzoned city: an analysis of the causes and effects of Houston's 1998 subdivision reform. J. Plan. Educ. Res., 0739456X20935156.
Greenhut, S., 2020. Abolishing Single-Family-Only Zoning Expands Freedom and Choice. Reason. 1/10/ https://reason.com/2020/01/10/abolishing-single-family-only-zoning-expands-freedom-and-choice/. (accessed 1/1/2021).
Hess, D.B., 2017. Repealing minimum parking requirements in Buffalo: new directions for land use and development. J. Urban. Int. Res. Placemak. Urban Sustain. 10 (4), 442–467.
Hirt, S., 2014. Zoned in the USA: The Origins and Implications of American Land-Use Regulation. Cornell University Press, Ithaca; London.
Jones, C., Kammen, D.M., 2014. Spatial distribution of US household carbon footprints reveals suburbanization undermines greenhouse gas benefits of urban population density. Environ. Sci. Technol. 48 (2), 895–902.
Kapur, T.M., 2004. Land use regulation in Houston contradicts the city's free market reputation. Environ. Law Rep. News Anal. 34, 10045.
KUSI News, October 9, 2019. Advocates Urge End to Zoning that they say Causes Housing Discrimination. Video clip https://www.kusi.com/advocates-urge-end-to-zoning-that-they-say-causes-housing-segregation/. (accessed 1/1/2021).
Lake, R.W., 1993. Planners' alchemy transforming NIMBY to YIMBY: rethinking NIMBY. J. Am. Plann. Assoc. 59 (1), 87–93.
Levine, J., 2006. Zoned Out: Regulation, Markets, and Choices in Transportation and Metropolitan Land Use. Resources for the Future, Washington, D.C.
Levine, J., Grengs, J., Shen, Q., Shen, Q., 2012. Does accessibility require density or speed? A comparison of fast versus close in getting where you want to go in US metropolitan regions. J. Am. Plann. Assoc. 78 (2), 157–172.
Levine, J., Merlin, L., Grengs, J., 2017. Project-level accessibility analysis for land-use planning. Transp. Policy 53, 107–119.
Levine, J., Grengs, J., Merlin, L.A., 2019. From Mobility to Accessibility: Transforming Urban Transportation and Land-Use Planning. Cornell University Press, Ithaca, NY.
Lewyn, M.E., 2004. How overregulation creates sprawl (even in a city without zoning). Wayne Law Rev. 50, 1171.
Maine State Housing Authority, 2020. (Accessed 2 March 2021).
Manville, M., Beata, A., Shoup, D., 2013. Turning housing into driving: parking requirements and density in Los Angeles and New York. Hous. Policy Debate 23 (2), 350–375.
Manville, M., Monkkonen, P., Lens, M., 2020. It's time to end single-family zoning. J. Am. Plann. Assoc. 86 (1), 106–112.
Mark, J., December 18, 2019. How the Environmental Movement Can Go Beyond NIMBY-ism. Sierra. https://www.sierraclub.org/sierra/2020-1-january-february/editor/how-environmental-movement-can-go-beyond-nimby-ism. (accessed 12/28/2020).
Mast, E., 2019. The Effect of New Market-Rate Housing Construction on the Low-Income Housing Market (No. 19–307). Upjohn Institute. https://research.upjohn.org/up_workingpapers/307/.

Matheny, A.R., Williams, B.A., 1985. Knowledge vs. NIMBY: assessing Florida's strategy for siting hazardous waste disposal facilities. Policy Stud. J. 14 (1), 70.

McCormick, K., January 16, 2020. Rezoning History: Influential Minneapolis Policy Shift Links Affordability, Equity. Lincoln Institute of Land Policy. https://www.lincolninst.edu/publications/articles/2020-01-rezoning-history-minneapolis-policy-shift-links-affordability-equity. (accessed 1/1/2021).

Minneapolis 2040, 2021. https://minneapolis2040.com/media/1644/height.pdf. (accessed 12/26/2020).

Mogush, P., Worthington, H., 2020. The view from Minneapolis: comments on 'death to single-family zoning' and 'It's time to end single-family zoning'. J. Am. Plann. Assoc. 86 (1), 120.

Molotch, H., 1976. The city as a growth machine: toward a political economy of place. Am. J. Sociol. 82 (2), 309–332.

Monkkonen, P., 2016. Understanding and Challenging Opposition to Housing Construction in California's Urban Areas. Available at SSRN 3459823, SSRN.

Myers, D., Park, J.H., 2019. A constant quartile mismatch indicator of changing rental affordability in US Metropolitan areas, 2000 to 2016. Cityscape 21 (1), 163–200.

Nall, C., Marble, W., 2020. Where Self-Interest Trumps Ideology: Liberal Homeowners and Local Opposition to Housing Development. The Southern Political Science Association. Preprint https://www-journals-uchicago-edu.proxy.lib.umich.edu/doi/pdf/10.1086/711717. (accessed 1/5/2021).

Nozzi, D., 2003. Road to Ruin: An Introduction to Sprawl and How to Cure it. Greenwood Publishing Group.

Oregon State Legislature, 2019. 2019 Regular Session. https://olis.leg.state.or.us/liz/2019R1/Measures/Overview/HB2001. (accessed 12/26/2020).

OregonLaws.org, 2020. ORS195.065. https://www.oregonlaws.org/ors/195.065. (accessed 12/29/2020).

Parolek, D.G., 2020. Missing Middle Housing: Thinking Big and Building Small to Respond to Today's Housing Crisis. Island Press, Washington, D. C.

Pendall, R., 1999. Opposition to housing: NIMBY and beyond. Urban Aff. Rev. 35 (1), 112–136.

Portland: Neighbors Welcome, 2020. https://portlandneighborswelcome.org/reasons-to-support-infill. (accessed 1/5/2021).

Ramey, C., June 24, 2020. Edmonton Removes Minimum Parking Requirements City-Wide. Global News. https://globalnews.ca/news/7101796/edmonton-removes-minimum-parking-requirements/#:~:text=Council%20voted%20on%20the%20bylaw,%2C%20transit%2Doriented%20and%20walkable. (accessed 1/1/2021).

Rider Levett Bucknall, 2018. North America Quarterly Construction Cost Report. Second Quarter. https://www.rlb.com/wp-content/uploads/2018/07/Q2-2018.pdf. (accessed 1/1/2021).

Rothstein, R., 2017. The Color of Law: A Forgotten History of How Our Government Segregated America, first ed. Liveright Publishing Corporation.

Schmitt, A., December 12, 2018. Minneapolis Moves to Eliminate Mandatory Parking. Streetsblog, USA. https://usa.streetsblog.org/2018/12/12/minneapolis-moves-to-eliminate-mandatory-parking/#:~:text=As%20part%20of%20a%20larger,a%20hidden%20subsidy%20for%20drivers. (accessed 1/1/2021).

Shaw, R., September 22, 2018. Why Can't YIMBYs and Tenant Activists Get Along? BeyondChron. https://beyondchron.org/why-cant-yimbys-and-tenant-activists-get-along/. (accessed 1/4/2021).

Shaw, R., October 15, 2019. New Progress in Battling Housing Crisis. BeyondChron. https://beyondchron.org/will-ca-boost-housing-in-2020/. (accessed 12/26/2020).

Seltzer, E., 2015. Land Use Planning in Oregon: The Quilt and the Striggle for Scale. In: Knaap, G., Nedović-Budić, Z., Carbonell, A. (Eds.), Planning for States and Nation-States in the U.S. and Europe. Lincoln Institute of Land Policy, p. 53. Chapter 2.

Shaw, R., 2020a. Generation Priced Out: Who Gets to Live in the New Urban America, with a New Preface. University of California Press.

Shaw, R., 2020b. Cambridge Passes Citywide Affordable Housing Overlay: A New National Model. BeyondChron. October 6 https://beyondchron.org/cambridge-passes-citywide-affordable-housing-overlay-a-new-national-model/. (accessed 12/30/2020).

Shaw, R., June 30, 2020. Want to Change Housing Policies? Elect Pro-Housing Candidates! BeyondChron. http://beyondchron.org/mobilize-to-elect-pro-housing-candidates/?fbclid=IwAR2FnCoG-nk9MxiCi-NTvHYktYsrhbDjq8AGCHpQ1KN0jyH44HUTXq5xDok. (accessed 1/1/2020).

Shoup, D.C., 2011. The High Cost of Free Parking. Updated, Planners Press, American Planning Association.

Shoup, D., 2018. Parking and the City. Routledge.

Siegan, B.H., 1972. Land Use Without Zoning. Lexington Books, Lexington, MA.

Sisson, P., June 28, 2019. YIMBY in Action: How Pro-Housing Policies Became a Political Rallying Cry. Curbed. https://archive.curbed.com/2019/6/28/19154146/yimby-real-estate-housing-apartment-rent-deveopment-zoning. (accessed 1/4/2019).

Stein, S., 2019. Capital City: Gentrification and the Real Estate State. Verso.

Strong Towns, November 15, 2019. Every City Should Abolish its Minimum Parking Requirements. Has Yours? https://www.strongtowns.org/journal/2019/11/24/every-city-should-abolish-its-minimum-parking-requirements-has-yours. (accessed 1/1/2021).

Takahashi, L.M., 1997. The socio-spatial stigmatization of homelessness and HIV/AIDS: toward an explanation of the NIMBY syndrome. Soc. Sci. Med. 45 (6), 903–914.

The Oregonian, June 23, 2019. Oregon Republican Senators Walkout: What You Need to Know Today. https://www.oregonlive.com/politics/2019/06/oregon-republican-senators-walkout-what-you-need-to-know-today.html. (accessed 12/29/2020).

The Upzoning Wave Finally Catches Up to California, 2021. (Accessed 05 March 2021).

Toderian, B., November 12, 2010. 'Hidden Density' Showing Up Across City. Planetizen blog post https://www.planetizen.com/node/46877. (accessed 12/26/2020).

Trickey, E., July 11, 2019. How Minneapolis Freed Itself From the Stranglehold of Single-Family Homes. Politico. https://www.politico.com/magazine/story/2019/07/11/housing-crisis-single-family-homes-policy-227265. (accessed 2/13/2021).

Vote Tracker, 2020. Natasha Harper-Madison. https://apps.statesman.com/votetracker/people/natasha-harper-madison/. (accessed 12/29/2020).

Walsh, E., July 30, 2019. City Council Approves Regulation Changes for Low-Income Housing Development. City News Service. https://www.wkyc.com/article/news/politics/san-diego-city-council-approves-regulation-changes-for-low-income-housing-development/509-1b829a1c-d2a9-46d9-a491-ed832c0afe61. (accessed 1/5/2021).

Wegmann, J., 2020. Death to single-family zoning… and new life to the missing middle. J. Am. Plann. Assoc. 86 (1), 113–119.

Whittemore, A.H., 2020. Exclusionary zoning: origins, open suburbs, and contemporary debates. J. Am. Plann. Assoc., 1–14.

Wylie, A., December 27, 2018. Eliminating Minimum Parking Requirements Makes San Francisco More Livable. San Francisco Examiner. https://www.sfexaminer.com/opinion/eliminating-minimum-parking-requirements-makes-san-francisco-more-livable/. (accessed 1/1/2021).

Ziegler, J., Edward, H., 1982. The twilight of single-family zoning. UCLA J. Environ. Law Policy 3, 161.

CHAPTER SEVEN

Linking off-street parking to local transport and resilience policies

David A. King*
School of Geographical Sciences and Urban Planning, Arizona State University, Tempe, AZ, United States
*Corresponding author: e-mail address: david.a.king@asu.edu

Contents

Abstract

Off-street parking is commonly required by cities, which leads to an ever-expanding supply of spaces. This chapter reviews the literature to assess how off-street parking affects travel choices. The supply of parking has direct effects on travel, where the ease of parking makes driving more attractive, and conversely, limited or expensive parking reduces driving and encourages use of alternatives. Parking also has indirect effects on travel choices, where parking becomes a dominant feature of the built environment and inhibits walking, biking or transit use, in addition to increasing the cost of housing in places where alternatives to driving are abundant. Recent moves by some cities to reduce or eliminate parking requirements suggests that an era of parking reform is underway, and cities have tied parking reform to environmental, economic, and equity goals. Ultimately, parking remains a powerful tool for influencing travel choices, where more parking leads to more driving, but managing parking through prices and reducing required parking can nudge travelers toward other modes.

Keywords: Parking requirements, Travel behavior, Transportation demand management, Parking cash out, Resilience

Advances in Transport Policy and Planning, Volume 9
ISSN 2543-0009
https://doi.org/10.1016/bs.atpp.2021.10.004

1. Introduction

Parking policies and management are typically municipal-level transport policies that strongly influence travel behavior. Off-street parking requirements, one aspect of local parking policy, are a source of severe distortions to land development, mode choices and the overall transport system. These requirements are part of local zoning codes that regulate land development. Off-street parking regulations were originally intended to address traffic concerns, namely, by attempting to minimize disruptions to the traffic flow on streets and surrounding communities (Collis, 2005). They have since evolved into a poor device for managing traffic concerns, while contributing to auto-centric urban development.

Parking influences travel behavior through supply and monetary costs of spaces, and to a lesser extent, the convenience of parking. This means that there are multiple levers of policy available that promote or inhibit driving. Parking requirements are, in many ways, the most consequential aspect of land use policy in terms of social, economic, and environmental goals cities pursue. In most US cities, and many cities throughout the world, land use is regulated through zoning codes. These codes describe allowable uses for development, set bulk and size requirements of buildings, and often require a minimum number of parking spaces to be built on site. At their most basic level, these parking requirements are, as transport economist Donald Shoup quips, fertility drugs for cars (Shoup, 2017). In more practical terms, parking policy "acts as glue between the implementation of land-use and transport policies" (Marsden, 2006).

Parking is largely a derived demand, where motorists want and seek a place to leave their vehicles at their destinations when they are not actively using it. If there were no place to park, few people would drive. How parking supply is managed matters a great deal, as well, because managed parking can include priced parking, shared parking, or other aspects of parking that affect driver behavior with respect to travel choices. In places where parking is constrained by supply or price, drivers respond by doing one or more of:

- Park somewhere else farther away,
- Change the location of their destination (i.e., go someplace else),
- Change the time of travel (e.g., leave earlier),
- Change the mode used for travel (e.g., take the bus, carpool), and
- Not travel at all.

Each of these responses has obvious implications for travel behavior.

Parking also affects the built environment in ways that influence the use of other modes, though these effects are less studied. Parking is part of a suite of policies that make driving cheaper and easier than it should be relative to the costs of driving borne by society, including congestion, air pollution and crash costs. By making driving cheaper and easier, planners and engineers inadvertently make all other modes more difficult and onerous because of the physical characteristics of parking lots, curb cuts and other infrastructure. Ample surface parking lots discourage walking and biking, which in turn make transit less desirable. Trains and buses are harder to reach because parking increases distances that people on foot have to walk to get to their destinations, as parking lots often sit between the sidewalk and a business' door. Parking lots are also designed for driving, not walking, which discourages people on foot and creates dangerous conditions. In the United States, over 60,000 people are injured in parking lot crashes annually, though there is scant research to assess how this may affect active travel modes. Such indirect effects on demand for other modes caused by the supply of parking have received less attention than direct effects on driving, but are an important component of how parking requirements influence personal travel.

Lastly, off-street parking shapes the built environment in ways that undermine efforts to increase transport choices to individuals. As a practical matter, off-street parking requirements act as the leading design principle, as well as local transport policy that favors driving. For example, required parking inhibits redevelopment of buildings by forcing developers to devote scarce land to parking provision rather than housing or commercial space. Some cities recognize that holding a building to current era parking requirements, even though the building may have been built prior to any parking regulations, results in perverse incentives to destroy buildings people seek to save. Washington, DC, as one example, has exempted historic districts from required parking (Rugaber, 2002). An oversupply of off-street parking diminishes the quality of places where people want to go to walk around, shop, and live.

Ultimately, American cities are overparked. Despite frequent cries from the public that they can never find a parking space, in truth they most often mean that they cannot find a free spot exactly where and when they want one. In one study of mixed-use neighborhoods, the amount of parking supplied was 65% more than what was the maximum observed occupancy (Weinberger and Karlin-Resnick, 2015). Even transit-oriented developments, which ostensibly should encourage residents to forego cars, consistently supply more parking than needed (Cervero et al., 2010).

The ample parking supplied in cities and suburbs is problematic for many reasons, but most directly, lots of free parking subsidizes cars and keeps the cost of driving low.

This chapter will describe the many ways that parking requirements affect travel behavior by distorting land development and the built environment, then turn to strategies for reform and areas in need of additional research. There are two previous reviews of parking policy to note at the onset. One of the first analyses of how parking policy affects travel demand was by Feeney (1989). Feeney reviewed the empirical evidence available up to that point, and evaluated some methodological issues associated with studying parking. The second study is Marsden (2006), who assesses the evidence base of parking policy. These two studies are worthy of their own reading by anyone reading this.

2. Parking is local transport policy

Minimum parking requirements, as regulated through local zonings codes, act in practice as local transportation policy by favoring driving at the expense of other modes. Whenever a developer wants to build a new building or rehabilitate an old one, they must adhere to the zoning code, which determines what can be built (the allowable uses), the building bulk (size and orientation of the buildings), and how many parking spaces they must include (minimum parking requirements). These parking requirements were ubiquitous by the 1950s in zoning codes across the United States and around the world (Ferguson, 2004), and despite some movement toward reform, remain common in local codes (Hess, 2017). Transport economist Donald Shoup, who has likely done more than any other academic to argue the importance of parking for how cities work, calls minimum parking requirements a "fertility drug for cars." Not only do parking requirements lead to an abundance of cars, but those cars are more likely to be driven when there is ample free parking. One recent study of housing lottery recipients examined the effect of free parking at home on travel behavior, and found that people who were randomly assigned housing with parking were more likely to buy and use cars than those who weren't (Millard-Ball et al., 2021).

Despite parking acting as *de facto* transport policy, the supply of parking is generally not part of a city or region's long range transport planning (Taylor and van Bemmel-Misrachi, 2017). While cities and regions present visions of transport futures that are not oriented around driving, such as through plans for expanded transit or active travel, these plans are likely to avoid treating the supply of parking as a strategic goal. Parking exists in liminal spaces between the way the built environment is planned and the transport systems are managed. Land use planners are responsible for assessing the requirements for parking. Transport planners are not required to account for the storage needs of all the vehicles that comprise traffic flow. This unique space where parking is a transport issue in land use planning and an invisible problem for traffic analysis creates necessary conflict among desirable planning goals, including reducing social harms from automobility, providing alternatives to driving and building denser, more walkable communities.

2.1 Required parking leads to more driving

Despite the direct connections between parking supply and travel outcomes, few studies of the built environment on travel directly examine parking. Rather, parking is treated as a subset of other elements of the built environment, such as the three D's of density, diversity and design (Cervero and Kockelman, 1997) or as urban form relates to travel choices (Saelens and Handy, 2008). As discussed above, the requirement of parking directly affects these explanatory variables of travel behavior. As parking reduces density, parking has the indirect effect of making streets less safe. In a study of street safety in Philadelphia, scholars examined traffic crashes and injuries in the context of urban form and found that denser neighborhoods have fewer crashes and injuries (Guerra et al., 2019). It follows that increased parking supply, which would lead to lower densities, will also lead to more dangerous streets. As street safety is a determinant of travel choices, parking requirements have an indirect, and understudied, influence on travel behavior.

The evidence is clear that more parking is associated with more driving. For example, in New York City, having a parking space at home is associated with higher likelihood of driving to work even in locations where origins and destinations are well served by transit (Weinberger, 2012). However, the associations between parking supply and travel behavior present a challenge for asserting causality (Feeney, 1989). Most studies are snapshots of parking and travel behavior at a particular time rather than time-series or before and after studies. In addition, at present off-street parking is so ubiquitous that it is hard to estimate the effects of additional marginal spaces on the demand for driving. One study that did seek to evaluate causality used data dating back to 1960 to assess the effects of additional spaces on driving (McCahill et al., 2016). The authors also applied Bradford Hill criteria, which are guides for determining potential causality from known associations, to existing research on the effects of off-street parking. Their findings show that an increase in parking spaces per person from 0.1 to 0.5 increased automobile mode share by 30%.

2.2 Parking reduces the land available for buildings

Supplying parking spaces on individual building parcels has many implications for land use planning and the built form of cities. The built form then influences travel behavior and travel options. One study used data from 12 US cities to estimate the contribution of parking to the overall density of the built environment. The authors found that a 10% increase in the portion of commuters traveling by car is associated with an increase of 2500 m^2 of parking per 1000 people and a decrease of 1700 people/ km^2 in overall population density (McCahill and Garrick, 2012). The implications of this are intuitively understood, but perhaps not as well spelled out in the literature as they should be. Increasing the supply of off-street parking negatively effects the elements of the built environment, such as proximity, density, diversity of land uses, and other elements that have been shown to influence travel behavior. Until off-street parking is reformed to not be required for development and re-development, it will be extremely difficult to make substantial progress with modes shifts or either changes to travel behavior that will help achieve environmental, economic or social goals, however desirable they may be. Increasing the supply of parking as cities develop effectively keeps the cost of driving low—and hidden from drivers.

The land use regulations that require parking tacitly acknowledge the harm that parking requirements cause. In many cities the space built for parking does not count against the Floor Area Ratio (FAR) as dictated in the zoning code (Davis et al., 2010a,b; Liu et al., 2019). This means that developers can build parking decks that occupy the first few floors of a building, and can then place the occupied building on top of the parking pedestal. This exemption recognizes that onerous parking requirements inhibit developers from building as much as they otherwise would. This exemption also has a few effects of note. First, this adds to the expense of the building overall. Second, the parking decks can contribute to a dead street presence, as opposed to a row of shops or businesses. Third, the parking structure will contribute a curb cut to the sidewalk, and with large parking pedestals these may be wide enough for multiple lanes of traffic crossing the sidewalk. This diminishes the pedestrian environment.

The supply of parking shapes urban form and is central to local land use planning. Scholars have long documented how the built environment influences travel behavior (Cervero, 2002; Ewing and Cervero, 2010), but less on how parking shapes the built environment (Mukhija and Shoup, 2006). Private automobiles are a transport technology that has substantial space requirements in order to work. Cars are large, so need large roads to move. Cars are also parked most of the time (around 95% of the time), so they need ample spaces to sit idle for hours on end. Cities began to require developers to provide parking on site as they sought to minimize parking spillover into surrounding neighborhoods. The immediate effects of these regulations were to reduce the amount of space available to build buildings on any parcel. Consider a typical American parking requirement of three spaces per 1000 square feet of commercial space. Each parking stall takes up almost 350 square feet of space, so a developer is required to build approximately as much space for parking as they build for commercial uses. A 10,000 square foot parcel cannot accommodate a 10,000 square foot building and what would 30 required parking spaces, except with expensive digging or structured spaces. A 5000 square foot building will occupy half of the parcel, leaving just enough space for 15 car parking spaces.

The implications of such parking requirements go beyond simply subsidizing cars. Importantly, cars are a transport mode that makes all other modes more difficult to use (Krizek and King, 2021). Required parking not only limits the amount that can be built on a site, it pushes activities apart. An extra few hundred feet (or meters) of travel may not seem a large issue to a driver as they cruise for parking, but such distances are substantial time commitments for people on foot (King and Krizek, 2020). The physical layout of places, including the entries and exits, has strong effects on the overall accessibility of the place. One study of transit station layouts estimated that the catchment area for a station increased substantially by realigning the doors and walkways (Lahoorpoor and Levinson, 2020). There have been no similar studies of parking lot configurations, as best as I can find, but this is an area for future research on how parking lot design affects active travel accessibility, comfort and safety.

Placing parking lots between sidewalks and shops discourages walking by increasing distances while reducing comfort and safety. Once enough developments are made to accommodate parking on site, compact neighborhoods with ease of walking or biking cease to exist. If people are unable to walk in comfort and safety, they are unlikely to do so, and this has additional effects on transit ridership and all other modes, though the degree parking discourages other modes is unknown. Conversely, cities that are easy to walk are also cities where alternatives to driving, such as mass transit, ridehailing, taxis, and bicycling, can succeed. Parking, as a physical object in the city, is a lynchpin blocking sustainable transport policy.

2.3 Housing is influenced by parking

Minimum parking requirements have been shown to affect the composition and price of housing (Lehe, 2018). Housing affects travel behavior in that if housing cannot be built near high quality transit or walkable communities, then people become drivers out of necessity rather than choice. Moreover, residential parking requirements result in guaranteed parking at home as a hidden cost bundled within monthly rents. When people have a dedicated parking space at home they are more likely own cars and drive under all circumstances (Guo, 2013; Weinberger et al., 2008).

The bundled nature of residential parking represents a sizable cost of driving that is obscured from drivers. A study in Los Angeles shows that apartments with bundled parking cost \$200 more than those without, and condominiums with bundled parking command a \$43,000 premium (Manville, 2013). More importantly, bundled parking is associated with less transit use and higher gasoline expenses, suggesting more miles traveled (Manville and Pinski, 2020). Bundled parking hides the costs of parking from people, but critically bundled parking incentivizes auto ownership and use.

2.4 Making transit-oriented development work

Transit-oriented development (TOD) is an approach to development that focuses housing and other opportunities in close proximity to high quality transit services, such as within 400 m of a light rail transit station. While the intent of TOD is to entice people to substitute transit travel for auto travel, in practice it has mixed results in spurring modes shifts. Partly this is due to self-selection, where people who are already inclined to take transit seek to live in places with transit (Cervero, 2004, 2007; Wolday et al., 2018). Although TOD does see lower rates of auto ownership, solo driving to work and daily trips by car (such as to the grocery store) when evaluated against control groups farther from transit, the rail transit provision does not seem to be the primary cause of these differences. Rather, overall density, bus services, and most importantly the supply of parking on and off street are the dominant reasons for these differences (Chatman, 2013). The supply of parking at TODs undermines a key promise of this development idea, and the issue of too much parking at TODs is widespread (Cervero et al., 2010). Moreover, the location of parking within the TOD matters, as if parking is located between homes and the train station it acts as a barrier to an easy walk to transit. It is not simply the availability of parking that matters (Arrington and Cervero, 2008; van Lierop et al., 2017).

2.5 Travel implications of paid parking

There are many reasons to charge motorists to park. Parking takes up space, so parking charges can reflect the costs of construction, maintenance and opportunity costs of land. Parking prices may also reflect strategic policy objectives, such as fees designed to shift where people park. Prices can also be used to shape travel behavior and mode choices as part of programs designed to reduce solo vehicle travel.

For most auto trips, parking is free. Unfortunately, most travel surveys and diaries do not ask questions about the cost of parking, though the 1995 National Household Travel Survey (NHTS) did ask whether people paid for parking during their travel days. The responses showed that 99% of car trips ended in free parking (Shoup, 2017). This lack of data about paid parking presents challenges for research and policy, as the studies that have examined price sensitivity show that parking prices can be very effective at changing travel choices.

Parking fees have been shown to have a strong influence on travel behavior. Though studies have presented a range of elasticities for the price of parking, scholars and policy makers generally use −0.3 as the elasticity for parking demand (i.e., the number of cars parked) (Federal Transit Administration, 2003). Yet overall parking demand is one potential change. The decision about parking has spatial and temporal dimensions—drivers may choose to park farther away where it may be cheaper, or they may shift their time of travel. There are also modal substitutes, where the cost of parking influences traveler decisions about how to travel. For example, high parking prices or overall scarcity are associated with higher use of ridehail services (Brown, 2019). For cities that rely on parking revenues to pay for services, substitution away from driving toward ridehailing as parking prices increase may negatively affect overall parking revenues (Clark and Brown, 2021). The precise elasticity associated with parking prices then is dependent on many factors, which will in turn influence the expected change.

The elasticity of parking prices also depends on the type of trip. Commute trips are less elastic than noncommute trips (Lehner and Peer, 2019). As parking is a derived demand, time spent at work is determined by the employer far more often than by the employee. In these cases, once the decision to drive has been made, then the employees have little choice but to pay the fees, whatever they may be. Of course, at least in the United States, employers are able to offer parking as a nontaxable employee benefit, which provides a substantial workplace incentive to drive.

However, the effectiveness of using parking prices to influence travel behavior depends on available alternatives, as well as the location of destinations. Drivers are more sensitive to price increases in central business districts, where alternatives are likely to be available. At suburban locations with little to no transit service and low walkability, drivers are more likely to be captive to driving.

3. Parking and transportation demand management

Transportation demand management (TDM) includes concepts where employers work with their employees to reduce solo-occupant commuting. Alternatives such as carpooling, transit passes, and telecommuting are all tools within the TDM toolkit. What is most effective for changing commute modes, however, is managing parking better. A study in Melbourne, Australia, used a survey of downtown workers to assess how parking availability affects commute choices (Pandhe and March, 2012). Over half of respondents said that if parking was not available they would not drive, though only about one-third of respondents said they would switch to transit. Other studies confirm that restricting parking access and implementing higher parking charges that employees pay are effective for reducing solo driving (Christiansen et al., 2017), though the overall effectiveness may depend on employer characteristics such as location within a Central Business District (Ko and Kim, 2017).

Employee-paid parking fees can also be used to moderate demand for parking and pay for other TDM strategies, such as program outreach, program staff and incentives for employees to change their commute. A case study of the US Berkeley campus suggests that higher parking prices can help the university both avoid costly construction of new parking facilities, needed to accommodate demand at low prices, and pay for staffing and incentives for a broader TDM approach (Rivadeneyra et al., 2017). While this particular study did not include an analysis of the success of the TDM programs for changing travel behavior, the findings point to the importance of parking as a key, but complementary, aspect of TDM programs.

One area of TDM that can reduce demand for parking while affecting travel behavior is a parking cash out program (Enoch, 2002; Evangelinos et al., 2018; Shoup, 1997, 2005; Watters et al., 2006). The way parking cash out works is employers offer their employees a cash bonus to not have a parking place at work. The employers should be able to save money by leasing fewer parking spaces, and the employees are often happy to pocket the extra money each month. The most common outcome of parking cash out is that carpooling increases as solo driving declines. An advantage of parking cash out is it takes advantage of existing transport networks and choices rather than waiting for future investments in some new technology.

4. Parking futures for policy and research

There is substantial pressure to change the status quo of required parking. Many cities are reviewing, and often eliminating, required parking within the zoning code to make housing cheaper and businesses easier to open. New transport technologies reduce the demand for parking, such as micromobility and ridehailing. Increases in electric vehicles, by contrast, may increase the need for places to charge cars. Growing recognition of how parking infrastructure affects resilience will lead to strategies to remove or adapt lots and structures. The pandemic of 2020–21 may have permanent effects on office work and commuting. As the future of transport is filled with uncertainty, so is the future of parking.

4.1 Parking reform and emerging technologies

There is growing recognition that land use regulations should not require parking with every development. Buffalo, New York eliminated parking requirements city-wide in 2016 (Hess, 2017). Minneapolis, Minnesota eliminated parking requirements in 2019 for most parts of the city in a recent zoning reform. In 2021, Saint Paul, Minnesota eliminated parking requirements as part of a city commitment to environmental and affordable housing goals. Other cities have followed suit for similar reasons. Overall, these changes are too recent to have a large literature of what happens after parking requirements are relaxed, but there is some evidence of the effects of relaxing these regulations. In 2012, Seattle, Washington reduced or eliminated parking requirements in most of the city. A 2020 study showed that after these reforms, developers built approximately 40% fewer parking spaces than had been required under previous regulations (Gabbe et al., 2020). Parking reform is unlikely to lead to no new parking spaces being built. Rather, elimination of parking requirements will free developers and businesses from building more than people are willing to pay for.

A challenge for parking reform is the structural issues associated with parking provision. There is substantial interest for improving data and analysis regarding trip generation and parking generation in order to better reflect actual behavior as well as account for new technologies. Conventionally, urban development is assessed through the Institute of Transportation Engineers (ITE) Trip and Parking Generation Manuals. These manuals present observed data of trip making and occupied parking for a wide variety of potential building uses. Despite their broad use, these manuals generally overstate the amount of trip making and parking generation (Clifton et al., 2017; Currans, 2017; Currans and Clifton, 2015; Millard-Ball, 2015). Case studies specifically examining TOD in the United States show that both trip generation and parking demand is less than half of what standard guidelines predict (Ewing et al., 2017).

Investigations into how new mobility technologies affect trip making are ambiguous (Jiao et al., 2020; King and Saldarriaga, 2018). Better understanding of how new technologies affect trip making, mode choice and parking demand is a needed area of research, but one that is growing quickly. For instance, studies of ridehail use show that ridehail tends to increase in use in places where parking fees are high (Brown, 2019). The promise of automated vehicles (AVs) has led many to study potential effects on parking demand if AVs become commonplace, especially used as taxi services (Sperling, 2018). The proponents claim that AVs may reduce or eliminate demand for parking, especially in dense urban neighborhoods, as cars that drive themselves will either find a new passenger or drive to a less congested location until needed again. If these assumptions hold, a tremendous amount of urban land that is currently used for parking would be free to be developed into other buildings offering a mix of uses. Simulations have estimated that automated vehicles may lead to sizable reductions in parking demand in central business districts under conditions where automated vehicles are shared (Zhang and Wang, 2020). Even if this holds true, other simulation studies show that driverless cars may instead cruise endlessly, increasing traffic congestion and reducing many potential gains from the technology (Millard-Ball, 2019). Overall, simulation studies suggest that even in an automated future for urban transport, historically effective yet unpopular policies that manage parking through prices will be warranted.

Together, however, the above referenced studies point to a need to develop new tools for assessing the transport effects of new development, especially in the context of new modes that are currently available or in development. New technologies will affect travel behavior, as will the built environment if real estate developers are allowed to build without supplying parking. Future research of travel behavior in cities that have reduced or eliminated parking requirements will make important contributions to the field.

4.2 Park once neighborhoods

Parking supplied on each development site in inefficient use of land and makes travel by mode other than driving more difficult. A policy reform that decouples building sites from parking supply will create better neighborhoods that support multimodal travel. A study from Vancouver suggests that existing underused parking spaces in residential buildings can be pooled and made available to the public, thus reducing demand for on-street spaces (Abbott and Bigazzi, 2017). These types of approaches are useful for managing supply and demand issues but offer less opportunity for mode switching. Whether park once neighborhoods reduce total vehicular travel is largely unexamined and an area of future work.

While shared parking makes more efficient use of land and contributes to better urban environments than accessory parking on each site, people tend to prefer parking close to their final destinations. One study used data from a commuter survey at the University of Michigan to simulate the effect parking policies have on mode choice (Yan et al., 2019). This study estimated the parking price elasticity average of −0.78, which is larger than the commonly used value of −0.3 (e.g., Hensher and King, 2001; Vaca and Kuzmyak, 2005). Moreover, the study shows that the egress time of parking, meaning the nonmonetary costs associated with getting from the parking lot to the final destination, has a larger effect on travel behavior than just the monetary costs of parking. City planners and engineers should account for the placement of shared parking as part of these reforms.

4.3 Resilience planning

Parking is one of the largest single use of land for cities. Roads and parking combined are over a third of all land in both the Los Angeles and Phoenix regions (Chester et al., 2015; Hoehne et al., 2019). The volume of pavement exacerbates many urban climate and resilience planning concerns, which suggests that pavement reductions and other strategies are worthwhile. Overall, parking lots have a large environmental footprint beyond the contribution to driving. In one study of the Upper Midwest in the United States researchers estimated that approximately 5% of all land area is comprised out parking lots (Davis et al., 2010a,b). This represents 43 million parking spaces for a region that has 15.5 million cars—if all cars were parked they would only use 40% of the available spaces. Not only does all this parking incentivize driving and associated emissions and air pollution, it carries substantial ecological and local environmental damage through increased heat island effects and polluted storm water run-off.

All of the pavement used for roads and parking contributes to urban heat effects, where surface sensible heat is approximately 20% higher than natural environments (Hoehne et al., 2020). Heat affects comfort and safety, which are factors that affect propensity to walk or bike. The presence of parking, regardless of shade trees or other heat mitigation interventions, will reduce the thermal comfort of travelers, and cities should include such effects in their climate resilience programs. A study of green parking in Korea, where green parking was an initiative to shift on-street parking to off-street in order to create spaces for tree planting at the curb, found that replacing parking with trees increased shade and reduced heat exposure (Park et al., 2016).

Another study from Serbia shows that contextual tree plantings, meaning trees that thrive in local conditions, can improve thermal comfort for people walking and reduce heat stress (Milošević et al., 2017). Other studies have shown that summer temperatures in parking lots can be reduced 1–5 °C with adequate cooling strategies including evaporative cooling and tree planting (Sharifi et al., 2021). Together, these studies suggest that reducing parking can improve the thermal conditions for pedestrians and cyclists. Additional research is needed to assess how this affects decisions to walk or bike.

5. Conclusions

Off-street parking strongly influences on travel behavior. The supply of parking on travel behavior has been well-studied. Ultimately, off-street parking requirements act as transport policy for cities, even as cities work to promote alternatives to driving. As the supply of parking increases, the costs of driving decline by making car storage easier. The evidence is clear that more parking leads to more driving. Cities can harness parking management through TDM programs. The most effective programs to affect travel behavior include pricing parking and offering worker cash in lieu of a parking space. These programs have successfully shifted some workers from solo drivers to carpoolers or transit users. Parking cash out is particularly effective at shifting travel choices, though for many suburban employers where parking is abundant and free developing such a program may be challenging.

As the built environment influences travel behavior, the role of parking in shaping the built form is critical though somewhat understudied. The supply of parking pushes buildings further apart, which leaves people on foot to navigate spaces designed for cars and driving. How neighborhoods with ample off-street parking affect propensity to walk or bike is an area of needed research, along with how to design parking lots that are safer for people regardless of their mode of travel. As many cities are implementing parking reform, off-street parking is tied to environmental, economic and social goals. As cities pursue resilience planning, the costs of parking lots in terms of urban heat and flooding will grow in importance. How these urban climate issues affect active travel or transit usage is growing as a research area (e.g., Martello et al., 2021). To sum, the causality of between parking supply and driving is clear and established. Less established are the indirect effects off-street parking has on other modes of travel. As more cities and developers view parking as an unnecessary cost or damaging to larger climate goals, parking reform is expected to continue and new avenues of research about the association between parking and travel behavior will open.

References

Abbott, N.T., Bigazzi, A.Y., 2017. Utilizing shared parking to mitigate imbalanced supply in a dense urban neighborhood: case study in Vancouver, British Columbia, Canada. Transp. Res. Rec. 2651 (1), 92–100.

Arrington, G.B., Cervero, R., 2008. TCRP Report 128: Effects of TOD on Housing, Parking, and Travel. Transportation Research Board of the National Academies, Washington, DC, p. 3.

Brown, A., 2019. Redefining car access: ride-hail travel and use in Los Angeles. J. Am. Plann. Assoc. 85 (2), 83–95.

Cervero, R., 2002. Built environments and mode choice: toward a normative framework. Transp. Res. Part D: Transp. Environ. 7 (4), 265–284.

Cervero, R., 2004. Transit-Oriented Development in the United States: Experiences, Challenges, and Prospects. Transportation Research Board.

Cervero, R., 2007. Transit-oriented development's ridership bonus: a product of self-selection and public policies. Environ. Plan. A 39 (9), 2068–2085.
Cervero, R., Kockelman, K., 1997. Travel demand and the 3Ds: density, diversity, and design. Transp. Res. Part D: Transp. Environ. 2 (3), 199–219.
Cervero, R., Adkins, A., Sullivan, C., 2010. Are suburban TODs over-parked? J. Public Transp. 13 (2), 3.
Chatman, D.G., 2013. Does TOD need the T? On the importance of factors other than rail access. J. Am. Plann. Assoc. 79 (1), 17–31.
Chester, M., et al., 2015. Parking infrastructure: a constraint on or opportunity for urban redevelopment? A study of Los Angeles County parking supply and growth. J. Am. Plann. Assoc. 81 (4), 268–286.
Christiansen, P., et al., 2017. Parking facilities and the built environment: impacts on travel behaviour. Transp. Res. Part A: Policy Pract. 95, 198–206.
Clark, B.Y., Brown, A., 2021. What does ride-hailing mean for parking? Associations between on-street parking occupancy and ride-hail trips in Seattle. Case Studies on Transport Policy 9 (2), 775–783.
Clifton, K.J., et al., 2017. Improving Trip Generation Methods for Livable Communities. NITC-RR-757. Transportation Research and Education Center (TREC), Portland, OR. https://doi.org/10.15760/trec.159.
Collis, H., 2005. Parking Strategies and Management. Institution of Highways and Transportation.
Currans, K.M., 2017. Issues in trip generation methods for transportation impact estimation of land use development: a review and discussion of the state-of-the-art approaches. J. Plan. Lit. 32 (4), 335–345.
Currans, K.M., Clifton, K.J., 2015. Using household travel surveys to adjust ITE trip generation rates. J. Transp. Land Use 8 (1), 85–119.
Davis, A.Y., et al., 2010a. Estimating parking lot footprints in the upper Great Lakes region of the USA. Landsc. Urban Plan. 96 (2), 68–77.
Davis, A.Y., et al., 2010b. The environmental and economic costs of sprawling parking lots in the United States. Land Use Policy 27 (2), 255–261.
Enoch, M., 2002. UK Parking Cash out Experience, and Lessons from California. Loughborough University.
Evangelinos, C., et al., 2018. Pricing workplace parking via cash-out: effects on modal choice and implications for transport policy. Transp. Res. Part A: Policy Pract. 113, 369–380.
Ewing, R., Cervero, R., 2010. Travel and the built environment. J. Am. Plann. Assoc. 76 (3), 265–294. https://doi.org/10.1080/01944361003766766.
Ewing, R., et al., 2017. Trip and parking generation at transit-oriented developments: five US case studies. Landsc. Urban Plan. 160, 69–78.
Federal Transit Administration, 2003. Traveler Response to Transportation System Changes. Transportation Research Board.
Feeney, B.P., 1989. A review of the impact of parking policy measures on travel demand. Transp. Plan. Technol. 13 (4), 229–244.
Ferguson, E., 2004. Zoning for parking as policy process: a historical review. Transp. Rev. 24 (2), 177–194.
Gabbe, C.J., Pierce, G., Clowers, G., 2020. Parking policy: the effects of residential minimum parking requirements in Seattle. Land Use Policy 91, 104053.
Guerra, E., Dong, X., Kondo, M., 2019. Do denser neighborhoods have safer streets? Population density and traffic safety in the Philadelphia region. J. Plan. Educ. Res. (p. 0739456X19845043).
Guo, Z., 2013. Home parking convenience, household car usage, and implications to residential parking policies. Transp. Policy 29, 97–106.

Hensher, D.A., King, J., 2001. Parking demand and responsiveness to supply, pricing and location in the Sydney central business district. Transp. Res. Part A: Policy Pract. 35 (3), 177–196.
Hess, D.B., 2017. Repealing minimum parking requirements in Buffalo: new directions for land use and development. J. Urban.: Int. Res. Placemaking Urban Sustain. 10 (4), 442–467.
Hoehne, C.G., et al., 2019. Valley of the sun-drenched parking space: the growth, extent, and implications of parking infrastructure in Phoenix. Cities 89, 186–198.
Hoehne, C.G., et al., 2020. Urban heat implications from parking, roads, and cars: a case study of metro Phoenix. Sustain. Resilient Infrastruct., 1–19. Online First.
Jiao, J., Bischak, C., Hyden, S., 2020. The impact of shared mobility on trip generation behavior in the US: findings from the 2017 National Household Travel Survey. Travel Behav. Soc. 19, 1–7.
King, D.A., Krizek, K.J., 2020. Revamping site design specifications to support human-scaled transport networks. In: *State of Transportation Planning 2020.* Moving People over Cars*: Mobility for Healthy Communities*. American Planning Association, Transportation Planning Division, pp. 176–181.
King, D.A., Saldarriaga, J.F., 2018. Measuring changes in taxi trips near infill development and issues for curbside management of for-hire vehicles. Res. Transp. Bus. Manag. https://doi.org/10.1016/j.rtbm.2018.10.006.
Ko, J., Kim, D., 2017. Employer-based travel demand management program: Employer's choice and effectiveness. Transp. Policy 59, 1–9.
Krizek, K.J., King, D.A., 2021. Advanced Introduction to Urban Transport Planning. Edward Elgar Publishing.
Lahoorpoor, B., Levinson, D.M., 2020. Catchment if you can: the effect of station entrance and exit locations on accessibility. J. Transp. Geogr. 82, 102556.
Lehe, L., 2018. Minimum parking requirements and housing affordability. J. Transp. Land Use 11 (1), 1309–1321.
Lehner, S., Peer, S., 2019. The price elasticity of parking: a meta-analysis. Transp. Res. Part A: Policy Pract. 121, 177–191.
Liu, Q., Zhu, M., Xiao, Z., 2019. Workplace parking provision and built environments: improving context-specific parking standards towards sustainable transport. Sustainability 11 (4), 1142.
Manville, M., 2013. Parking requirements and housing development: regulation and reform in Los Angeles. J. Am. Plann. Assoc. 79 (1), 49–66.
Manville, M., Pinski, M., 2020. Parking behaviour: bundled parking and travel behavior in American cities. Land Use Policy 91. https://doi.org/10.1016/j.landusepol.2019.02.012, 103853.
Marsden, G., 2006. The evidence base for parking policies—a review. Transp. Policy 13 (6), 447–457.
Martello, M.V., et al., 2021. Evaluation of climate change resilience for Boston's rail rapid transit network. Transp. Res. Part D: Transp. Environ. 97, 102908.
McCahill, C., Garrick, N., 2012. Automobile use and land consumption: empirical evidence from 12 cities. Urban Des. Int. 17 (3), 221–227.
McCahill, C.T., et al., 2016. Effects of parking provision on automobile use in cities: inferring causality. Transp. Res. Rec. 2543 (1), 159–165.
Millard-Ball, A., 2015. Phantom trips: overestimating the traffic impacts of new development. J. Transp. Land Use 8 (1), 31–49.
Millard-Ball, A., 2019. The autonomous vehicle parking problem. Transp. Policy 75, 99–108.
Millard-Ball, A., et al., 2021. What do residential lotteries show us about transportation choices? Urban Stud. 1–19. Online First.

Milošević, D.D., Bajšanski, I.V., Savić, S.M., 2017. Influence of changing trees locations on thermal comfort on street parking lot and footways. Urban For. Urban Green. 23, 113–124.

Mukhija, V., Shoup, D., 2006. Quantity versus quality in off-street parking requirements. J. Am. Plann. Assoc. 72 (3), 296–308.

Pandhe, A., March, A., 2012. Parking availability influences on travel mode: Melbourne CBD offices. Aust. Plan. 49 (2), 161–171. https://doi.org/10.1080/07293682.2011.616177.

Park, J.-H., et al., 2016. The influence of Korea's green parking project on the thermal environment of a residential street. Habitat Int. 56, 181–190.

Rivadeneyra, A.T., et al., 2017. Building more parking at major employment centers: can full-cost recovery parking charges fund TDM programs? Case Studies on Transport Policy 5 (1), 159–167.

Rugaber, E.W., 2002. The Special Merit Exemption under DC's Historic Preservation Act: An Analysis of 20 Years of Application and Suggestions for the Future. Georgetown University Law Center.

Saelens, B.E., Handy, S.L., 2008. Built environment correlates of walking: a review. Med. Sci. Sports Exerc. 40 (7 Suppl), S550.

Sharifi, E., Zawarus, P., Lehmann, S., 2021. Optimization of urban cooling strategies for parking lots in hot and dry climates: case study of Las Vegas and Adelaide. In: Urban Heat Island (UHI) Mitigation. Springer, pp. 169–182.

Shoup, D.C., 1997. Evaluating the effects of cashing out employer-paid parking: eight case studies. Transp. Policy 4 (4), 201–216.

Shoup, D.C., 2005. Parking Cash out. American Planning Association.

Shoup, D., 2017. The High Cost of Free Parking: *Updated Edition*. Routledge.

Sperling, D., 2018. Three Revolutions: Steering Automated, Shared, and Electric Vehicles to a better Future. Island Press.

Taylor, E.J., van Bemmel-Misrachi, R., 2017. The elephant in the scheme: planning for and around car parking in Melbourne, 1929–2016. Land Use Policy 60, 287–297. https://doi.org/10.1016/j.landusepol.2016.10.044.

Vaca, E., Kuzmyak, J.R., 2005. Traveler response to transportation system changes. In: Chapter 13-Parking Pricing and Fees.

van Lierop, D., Maat, K., El-Geneidy, A., 2017. Talking TOD: learning about transit-oriented development in the United States, Canada, and the Netherlands. J. Urban.: Int. Res. Placemaking Urban Sustain. 10 (1), 49–62. https://doi.org/10.1080/17549175.2016.1192558.

Watters, P., O'Mahony, M., Caulfield, B., 2006. Response to cash outs for work place parking and work place parking charges. Transp. Policy 13 (6), 503–510.

Weinberger, R., 2012. Death by a thousand curb-cuts: evidence on the effect of minimum parking requirements on the choice to drive. Transp. Policy 20, 93–102.

Weinberger, R.R., Karlin-Resnick, J., 2015. Parking in mixed-use US districts: oversupplied no matter how you slice the pie. Transp. Res. Rec. 2537 (1), 177–184.

Weinberger, R., et al., 2008. Guaranteed Parking— Guaranteed Driving. Transportation Alternatives, New York. *http://www. (transalt. org/files/news/reports/guaranteed_parking. pdf* [Preprint).

Wolday, F., Cao, J., Næss, P., 2018. Examining factors that keep residents with high transit preference away from transit-rich zones and associated behavior outcomes. J. Transp. Geogr. 66, 224–234.

Yan, X., Levine, J., Marans, R., 2019. The effectiveness of parking policies to reduce parking demand pressure and car use. Transp. Policy 73, 41–50.

Zhang, W., Wang, K., 2020. Parking futures: shared automated vehicles and parking demand reduction trajectories in Atlanta. Land Use Policy 91. https://doi.org/10.1016/j.landusepol.2019.04.024, 103963.

CHAPTER EIGHT

Pathway toward integrated transportation-land use planning in China

Jiawen Yang* and Yuling Yang
School of City Planning and Design, Peking University Shenzhen Graduate School, Shenzhen, GD, China
*Corresponding author: e-mail address: yangjw@pkusz.edu.cn

Contents

Abstract

As traffic congestion and fertile land loss arise in China's urbanization, integrated transportation-land use planning (ITLUP) begins to play a central role in China's pursuit for sustainable development. This chapter reviews China's practice in ITLUP. It explains the relevant governance arrangement, planning processes and ITLUP initiatives and tools. It also illustrates Shenzhen's pathway toward ITLUP, which features integrated planning for land management and multimode transportation management. Overall, Shenzhen's approaches have preceded the national government's endeavor and inspired other Chinese cities. It provides a window, through which one can observe China's planning innovation. It offers insights for other megacities constrained by land availability.

Advances in Transport Policy and Planning, Volume 9
ISSN 2543-0009
https://doi.org/10.1016/bs.atpp.2021.10.001

Keywords: Integrated transportation-land use planning, Governance arrangement, Planning process, Transit-oriented development

1. Introduction

As traffic congestion arises in the urbanizing world, there have been increasing calls for integrated transportation-land use planning (ITLUP), with a hope that better-coordinated transportation-land development could result in more accessible urban space. Given the broad implications of transportation and land development, the initiative of ITLUP has been linked to various policy agendas in different parts of the world. In North America, ITLUP is more likely to suggest the development of higher density and better transit services. It has been promoted as a venue to revitalize city centers and to contain urban sprawl. In Europe, ITLUP has been marketed as a venue for environmental protection as it helps to decrease vehicular emissions (Yekyeong, 2012). In China, where fertile land per capita is low, ITLUP is part of a broad agenda of sustainability which targets not only traffic congestion and air quality, but also strategic issues such as food security, as China's legendary economic development has been accompanied by fast loss of fertile land.

The movement toward ITLUP always suggests some changes in the status quo, and the exact changes depend on the specific institution arrangement and urban contexts. What is China's typical movement toward ITLUP? One would expect that it should be significantly different from its counterpart in other countries. China's state ownership of land, the deep involvement of local government in land development, and the scarcity of the fertile land for food security all suggest that China might have an ITLUP path of its own characteristics. This chapter explains China's rationale for and approaches to ITLUP, which was illustrated in relatively details with the case of Shenzhen. This book chapter is organized as follows. Section 2 reviews typical measures and practices to implement ITLUP in example countries of different parts of the world, with a description of relevant governance arrangement, coordination mechanism, and planning initiatives. Section 3 presents a brief review of the Chinese planning system in relevance to ITLUP, with a reference to land management, multimode transportation integration, and coordination between transportation and land development. Section 4 further illustrate China's ITLUP pathway with the story of Shenzhen. Section 5 summarize China's ITLUP pathway with a reference to governance reform, new planning processes and new planning initiatives.

2. Integrated planning and integrated transportation-land use planning

The term "integrated planning" refers to a holistic approach to planning, which ensures planning coordination among different sectors or different jurisdictions, or between different levels of governments. Planning integration is viewed as necessary or desirable because of noticeable interaction among relevant sectors, jurisdictions, or governments. Planning integration can be aided with governance arrangement or appropriate planning process (Abukhater, 2009; Fairfax, 2005).

Among different kinds of integrated planning, ITLUP has been a common means to achieve sustainability over the past decades in many cities of either developed or developing countries. Transportation and land development are two elements in a two-way dynamic feedback cycle. On the one hand, the developed land feeds the transportation system with various passengers and goods to be carried to the destinations. On the other hand, transportation can increase accessibility to land parcels and attracts activities to move to places of high accessibility. This growth process can trigger further transportation demands on more and better transportation infrastructures and services. The expansion of the transportation system again increases accessibility to relevant places, which encourages densification and infill development. This feedback process fuels the fundamental dynamics of urban development and poses transportation-land use integration as a planning challenge (Acheampong and Silva, 2015; Fairfax, 2005; Guiliano, 2004; Lee, 2020).

ITLUP implies that planning for land development and transportation should not be separated from each other. Instead, land development planning and transportation planning should be carefully coordinated or even integrated into one coherent planning process (Geerlings and Stead, 2003). This integration is conditioned on governance arrangement, the existence of coordination mechanism, and/or relevant planning initiatives.

2.1 Governance arrangement

Governance arrangement plays a significant role in interconnecting different sectors for an agreement on integrated planning (Transport and Infrastructure Council, 2006). The responsibility of transportation planning and land development planning can be put either into one authority or two separate ones. If they are put under one authority, the integration between land and transportation can be woven into the work routine (Stanley, 2015).

Such an arrangement happens in the South Australia government, where the authority has fewer restrictions when it releases an integrated transportation-land use plan (Transport and Infrastructure Council, 2006). If cities keep these two sectors separate, a specific communication protocol is warranted to ensure a smooth integration (Stanley, 2015). When transportation planning and land-use planning are conducted by governments of different geographical levels, a vertical integration is desired. In the USA, for example, municipal governments, who are responsible for local land use planning, are expected to coordinate with metropolitan planning organizations, who are responsible for regional transportation planning (Meyer, 2016).

2.2 Coordination mechanism

It is rare for cities to keep land use planning and transportation planning under a single authority. An integrated planning procedure, therefore, is expected for interinstitute collaboration. The exact format depends on the local context.

First, a government official can be appointed or a government office can be created to take charge of the integration. In London, the elected Mayor is responsible for economic development, land use planning, and transportation planning. This gives the Mayor's office as a bridge between land use planning and transportation planning to ensure that those plans are in concert with each other (Stanley, 2015).

Integration mechanism ensures coordination between land-use planning and transportation planning. Bristol prepares a land-use plan and a transportation plan separately. These two plans are then coordinated by incorporating the transportation strategy in the land-use plan (Hull, 2005). In the United Kingdom, an integrated transportation plan of different modes and a place-based transportation plan are both interventions for ITLUP. The integrated transportation plan sets the land-use plan as the planning background (Department for Transport, 2002). The place-based plan requires transportation planners to pay attention to the built environment and land-use patterns (James, 2005). A few cities employ a spatial development framework that integrates their strategic land-use plan and transportation plan (Hull, 2005; Planning Institute of Australia (South Australian Division), 2010).

Planning processes are typically created for ITLUP. For example, Amsterdam sets up a five-step intervention process: framing the problem, shaping the process, discussing and selecting relevant information, developing alternative strategies, and identifying "no regrets" and interdependencies. In the first step, land use and transportation planners can arrive at a shared problem statement. Then, they discuss the approaches to enhancing integration between land use and transportation. In the third and fourth steps, planners work together and discuss shared strategies (Te Brömmelstroet and Bertolini, 2010).

2.3 Integration tools or initiatives

Tools and initiatives can bring integrated planning to reality and enhance positive outcomes. Transit-oriented development (TOD) is one of the most frequently employed initiatives for ITLUP in the world. TOD aims to achieve a compact, mixed-use, and pedestrian-friendly community around a public transit node (Calthorpe, 1993; Cervero et al., 2002, 2004). Cities like Hong Kong have adopted TOD as a tool to integrate land development and transportation in their spatial development plan (Development Bureau and Planning Department, 2016).

Required analysis of the mutual impacts between land use and transportation at a project scale can also improve integration. In the United States, National Environmental Policy Act requires an analysis of environmental impacts, including land-use impacts, of transportation infrastructure projects. Environmentalists and community groups have used this policy to battle against undesirable impacts of transportation projects. In high-density Chinese cities, transportation impact analysis has been instituted as a preventive measure for traffic congestion stemming from land development projects (Lin and Yang, 2019).

Transportation service index could also play as an integration tool. In London, Public Transport Accessibility Level (PTAL) is a measure of access quality to public transportation. In the London Plan, an overall strategy for London's future development, PTAL has been used as a benchmark to match land development with corresponding levels of transportation service. In particular, PTAL helps to make decisions on housing density, as a location with good public transportation service can support the development of higher density (Transport for London, 2015).

3. The challenges for integrated transportation-land use planning in China

Several aspects of ITLUP in China should be mentioned before any detail is introduced. These features may distinguish China from many other countries. First, owing to the conflicts between the central government's top-down approach to land preservation and local governments' motivation for local economic development, there existed purposeful mis-integration in urban planning and land planning in many Chinese cities. Second, both transportation sectors and land development sectors had their own integration problems, which had to be addressed before ITLUP can be achieved. Third, ITLUP is under constant changes, subject to the evolving arrangement for transportation planning and land planning, which in turn is affected by the fast growth of Chinese cities.

3.1 The struggle for consolidated land management and planning

Since China launched market-led urban development in the early 1980s, local governments began to play an increasingly active role in leading local economic development (Yeh and Wu, 1999). During this marketization and decentralization process, one primary resource for the arising power of local governments is the urban land within their local jurisdictions. Land in China is owned by either the state or village collectives. Local governments, who represent the state to manage local land resources, could make their own decisions to lease land development rights to developers and collect a big amount of lump-sum payment for multidecade land usage. Those revenues have served as primary resources to fuel local infrastructure investment and economic development (Yang and Fang, 2015; Yang et al., 2007). The amount of land available for urban development or redevelopment becomes an important indicator of local governments' ability to raise municipal revenues. As a result, local governments always try to put as much land as possible into their planned developable area, which sets up the upper limit of land the city government can lease in a few years. The specific amount and location of leasable land are determined through two distinct planning processes: an urban planning process and a land planning process. Discrepancy often arises between them, either by intention or negligence.

Urban planning in China has been used as a comprehensive platform to coordinate various sectors relevant to urban development. China's state government specified an urban planning process for every city government to follow. Within each city, this process was led by corresponding bureau of urban planning.[a] Out of this process was a new or updated city master plan, which specified the land that might be serviced by urban infrastructures within 5 or even 20 years. It laid out functional zones, land use, comprehensive urban transportation system, sewage, and electricity networks. The city

[a] The exact name of this bureau should be slightly different across cities.

master plan served as a blueprint for future development. It reflected in general the local leadership's ambition for a prosperous future. Since urban land was used as a funding venue for urban infrastructure, including transportation infrastructure, it became a natural choice for local governments to incorporate into urban service areas as much land as possible (Yeh and Wu, 1999).

The scarcity of fertile land in China eventually drove the central government to create a separate land planning process, hoping to restrict the abovementioned local government behavior. The State Land Administration was created in 1987 and further upgraded to the Ministry of Land and Resources in 1998. The first nationwide land-use plan was published in 1993, which initiated a top-down system of land quota allocation. The corresponding land planning bureaus at the local level were also created and then upgraded. Their responsibility was to carry out the land planning process at the locality, which was subject to the total land quota granted by the higher-level government. The central government expected the land planning process to serve as an instrument for reducing land consumption at the local level (Han, 2012).

However, discrepancies between these two planning processes happened frequently in two situations. First, the amount of developable land specified in the city master plan tended to be bigger than that in the land plan. Second, the location of the developable land in the city master plan may fall within the area prohibited from development in the land plan.[b] Those discrepancies happened frequently because these two planning processes were driven by contrastingly different objectives. It was economic development for urban planning, but land conservation for land planning. One might expect that the higher-level government might be able to ensure consistency while they review and (dis)approve local plans, but these two plans were not reviewed by the same government unit at the higher level. Within the central government, the Ministry of housing and Urban-Rural Development reviewed the city master plans, but the Ministry of Land and Resources reviewed the land plans. The pro-growth planning sector and the pro-conservation land sector needed a coordination mechanism to work together. This problem was not solved until the national government replaced these two separate planning processes with a consolidated spatial planning process in 2019.[c]

[b] The term land plan here denotes the planning document created out of the land planning process, while the term land use plan denotes the land relevant component in the city master plan.

[c] There was a mitigating measure for this problem, which has proved to be ineffective. The national government once required both plans to comply with the economic and social development plan, which was compiled by the Commission of Economic development and Reform.

3.2 Multimodal transportation integration

The planning and management for the transportation system in China for a period of time were urban-rural divided and mode-specific. Inheriting from the period of planned economy, when urban area and rural area were managed as two systems, urban transportation at each locality was managed by the local bureau of urban planning. Regional and rural transportation was managed by the local bureau of transportation[c] (Huang, 2003). The responsibilities for region-wide or rural transportation planning were mode-specific. The local bureau of transportation only took charge of regional and rural roads. Railway, waterway, and aviation are under the authorities of their own bureaus. Urban transportation planning was part of urban planning process and compiled by the local bureau of urban planning. The city master plan includes sections for urban roads, streets, and public transportation. The urban planning process thus served to compile relevant components of varied transportation modes. As city area becomes bigger and urban transportation problems become more complicated, a comprehensive urban transportation planning process was added, which provided references for urban transportation management and ensured that necessary transportation infrastructure would be provided for forthcoming land development.

The usage of urban planning as a process to integrate urban transportation and land development planning worked well when the city size and the transportation system size were relatively small. Fast economic development and urban expansion in the post-reform period, however, required an integrated transportation system coordinating various transportation modes in urban and rural areas. As urban areas became bigger and transportation planning and management became more multimode, discrepancies among different plans and modes can easily arise, particularly in suburban areas and at multimode hubs. It was difficult for urban planning process alone to continue to serve as an integrated platform across urban and suburban areas as well as for different modes. Synthesizing plans and management of various modes in urban and rural areas became challenging (Yang and Fang, 2015). In 2009, the central government initiated a national transportation reform, which created a national Ministry of Transportation and mandates a bureau of transportation for each city. This reform also instituted a truly comprehensive transportation planning process, which unified the planning and management for various transportation modes (Guo and Wang, 2014). The responsibility for urban transportation planning was then transferred from the municipal bureau of urban planning to the bureau of transportation.

3.3 Initiatives for transportation-land use integration

China does not have specific law requiring ITLUP, which largely relies on initiatives enacted by city governments. ITLUP in its primitive format is to ensure necessary transportation infrastructure for land development.

Local governments in China have always paid attention to the road system, which provides necessary access to leasable land. A road network plan has always been required as a vital component in the city master plan. Transit services and expensive metro systems, for a period of time, were not prioritized by Chinese city governments, as they were not directly linked to land lease revenues (Yang et al., 2007). Changes, however, happened as urban population grows and roads become saturated with traffic. In 2004, China's national government initiated Urban Public Transportation Priority Development Strategy. It was further upgraded to Transit Metropolis Initiative in 2011. This new version of transit priority policy encourages land development around transit nodes. Expensive metro systems have been gradually added into Chinese cities. Land value capture has been employed to collect revenues and to fund metro systems. This financial linkage between metro and land development stimulates the widespread use of transit-oriented development (TOD) in China.

4. The development of integrated transportation-land use planning in Shenzhen

As a pioneer city in China, Shenzhen's story of ITLUP preceded nation-wide effort for ITLUP. How Shenzhen addressed the above needs for consolidated land development planning, comprehensive transportation planning and management, and carried forward effective ITLUP has served as the role model for other Chinese cities. Shenzhen is one of the four first-tier cities in China, which also include Beijing, Shanghai and Guangzhou. It is located in Guangdong Province and on the north side of Hong Kong. In the late 1970s when China started to reform and open up to the global economy, Shenzhen became one of the earliest Special Economy Zone (SEZ) in 1980. The SEZ was smaller than today's Shenzhen. It included only four inner districts, namely, Futian, Luohu, Nanshan, and Yantian (Fig. 1). The SEZ was granted the flexibility to experiment with various new ideas. Since then, the SEZ has experienced fast development. In 2010, the SEZ, was expanded to the whole Shenzhen area.

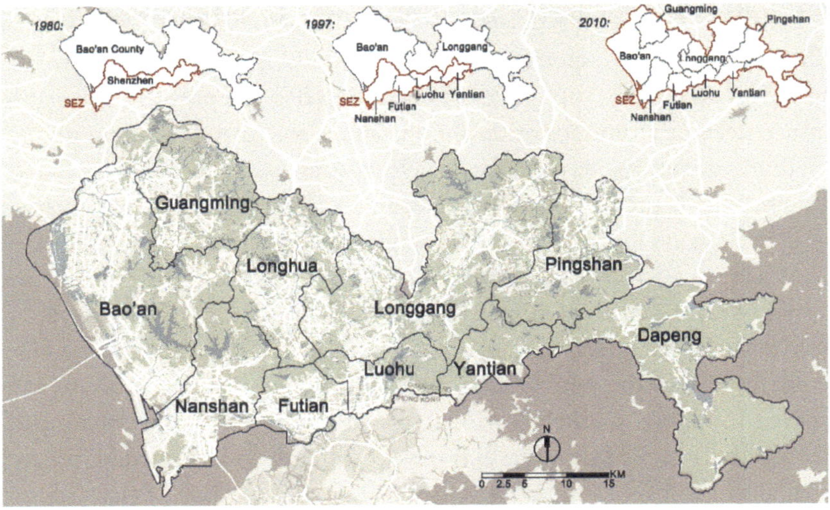

Fig. 1 Boundaries of Shenzhen SEZ and Districts.

Shenzhen was selected as the primary case for the following reasons. First, fast urban development in Shenzhen creates a window to observe how the city government uses ITLUP strategies to accommodate fast urbanization. When Shenzhen SEZ was expanded to include all districts in 2010, the focus of the new development shifted to the outer districts. New transportation infrastructures have to be provided. Meanwhile, as China's central government began to prioritize transit services, Shenzhen has invested heavily in metro systems and targeted compact and mixed-use development. Inspired by the concept of TOD and land value capture, Shenzhen City Government has successfully funded expensive metro infrastructure with land sector revenue.

Second, Shenzhen has served as the role model of institutional and political innovations in China. In the past four decades, policies that have successful implementations in Shenzhen have been promoted by the national government and replicated in other Chinese cities. Shenzhen's efforts to integrate multisector transportation management has enlightened the national reform for a consolidated urban transportation authority for multisector transportation planning at each city. Shenzhen's efforts to integrate urban planning and land planning have preceded the national reform for today's territory spatial planning. Shenzhen's efforts in ITLUP, particularly in TOD, has been emulated by other Chinese cities. Shenzhen, therefore, serves as the window for other parts of the world to watch how Chinese cities innovate in integrated planning. An examination of Shenzhen's experience can help to reveal the rationale for and approaches to ITLUP in China. Shenzhen's pathway toward ITLUP can be roughly divided into four stages, with each stage containing milestone efforts (Table 1). The following sections explain these stages.

4.1 The First Stage: Inheritance from the planned economy (1979–1986)

When the central coastal area of the territory of the former Bao'an County was branded as Shenzhen Special Economic Zone (SEZ) in 1979, it was assigned the role to experiment with new ideas and policies. The governance structure inherited from the period of planned economy, however, did not change overnight. The planning responsibility for urban planning and transportation planning was assigned to the local bureau of urban planning. Shenzhen's first city master plan was made in 1986, which included relevant plans for land use, transportation, sewage and electricity for SEZ. The process of the city master plan, therefore, served as the platform for relevant government units to identify possible discrepancies, which were not a big issue given the small size of the city then. Roads were the major transportation infrastructure, and road network planning was expected to comply with urban planning. The conventional four-step transportation forecasting process was introduced for Shenzhen's city master plan, which helped to assess the increase in travel demand resulting from planned development (Ma, 2019).

4.2 The Second Stage: Consolidation in land management and transportation management (1987–2004)

No formal real estate market existed during the period of communism China. Following Hong Kong's practice, Shenzhen was the first to introduce land and housing markets into post-reform China. The availability of developable land at a discounted price has helped Chinese cities to attract manufacturing plants (Liu, 2019). However, compared to other typical Chinese cities, the availability of developable land in Shenzhen is much more limited, particularly considering its unprecedented growth. First, Shenzhen is a mountainous coastal city. The mountains and oceans are not suitable for development. The developable basin accounts for at most half of the total land area. Second, the whole area of Shenzhen is <2000 sq. km, and the SEZ then was only 327 sq. km. Shenzhen from its very beginning has to economize land consumption.

Table 1 Stages of ITLUP in Shenzhen (1979–2018).

			1979–1986	1987–2004	2005–2009	2010–2018
Land Management	*Governance Arrangement*	*Land planning*	Bureau of Land and Resource	Bureau of Planning, Land, and Resource	–	–
		Urban planning	Bureau of Urban planning			
	Planning Process	*Land planning*	–	Common spatial framework	–	Comprehensive development planning; GIS techniques for the same baseline
		Urban planning				
Multimodal transportation integration	*Governance Arrangement*	*Planning* *Urban*	Bureau of Urban Planning		Transportation Commission	–
		Rural	Transportation Authority			
	Planning Process	*Transportation planning*	–		Comprehensive transport planning	
Integration between land use and transportation	*Integration Mechanism*		Transportation planning complied with urban planning	GIS techniques for the same baseline	Common spatial framework	Comprehensive development planning
	Tools or initiatives		Conventional four-step transportation forecasting process	–	TOD: joint development	TOD: vertical division of land development rights

When China's central government tried to reduce land consumption by instituting a separate land planning process, many city governments purposefully created discrepancies between city master plans and land plans. The local leadership used the land plan to meet the requirement from the higher-level government on land conservation, but used the city master plans to permit land leasing. In contrast, the scarcity of land supply in Shenzhen has moved the city government to a different path. Instead of creating purposeful discrepancies between the land plan and the city master plan, Shenzhen city government unified the two separate planning processes. In 1989, Shenzhen's Bureau of Land and Resource (responsible for land planning and conservation) and Bureau of Urban Planning (responsible for city planning and land development management) were merged into the Bureau of Planning, Land, and Resource (PLRB) (Wang and Xiang, 2009). This merged bureau still produced two sets of plans, i.e., the city master plan and the land plan, both of which are required by the central government. However, there was no reason for the discrepancies to exist anymore, as Shenzhen City Government itself was quite motivated to economize land consumption.

On the transportation side, as economic development continued and integration among different transportation modes became essential, Shenzhen created a new bureau of transportation in 1988. This bureau was responsible for the management of all transportation modes, covering roads, urban transit, waterway, seaports, railway, urban rail, airport, freight logistics, and postal services (Guo and Wang, 2014). It was the first municipal bureau to manage a comprehensive transportation system in China.[d] The reform was later promoted by the central government in 2008, when China's Ministry of Transportation was created and local governments were required to create their own government departments for comprehensive transportation planning, policy-making, and management.

In order to bridge transportation planning and land-use planning, Shenzhen started with sharing baseline data between the land sector and transportation sector. Geographic Information System (GIS) was employed to compile relevant data. It provided urban planning and transportation planning a common baseline, which was an important step toward ITLUP.

[d] Efforts to consolidate transport management were first made in 1882 when Shenzhen decided to set up a transport management headquarter. The headquarter was designated to manage all modes of transportation (Guo and Wang, 2014).

4.3 The Third Stage: A common spatial framework for ITLUP (2005–2009)

During this period, Shenzhen's Bureau of Transportation began to conduct comprehensive transportation planning, which was updated with the same schedule as the city master plan (Zhang et al., 2016). The comprehensive transportation plan synthesized relevant plans for different transportation modes (Zhang et al., 2010). This plan was not required by law in China until 2010 (Ma, 2019). It was up to Shenzhen to decide whether a separate multimodal transportation plan was needed (Yang and Fang, 2015). Shenzhen noticed the problems stemming from lacking integration of multimodal transportation systems and initiated this comprehensive transportation planning process without national government requirement. Shenzhen also updated the spatial framework for transportation planning. The new framework includes five geographic levels, which matched that of the urban planning process (Zhang et al., 2010, 2016). This updated framework made cross-verification between transportation planning and land use planning much easier at varied geographical levels.

During this period, the central government began to promote transit development for big cities as traffic congestion rose. Transit-oriented Development (TOD) emerged as a new planning initiative in Shenzhen as the city government moved forward with metro investment. Since the city government compiled its first metro plan in 1996, TOD was proposed to encourage land development around metro stations. In 2001, Shenzhen issued the Provisional Rules of the Shenzhen Municipality on the Administration of Metro Construction, which enabled joint development of transit stations and real estate properties.

4.4 The Fourth Stage: Comprehensive development planning and TOD (2010–2018)

In 2010, the government applied the SEZ policy from the inner four districts to every corner of Shenzhen. In the newly incorporated SEZ area (Fig. 1), the coordination between transportation and land use planning was further strengthened with the creation of a few new districts, where the new district government tried a holistic planning approach (Wang, 2013; Zou, 2013). They consolidated economic development planning, urban planning, land planning, and transportation planning into a comprehensive development planning process. The local Bureau of Development and Reform oversaw the whole process. The related government units were expected to reach agreement on development sequences, key issues, strategic management, and objectives for future development before adding details into the plan. A key part of the job was to figure out the amount of leasable land. Relevant government units shared data with a common GIS database (Wang, 2013). This practice resulted in a tight connection between land development plans and transportation plans.

During this period, land shortage in Shenzhen became more obvious. Shenzhen city government realized the potential to locate urban activities around transit nodes and began to emphasize the incorporation of rail transit planning in urban planning. The result is a spatial framework for rail transit planning, which matches that of urban planning, so that these two can be cross-checked at different spatial levels and development stages (Li, 2015).

As for TOD implementation, Shenzhen Metro, the rail transit operator owned by the city government, was authorized to develop real estate property in conjunction with the metro infrastructure. Shenzhen Metro was asked to make development plans around transit stations, which preceded the joint development of rail infrastructure and real estate properties. In this process, the metro corporation played a key role in ITLUP. In addition, the city government leased to or granted Shenzhen Metro development rights on-top or nearby transit stations, so that a Hong Kong-style rail plus property model began in Shenzhen (Yang, 2016). Some pre-existing rules had to be altered in order to enable this new development practice. By China's pre-existing law, the land for metro infrastructure was not allowed for market-oriented real estate development. Under the new TOD framework, rights for underground development and air development were created and separated from the development right for metro stations, which enabled Shenzhen Metro to build real estate projects on top or under the metro system (Yang et al., 2020).

The inspiration from Shenzhen's comprehensive development planning by some extent encouraged the most recent national planning reform. In 2018, China's central government rehauled the whole planning system. The new planning system, named Territorial Spatial Planning (TSP), requires authorities for land planning and urban planning to merge into one. At the national level, the responsibilities for policy-making and planning review of local urban plans were transferred from the Ministry of Housing and Urban-Rural Development to the Ministry of National Resources, who now serves not only as the national authority for land planning and management, but also for urban planning. At the municipal level, the TSP governance arrangement is something that already happened in Shenzhen, i.e., assigning the responsibility for urban planning and land planning to a single municipal department. Shenzhen had instituted this governance arrangement two decades ahead of the national requirement.[e] Under this new national TSP program, Shenzhen is no longer required to produce two separate planning documents for upper-government approval.

The central government takes TSP as a chance to promote integrated planning. TSP adopts a five-level framework, namely, national, provincial, municipal, county, and township. At each level, TSP not only serves as the process for land planning, but also to integrate other plans, including transportation plans (Li, 2021; Liu and Zhou, 2021; Qian et al., 2020). This framework ensures that other plans will be compatible with land plans. Any conflict with the land plan will be identified in the TSP process. This is similar to the comprehensive plan in Shenzhen's new district.

5. Conclusion

As problems like traffic congestion and loss of fertile and ecological land arise, China raises its ambition for a sustainable future. ITLUP as an approach to reducing sprawling development and mitigating traffic congestion has gained lots of attention, particularly in those megacities with an ambition for metro systems. Shenzhen, the city of fast urbanization and economic growth, has served as China's testbed for ITLUP. Benefiting from its role as China's special economic zone and flexibility in policy innovation, Shenzhen's efforts to coordinate land and transportation development serve as a window, through which one can watch how Chinese cities have responded to the challenge of ITLUP in the past decades of fast urbanization and motorization. The case of Shenzhen suggested that land management, multimode transportation integration, and the integration between land use and transportation are three critical aspects of ITLUP in China. They can be achieved by reforming governance arrangement, planning processes as well as employing new planning tools or initiatives.

The pre-existing urban planning, land planning, and transportation planning in China were managed by different government units and with

[e] For bureaucratic reasons, the bureau for land management and the bureau for urban planning was separated in 2004, and then reunited in 2009.

separate planning processes. Purposeful mis-coordination existed between urban planning and land planning. Different modes of transportation systems were funded and developed under different government units. Integrated planning between land use and transportation imposed significant challenges as the pace of economic growth drove up urban area expansion and traffic congestion.

To avoid possible mismatches between land development and transportation development, government leaders in Shenzhen innovated governance arrangement and coordination mechanism. First, the two separate bureaus for urban planning and land planning were merged to ensure better consistency between land development and conservation. Second, a comprehensive transportation authority was created to oversee plan-making for all transportation modes. Third, the integration of transportation and land use has been experimented in different circumstances. In Shenzhen's new suburban districts, a framework for comprehensive development planning was created, which incorporated land planning, urban planning, and transportation planning. Shenzhen's merge of land planning and urban planning and the innovation of a comprehensive development planning framework preceded China's territorial spatial planning framework. Shenzhen's creation of a comprehensive municipal authority and comprehensive planning for urban transportation was 25 years ahead of the national requirement.

The application of transit-oriented development (TOD) is a particular example demonstrating how constructive ITLUP is in Shenzhen. New government regulations were created so that vertical division of land development rights for different usage categories can be defined and land development rights can be sold to different developers on the same land parcel. Underground space can be reserved for transportation and public purposes. Ground-level and air right can be sold for retail, office, and housing development. While this development outcome can be observed in many parts of the world, Shenzhen City Government enabled this practice in China's institutional context, which has been soon emulated in other Chinese cities. All above-mentioned innovation happens under a circumstance of land scarcity, which not only shared by other leading cities in China, but also megacities in other parts of the world. How China has tried to economize land development and preserve ecological resources by tightening the feedback loop between transportation and land development could inspire other countries and cities that are struggling to enhance the vibrancy and livability of their own cities.

Reference

Abukhater, A.B.E.D., 2009. Rethinking planning theory and practice: a glimmer of light for prospects of integrated planning to combat complex urban realities. Theor. Empir. Res. Urban Manag. 4 (2(11)), 64–79.

Acheampong, R.A., Silva, E.A., 2015. Land use–transport interaction modeling: a review of the literature and future research directions. J. Transp. Land Use 8 (3), 11–38.

Calthorpe, P., 1993. The Next American Metropolis: Ecology, Community, and the American Dream. Princeton Architectural Press, New York.

Cervero, R., Ferrell, C., Murphy, S., 2002. Transit-Oriented Development and Joint Development in the United States: A Literature Review. Transportation Research Board, Washington.

Cervero, R., Murphy, S., Ferrell, C., et al., 2004. Transit-Oriented Development in the United States: Experiences, Challenges, and Prospects. The National Academies Press, Washington, DC.

Department for Transport, 2002. Guidance on the Methodology for Multi-Modal Studies. Government of the United Kingdom, London.

Development Bureau and Planning Department, 2016. Hong Kong 2030+: Towards a Planning Vision and Strategy Transcending 2030. Government of Hong Kong S.A. R, Hong Kong.

Fairfax, V., 2005. Handbook on Integrating Land Use Considerations into Transportation Projects to Address Induced Growth. Transportation Research Board, Washington.

Geerlings, H., Stead, D., 2003. The integration of land use planning, transport and environment in European policy and research. Transp. Policy 10 (3), 187–196.

Guiliano, G., 2004. Land Use Impacts of Transportation Investments - Highway and Transit. The Geography of Urban Transportation, Third. Guilford Press, New York, pp. 237–273.

Guo, W., Wang, Y., 2014. The experience and enlightenment of Shenzhen's comprehensive traffic management system reform (in Chinese: 深深圳市综合交通管理体制改革的经验与启示). Comp. Transp. 8, 20–24.

Han, H., 2012. National Land use Management in China: an analytical framework. J. Urban Manag. 1 (1), 3–38. Zhejiang University and Chinese Association of Urban Management.

Huang, Z., 2003. Data Integration for Urban Transport Planning. Utrecht University.

Hull, A., 2005. Integrated transport planning in the UK: from concept to reality. J. Transp. Geogr. 13 (4), 318–328.

James, B., 2005. Institutional arrangements for land use and transport integration. In: State of Australian Cities National Conference, Brisbane, Queensland, 2005.

Lee, J., 2020. Reflecting on an integrated approach for transport and spatial planning as a pathway to sustainable urbanization. Sustainability 12 (10218), 1–6.

Li, L., 2015. The exploration of urban rail transit planning and Design in Shenzhen (in Chinese: 城市轨道交通规划设计体系探索与思考 —— 以深圳为例). Ann. Nat. Plan. Conf. 2015, 1–11.

Li, R., 2021. Territorial planning: practical dilemma and system reconstruction. City Plan. Rev. 45 (2), 58–72.

Lin, X., Yang, J., 2019. Supporting green transportation with transportation impact assessment in China. Transp. Res. D: Transp. Environ. 73, 67–75.

Liu, Z., 2019. Land-based finance and property tax in China. Area Dev. Policy 4 (4), 367–381.

Liu, Y., Zhou, Y., 2021. Territory spatial planning and national governance system in China. Land Use Policy 102 (105288), 1–9.

Ma, L., 2019. The exploration and development of new China's urban transportation planning (in Chinese: 新中国城市交通规划的探索与发展). Urban Plan. Int. 34 (4), 49–53.

Meyer, M.D., 2016. Transportation Planning Handbook. John Wiley & Sons, Inc., Fourth edi. New Jersey.
Planning Institute of Australia (South Australian Division), 2010. Integrated Landuse and Transportation: Policy Position Statement. Planning Institute of Australia, Adelaide.
Qian, J., Zheng, Q., Lai, Q., 2020. Consideration on the reconstruction of Shenzhen's spatial planning system in the new era (in Chinese: 新时期深圳市国土空间规划体系重构的思考). Land Res. Inf. 8, 51–56.
Stanley, J., 2015. Governance for Integrated Urban Land Use Transport Policy and Planning. Bus Industry Confederation Inc., Barton.
Te Brömmelstroet, M., Bertolini, L., 2010. Integrating land use and transport knowledge in strategy-making. Transportation 37 (1), 85–104.
Transport and Infrastructure Council, 2006. National Guidelines for Transport System Management in Australia. Transport and Infrastructure Council, Canberra.
Transport for London, 2015. Assessing Transport Connectivity in London. Transport for London, London.
Wang, J., 2013. Decentralization and fragmentation: development stages and trend of metropolitan area in China (in Chinese:分权下的多规合一 ——深圳新区发展历程与规划思考). Urban Dev. Stud. 20 (1), 23–30.
Wang, W., Xiang, W., 2009. Planning in Shenzhen for the past 30 years: institution, technique, and mechanism (in Chinese:深圳规划 30 年:机构·技术·体系). Ann. Nat. Plan. Conf. 2019, 203–210.
Yang, J., 2016. The study on land preparation for rail plus property model (in Chinese: 轨道交通物业开发用地获取方式研究). Railway Technical Innovation 4, 91–95.
Yang, J., Fang, C., 2015. Assessing public-sector transportation finance and planning in urban China. In: Building Resilient Cities in China: The Nexus between Planning and Science, pp. 321–337.
Yang, J., Feng, C., Cao, G., 2007. Land and transportation development in China: economic analysis of government behavior. Transp. Res. Rec.: J. Transp. Res. Board 2038, 78–83.
Yang, J., Zhu, L., Duan, Y., Zhou, J., Ma, H., 2020. Developing metro-based accessibility: three aspects of China's rail + property practice. Transp. Res. D: Transp. Environ. 81, 102288.
Yeh, A.G., Wu, F., 1999. The transformation of the urban planning system in China from a centrally-planned to transitional economy. Prog. Plan. 51 (3), 167–252.
Yekyeong, S., 2012. TOD as a rail integrated urban regeneration strategies of Old City through case study about Toyama Station and surroundings area in Japan. In: Computer Applications for Software Engineering, Disaster Recovery, and Business Continuity. Springer, Berlin, pp. 429–436.
Zhang, X., Xu, H., Lin, Q., et al., 2010. Integrated transportation planning and design system in Shenzhen (in Chinese: 深圳市交通规划设计技术体系). Urban Transp. China 8 (5), 36–46.
Zhang, X., Shao, Y., Sun, H., 2016. The innovation and implementation of urban transportation in Shenzhen (in Chinese:深圳市城市交通规划创新与实践). In: China Annual Urban Transport Conference, Shenzhen, 2016.
Zou, B., 2013. Action plan, institutional design and policy support: analysis of Shenzhen's urban implementation in the last decade (in Chinese: 行动规划·制度设计·政策支持——深圳近10年城市规划实施历程剖析). Urban Plan. Forum 1 (206), 61–68.

CHAPTER NINE

Advances in integrated land use transport modeling

Ming Zhong[a,b,c,*], John Douglas Hunt[b,f], John Edward Abraham[g], Wanle Wang[a,b,c,d], Yiming Zhang[a,b,c], and Rui Wang[a,b,c,e]

[a]National Engineering Research Center for Water Transportation Safety, Wuhan, Hubei, China
[b]Intelligent Transport Systems Research Center, Wuhan University of Technology, Wuhan, Hubei, China
[c]Engineering Research Center for Transportation Safety, Ministry of Education, Wuhan, Hubei, China
[d]College of Air Traffic Management, Civil Aviation University of China, Tianjin, China
[e]School of Foreign Language, Wuhan University of Technology, Wuhan, China
[f]Department of Civil Engineering, University of Calgary, Calgary, Canada
[g]HBA Specto Incorporated, Calgary, Canada
*Corresponding author: e-mail address: mzhong@whut.edu.cn

Contents

Abstract

This chapter presents the concept and history of integrated land use transport models (ILUTMs), the reasons of creating and developing such models, recent progresses and the details of some typical "operational models," the challenges and implications of developing such models, and proposes an agenda for future research directions, based on the trend and the needs identified. By representing and considering land use (the spatial distribution of economic activities and resulting space pattern) and transportation system together, the ILUTMs are expected to be able to assess the impacts of different policies and their combined/compound effects onto the economy, land use, transportation, environment and more. Over the last decade, the developments in computing, AI and big data have helped to advance the integrated modeling with

Advances in Transport Policy and Planning, Volume 9
ISSN 2543-0009
https://doi.org/10.1016/bs.atpp.2021.10.002

more completed and disaggregated representations of relevant agents and processes, and overcoming quite a few challenges associated with traditional aggregated models. Still, efforts are needed in order to make the integrated models versatile tools for addressing the changing needs of planning community. Researchers and modelers are expected to work closely with the cutting-edge technologies and practitioners to advance the integrated modeling along the right directions.

Keywords: Integrated land use transport modeling (ILUTM), Planning, Microsimulation

1. Introduction

The interactions between transportation and land use are always in a complex and changing state with the development of cities and regions. At present, most of the researchers and modelers, especially those studying the relationship between transportation and land use system, focus on "integrated land-use transport modeling" (ILUTM) or "integrated modeling" (IM). Under the concept of the integrated planning, transportation planning should not only consider the supply and demand of transportation infrastructure and the corresponding external problems and effects (such as congestion and air pollution), but more importantly, examine the combined/compound impact of the corresponding transportation infrastructure development, economic, land use and social/environmental policies onto the benefits of various social and economic activities, their temporal and spatial distribution, and long-term development pattern. In addition, integrated models can study other issues that should be considered for sustainable development, such as those related to environment and equity.

The Lowry model developed in 1964 is seen as the "classic" integrated land use transport model (ILUTM), which is the first operational framework that can explicitly consider the interactions between land use and transportation (Lowry, 1964). Then it was further enhanced to DRAM/EMPAL and then to ITLUP/METROPILUS by Putman (1983, 1991, 1994, 1996). Echenique and Lindsay (1969) and Echenique et al. (1990) introduced the MEPLAN model and used the model in Spain, West Germany and England, in order to study the effects of local land use and transport policies. Boyce et al. (1985) proposed a combined model of urban travel and location for the Chicago region—*Urbana*, which provided transportation planners one of early computer-based decision-making tools for integrated land-use transport planning. Miller and Salvini (2001) presented the architecture of the Integrated Land Use, Transportation, Environment (ILUTE) system, making it possible to simulate and analyze the environmental impact of different land use and transport plans. Waddell (2000) and Waddell et al. (2004) proposed UrbanSim, which is featured with microsimulation of urban land, real-estate, transport markets without requiring an equilibrium solution. Recent studies took more disaggregated approaches, featured with disaggregated land use and/or transport representation inside their models (Emberger and Pfaffenbichler, 2020; Hunt et al., 2008; Ziemke et al., 2016).

Research on the development of mathematical models for studying the relationship between transportation and land use mostly took place in developed countries, started in the 1960s and has been advanced in a much faster speed and larger scale since the 1980s, resulting in substantial experiences and achievements to date. Recent advancements in computing and data technologies have accelerated the development of the field in different ways and with important features, such as modeling with a greater disaggregation and details, using data driven and microsimulation approach and staying away from traditional equilibrium assumption.

This chapter focuses on providing an overview of ILUTMs, including the reason and history of creating or developing such models, their development and recent progress, the challenges and implications of developing and applying these models in planning practice and a research agenda identified in order to take up the challenges and best use these models to serve our societies. The chapter is concluded with a few concluding remarks.

2. What is ILUTM and why?

Integrated land use transport models (ILUTMs) explicitly consider the interactions among socioeconomic activities, land use, transportation and other components as needed, such as social/natural environment, for policy analysis and for guiding the progressive urbanization process, as shown in Fig. 1.

The issues of urban sprawl, traffic congestion, long-distance travel and air pollution have been becoming ever more challenging with the expansion of the cities and skyrocketing car ownership. ILUTMs, with their capacity for considering the interactions between social/economic development, land use, transport and possibly social/natural environment, have been developed and used to tackle the above issues in the context of both developed and developing countries alike (Hunt et al., 2005; Iacono et al., 2008; Wegener, 2004; Zhong et al., 2015). These studies show the potentials of ILUTMs in studying various policies related to economy, transportation,

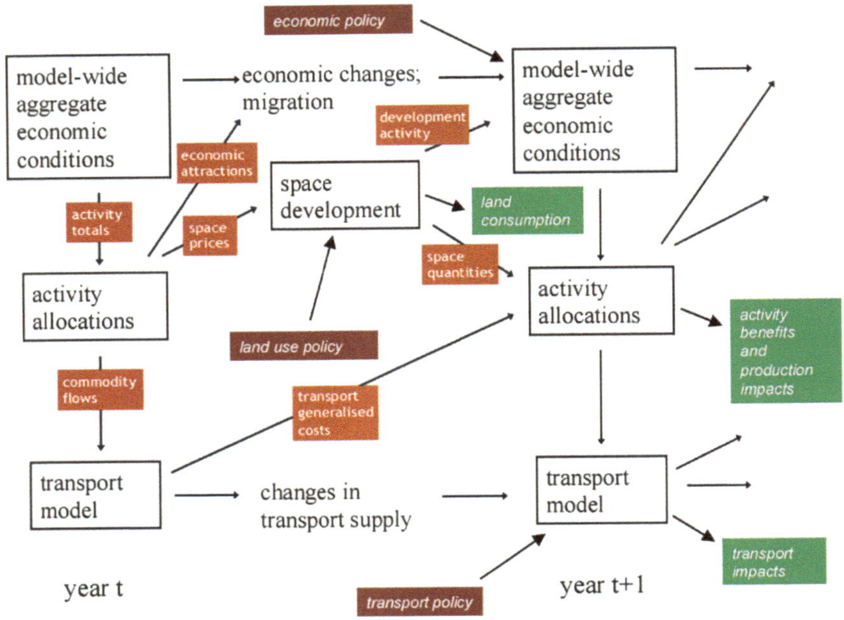

Fig. 1 Functional view of integrated land use transport models.

land use and social/natural environment in a holistic and realistic manner, which potentially eliminates the possibility of incomplete understanding of the impact of various policies and myopic solutions.

Integrated land use transport models are computer-based simulations of the evolution of the spatial form of a region over many years, and how people and businesses interact between locations using the transportation system. They are representations of how the built form, land use, and transportation system support the people and economy of a city, province/state and/or region (HBA Specto Incorporated, 2013). ILUTMs are intended to represent the spatial evolution of a given urban or regional system over time, as a function of various socio-economic, demographic, physical and political processes. These models should not only be able to simulate the current state but also to predict changes to and influences on transportation and land use systems based on policy measures. Two basic purposes served are:

- forecasting, which is predicting future activity locations and interactions and the resulting patterns of travel and freight movements, and
- policy analysis, which is assessing the impacts and effectiveness of specific policies, regulations and infrastructure designed to improve travel conditions, environmental conditions, social well-being, economic performance, and equity.

The popular "four-step" transportation demand forecasting models are used in most cities and regions at the current stage to support decision-makings related to transportation planning, but compared to integrated models, they have the following limitations:

(1) First, high-speed urban expansion has resulted in numerous changes in activity distribution and land use, but the existing "four-step" models cannot predict such changes simply because land use dynamics are not represented and modeled within these models. The "four-step" models only indirectly represent land use based on the distribution of population and employment. Future population and employment distribution pattern is usually forecasted in a very rough and subjective manner, which is basically done through incremental forecasts of local zonal population/employment and then modified based on planners' subjective adjustments according to a master plan. However, these adjustments often do not have a sound, scientific basis and are basically carried out based on the experiences or the judgment of planners. Different from the "four-step" model, the integrated models use microeconomics methods to predict the type (such as residential or commercial use) and the intensity of land/space development scientifically based on corresponding demand, supply and zoning rules (e.g., land supply for different uses and corresponding density (Floorspace area ratio—FAR)).

(2) Second, due to the fact that the "four-step models" don't have a representation for economy and environment, they therefore won't be useful for studying the wider impacts of transportation investments and programs.

(3) Third, the existing "four-step" model is based on the assumption that travel is a "rigid demand," meaning that people must travel in their lives. Compared with the integrated models, they lack economic basis to explain travel behavior. It is well understood that travel or transport itself is not purpose, but with sound socioeconomic motivations.

(4) Lastly, most of the existing "four-stage" models only model passenger flow rather than those related to goods. Hunt and Stefan (2007) and Stefan et al. (2005) found that commercial vehicles responsible for intra-city delivery, maintenance and other home services accounted for about 13–15% of the total traffic in Canadian cities such as Calgary and Edmonton. Therefore, it is necessary to take the goods transportation into consideration in the urban transport demand forecasting.

In summary, based on the above issues of the "four-step" models, it is not sensible to totally depend on such models for decision-makings of urban and transportation planning. On the other hand, integrated models provide a defensible and consistent system to forecast land use patterns that are likely to occur under different economic development, land use and transportation infrastructure development plans, allowing each of above policy option to be evaluated in a realistic and consistent manner (Table 1).

Table 1 Comparison of characteristics between "four-step" transportation demand forecasting models and integrated models.

Features	Transport models	Integrated models
Impact of transport policies on transportation conditions	Comprehensive	Comprehensive
Impact of transport policies on land use	Limited	Comprehensive
Impact of transport policies on employment/population	None	Comprehensive
Impact of land policies on transport conditions	Limited: require assumptions on land policies and urban development	Comprehensive
Impact of land policies on urban development pattern	None	Comprehensive
Impact of land policies on economic growth	None	Comprehensive
Impact of policies on economic growth	None	The transition from limited to comprehensive depends on the investment and scope of modeling
Impact of policies on environment	Limited: only evaluating the impact of the transportation policy on environment	The transition from limited to comprehensive depends on the scope of modeling

3. Review of development and progress

3.1 Theory

Generally, theories related to the land use modeling and those to the transportation are developed in isolation, but recently they were combined in an effort to develop ILUTMs, in order to address complicated regional/urban issues that cannot be tackled by either of them.

Back in 1826, German economist Von Thünen made the first attempt to explain the effect of transport costs on the location of activities and the functioning of the land market. In his theory of location, the distance between agricultural producers and the market-place affects the land allocation and rent, and the price of agricultural commodities. Later, Wingo and Alonso studied the relationship among accessibility, residential and employment choices and land value in urban settings (Alonso, 1964; Wingo, 1961). Based on Alonso's work, bid-rent theory was developed, which provided the theoretical foundation for several of later ILUTM models, e.g., MUSSA, RURBAN (Martínez and Donoso, 1995; Miyamoto et al., 2007). Concentric Zones, Sectors and Multiple Nuclei land use models are all based on this line of research.

Compared to the microeconomic theories of land use, the approach taken by spatial interaction models is of an aggregate nature, in which zones containing a large number of activities are defined and analyzed. The modern spatial interaction models originated from the work of Hansen (1959). Based on the gravitational analogy, he elaborated on the location of residents as a function of accessibility to employment. A decade later, Wilson proved that the gravity-based spatial interaction formulation is equivalent to an entropy maximization problem, which created the basis for the development of many operational models (Wilson, 1970).

Another theory for ILUTM is from the macroeconomics: the input-output model, in which, the spatial distribution of socioeconomic activities and resulting urban or regional structure, their production and consumption, corresponding interactions and travel/transport demand can be explicitly represented and modeled using production/consumption functions, with transport cost being considered within the exchange process (De la Barra, 1989; Hunt et al., 2005; Hunt and Abraham, 2005).

With the development of the random utility theory and discrete choice models (McFadden, 1978), the behavior of individuals and the system can be better explained and modeled, and the relationship between the two can be established, thus providing an acceptable causal interpretation. Later, the discrete choice modeling became the "core" modeling technique of the Second-generation ILUTMs during the 1980s and the 1990s. In random utility theory, the probability of an individual choosing a given alternative is a function of the socioeconomic characteristics of the individual and the relative attractiveness of the alternatives. The attractiveness of alternatives is represented using the concept of utility, which is derived from a set of attributes of the alternatives as perceived by the individual. The individual always chooses the alternative with the highest utility. However, since there are unobserved attributes of the alternatives, differences in taste between the individuals and uncertainty or lack of information, the utility function is assumed to consist of two parts: a measurable component and a stochastic error term. With different assumptions on the distribution of the error term, there are different types of models, such as logit and probit, based on either Generalized Extreme Value (GEV) distribution or Normal distribution.

In recent years "microsimulation" approaches have become more and more popular (Hunt et al., 2019; Ziemke et al., 2016). Microsimulation models, due to their flexibility of modeling processes that cannot be materialized in the aggregate models, are becoming more and more popular. Two classes of models that have been widely applied are Cellular automata (CA) and agent-based models (Clarke, 2014). In microsimulation approaches, rather than representing quantities of categories of modeling elements (of economic activity, jobs, households, population, goods, services, land, etc.), individual agents are created and represented inside the ILUTMs. The decisions of these agents are simulated, using random numbers to choose from (more flexible) observed/expected probability functions, and the total effect of the decisions by the population of agents conforms to the traditional theories but through a more intuitive and flexible computer system operation. Microsimulation approaches are able to enhance the representation of the variety and heterogeneity in individual agents and the complexity of a region in a much greater detail than the traditional aggregate models. Waddell (2009) agreed with Wegener (2011) in that integrated microsimulation models are likely to be unstable and suffer from excessive stochasticity. He also suggested that uncertainty in models should be taken seriously.

As stated before, transport modeling has been developed separately from their land use counterpart, from the most famous "four-step" model to advanced activity-based model. The activity-based travel demand forecasting theory believes that the demand for travel is derived from the demand for activities and there are many temporal-spatial constraints that need to be considered, e.g., people have to return to a home base for rest (Bowman and Ben-Akiva, 2000). Recently, microsimulation has become the standard in best-practice travel demand models (Miller, 2018). However, due to their complexity, the adoption of activity-based travel demand models in practice has been slow and most of the existing operational ILUTMs use the traditional four-step model (Acheampong and Silva, 2015) as one of their components.

It was after 1970 that the first generation of integrated land use transport models came into being. When the land use side and the transport side are combined, in terms of the modeling structure for the two to interact with each other, they can be either "connected (or linked)" or "integrated." In an "integrated" model, the land-use submodel feeds the spatial distribution of flows of economic interactions between zones as origin and destination movements into the transport submodel, and the transport submodel performs the remaining two steps: modal split and network assignment. On the other hand, under the "connected" structure, the land use submodel is used to simulate or forecast population/employment pattern, then the transport submodel performs the classical four-step modeling process, including trip generation, trip distribution, modal split and network assignment. Compared with a "connected" structure, the "integrated" option assures the best integration of the two components and avoids inconsistency in the use of Origin-Destination matrix in the two submodels.

3.2 Methods

Research on the integrated land use transport modeling started in the 1960s and has been developed in a much faster pace since the 1980s. Much experience and academic advancements have been accumulated since then. According to Cordera and Ibeas (2017), there are multiple ways of classifying ILUTMs due to their complexity.

From the perspective of research methods and theoretical foundations, the modeling framework of the interactive relationship between urban transportation and land use can be roughly divided into: (1) the spatial interaction models, such as LILT (Mackett, 1990), IPRUD (Wegener, 1982), DRAM/EMPAL (Putman, 1997), ILUTP/METROPILUS (Putman and Chan, 2001) and their variants based on the Lowry model); (2) spatial input-output models, such as the MEPLAN (Hunt and Echenique, 1993),

TRANUS (De la Barra, 1982) and PECAS model (Hunt and Abraham, 2005); (3) CATLAS (Anas, 1982; Anas et al., 1998)/METROSIM (Anas and Liu, 2007), MUSSA (Martínez, 1992) and HUDS (Kain and Apgar, 1985) systems based on urban economic bidding theory and discrete choice model; (4) microsimulation models based on cellular automata, SLEUTH (Silva and Clarke, 2002) and CLUE (Verburg et al., 1999), and those based on agents SWARM (Minar et al., 1996), UrbanSim (Waddell, 1998a,b,c), ILUMASS (Strauch et al., 2004) and ILUTE (Salvini and Miller, 2005); (5) Models based on optimization and linear programming, such as TOPAZ (Brotchie et al., 1980) and POLIS (Caindec and Prastacos, 1995); and (6) those land-use models based on land development rules, such as CUF (Landis, 1994) and WHATIF (Acheampong and Silva, 2015; Iacono et al., 2008; Klosterman, 1999). Spatial interaction was the mainstream modeling tool that simulates the interactions between transport and land use in the earlier models (e.g., ILUTP and LILT), but it was replaced by the logit model within the latter models (e.g., MUSSA, MEPLAN and UrbanSim).

The Lowry model is seen as the seminal ILUTM, which integrates the spatial distribution of population, basic industry employment, retail employment (all services and nonbasic industries) and land use in an iterative process. In the following decades, scholars and planners have continuously improved and expanded it since the Lowry model was published. The DRAM/EMPAL model, as a representative example, was proposed by Putman in 1983–1991 based on the Lowry model. Based on DRAM/EMPAL, Putman later developed an integrated transportation land use planning software—ITLUP (Integrated Transportation Land Use Package) (Putman, 1997). Then it was enhanced with the visualization function, and the METROPILUS model was developed in conjunction with GIS (Putman, 1997).

Based on microeconomic and discrete choice theory, Anas (1982) developed a series of models to simulate the impact of improved transportation facilities on the land and real estate market. In his models, 656 mathematical formulas are used to describe the behavior of consumers, producers, landowners and developers. Under the expected travel time and cost, the model system can reach an equilibrium state when the utility of all consumers is maximized, the cost of producers is minimized, and the benefits of all land owners and developers are maximized (Anas and Liu, 2007). CATLAS was improved and named as "METROSIM" and applied to the City of New York (Anas and Arnott, 1994), which integrated submodels such as employment, residential areas, commercial areas, vacant areas, work-related travel and nonwork-related travel, and trip distribution (Iacono et al., 2008).

SLEUTH (Clarke et al., 1996; Silva and Clarke, 2002) and CLUE-S model (Verburg et al., 1999) are the two representatives of integrated land use transportation models based on cellular automata models, both of which can simulate the transformation of non-urban land use (e.g., farmland and forest) at the edge of cities to urban land use (urban residential, commercial and industrial land, etc.). However, the cellular automata in these models are mostly grid-based, and all cellular units in this model need to perform certain decisions and tasks simultaneously, which is called as "Synchrony." However, a model with the "synchronized task mode" in cellular automata can hardly reflect the complex changes and influences of population/employment, policies, economy, land use, and transportation.

Different from cellular automata, agents have automaticity and do not have to follow the principle of "synchronization" of cellular automata. The agents can interact with each other and the environment at different points in time, and then make their own decisions and reactions. In recent years, scholars have begun to develop agent-based models in order to better model land use changes, such as Hunt (2002), Parker and Meretsky (2004) and Torrens (2002). Hunt (2002) introduced a large-scale collaborative research project for ILUTMs funded by Canadian research funding agencies. The integrated models developed through this project included seven submodules, some of them were based on agents, and others were based on aggregate equilibrium models. He introduced the representation of time, space, system behavior and the structure and function of each submodule in the model in detail. Besides, he also raised a series of questions on how to improve traditional integrated models based on the concept of agent.

Hunt et al. (2008) applied a nested logit model at the parcel level to simulate the changes in land use in Baltimore, USA. In their studies, each parcel is seen as an agent. The upper level logit model considers whether to maintain the original type of land use or whether to build, increase, or convert to other types. Conditional upon the upper level choice, the lower level uses a continuous logit model to decide upon the amount of new construction, increase or change of building area.

Parker and Meretsky (2004) developed the SLUDGE model, which includes a submodule for simulating urban land use with cellular automata and a submodule for simulating the behavior of landowners with an agent.

This model is used to study the impact of transportation costs and other related external spatial characteristics (such as land rent) on urban expansion and land use. Very recently, Moeckel et al. (2020) have been taking the lead to integrate microscopic land use and travel demand models for enhanced representation on land use/transportation interactions.

3.3 Operational models

There are more than 30 types of ILUTMs worldwide with different characteristics. Based on the selection of Wegener (1994), Southworth (1995) and Hunt et al. (2005), this section focuses on a set of selected, representative, operational models that have been used in planning practice, so they are classified as "operational models," which include the following eight models: ITLUP, MEPLAN, TRANUS, MUSSA, NYMTC-LUM, UrbanSim, PECAS and DELTA , shown in Table 2.

(1). ITLUP (DRAM/EMPAL)

ITLUP may be the most widely used spatial allocation model in the World currently. According to Putman (1997), the model has more than a dozen applications in the United States and other places with more than 40 calibrations. It includes a number of submodels, the best known of which are DRAM (Disaggregate Residential Allocation Model) and EMPAL (Employment Allocation Model). It includes a multinomial logit model that can be divided into multiple submodels, and also provides a traffic assignment submodel that can carry out different traffic assignment algorithms. Southworth (1995) pointed out that only needing the generally available data (such as data related to population, households, and employment) is an important advantage of DRAM/EMPAL, when compared to other modeling frameworks. However, the framework does not consider the land market clearing (or other market clearing processes). The latest development of this model is the METROPILUS, which aims to improve the integration with the geographic information system (GIS) database and the calibration process, thereby enabling the system to achieve a greater degree of modularity.

(2). MEPLAN

Many scholars discussed MEPLAN in detail, such as Echenique and Williams (1980); Echenique (1985); Hunt and Echenique (1993); Hunt and Simmonds (1993) and Hunt (1994). MEPLAN is an ILUTM with a truly "integrated" structure. It divides the space into multiple zones, and allocates the number of households and economic activities (called "elements") to these zones. The interactions of elements in different zones

Table 2 Comparison of selected operational ILUTMs.

Model	ITLUP	MEPLAN	TRANUS	MUSSA	NYMTC-LUM	UrbanSim	PECAS	DELTA
Developer	S.H. Putman	M. Echenique	T. de la Barra	F. Martinez	A. Anas	P. Waddell	J.D. Hunt	D. Simmonds
Distinguishing features	Comprehensive urban system microsimulation model; structured to accurately capture temporal elements of urban change; activity-travel mode includes household member interactions; disequilibrium model framework	Incorporation of spatial input-output model with economic evaluation component; able to forecast business trip generation; travel treated as a derived demand	A supply model simulates choices of developers; sophisticated travel model with combined mode-route choice	Incorporation of bid-rent framework for land, floor space markets; detailed representation of transit network in travel model; high level of household type disaggregation	Endogenous determination of housing prices, floor space rents, and wages; high level of spatial disaggregation suitable for transit and land use policy evaluation	Land use model incorporating microsimulations of demographic processes of land use development; parcel-level land use representation; high level of household type disaggregation; open-source software developed for general use	Regional econometric model with microsimulation of land development at the parcel level; ability to couple with an activity-based travel model and to apply at super-regional level	Microsimulation of demographic changes; treatment of space to be developed as a fraction of existing buildings
Operational history	Developed over the last 25 years; operationally applied in many US cities and overseas (40 plus calibrations)	Much shared history over 25-year development. Operational applications throughout the world, including the USA (Sacramento for both; Washington State for MEPLAN; Oregon State and Baltimore for TRANUS)		Operational in Santiago, Chile. developed over the last 8–10years	Currently being implemented in New York City. Based upon previous models(CATLAS, CPHMM, NYSIM) developed in Chicago and New York over the last 20 years	Currently being implemented in Honolulu, Eugene/ Springfield and Salt Lake City. Historical validation performed in Oregon	Relying on the University of Calgary in Canada, it has been gradually improved and applied over the past 20 years, mainly in North American states/ provinces and cities	More than 15 applications in UK since 1997 and 1 in Auckland, New Zealand.

Continued

Table 2 Comparison of selected operational ILUTMs.—cont'd

Model				ITLUP	MEPLAN	TRANUS	MUSSA	NYMTC-LUM	UrbanSim	PECAS	DELTA
Policy capabilities	Land use	Pricing	Taxation (property taxes)	✗	✓	✓	✓	✓	✓	✓	✓
			Subsidies	✗	✓	✓	✓	✓	✓	✓	✓
			Development charges	◆	✓	✓	✓	✓	✓	✓	✓
		Infrastructure and services	Public housing	✗	✓	✓	✓	✓	✓	✓	✓
			Servicing land	◆	✓	✓	✓	✓	✓	✓	✓
			Government buildings/other not-for-profit institutions	✗	✓	✓	✓	✓	✓	✓	✓
		Regulatory	Zoning (uses, densities)	◆	✓	✓	✓	✓	✓	✓	✓
			Microdesign building/neighborhood issues	✗	✗	✗	✓	✗	✓	✓	✓
		Education/marketing	Changing/how to change attitudes and sensitivities	◆	◆	◆	◆	◆	◆	◆	◆
	Transportation	Pricing	Road tolls/congestion pricing	✶	✓	✓	✶	✶	✶	✓	✶
			Gas taxes	✶	✓	✓	✶	✶	✶	✓	✶
			Subsidies	✗	✗	✗	✗	✗	✗	✗	✗
			Transit fares	◆	✓	✓	✶	✶	✶	✓	✶
			Parking pricing	◆	✓	✓	✶	✶	✶	✓	✶
		Infrastructure and services	Build roads, high-occupancy vehicles	✓	✓	✓	✓	✓	✓	✓	✓
			Build rail/dedicated transitways	◆	✓	✓	✓	✓	✓	✓	✓
			Operate transit services	◆	✓	✓	✓	✓	✓	✓	✓
			ITS (i.e., infrastructure technology)	✗	✗	✗	✗	✗	✗	✗	✗
			Parking	✗	✗	✗	✗	✗	✗	✓	✗

	Regulatory	Parking provision regulations (off-street)	✗	✗	✗	✗	✗	✗	✗	✗
		Rules of the road	◆	◆	◆	✓	✓	✓	✓	✓
		Non-pricing TDM	✗	✗	✗	✗	✗	✗	✗	✗
		Vehicle/driver licensing	◆	◆	◆	✗	✗	✗	✗	✗
		Inspection/maintenance programs	✗	✗	✗	✗	✗	✗	✗	✗
	Education/ marketing	Changing/how to change attitudes and sensitivities	◆	◆	◆	◆	◆	◆	◆	◆
Other	Pricing	Car purchase tax	✗	✗	✗	✗	✗	✗	✗	✗
		License charges	✗	✗	✗	✗	✗	✗	✗	✗
		Income redistribution	◆	✓	✓	✓	✓	✓	✓	✓
	Regulatory	Air quality standards	✗	✗	✗	✗	✗	✗	✗	✗
		Emissions standards	✶	✓	✓	✓	✶	✶	✓	✓
		Noise	✶	✶	✶	✶	✶	✶	✓	✶
		Safety	✶	✶	✶	✶	✶	✶	◆	✶
		Vehicle technology standards	✗	✗	✗	✗	✗	✗	✗	✗
	Education/ marketing	Changing/how to change attitudes and sensitivities	◆	◆	◆	◆	◆	◆	◆	◆

✓, Explicit and normally/could be done; ✗, no; ✶, implicit; ◆, can respond, but only through exogenous change in parameters.

Adapted after Hunt, J.D., Kriger, D.S. and Miller, E, 2005. Current operational urban land-use transport modelling frameworks: a review. Transp. Rev., 25(3), 329–376.

is the basis of transport demand. Considering congestion, the logit function is used to represent the mode and route selection, and the travel demand generated at a given time point is assigned to the multimodal transportation network. The disutility of transportation will act in the next period, indicating the time lag effect of transportation conditions. Exogenous demands that are similar to the basic elements of "Lowry" are the basic driving force of the economic activities. The external demands and the changes in the amount of land use in each zone from one period to another drive the economy, which will be allocated into the zones.

(3). MUSSA

MUSSA is an operational model for modeling urban land and real estate development developed by Professor Francisco Martínez for the Santiago, Chile. It can be seamlessly integrated with the complete four-stage model (ESTRAUS) of the city, and that is why it is also called the "five-step model" (5-LUT). The equilibrium of land use and transportation is forecasted for the City of Santiago through this model. Meanwhile, the model has been used to test a variety of transportation/land use policies, usually with the related transport policies as the "core" of analysis. Details about this model can be found in Martínez (1992) and Martínez and Donoso (1995).

(4). NYMTC-LUM

The framework of NYMTC-LUM was developed by the New York Metropolitan Transportation Commission with the Professor Alex Anas as the consultant. It is a simplified version of METROPOLIS and the latest model is one of a series of land use and real estate models developed by Professor Anas (1982) in the past two decades. The model is based on the microeconomic theory, representing the interactions between residential and commercial land-use, as well as labor and nonwork-based travel. It represents the process of demand and supply in different cases, and solves the static equilibrium problem of the forecast year by finding the prices and wages that enable the equilibrium of market supply and demand. The model currently has not been "integrated" but "connected" to the existing travel demand model developed by the Metropolitan Transportation Commission (MTC), and takes the output of the mode split of the MTC model as the input. This is similar to the interaction structure of DRAM/EMPAL, MUSSA and UrbanSim, when interacting with corresponding transport model.

(5). TRANUS

The TRANUS package is a proprietary software developed by Modelistica of Venezuela, a private company run by Dr. Tomas de la Barra. It was developed based on similar modeling experiences as MEPLAN, initially developed in the 1980s. The main feature of TRANUS is to support the use of a more restricted set of functional forms and modeling options in the framework, and to allow a more focused approach to develop models than MEPLAN. Currently, it has been used in Central and South America and quite a few cities/regions in Europe. TRANUS models have been developed or under development in Sacramento and Baltimore, Maryland, Oregon in the United States and other regions. See De la Barra (1982) for more information on TRANUS.

(6). UrbanSim

UrbanSim is an operational model for modeling urban land and built space market developed by Professor Paul Waddell for Hawaii, Oregon and Utah in the United States. Its prototype has been completed in Eugene-Springfield. The model is intended to be linked with the traditional four-step travel demand model of Eugene-Springfield and the activity-based travel demand model of Honolulu. UrbanSim was originally developed by a company called Urban Analytics, but latter it was further developed and maintained by the University of Washington. The model operates in a dynamic and disequilibrium manner on an annual basis, and adjusts real estate development plan according to the expected profit (the expected revenue minus costs). Besides, the floorspace demand depends on the price of the previous year and the current supply level while the price is adjusted according to the supply and demand in each market each year. This model takes the parcel as the unit of land development, making it one of a few models that uses the parcel as the basic unit of analysis so far. The detailed information can be found in Waddell (1998a,b,c) and Waddell et al. (1998).

(7). PECAS

Based on the experience of the MEPLAN and TRANUS models, the PECAS was developed in recent years as a newer version of an integrated model using the spatial input-output analysis framework. It includes three submodels: (1) The space development submodel simulates the development behavior of developers providing real estate for various socioeconomic activities, including no change, new development, demolition and redevelopment from one point to another (by the categories of land use); (2) The activity allocation submodel of socioeconomic activities simulates the spatial allocation of various social economic activities and the interaction between them in the same time period; (3) In the transportation submodel, the social and economic activities allocated to the zones in the activity allocation module and their exchanges are the basis for transportation demand. Their interaction determines the transportation demand and transportation cost, and has an important impact on the improvement or deterioration of the transportation condition, and the spatial distribution of economic activities and their interactions in society (Hunt and Abraham, 2005).

(8). DELTA

DELTA is a land-use/economic modeling package by David Simmonds Consultancy, Cambridge, UK (Simmonds, 1999). DELTA is inspired by Wegener's IRPUD model and has more than 15 applications in UK since 1997 and 1 in Auckland, New Zealand. The unifying theoretical basis of DELTA is that there is no one unifying theoretical basis, in that different submodels should be modeled based on different theoretical frameworks. The theoretical framework for each submodel should be drawn from research in the relevant discipline; for example, the demographic model should use survival probabilities derived from studies of regional demographics rather than being calibrated directly along with the rest of the model system. DELTA contains five submodels: Development, Employment, Location, Transition/growth, and Area quality. Economic and Migration models were added to simulate larger-scale interactions between regions. Car ownership model was integrated into DELTA as well. The order of model running is now: Migration, Development, Transition, Car ownership, Economic, Location, Employment and Area quality (HBA Specto Incorporated, 2013).

3.4 Empirical findings

The existing models are different in terms of completeness, availability, capacity and details of the representation of activities, time, land, building stock, and transportation system. In general, most operational models are "static equilibrium" models because they set an annual step size or jump directly to the balance year with an assumed "equilibrium" within each modeling year. However, UrbanSim is a dynamic disequilibrium model (operates at a step length of 1 year, and do not assume the state of equilibrium). There is no unified and reliable population forecast method across the models, and there are large differences in the classification of households. However, for nearly all of the operational models discussed above, a composite utility value derived from the random utility theory is transferred from the transportation model to the land use model as the input in almost the same way, as a kind of "accessibility" measure. Almost all models are based on households, rather than individual persons since the former is more appropriate as an "economic unit."

The early ILUTMs were based on a relatively macroscopic spatial and temporal resolution. For example, the time step of the models was mostly based on the calendar year, and the spatial resolution was based on "land use or transportation zones." With the fast development of information technologies, the limitation of computing power and data gradually disappeared, and microsimulation models began to come onto the stage after 2000. These models, such as UrbanSim, PECAS and ILUMASS, simulate the behavior of land development (such as those at land parcels or grids) and decision-making agents (such as households, enterprises or developers) from a microscopic perspective, and analyze the impact of various planning policies (e.g., zoning and subsidy) through computer-based simulation analysis.

3.5 Recent progress

As can be seen from Fig. 2, Wegener (2004) pointed out that activity-based or agent-based models should be the long-term development direction of the field. Today, we can see that more agent-based models have been developed (e.g., ILUMASS). In the book edited by Bierlaire et al. (2015), the state-of-the-art agent-based ILUTM and the challenges of implementing it in European cities are described, including how to address

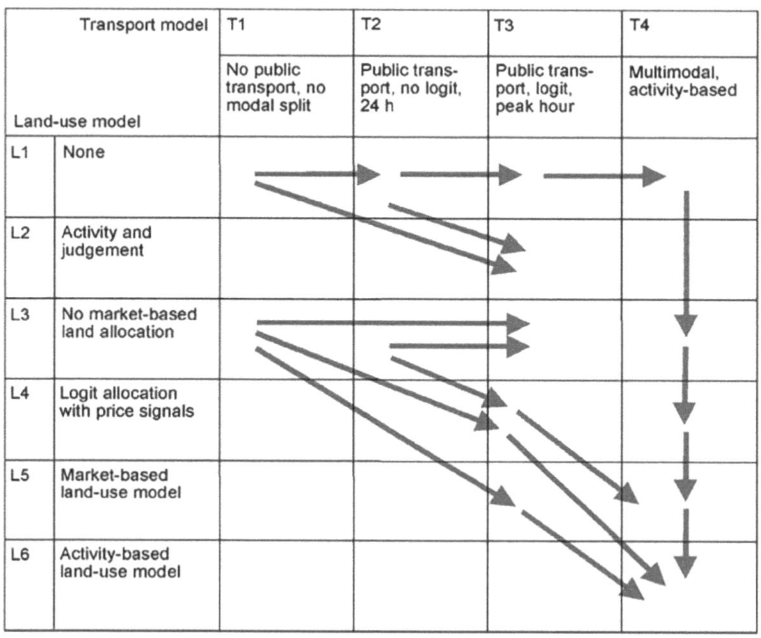

Fig. 2 The development trend of land use and transport modeling. *(See Wegener (2004))*

the modeling and computational issues of integrating modern mobility simulations with the latest microsimulation land use models (see http://www.sustaincity.org). Miller (2018) argued that although integrated urban microsimulation models are not yet commonplace, they are needed in order to successfully model the complexities of the urban systems and their behavior.

It should be noticed that the development of agent-based ILUTMs requires much larger amount of microscopic data than traditional ones. Therefore, it is necessary to take advantages of the progress in other fields, such as big data and internet of things (IOT), in order to advance the field in a successful way.

There are ongoing studies on how to integrate existing independent models to develop an integrated framework with the capacity of carrying out relevant analysis related to land use, economy, demographics and transport (Harvey et al., 2019). The authors believed that it is desired to integrate existing models rather than to develop a completely new integrated model considering the large amounts of time and money invested into developing them. However, many challenges lie ahead and need to be tackled.

Ziemke et al. (2016) integrated the microscopic land use simulation system SILO with an agent-based transport simulation system MATSim, based on which, the authors conducted further study on the impact of population scaling and simulation intervals of the transport model on run times (Llorca et al., 2020). They also calculated individual travel times based on x/y coordinates (rather than zones) and applied a detailed temporal resolution for synthetic agents, which is expected to reduce the spatial biases (Kuehnel et al., 2020).

Ho et al. (2017) applied endogenous treatment of location choices in an integrated framework, and studied simultaneous location choice behavior of firms and jobs in an ILUTM, which enables endogenous treatment of firm location choice in the model, allowing for feedback between travel and firm location (Hensher et al., 2019).

Emberger and Pfaffenbichler (2020) studied the impact of automatic vehicles using a dynamic LUTI model; Manrique et al. (2020) conducted equity analysis in access to public transport through an ILUTM; Penazzi et al. (2019) applied an integrated land-use transport model for low carbon, urban-rural ecosystems planning; Yin et al. (2017) assessed the impact of ridesharing on congestion reduction and pollutant emissions mitigation in the Paris region with an ILUTM; Noviandi et al. (2017) discussed the development of a model for understanding the dynamics and the complexity of the interactions between land use and transport in megapolitan urban fringe of Indonesia.

In addition, integrated land use transport models are recommended by the Department of Transport (DfT) of the UK for assessing the Wider Economic Impacts (WEIs) of transformational transport infrastructure development (Department for Transport (DfT), 2018). Example is the model DEIM (based on DELTA package) by Simmonds, which allows changes in endogenous variables (e.g., vary the overall quantities of households and jobs) in the model over a forecast (Simpson et al., 2016). When applied to the West Midlands project, a productivity model was added to provide a detailed matrix of productivity (Gross Value Added (GVA)/worker) estimates by zone, industry, and socio-economic level and then calculate how changes in location and density affect GVA/worker (Simmonds, 2017; Simpson et al., 2016).

4. Challenges and implications

Zhong et al. (2018) described the challenges and implications of developing and applying ILUTMs in urban planning field and planning organizations in particular. The main challenges and implications identified are summarized as follows:

1) Challenges
  - **i.** Lack of modeling legislation and culture;
  - **ii.** Institutional barrier;
  - **iii.** Distrust from engineers and politicians regarding ILUTMs;
  - **iv.** Lack of human resources required for ILUTM work;
  - **v.** Limited resources and urgency of decision making faced by modelers;
  - **vi.** Scissor differences between rural and urban areas;
  - **vii.** Lack of socio-economic and freight data at the spatial scale required for modeling;
  - **viii.** Data inconsistency; and
  - **ix.** Complexity of developing, calibrating, validating and using ILUTMs.

2) Implications
  - **a)** The distrust from engineers and politicians regarding ILUTMs makes it difficult to reach a consensus for developing an integrated

model in the first place. Due to weak modeling culture, politicians, engineers and even transport modelers doubted the usefulness of integrated models and successfulness of developing such a "complicated" model based on limited data and resources (e.g., funding and staff). In such a case, it is necessary to develop a Demo model to demonstrate that it is feasible to develop such a model within a reasonable time and budget. It should be clear that modeling is not about to provide an accurate forecast of the future, but a tool for understanding relative impacts of a range of policies and corresponding actions. A set of assumptions exist behind every type of models. Most likely these assumptions won't be all met in the real-world and therefore, no model is supposed to accurately forecast the future.

b) Lack of human resources required for ILUTM development at both universities and planning agencies is a hard fact the modeling community has to face. The development of an ILUTM requires the expertise in various subjects, such as transportation planning and modeling, land-use planning, geography, computer science, statistics and economics. Dedicated education and training programs are needed.

c) The development of ILUTMs requires a long-term commitment and investment, but limited resources and urgency of decision-makings make the efforts of integrated modeling suspicious. Due to the shortage of time, budget and data, it is often impossible to develop a full-fledged, operational model at once.

5. A research agenda

5.1 Changing paths

Despite significant improvement has been made in the ILUTM field in the past several decades, it is still not widely accepted by the planning community (Saujot et al., 2016; Te Brommelstroet and Bertolini, 2008; Zhong et al., 2018). Saujot et al. (2016) proposed a "sound" perspective for the development of integrated modeling and suggested that the model development be based on user expectation rather than model specifications. The authors believed that, while the top-down approaches have been useful to provide different structures of integrated models, more bottom-up approaches are needed to make them popular.

With the rapid development of new technologies, unprecedented computing capacity is available and advanced sensors provide huge datasets. The ILUTM has been seen to move away from static, equilibrium-based, aggregate structure with strong theories and assumptions to dynamic, dis-equilibrium, disaggregate, data-driven and more behavioral. In terms of the types/number of modeling units and temporal and spatial resolution, more comprehensive, larger-scale modeling or more detailed representation has been attempted (Zhong, 2017).

5.2 Extending the empirical focus

There is a tendency for ILUTMs being used to look at the impact of various policies onto the economic, environmental, and social impact. For example:

1) There is a tendency of extending ILUTMs for estimating environmental (ILUTME from the University of Toronto) (Miller and Salvini, 2001) and societal impacts (Baltimore PECAS for looking at social segregation/separation) (Hunt et al., 2008). Automated vehicles and new way of travel (i.e., ridesharing) are expected to bring changes to the transport system, land use and environment. We recommend more research into these areas (Emberger and Pfaffenbichler, 2020; Yin et al., 2017).
2) There is a tendency of extending ILUTMs for estimating Wider Economic Impacts (WEIs) of transportation infrastructure plans. Transformational transport infrastructure development (e.g., high-speed railway) could bring wider economic benefits which is normally excluded from the conventional transportation infrastructure cost and benefit analysis. ILUTMs could be a supplementary economic modeling tool which helps to capture the WEIs (Department for Transport (DfT), 2018; Simmonds, 2017; Wang et al., 2019) and thus provide a much better accounting of the benefits of transportation investments.
3) Equity issue (California PECAS). In terms of equity, the distribution of impacts, benefits and costs of policies across the population is of great importance. To meet the requirement of equity legislation or to evaluate effective policies with their equity effects, ILUTMs could be a powerful tool (Kuehnel et al., 2020; Manrique et al., 2020; Rodier et al., 2010).
4) Extending ILUTMs for studying the interactions between multimodal transportation and mixed land use systems, as they have been identified as the two very important features of cities in developing countries.

5) AI & big data and "high-fidelity modeling." With the development in AI technology and availability of big data, high-fidelity modeling becomes possible (Wang et al., 2016). The new technologies can be applied in different ways for the enhanced modeling capacity, ranging from land use classification (Beykaei et al., 2015) and building extraction using remote sensing (Shiravi et al., 2015) to model estimation and calibration (Gong et al., 2015).

6. Concluding remarks

In this chapter, a brief introduction to ILUTMs and why using ILUTMs are provided. Then, the theory and methods for developing ILUTMs and the eight "operational" ILUTMs are presented in order to illustrate how the theory and methods are applied to develop each of them. In addition, the challenges and implications of developing and using ILUTMs are also identified and briefly discussed. Finally, a research agenda is proposed with an aim to identify the trend of the field and address the issues and challenges in the process of advancing the field. With a synthesis of the literature and the observations of recent developments of the field, it is believed that the mircosimulation-based integrated modeling will be the future direction. And as we are marching into IT age and big data era, it is believed that such models will become more practical, popular and powerful. More studies should be devoted to the detailed interactions among agents and stability of this type of model. At the same time, modelers should collaborate more closely with the decision-makers, making ILUTMs more practical for urban planning.

It has been noticed by the research community that ILTUM has been moving away from static, equilibrium-based to dynamic, disequilibrium-based. "High-fidelity" ILUTMs become the reality, as big data and AI become more and more available.

Integrated land-use transportation models (ILUTMs) have a dual role. First, these tools should be able to produce consistent forecasts of land development patterns, local demographics and local business (firmographics), travel patterns and transportation system performance, in addition to other detailed forecasts (e.g., environment impacts or equity issue). Second, these models should be able to support policy analysis, exploring how policies in one domain have an influence on others, and focusing on final goals (economic performance, quality of life, equity, etc.) vs intermediate objectives (congestion relief, budget reduction, etc.).

Integrated models can contribute to policy analysis in several ways. They provide a quantitative method of evaluating the benefits of a policy or investment alternative, taking into account sources and directions of benefit that would otherwise be difficult to measure. They enforce a linkage between transportation and land use policy implementation, so that both types of policies can work toward common goals. Transportation policy cannot be as effective without considering land use impacts and coordinated implementation of land use policies and vice versa. ILUTMs can be used to explore both the short-term and long-term feedback effects of a policy as its effects propagate through the complicated urban or regional systems over time with intended or sometimes unintended consequences.

References

Acheampong, R.A., Silva, E., 2015. Land use-transport interaction modeling: a review of the literature and future research directions. J. Transp. Land Use 8 (3), 11–38.

Alonso, W., 1964. Location and Land Use. Harvard University Press, Cambridge, MA.

Anas, A., 1982. Residential Location Models and Urban Transportation: Economic Theory, Econometrics, and Policy Analysis with Discrete Choice Models. Academic Press, New York.

Anas, A., 1982. Residential Location Markets and Urban Transportation. Economic Theory, Econometrics and Policy Analysis with Discrete Choice Models. Academic Press.

Anas, A., Arnott, R.J., 1994. The Chicago prototype housing market model with tenure choice and its policy applications. J. Hous. Res. 5 (1), 23–90.

Anas, A., Arnott, R., Small, K.A., 1998. Urban spatial structure. J. Econ. Lit. 36 (3), 1426–1464.

Anas, A., Liu, Y.A., 2007. Regional economy, land use, and transportation model (Relu-Tran©): formulation, algorithm design, and testing. J. Reg. Sci. 47 (3), 415–451.

Beykaei, S.A., Zhong, M., Zhang, Y., 2015. Development of a land use extraction expert system through morphological and spatial arrangement analysis. Eng. Appl. Artif. Intel. 37, 221–235 (January).

Bierlaire, M., de Palma, A., Hurtubia, R., Waddell, P., 2015. Integrated Transport and Land Use Modelling for Sustainable Cities. EPFL Press, Routledge.

Bowman, J.L., Ben-Akiva, M.E., 2000. Activity-based disaggregate travel demand model system with activity schedules. Transp. Res. A. 35, 1–28.

Boyce, D.E., Chon, K.S., Ferris, M.E., Lee, Y.J., Lin, K.-T., Eash, R.W., 1985. Implementation and evaluation of combined models of urban travel and location on a sketch planning network. In: Paper Presented at the Transportation Research Board 64th Annual Meeting. Washington, DC.

Anon., 1980. TOPAZ—General Planning Technique and Its Applications at the Regional, Urban and Facility Planning Levels. Lecture Notes in Economics and Mathematical Systems. Springer-Verlag, New York.

Caindec, E.K., Prastacos, P., 1995. Description of POLIS. The Projective Optimization Land Use Information System. Working Paper 95/1of Association of Bay Area Governments.

Clarke, K.C., 2014. Cellular automata and agent-based models. In: Fischer, M.M., Nijkamp, P. (Eds.), Handbook of Regional Science. Springer-Verlag, Berlin Heidelberg, pp. 1217–1233.

Clarke, K.C., Hoppen, S., Gaydos, L., 1996. Methods and techniques for rigorous calibration of a cellular automaton model of urban growth. In: Third International Conference/ Workshop on Integrating GIS and Environmental Modeling, Santa Fe, New Mexico.

Cordera, R., Ibeas, Á., 2017. A Classification of Land Use–Transport Interaction Models. Land Use–Transport Interaction Models. CRC Press, pp. 11–22.

De la Barra, T., 1982. Modelling regional energy use: a land use, transport and energy evaluation model. Environ. Plan. A. 9B, 429–443.

De la Barra, T., 1989. Integrated land use and transport modelling: Decision chains and hierarchies. Cambridge University Press.

Department for Transport (DfT), 2018. Transport Analysis Guidance (TAG) Unit A2.1 Wider Impacts. DfT, London, UK.

Echenique, M.H., 1985. The use of integrated land use and transport models: the cases of Sao Paulo, Brazil and Bilbao, Spain. In: Florian, M. (Ed.), The Practice of Transportation Planning. Elsevier, The Hague, pp. 263–286.

Echenique, M., et al., 1990. The MEPLAN models of Bilbao, Leeds and Dortmund. Transp. Rev. 10 (4), 309–322.

Echenique, M.D., Lindsay, W., 1969. A spatial model of urban stock and activity. Reg. Stud. 3 (3), 281–312.

Echenique, M.H., Williams, I.N., 1980. Developing theoretically based urban models for practical planning studies. Sistemi Urbani 3, 13–23.

Emberger, G., Pfaffenbichler, P., 2020. A quantitative analysis of potential impacts of automated vehicles in Austria using a dynamic integrated land use and transport interaction model. Transp. Pol. 98, 57–67.

Gong, Z., Thill, J.-C., Liu, W., 2015. ART-P-MAP neural networks modeling of land-use change: accounting for spatial heterogeneity and uncertainty. Geogr. Anal. 47 (4), 376–409.

Hansen, W.G., 1959. How accessibility shapes land use. J. Am. Inst. Plann. 25, 73–76.

Harvey, E.P., Carwell, R.C., McDonald, G.W., van Delden, H., Vanhout, R., Smith, N.J., Kim, J., Forgie, V.E., van den Belt, M., 2019. Developing integrated models by coupling together existing models; land use, economics, demographics and transport in Wellington, New Zealand. Comp, Environ. Urb. Syst. 74, 100–113.

HBA Specto Incorporated, 2013. Best Practice Review of Integrated Land Use –Transportation Models Scope for Model Development and Final Report. Calgary, Alberta, August.

Hensher, D.A., Ho, C.Q., Ellison, R.B., 2019. Simultaneous location of firms and jobs in a transport and land use model. J. Transp. Geogr. 75, 110–121.

Ho, C.Q., Hensher, D.A., Ellison, R., 2017. Endogenous treatment of residential location choices in transport and land use models: introducing the MetroScan framework. J. Transp. Geogr. 64, 120–131.

Hunt, J.D., 1994. Calibrating the Naples land use and transport model. Environ. Plan. A. 21B, 569–590.

Hunt, J.D., 2002. Agent behaviour issues arising with urban system micro-simulation. European J. Transp. Infrastruc. Res. 2 (3), 233–254.

Hunt, J.D., Abraham, J.E., 2005. Design and implementation of PECAS: a generalized system for the allocation of economic production, exchange, and consumption quantities. In: Chapter 11. In: Foundations of Integrated Land-Use and Transportation Models: Assumptions and New Conceptual Frameworks. Elsevier, Oxford UK, pp. 217–238.

Hunt, J.D., Echenique, M.H., 1993. Experiences in the application of the MEPLAN framework for land use and transport interaction modelling. In: Proceedings of the 4th National Conference on the Application of Transportation Planning Methods, Daytona Beach, FL, USA, May, pp. 723–754.

Hunt, J.D., Simmonds, D.C., 1993. Theory and application of an integrated land-use and transport modelling framework. Environ. Plan. A. 20B, 221–244.

Hunt, J.D., Kriger, D.S., Miller, E., 2005. Current operational urban land-use transport modelling frameworks: a review. Transp. Rev. 25 (3), 329–376.

Hunt, J.D., Abraham, J.E., 2005. Design and implementation of PECAS: a generalised system for allocating economic production, exchange and consumption quantities. In: Lee-Gosselin, M.E.H., Doherty, S.T. (Eds.), Integrated Land-Use and Transportation Models. Emerald Group Publishing Limited, Bingley, pp. 253–273. https://doi.org/10.1108/9781786359520-011.

Hunt, J.D., Abraham, J.E., Silva, D.D., Zhong, M., Bridges, J., Mysko, J., 2008. Developing and applying a parcel-level simulation of developer actions in Baltimore. In: Transportation Research Board 87th Annual Meeting. (08–2593).

Hunt, J.D., Hill, G.T., Araham, J.E., 2019. Controlled deterministic microsimulation modelling: expected value calculation of development events in Alberta. In: Compendium of Annual Papers. Washington, D.C, pp. 19–05229.

Hunt, J.D., Stefan, K.J., 2007. Tour-based microsimulation of urban commercial movements. Transp. Res. B: Methodol. 41 (9), 981–1013.

Iacono, M., Levinson, D., El-Geneidy, A., 2008. Models of transportation and land use change: a guide to the territory. J. Plan. Lit. 22, 323–340.

Kain, J.F., Apgar, W.C., 1985. The Harvard urban development simulation model. Microeconomic Models of Housing Markets. Springer, Berlin, Heidelberg, pp. 27–71.

Klosterman, R.E., 1999. The what if? Collaborative planning support system. Environ. Plann. B: Plann. Des. 26 (3), 393–408.

Kuehnel, N., Ziemke, D., Moeckel, R., Nagel, K., 2020. The end of travel time matrices: individual travel times in integratd land use/transport models. J. Transp. Geogr. 88, 102862.

Landis, J.D., 1994. The California Urban Futures Model: a new generation of metropolitan simulation models. Environ. Plann. B Plann. Des. 21B, 399–422.

Llorca, C., Kuehnel, N., Moeckel, R., 2020. Agent-based integrated land use/transport models: a study on scale factors and transport model simulation intervals. Procedia Comp. Sci. 170, 733–738.

Lowry, I.S., 1964. A Model of Metropolis. Rand Corp, Santa Monica, CA.

Mackett, R.L., 1990. Comparative analysis of modeling land-use transport interaction at the micro and macro levels. Environ. Plan. A 22, 459–475.

Manrique, J., Cordera, R., Moreno, E.G., Orena, B.A., 2020. Equity analysis in access to public transport through a land use transport interaction model- application to Bucaramanga metropolitan area Colombia. Res. Transp. Bus. Manag. 100561.

Martínez, F.J., 1992. Towards the 5-stage land use–transport model. In: Selected Papers of the 6th World Conference on Transportation Research ; Land Use Development and Globalization, Lyon, France, July, pp. 79–90.

Martínez, F.J., Donoso, P.P., 1995. MUSSA model: the theoretical framework. In: Proceedings of the 7th World Conference on Transportation Research, Vol. 2, Sydney, Australia, July, pp. 333–343.

McFadden, D., 1978. Modeling the choice of residential location. Transp. Res. Rec. 673, 72–77.

Miller, E., 2018. The case for microsimulation frameworks for integrated urban models. J. Trans. Land Use 11 (1), 1025–1037.

Miller, E.J., Salvini, P.A., 2001. The integrated land use, transportation, environment (ILUTE) microsimulation modelling system: description & current status. In: Hensher, D., King, J. (Eds.), Travel Behaviour Research: The Leading Edge. Elsevier, pp. 711–724.

Minar, N., Burkhart, R., Langton, C., et al., 1996. The Swarm Simulation System: A Toolkit for Building Multi-agent Simulations. Santa Fe Institute.
Miyamoto, K., Vichiensan, V., Sugiki, N., Kitazume, K., 2007. Applications of RURBAN integrated with a transport model in detailed zone system. In: Paper presented at the World Conference on Transport Research, Berkeley, CA.
Moeckel, R., Heilig, M., Hilgert, T., Kagerbauer, M., 2020. Benefits of integrating microscopic land use and travel demand models: location choice, time use & stability of travel behavior. Transp. Res. Procedia 48, 1956–1967.
Noviandi, N., Pradono, P., Tasrif, M., Kusumantoro, I.P., 2017. Modeling of dynamics complexity of land use and transport in megapolitan urban fringe (case of Bekasi city). Transp. Res. Procedia. 25, 3314–3332.
Parker, D.C., Meretsky, V., 2004. Measuring pattern outcomes in an agent-based model of edge-effect externalities using spatial metrics. Agr Ecosyst Environ 101 (2), 233–250.
Penazzi, S., Accorsi, R., Manzini, R., 2019. Planning low carbon urban-rural ecosystems: an integrated transport land-use model. J. Clean. Prod. 235, 96–111.
Putman, S.H., 1983. Integrated Urban Models. Pion, London.
Putman, S.H., 1991. Integrated Urban Models 2. Pion, London.
Putman, S.H., 1994. Integrated land use and transportation models: an overview of progress with DRAM and EMPAL, with suggestions for further research. In: Paper Presented at the Transportation Research Board 73rd Annual Meeting, Washington, DC.
Putman, S.H., 1996. Extending DRAM Model: theory–practice nexus. J. Transp. Res. Rec. 1552, 112–119.
Putman, S.H., 1997. LINKAGES Newsletter of Integrated Transportation and Land Use Analyses. S. H. Putman Associates, Townsend, DE.
Putman, S.H., Chan, S.L., 2001. The METROPILUS planning support system: urban models and GIS. In: Planning Support Systems: Integrating Geographic Information Systems, Models and Visualization Tools. ESRI Press, pp. 99–128.
Rodier, C., Abraham, J.E., Dix, B.N., Hunt, J.D., 2010. Equity analysis of land use and transport plans using an integrated spatial model. In: Proceedings of the 89th Annual Meeting of the Transportation Research Board, Washington, DC, USA.
Salvini, P., Miller, E.J., 2005. ILUTE: an operational prototype of a comprehensive microsimulation model of urban systems. Netw. Spat. Econ. 5 (2), 217–234.
Saujot, M., de Lapparent, M., Arnaud, E., Prados, E., 2016. Making land use-transport models operational tools for planning: from a top-down to an end-user approach. Transp. Pol. 49, 20–29.
Shiravi, S., Zhong, M., Beykaei, S.A., Hunt, J.D., Abraham, J.E., 2015. An assessment of the utility of LiDAR data in Extracting Base-year Floorspace and a comparison with the census-based approach. Environ. Plan.: B 42 (4), 708–729.
Silva, E.A., Clarke, K.C., 2002. Calibration of the SLEUTH urban growth model for Lisbon and Porto, Portugal. Comp., Environ. Urb. Syst. 26, 525–552.
Simmonds, D., 1999. The design of the DELTA land-use modelling package. Environ. Plan. B: Plan. Design 26 (5), 665–684.
Simmonds, D., 2017. The DELTA models and their applications. In: Paper based on presentations to the Applied Urban Modelling Symposia, Cambridge.
Simpson, T., Bosredon, M., Dobson, A., Minta, P., Revill, E., Simmonds, D., 2016. Illustrating recent variations in land-use transport interaction (LUTI) modeling methodologies. In: Paper presented at the Annual Transport Practitioners' Meeting.
Southworth, F., 1995. A Technical Review of Urban Land Use–Transportation Models as Tools for Evaluating Vehicle Travel Reduction Strategies. Report 6881, Oak Ridge National Laboratory, Oak Ridge, TN.
Stefan, K.J., McMillan, J.D.P., Hunt, J.D., 2005. Urban commercial vehicle movement model for Calgary, Alberta, Canada. Trans. Res. Rec. 1921 (1), 1–10.

Strauch, D., Moeckel, R., Wegener, M., et al., 2004. Linking transport and land use planning: the microscopic dynamic simulation model ILUMASS. Geodynamics. CRC Press, pp. 319–336.

Te Brommelstroet, M., Bertolini, L., 2008. Developing land use and transport PSS: meaningful information through a dialogue between modelers and planners. Trans. Policy 15 (4), 251–259.

Torrens, P.M., 2002. SprawlSim: modeling sprawling urban growth using automata-based models. In: Agent-Based Models of Land-Use/Land-Cover Change, pp. 69–76.

Verburg, P.H., Veldkamp, T., Bouma, J., 1999. Land use change under conditions of high population pressure: the case of Java. Glob. Environ. Chang. 9 (4), 303–312.

Waddell, P., 1998a. The Oregon prototype metropolitan land use model. In: Proceedings of the ASCE Conference on Transportation, Land Use and Air Quality: Making the Connection, Portland, OR, USA, May, pp. 549–558.

Waddell, P., 1998b. Final Report on the Oregon Prototype Metropolitan Land Use Model, Phase II. Report. Oregon Department of Transportation, Salem, OR.

Waddell, P., 1998c. An urban simulation model for integrated policy analysis and planning: residential location and housing market components of UrbanSim. In: Paper presented at the 8th World Conference on Transport Research, Antwerp, Belgium, July.

Waddell, P., 2000. A behavioral simulation model for metropolitan policy analysis and planning: Residential location and housing market components of UrbanSim. Environ. Plann. B 27 (2), 247–264.

Waddell, P., 2009. Parcel-level microsimulation of land use and transportation: the walking scale of urban sustainability. In: Paper Presented at 2009 IATBR Workshop on Computational Algorithms and Procedures for Integrated Microsimulation Models. Jaipur, Rajasthan, India.

Waddell, P., Moore, T., Edwards, S., 1998. Exploiting parcel-level GIS for land use modeling. In: Proceedings of the ASCE Conference on Transportation, Land Use and Air Quality: Making the Connection, Portland, OR, USA, May, pp. 632–641.

Waddell, P., Peak, C., Caballero, P., 2004. UrbanSim: Database Development for the Puget Sound Region. (Technical Report). Center for Urban Simulation and Policy Analysis. University of Washington.

Wang, H.N., Zhong, M., Hunt, J.D., 2016. Opportunity for "high-Fidelity" ILUTMs: a study of high-resolution urban building and land-use classification. In: Presentation presented at 2016 World Conference on Transport Research (WCTR), Shanghai, July 10-15th.

Wang, W., Zhong, M., Hunt, J.D., 2019. Analysis of the wider economic impact of a transport infrastructure project using an integrated land use transport model. Sustainability 11 (2), 364. https://doi.org/10.3390/su11020364.

Wegener, M., 1982. Modeling urban decline: a multilevel economic-demographic model for the Dortmund region. Int. Reg. Sci. Rev. 7 (2), 217–241.

Wegener, M., 1994. Operational urban models: state of the art. J. Am. Plann. Assoc. 60, 17–29.

Wegener, M., 2004. Overview of land use transport models. In: Hensher, D.A., Button, K. (Eds.), Transport Geography and Spatial Systems. Pergamon/Elsevier Science, Kidlington, pp. 127–146.

Wegener, M., 2011. From macro to micro—how much micro is too much? Trans. Rev. 31 (2), 161–177.

Wilson, A.G., 1970. Entropy in Urban and Regional Modelling. Pion, London.

Wingo, L., 1961. Transportation and Urban Land. John Hopkins Press, Baltimore.

Yin, B., Liu, L., Coulombel, N., Viguie, V., 2017. Evaluation of ridesharing impacts using an integrated transport land-use model: a case study for the Paris region. Transp. Res. Procedia. 27, 824–831.

Zhong, M., 2017. Where is integrated land-use transport modeling/planning moving to: from theory, assumptions to big data and high-Fidelity? In: Invited speech, presented at the 4th International Conference on Transportation Information and Safety, Banff, Alberta, Canada, August 8 – 10th.
Zhong, M., Shan, R., Du, D., et al., 2015. A comparative analysis of traditional four-step and activity-based travel demand modeling: a case study of Tampa, Florida. Trans. Plann. Technol. 38 (5), 517–533.
Zhong, M., Wang, W., John, D.H., Pan, H., Chen, T., Li, J., Yang, W., Zhang, K., 2018. Solutions to cultural, organizational, and technical challenges in developing PECAS models for the cities of Shanghai, Wuhan and Guangzhou. J. Transp. Land Use 11 (1), 1193–1229.
Ziemke, D., Nagel, K., Moeckel, R., 2016. Towards an agent-based, integrated land-use transport modeling system. Procedia Comp. Sci. 83, 958–963.

CHAPTER TEN

Transit oriented development: A bibliometric analysis of research

Farjana Shatu[a], Laura Aston[b], Lipi Bhavesh Patel[b], and Md. Kamruzzaman[b,*]

[a]Freelance Researcher, Narre Warren South, VIC, Australia
[b]Urban Planning and Design, Monash Art, Design and Architecture (MADA), Monash University, Caulfield East, VIC, Australia
*Corresponding author: e-mail address: md.kamruzzaman@monash.edu

Contents

Abstract

Transit-oriented development (TOD) is a popular planning concept both in policy circles and in academia. The field has grown over the last 30 years with hundreds of research articles. However, a comprehensive review of the field in its entirety is missing in the literature. This chapter uses bibliometric analysis techniques and examines bibliographic data of 677 research outputs on TODs to explore: (a) the knowledge structure in TOD research in terms of its thematic evolution over time; (b) the various entities (author, journal, country) that are driving the field with greater productivity and influence; and (c) if a concerted effort has been made by the various entities to progress the field of research. Findings show that nine thematic research foci evolve in the TOD literature (e.g., various contextual effects of TODs, TOD design and behavioral outcomes, TOD typology and accessibility) with differential impacts on the field. The various factors that have a greater influence in the field include an overall productivity of authors, their

Advances in Transport Policy and Planning, Volume 9
ISSN 2543-0009
https://doi.org/10.1016/bs.atpp.2021.06.001

capability to generate high quality publications, and the strength of their broader collaborative networks. However, evidence shows that most of the researchers have been working in silos and lack effective collaboration. The findings of this chapter provide a bird's eye view of the field for researchers interested in TOD.

Keywords: Transit-oriented development, Land use, Bibliometric analysis, Bibliographic coupling, Citation analysis, Co-authorship analysis, Co-occurrence analysis, Network visualization, Research productivity, Research performance

1. Introduction

Transit-oriented development (TOD) has traditionally been conceptualized as a neighborhood planning tool (Calthorpe, 1993). More recently, the concept has been expanded as a city shaping strategy (Liu et al., 2020). As a neighborhood planning concept, TODs are characterized by moderate to high density, diverse land use patterns, well-connected street patterns and centered on high-frequency mass transit services (Cervero and Kockelman, 1997; Renne, 2009). As a city shaping strategy, multiple TODs are now planned in tandem with transport network to form a hierarchical network of TODs with variations in their size, form, and functions depending on the spatial context in which a TOD node is located (Center for Transit-Oriented Development, 2010).

TODs are conceived as one of the best practice examples of integrated transport and land use planning, in which both transport services and urban development complement each other to maximize their own economic goals (e.g., increased ridership from urban development, value uplift from mass transit) (Cervero et al., 2004; Chen et al., 2019; Curtis et al., 2009; Falconer and Richardson, 2010; Knowles, 2012; Pritchard and Frøyen, 2019). Research has also shown that this integration creates an environment conducive to achieving broader policy agendas such as climate change due to reduced emissions (Dou et al., 2016; Wang et al., 2017a), social sustainability due to enhanced interactions among residents (Kamruzzaman et al., 2014b), social sustainability due to enhanced interactions among residents (Langlois et al., 2016), urban vibrancy created by agglomeration of opportunities (Yang et al., 2021), and quality of life (Lang et al., 2020).

TOD is a heavily-researched field, with hundreds of published research outputs. A number of review papers have already been published to consolidate research on various themes of TODs (Addison et al., 2013; Aston et al., 2021; Crane, 2000; Ewing and Cervero, 2001, 2010; Handy, 2005; Holz-Rau and Scheiner, 2019; Ibraeva et al., 2020; Jamme et al., 2019;

Kasraian et al., 2016; Padeiro et al., 2019a; Stevens, 2017). These studies summarize important aspects of TODs but each focuses on only one aspect of TOD. Little attempt has been made to map out the entire field to determine if there is a trend in the type of research conducted in particular regions, collaborators and sources. This understanding is important as it may reveal gaps, biases, over- and under-researched topics; as well as the influence of particular sources and authors in the field. However, the review of an entire field of research has proven to be difficult in a qualitative way (e.g., by reading every document and extracting the overall patterns), which necessitates the application of a quantitative approach for review, such as bibliometric review.

Most traditional approaches review the substantive content of published articles (Aromataris and Munn, 2020; Grant and Booth, 2009; Wee and Banister, 2016). Unlike these traditional approaches, a bibliometric review uses the bibliographic data of a publication for review such as citations, journals, keywords, and authors (Jarneving, 2005). To the knowledge of the authors, no bibliometric review has been undertaken in the field of TOD to date. This chapter addresses this gap and explores bibliographic linkages of TOD research. It aims to:

1. Synthesize the vast body of literature on TOD to gain a bird's eye view of the filed;
2. Examine trends in publications and patterns of topics surrounding TOD research, revealing stage of maturity and growth in the field; and
3. Visualize the interrelationships among authors, topics, sources and geographies to understand their influence and importance in the field.

The remainder of this chapter is structured as follows. Sections 1.1 and 1.2 frame the rationale for conducting a bibliometric review of TOD research. Section 2 presents the steps followed to synthesize the TOD research field using bibliographic data. Section 3 presents visualizations of linkages organized according to four bibliographic unit/elements: keywords, authors, geography and sources. The patterns emerging for each element are discussed in turn. The final section summarizes the key insights produced through the bibliometric analysis.

1.1 Transit-oriented development: A brief history and research

The concept of transit-oriented communities was introduced as a planning idea with the potential to herald more sustainable community design for modern cities, in 1993, Peter Calthorpe's book "The Next American

Metropolis: Ecology, Communities, and the American Dream" (Calthorpe, 1993). Although the notion of integrating transport and the built environment was not new, Calthorpe's theory of community design aimed to improve regional growth, increase economic returns on transit investment, ameliorate social gaps and issues, and also reduce environmental impacts by providing transportation alternatives (Carlton et al., 2009). A similar ideology was shared by Ebenezer Howard at the turn of the 20th century, through the Garden City movement that focused on real-estate development with rail as primary connection between developed areas (arguably the concept did not consider a central location for the train stations). Auto-oriented transit arose in the United States in the 1960s, until research in the 1970s identified that land use intensification around rail gave rise to more benefits than the existing park-n-ride model (Parsons Brinckerhoff Quade and Douglas Inc et al., 1996).

The term "transit-oriented development" evolved from the notions of "transit-supportive development" and "development-oriented transit" (Carlton, 2009; Cervero, 1993). Key pillars of TOD, derived from Calthorpe's vision of the Next American Metropolis, were codified in New Transit Towns in the early 21st century (Dittmar and Ohland, 2004). Later, the notion of the land use determinants of travel demand, including density, diversity, design and afterwards destination accessibility, distance to transit and other "D" variables, have also been used to guide transit-oriented development (Cervero and Kockelman, 1997). This design concept has been adopted in many cities in order to leverage the concept of TOD in city plans, and thereby to enhance social, environmental, and economic benefits such as Sydney, Melbourne, Brisbane, Perth, Taipei, Seoul, Hong Kong, Jinan, Louisville, New York, Phoenix, San Francisco Bay Area, Los Angeles, San Diego, Denver, Copenhagen, Stockholm, Freiburg, Toronto, Portland, Vancouver, Montreal, and San Francisco (Kamruzzaman et al., 2016; Padeiro et al., 2019b). Nevertheless, the applied design principles are not identical in every city but are adopted based on local contextual factors including a variability in focused transport modes (rail, bus, corridors, ferries, and bicycle) (Bertolini, 1996; Cervero and Dai, 2014; Chorus and Bertolini, 2016; Lee et al., 2016; Sipe and Burke, 2011).

More recently, the need for TOD at a scale reflective of the areas that can be accessed by transit, has been recognized (Thorne-Lyman and Wampler, 2010). Liu et al. (2020) conceptualize the notion of corridor-level transit-oriented development (C-TOD) as planning that strives to optimize access and amenity in transit "travel-sheds," which are areas that can be reached by transit within a typical daily travel budget of 60–90 min. Where previously TOD has focused on pedestrian travel-sheds within reach of the transit as node (Bertolini, 1996; Ibraeva et al., 2020), focus has now shifted to regional-scale planning of TOD to capture its network effects (Renne et al., 2016). Transit corridors are considered appropriate units for TOD planning, since they present an opportunity to plan for transit-oriented mobility to destinations, within a pragmatic development boundary, which reduces implementation complexities (Chorus and Bertolini, 2016; Ferrell et al., 2016).

Despite repeated attempts, the realization of TODs remains a challenge and requires a deliberate shift in institutional context to overcome implementation barriers including financial, legal, and socio-cultural (Tan et al., 2014). Evidence from well-known TOD cases, such as Perth Metropolitan Region, Portland Metropolitan Area and Greater Vancouver Region, confirms that both formal and informal stakeholder engagement, incentives, utilization of workable project structures, private and public balance, resources, and market dynamics play a key role toward a successful realization of TODs (Hale and Charles, 2006). A successful implementation process ensures an effective development and delivery of multi-stakeholder TOD projects and includes four broad phases: literature review to gather information, formulation of step-by-step procedure, stakeholder research, and formative evaluation (Curtis, 2012).

A successful implementation of a TOD does not necessarily mean that the TOD would bring successful outcomes. The success of TODs in terms of outcomes depends on a multitude of factors, beyond transport and density. These include a rich mix of choices in housing, employment, and other services; and place-making in terms of community living and social cohesion (Jamme et al., 2019). This is due to the fact that residents choose TODs for living mainly for their diversity of housing options, neighborhood quality, access to shops and services; and transit is ranked fifth in that preference list (Handy, 2005; Lund, 2006). As a result, studies have identified a large number of dissonant residents in TODs—i.e., they live in TODs but do not use public transport, which goes against the goal of TOD planning (Cao, 2015; Kamruzzaman et al., 2015a; Phani Kumar et al., 2018). Nevertheless, ample studies have shown that TODs have been successful in achieving their intended goals—i.e., to promote the use of public transport services (Crowley et al., 2009; Kamruzzaman et al., 2013, 2015b; Lee et al., 2010; Renne, 2009), and increasing property value (Chen et al., 2019; Higgins and Kanaroglou, 2016a, 2018). Despite the benefits, studies have identified that the implementation of equitable and sustainable TODs is difficult in practice due to the complex partnerships and supportive zoning and design policies required (Wood, 2009).

1.2 Bibliometric analysis as a research synthesis method

Bibliometric analysis uses research bibliographies or citations to map scientific output within a specific field of research. It has its origins in citation indexing, which gave rise to the Science Citation Index (SCI) (Garfield, 1970). It has evolved to leverage advanced visualization and big data processing to classify and map different research fields under a discipline (Ellegaard and Wallin, 2015). The process identifies and quantifies the performance, research patterns and cooperation patterns of authors, journals, publications, countries and institutes (Guo et al., 2019). It also helps identify over- and under-researched topics in the field. Analysis conducted using these methods provide a valuable point of reference for entrants to a field of research, as well as researchers who may be keen to unpack the linkages and even biases in that field.

Bibliometric analysis has been used in many research fields, including different branches of transportation, to scope the literature and identify strengths or weaknesses of existing research. For example, a bibliometric analysis of intelligent transportation systems (ITS) research for the period of 1992–2011 evaluated the conceptual evolution of the various themes and topics under the subject (Cobo et al., 2014). The editors of the Journal of Transport Geography leveraged bibliometric analysis to understand the Journal's role relative to the wider literature at the intersection of the geographical and transport sciences (Derudder et al., 2019).

Many techniques are available for mapping bibliographic linkages in research (Leydesdorff, 1987). The approach used to build a bibliometric network affects the results (Leydesdorff, 1987; Perianes-Rodriguez et al., 2016). Two prevailing techniques include multi-dimensional scaling and Visualization of Similarities (van Eck et al., 2010). For more insight about the bibliometric review method, readers may wish to refer to. The next section briefly explains the approach used in this review to visualize bibliometric TOD research. Readers are referred to Garfield (1970), Jarneving (2005), Leydesdorff (1987) or Moed (2005) for further insight into bibliometric review.

2. Methodology

In this review chapter, we conducted a graphical review of the TOD literature based on the bibliometric data of 677 research outputs by using the

Visualization of Similarities technique (van Eck et al., 2010). These visualizations are produced using the VOSviewer software package (Centre for Science and Technology Studies, L.U, 2020). Bibliometric analysis follows a three-step methodology: gathering of bibliographic data, analyzing bibliographic data and visualizing bibliometric linkages. A brief explanation of these steps, as applied to this chapter, are explained below.

2.1 Gathering of bibliographic data

Unlike other review methods, a key strength of the bibliometric technique is its ability to synthesize all published literature related to a topic. As a result, it is important to identify a comprehensive body of research, but also to ensure it is relevant. This study gathered data from two sources, Scopus and Web of Science, to generate bibliographic database for analysis. The initial results were further refined by three limiting factors:

1. Document type: book, book chapter, journal, conference paper, review
2. Publication language: English
3. Publication date: January 1993–September 2020.

Table 1 outlines the search terms, limiters and results of the database search for the TOD literature. The 1993 was set as the initial search period because the TOD concept was first published in a study in this year (Calthorpe, 1993). A full bibliographic record (e.g., author, year, journal, keywords, abstract, institutions, cited references, etc.) for each of the selected research output were extracted from both sources. These two extracted datasets were then merged and duplicate records were removed from the merged dataset. A manual screening was then conducted to ensure that only studies with a core focus on TODs are included through a review of the abstract of the research outputs. This screening resulted in a total of 677 research outputs for analysis with a share of 75% journal articles, 21% conference papers, and 4% book chapters. The bibliographic records (e.g., author's name, publication title, etc.) of these 677 research outputs were then checked for consistency and corrected if necessary by trial and error. For example, the name of the same journal (source) was documented differently in different publications (documents) such as Transportation Research Part A—Policy and Practice, Transportation Research Part A: Policy and Practice, Transportation Research Part A, etc. A problem with this type of inconsistency is that, for example, if these variations in the source name were retained in the database, the analysis would consider them as different sources, and as a result, the overall influence of a source might not be captured properly.

Table 1 Data extraction process and results.

Database	Search identifier	Search field	Research outputs	Limiter	Refined research outputs
Scopus	("TOD") OR ("Transit-oriented development") OR ("Transit oriented development")	Title or Abstract or Keywords	4151	Language: English Documents Type: Article, Conference Paper, Review, Book Chapter, Book Time Period: 1993–2020	762
Web of Science Core Collection	("TOD") OR ("Transit-oriented development") OR ("Transit oriented development")	Topic	2990	Language: English Documents Type: Article, Proceeding Paper, Book, Book Chapter, Book Review, Review, Early Access Time Period: 1993–2020	504

2.2 Bibliometric analysis: Units and metrics

The term bibliometric refers to a quantitative study of bibliographic data. Bibliographic data can be analyzed in two ways: performance and scientific mapping (network). The performance analysis outlines both productivity (e.g., number of research outputs) and influence (number of citations) of a bibliographic unit (also referred to as item, node, or entity) (Merigó et al., 2018). An entity can be a keyword, a publication (document), an author, a source (journal/conference), an organization or a country (Broadus, 1987). Citation count, average citation rate and h-index are the three important measures to determine the influence of an entity in their field. Evidence suggests that citation-based metrics (influence) are superior to document counts for an understanding of the impact of a unit (Cole and Cole, 1967; Podsakoff et al., 2008).

A performance analysis is useful for identifying, for example:

(a) The knowledge status, structure, maturity and growth/trend of a research area;

(b) Who and where the researchers are that drive the field;

(c) Which journal is the most influential; and

(d) What kind of research is being conducted on a particular topic.

This bibliometric review uses performance mapping to produce a ranking of authors, publications, countries and journals based on both volume of productivity and citations. This provides insight to the authors, regions or sources that have had the greatest influence in shaping the concepts and methodology of the TOD field (Podsakoff et al., 2008). Keyword frequency is also examined to understand the most common language and themes used in the field. Their variations over time are also investigated to understand if the thematic focus of the field has shifted.

The network analysis, on the other hand, is based on links between nodes/entities. A link is said to be created if, for example:

- A paper is co-authored (co-authorship link);
- A paper is cited by another (citation link);
- Two papers are cited by another paper (co-citation link);
- Two papers cite another paper (bibliographic coupling link); or
- A keyword appears in two or more publications (co-occurrence link).

A combination of nodes and links forms a network—hence the name "network analysis." The network analysis is useful for understanding, for example: (a) the co-operative relationship between countries; (b) the cited relationship between authors; and (c) the most important and influential node.

The strength of a link can be quantified (positive numeric value) based on, for example:

- The number of cited references two publications have in common (bibliographic coupling);
- The number of publications two researchers have co-authored (co-authorship links); or
- The number of publications in which two keywords occur together (co-occurrence links).

Overall, four types of analysis techniques were applied in this study:

(a) Co-occurrences of keywords to understand various theme of TOD research and their dynamics;

(b) Bibliographic coupling to understand the underlying thematic structure of TOD research. This analysis complements the co-occurrence analysis conducted in this study.

(c) Productivity and citation analysis to outline the performance of different authors, documents, sources, and countries; and
(d) Co-authorship analysis to visualize the collaborative networks of authors and countries.

The definitions, interpretations, unit of analysis, and other parameters as applied in this study for these four types of analysis techniques are provided in Table 2.

2.3 Visualizing research linkages

The study utilized both traditional and bibliometric visualization techniques to present the study findings. Traditional techniques were employed to present findings from the performance analysis and included tables and charts. On the other hand, two types of graph-based bibliometric visualization techniques were employed to represent bibliometric networks: network visualization, and overlay visualization (van Eck et al., 2010). In all visualizations, the items/nodes are presented as circles, which are also labeled by their names (e.g., the name of an author/organization/country/source). The size of a label/circle is determined by its weight. Weights are typically assigned on the basis of the number of:

- occurrences of a keyword appear in different outputs;
- citations received by a document/author/country; and
- documents published (co-published) by an author/country, etc.

An overlay visualization presents an additional information (score) in addition to weights using different coloring schemes. Typical scores include:

- average citation of an author (in addition to total citation), and
- average publication year.

Different colors are also used in a network visualization; however, they represent the membership of different units into different groups (clusters). The different weights and scores used in each visualization are noted in Table 2.

Nodes are connected by lines in a network, which are referred to as links. The distance between two nodes represents their relatedness (van Eck et al., 2010). The closer the two nodes, the stronger their relatedness. The thickness of the line between two nodes represents the link strengths. The thicker the line, the stronger the link between two nodes. Clusters are formed on the basis of link strength, and are represented by proximity in a network. For example, the authors that are close to each other in a visualization tend to be strongly related (e.g., published research outputs have similar thematic focus) than authors that are located far away from each other.

Table 2 Definition and application of bibliometric techniques to review the TOD literature.[a]

Analysis techniques	Definition	Purpose and interpretation	Figure	Item/unit of analysis	Visualization method	Weights/ strengths	Score (average)
Co-occurrence analysis	Co-occurring keywords are those which are used together to describe the content of a document	Identify the most popular keywords and the themes in research	2, 3A, 3B	Keyword	Network and overlay	Occurrences	Average publication year, and average citation
Bibliographic coupling	A bibliographic coupling is a link between two documents that both cite the same document. The number of bibliographic coupling links between two documents is equal to the number of pairs of cited references in the two documents. The bibliographic coupling link can be aggregated at the author, source, organization and country levels	Identify coupling of research themes, high impact authors, life span of a paper	4	Document	Network	Citations	N/a
Citation analysis	A citation link between two items reflects how the work of an item is influenced by the work of another item. It estimates the linkage and proximity between two items, but not the direction of the citing link	Quantify the performance and influence of an item	5	Author	Network and overlay	Citations	Average publication year, and average citation
			6	Document	Network	Citations	publication year
			7	Source	Network	Citations	N/a
			–	Country	Overlay	Citations	Average publication year, and average citation
Co-authorship analysis	Co-authorship links are formed between authors, or the country with which they are affiliated, who co-author a document	Understand scientific collaboration patterns between authors or geographic regions	8	Authors	Network and overlay	Documents	Average citation
			9	Country	Network	Documents	N/a

[a]Summary of: Fonseca et al. (2016), Surwase et al. (2011), van Eck and Waltman (2010).

"Counting" is a key methodological consideration for building the networks. Counting refers to the way weights are assigned to references when dividing them among multiple keywords, authors or other bibliographic elements. "Full counting" assigns a weight of one to each unit—e.g., if there are five authors in a document, all five authors receive a weight of one (Perianes-Rodriguez et al., 2016). In fractional counting, the total weight of one is distributed among the different members associated with a unit—e.g., each author will receive a weight of 0.2 if there are five authors in a document. Under fractional counting, the weights in each network add to the number of documents, which aids interpretation and mitigates inconsistencies that may arise if weights are apportioned differently (Leydesdorff and Park, 2016). The fractional counting method was applied to all analyses presented in this chapter.

3. Results

3.1 Overall trend of research outputs on TODs

As described previously, this study identified 677 research outputs on TODs. Fig. 1 outlines the trend in the number of research outputs published on TODs per year. The earliest published document retrieved by the search was published in 1995. The number of outputs produced increased slightly in the first 10 years until 2005, and since then, the rate of publication increased rapidly, reached its peak in 2019 with 92 outputs. Overall, an increasing trend in research outputs on TODs is observed in this study. Note that the 2020 represents a fraction of total outputs produced in this period given that the search period ended in September.

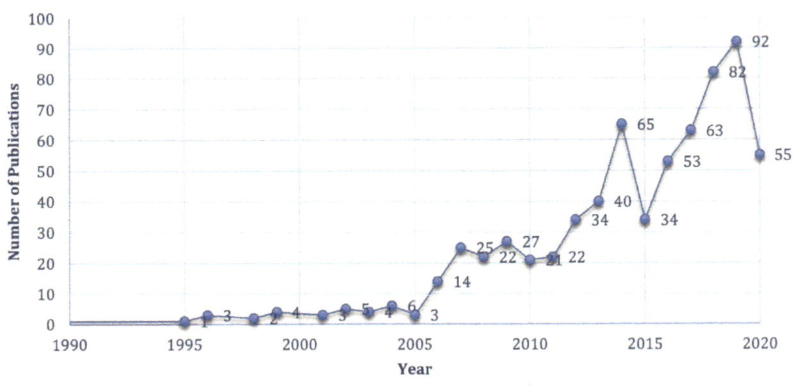

Fig. 1 Yearly publication rate of TOD research.

3.2 Knowledge structure in the TOD research field

The knowledge structure in TOD research is identified by examining the association of the 677 research outputs published in the TOD literature. An association between two documents is established when both documents have a high proportion of common keywords and citations (Meetham and Hudson, 1969). As a result, both the keywords and citations as used in the 677 documents are separately investigated with the aim of identifying a wide array of research themes that exist in the TOD literature.

3.2.1 Mapping research trends on TODs by co-occurrences of keywords

This section presents findings on the co-occurrence link of keywords—i.e., if a certain keyword was evident in two or more publications. Keyword co-occurrence has been considered as the main method of identifying research themes (Wang et al., 2017b). The analysis helped to identify the most popular keywords (themes) used in the TOD literature. The term TOD and its synonyms (e.g., transit-oriented development, transit oriented development) were excluded from this analysis because this was the fundamental inclusion criteria for the selected 677 research outputs. Notably, the most common synonym of TOD was found to be "transit-oriented development," which appeared 222 times in the keyword list; followed by "transit oriented development" (181 occurrences), and "TOD" (73 occurrences).

A total of 2935 keywords, including author keyword and index keyword, as used in the 677 research outputs were analyzed and visualized in a keyword co-occurrence network (Fig. 2). The network reflects the knowledge structure and displays the relationship between keywords (Lee and Su, 2010). In a keyword co-occurrence network, nodes represent keywords, while edges represent co-occurrence relationships among nodes. The co-occurrence analysis was conducted using 10 research outputs as a minimum threshold—i.e., a keyword must have used in at least 10 research outputs. This minimum threshold resulted in 82 eligible keywords for visualization and further analysis (Fig. 2).

The size of the circles in Fig. 2 represents the number of occurrences of each of the 82 keywords in the 677 documents. The bigger the circles, the more frequent the keywords appeared in the TOD literature. The distance between two keywords outlines their relative strength and topic similarity. The keywords are distinguished by four different colors (Red, Yellow, Green, and Blue) in Fig. 2, which suggest that they formed four different

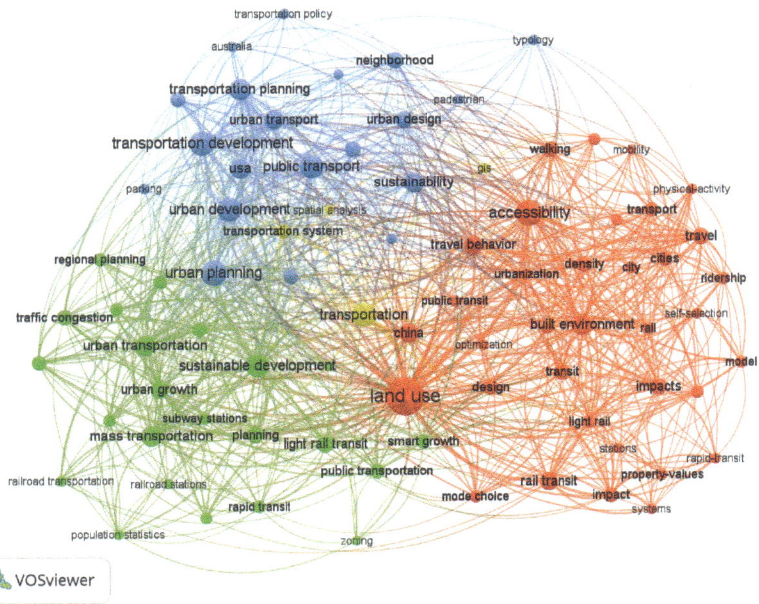

Fig. 2 Network visualization of keywords co-occurrence (weights = occurrences).

clusters—i.e., the associated research outputs have topic similarities and represent a subfield within the TOD field of research. Based on the frequently occurring keywords within each of the cluster as shown in Table 3, the four clusters can arguably be interpreted as: (a) Red—TOD design and outcomes; (b) Green—broader policy priorities and goals; (c) Blue—TOD planning; and (d) Yellow—analytic methods.

The largest (red) cluster includes keywords related to both the design of TODs (land use, built environment) and the outcomes of TODs such accessibility, impacts, walking, travel, and travel behavior (Fig. 2). The smallest (yellow) cluster includes four keywords, two of which clearly relate to analysis methods (spatial analysis and GIS). This cluster is located in close proximity to the other three clusters, suggesting the dependency of the Red, Green and Blue clusters on the analytic methods contained in Yellow cluster. Despite similarities in keywords between green and blue clusters; further investigation shows that the Blue cluster focuses more on TOD planning (e.g., urban planning, transportation planning, urban development, transportation development) whereas the Green cluster focuses on broader policy agendas associated with TODs such as sustainable development, mass transportation, urban growth, congestion, housing, and the economy.

Table 3 Description of co-occurring keyword clusters.

Cluster	Inferred theme	Total number of keywords within the cluster	Five most frequently used keywords	Occurrences	Links	Average publication year	Average citations
Red	TOD design and outcomes	35	Land use	154	79	2015.3	10.89
			Accessibility	70	71	2016.8	16.31
			Built environment	43	57	2016.3	11.91
			Travel behavior	35	54	2014.9	26.83
			Rail transit	33	58	2015.9	14.39
Green	Broader policy priorities and goals	23	Sustainable development	52	61	2015.4	12.73
			Mass transportation	44	54	2013.7	3.98
			Urban transportation	43	48	2016.4	2.26
			Urban growth	31	49	2016.6	7.77
			Light rail transit	29	47	2015.9	3.83
Blue	TOD planning	20	Urban planning	70	62	2012.6	15.09
			Transportation development	61	64	2015.8	19.13
			Urban development	60	63	2015.1	13.20
			Public transport	57	62	2015.4	10.05
			Transportation planning	47	56	2014.9	17.38
Yellow	Analysis method	4	Transportation	59	70	2014.9	17.88
			Transportation system	22	47	2015.4	13.82
			GIS	11	30	2016.2	8.64
			Spatial analysis	10	28	2016.4	6.70

Fig. 3A and B show the same keyword co-occurrences as shown in Fig. 2, but an overlay visualization technique was used to represent temporal dynamics in the occurrences of the keywords (3a) and to identify keywords associated with a higher (average) number of citations. Different colors were used to represent time-varying (from 2013 to 2017) and citation-varying (from 10 to 30) keyword occurrences in Fig. 3A and B, respectively.

A visual comparison between Figs. 2 and 3A indicates that the literature focusing on "TOD design and outcomes" (Red Cluster in Fig. 2) are relatively recent (yellow color in Fig. 3A). This is also evident in Table 3—average publication year ranges between 2015 and 2017 for the "TOD design and outcomes" cluster. In contrast, studies focusing on "TOD planning" (Blue cluster in Fig. 2) are relatively dated (more keywords with blue color in Fig. 3A). The average publication year of the frequently occurrence keywords ranges between 2012 and 2016 within this cluster (Table 3).

The average number of citations received by publications focusing on different topics of TODs are shown in Fig. 3B. Clearly research outputs having a focus on the most frequently occurring keyword (land use) were not cited the most. On average, studies focusing on land use received 11 citations (Table 3). The most cited publications had a focus on travel behavior with 27 citations on average, followed by transportation development (19 citations), transportation (18 citations), and transportation planning (17 citations). This does not necessarily mean that these publications were relatively dated, rather Fig. 3A and Table 3 shows that the average publication year of these studies was 2015. Interestingly, studies focusing on accessibility theme are relatively recent (2017) but received a higher rate of citation (16 citations on average).

3.2.2 Bibliographic coupling network

Kessler (1962) introduced the bibliographic coupling concept stating that "a number of scientific papers bear a meaningful relation to each other (they are coupled) when they have one or more references in common." The concept lies on the assumption that if two papers have common bibliographies, there is a possibility that their research focus is similar. The thematic relationship/focus increases with the increase in the number of common bibliographies between two papers (Wu et al., 2020). Fig. 4 shows the bibliographic coupling networks as derived in this study. The figure was prepared using only those research outputs (out of 677) that were cited at least 20 times in the TOD literature to ensure that the thematic patterns are extracted from the influential publications in the field. This resulted in 95 documents, which are visualized in Fig. 4.

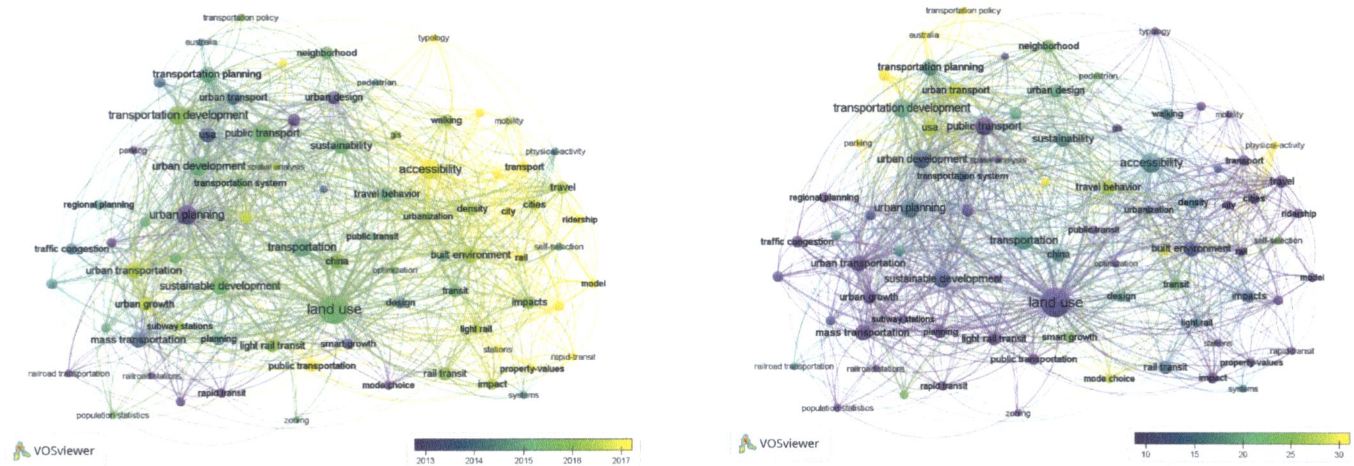

Fig. 3 Overlay visualization of keywords co-occurrence: (A) weights = occurrences, score = average publication per year; and (B) weights = occurrences, score = average citation.

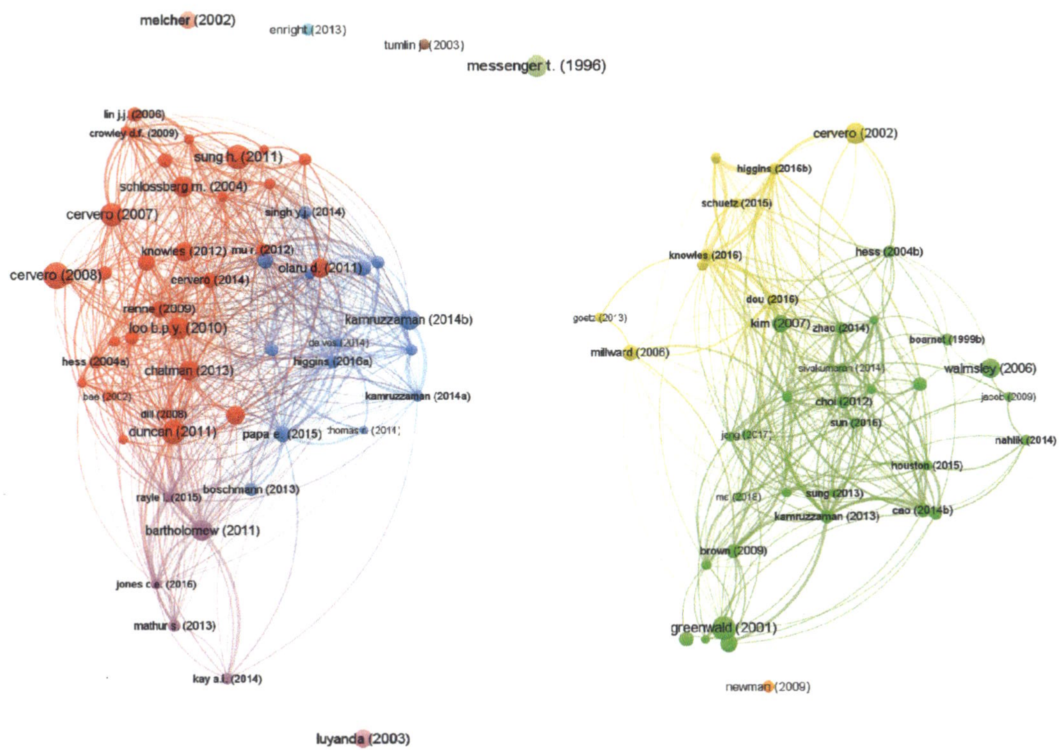

Fig. 4 Bibliographic coupling networks of TOD publications/documents (weight = citation). Note: The locations of the different clusters are adjusted to enhance visualization. The size of the circle is not to scale.

Fig. 4 shows that not all of the 95 documents are bibliographically coupled together. The largest and the second-largest sets of connected networks in Fig. 4, respectively consists of 51 and 36 documents. The remaining 6 documents are not bibliographically coupled at all with the remaining 94 documents as shown in the top and bottom of Fig. 4. There are two possible reasons for the disconnection between the two larger sets: (a) the documents that potentially bridge the two sets were omitted from the analysis—note that only documents with more than 20 citations are included; and (b) the two sets potentially focus on unique aspects of TOD research that they do not have common bibliographies.

The network visualization resulted in five major clusters, represented by different colors in Fig. 4. The different clusters illustrate the varied themes of TOD research, whereas the documents within a cluster have similar bibliographies. The largest cluster (Red) consists of 32 documents, focuses on the contextual effects of TODs such as suburbanization (Cervero and Day, 2008), New York vs Hong Kong (Loo et al., 2010), Copenhagen Finger Plan (Knowles, 2012), walkability level (Schlossberg and Brown, 2004). Cluster 2 (Green) is the second largest cluster with 29 documents where most studies are related to the design of TODs (built environment) and travel behavior outcomes. Within this cluster, for example: Greenwald and Boarnet (2001) examined the impact of the built environment on walking behavior; Walmsley (2006) emphasized to include greenways as part of TOD design; and Kim et al. (2007) examined travel behavior of light rail riders. Cluster 3 (Blue) is based on 14 document and focuses on the accessibility and typologies of TODs (Kamruzzaman et al., 2014a; Singh et al., 2017). Cluster 4 (Olive) comprises 9 documents with a focus on the economic effects of TODs including commercial values, land prices, and property values (Cervero and Duncan, 2002; Xu et al., 2016), and wider economic impact (Knowles and Ferbrache, 2016). Cluster 5 (Purple) contains 5 documents focusing on the social consequences of TODs such as displacement (Rayle, 2015), home values (Mathur and Ferrell, 2013), gentrification (Jones and Ley, 2016).

3.3 The best performing entities in the TOD literature

The performance of four different entities are analyzed in this study including author, document, source, and countries. The performance of these entities is measured in two ways: (a) by their productivity in terms of the number of documents they published; and (b) by their influence in terms of the number of citations they received.

3.3.1 The most productive authors in TOD research

A total of 1060 authors are linked (authored/co-authored) to the 677 research outputs published in the TOD literature. This means that these 1060 authors have at least one publication on TODs. Table 4 lists the most productive authors in the field. Despite the large number of authors involved in TOD research, very few, however, have published more than one documents. Table 4 shows that 908 authors have only one document and the remaining 152 authors (14.3%) have more than one documents. The researchers with the highest number of research outputs (10 in this case) are Luca Bertolini, Carey Curtis, and John Renne; followed by Robert Ewing, Md Kamruzzaman, and Robert Cervero with 7 research outputs. Andrew Allan and Robert Noland have published six documents, followed by Lei Zhang and Gavin Turrell with five documents. This means that only 10 authors have five or more publications in the field.

3.3.2 The most influential researchers in the TOD literature

The most influential authors were visualized in a network of authors connected by citation (Fig. 5). The network was constructed based on authors

Table 4 Rate of TOD publications by author.

N: Number of publications ("documents")	Authors reaching threshold	Number of authors with exactly N number of publications	Name of the authors
1	1060	908	–
2	152	103	–
3	49	28	–
4	21	11	–
5	10	2	Zhang, L.; Turrell, G.
6	8	2	Allan, A.; Noland, R.B.
7	6	3	Ewing, R.; Kamruzzaman, M.; Cervero, R.
10	3	3	Bertolini, L.; Curtis, C.; Renne, J.L.

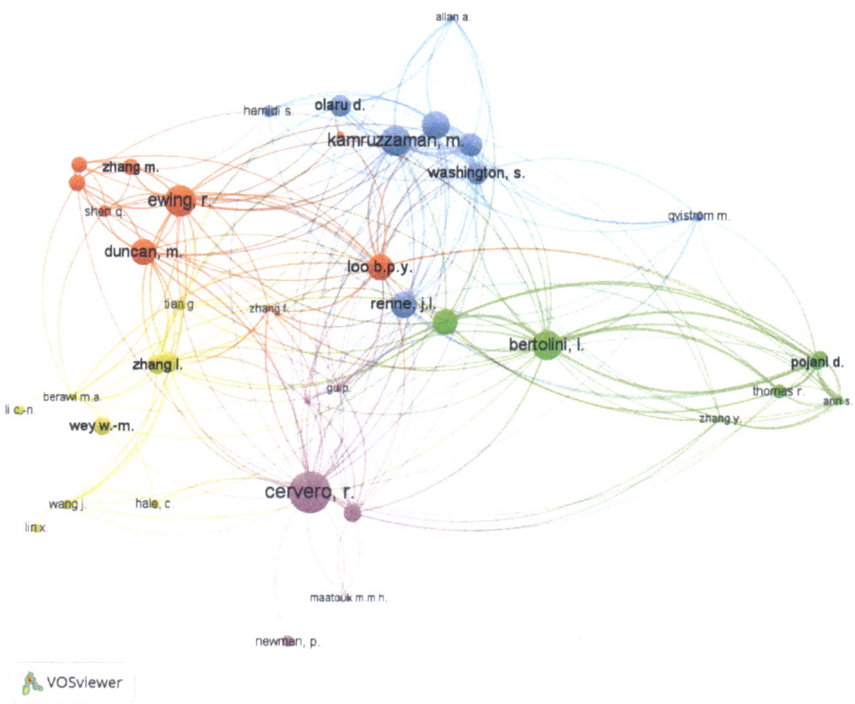

Fig. 5 Network visualization of authors' citation: weights = number of citations.

with at least 3 publications, which qualified 49 authors (nodes) to form the network. However, 6 of these authors were not connected to the main networks of 43 nodes, and as a result, they were excluded from this analysis.

Fig. 5 shows that the authors are grouped into five clusters. The size of the circle represents the number of times that each author is cited in the TOD literature.[a] Among the most productive authors as listed in Table 4 (based on article count), a number of them were identified to have similar sub-fields as shown in the five-cluster solution in Fig. 5. The clusters represent the authors that are closely linked by citation (without knowing who is cited by whom). As shown in Fig. 5, the central nodes in terms of the number of citations of the five clusters are: Robert Ewing in Cluster 1 (Red); Luca Bertolini in Cluster 2 (Green); Md Kamruzzaman in Cluster 3 (Blue); Lei Zhang in Cluster 4 (Yellow); and Robert Cervero

[a] The citation count refers to the number of times each entity (e.g., author, publication) is cited within the 677 documents analyzed in this study. An author may have received more citations than the one reported in this study because their works might have cited in many other fields beyond TOD. The intent here is to identify the entity with the most influence in the TOD literature, not in other fields.

in Cluster 5 (Purple). The findings point to the fact that the citation in TOD literature have a strong focal bias—i.e., citation is cluster dependent.

Table 5 shows the top 10 highly cited authors in the TOD literature. Clearly, Robert Cervero has a greater influence in the field with 422 citations, followed by Robert Ewing (288 citations), Md Kamruzzaman (211 citations), and Luca Bertolini (208 citations). They are also the cluster leaders as shown in Fig. 5. Despite leading the Cluster 4, Lei Zhang was not found to be listed among the highly cited authors in the field. It appears that there is a strong correlation between the most productive researchers as shown in Table 4 and the most influential researchers as shown in Table 5. Among the top 10 cited authors as listed in Table 5, only three of them are not named in Table 4 (highlighted bold). The USA, Australia, the Netherlands, and China were the home of these most influential authors in the TOD field. Also noticeable from Table 5 is that the influential authors are a mix of experienced (Robert Cervero, Carey Curtis) and young researchers as captured in their average publication year.

3.3.3 The most influential document in TOD research

To identify the influential documents in TOD research, the 677 research outputs are visualized in a network (Fig. 6). This network visualization also enables to identify the group of documents that have citation interdependency as captured in the 11 clusters in Fig. 6. The analysis was refined with documents that have at least 20 citations, which qualified 96 documents for inclusion. However, 18 of these documents are not connected to the broader citation networks. These are excluded and the remaining 78 documents are shown in Fig. 6 with their citation network. To visualize with clarity, only the first author's name and year of publication is displayed in Fig. 6, rather than the title of the document. However, a full reference to these documents is provided at the end.

Table 6 lists the 15 most cited papers in the TOD literature. A comparison between Tables 5 and 6 shows that 70% of the top cited authors have at least one top cited document. They are: Robert Cervero, Robert Ewing, Md Kamruzzaman (and his co-author Gavin Turrell, and Douglas Baker), Michael Duncan, and Becky Loo. Robert Cervero is the only top cited author with more than one (3) top cited papers (Table 6). The remaining three authors became a top cited author probably because they have more documents (Luca Bertolini, John Renne, and Carey Curtis) with an average citation rate per document as shown in Table 5.

Table 5 Most cited authors in the TOD literature with average publication year, country and cluster membership.

Rank	Authors	Number of documents	Total citation	Average citation	Average publication year	Cluster	Country
1	Robert Cervero	7	422	60.29	2010	5: Purple	USA
2	Robert Ewing	7	288	32.57	2013	1: Red	USA
3	Md Kamruzzaman	7	211	30.14	2015	3: Blue	Australia
4	Luca Bertolini	10	208	20.80	2014	2: Green	The Netherlands
5	Gavin Turrell	5	187	37.40	2015	3: Blue	Australia
6	John Renne	10	162	16.20	2012	3: Blue	USA
7	**Becky Loo**	4	157	39.25	2013	1: Red	China
8	**Michael Duncan**	4	156	39.00	2014	1: Red	USA
9	Carey Curtis	10	142	14.20	2011	2: Green	Australia
10	**Douglas Baker**	3	123	41.00	2015	3: Blue	Australia

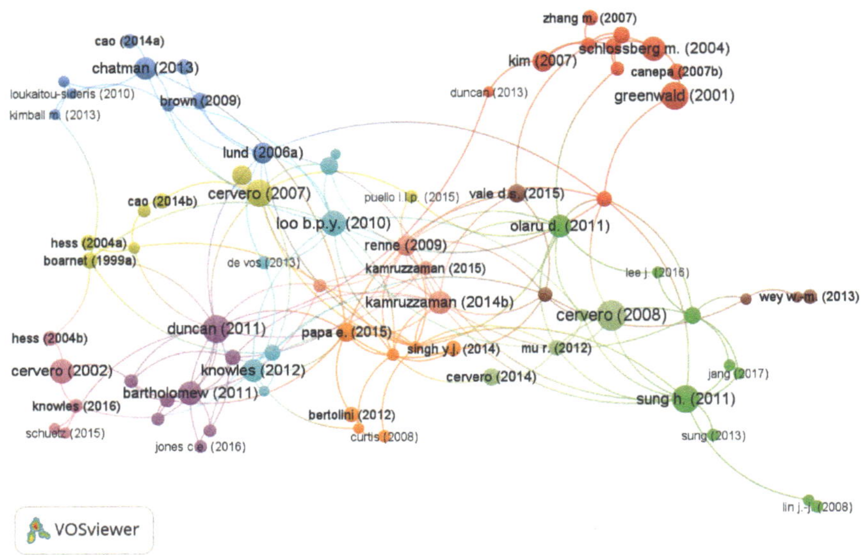

Fig. 6 Network visualization of the influential documents in the TOD literature (weights = citations). The citation of the listed documents are: (Atkinson-Palombo and Kuby, 2011; Bae, 2002; Bartholomew and Ewing, 2011; Bertolini et al., 2012; Boarnet and Compin, 1999; Boschmann and Brady, 2013; Brown and Werner, 2008; Canepa, 2007; Cao and Cao, 2014; Cao and Schoner, 2014; Cervero, 2007; Cervero and Dai, 2014; Cervero and Day, 2008; Cervero and Duncan, 2002; Cervero and Sullivan, 2011; Chakour and Eluru, 2016; Chatman, 2013; Choi et al., 2012; Curtis, 2008; De Vos and Witlox, 2013; De Vos et al., 2014; Dill, 2008; Dou et al., 2016; Duncan, 2011; Duncan and Christensen, 2013; Goetz, 2013; Greenwald and Boarnet, 2001; Hess and Lombardi, 2004; Higgins and Kanaroglou, 2016a,b; Houston et al., 2015; Jang et al., 2017; Jones and Ley, 2016; Kamruzzaman et al., 2013, 2014a,b, 2015b; Kay et al., 2014; Kim et al., 2007; Kimball et al., 2013; Knowles, 2012; Knowles and Ferbrache, 2016; Lee et al., 2013, 2016; Lin and Gau, 2006; Lin and Shin, 2008; Loo et al., 2010; Loo and du Verle, 2017; Loukaitou-Sideris, 2010; Lund, 2006; Lyu et al., 2016; Ma et al., 2018; Mathur and Ferrell, 2013; Mu and de Jong, 2012; Nahlik and Chester, 2014; Nasri and Zhang, 2014; Olaru et al., 2011; Papa and Bertolini, 2015; Puello and Geurs, 2015; Rayle, 2015; Renne, 2009; Schlossberg and Brown, 2004; Schuetz, 2015; Singh et al., 2014, 2017; Sivakumaran et al., 2014; Sun et al., 2016; Sung et al., 2013; Sung and Oh, 2011; Thomas and Bertolini, 2014; Vale, 2015; Wey et al., 2016; Wey and Chiu, 2013; Zhang, 2007; Zhao et al., 2013).

The paper, entitled Suburbanization and transit-oriented development in China, by Cervero and Day (2008) is the most cited document in the TOD literature (Table 6). Sung and Oh (2011) and Greenwald and Boarnet (2001) are the second and third most cited documents, respectively. However, none these authors were listed as a top cited author in Table 5. The number of citations they received in their single document (141 and 140) are greater than the total number of citations received by Douglas

Table 6 Fifteen most cited papers in the TOD research field.

Rank	Title	Author	Year	Journal	Top TOD source?[a]	Citations	Country
1	Suburbanization and transit-oriented development in China	Cervero and Day (2008)	2008	Transport Policy	Y	167	USA
2	Transit-oriented development in a high-density city: identifying its association with transit ridership in Seoul, Korea	Sung and Oh (2011)	2011	Cities	Y	141	South Korea
3	Built environment as determinant of walking behavior: analyzing nonwork pedestrian travel in Portland, Oregon	Greenwald and Boarnet (2001)	2001	Transportation Research Record	Y	140	USA
4	The impact of transit-oriented development on housing prices in San Diego, CA	Duncan (2011)	2011	Urban Studies	Y	137	USA
5	Transit-oriented development's ridership bonus: a product of self-selection and public policies	Cervero (2007)	2007	Environment and Planning A	N	133	USA
6	Rail-based transit-oriented development: lessons from New York City and Hong Kong	Loo et al. (2010)	2010	Landscape and Urban Planning	Y	119	Hong Kong
7	Transit's value-added effects: light and commuter rail services and commercial land values	Cervero and Duncan (2002)	2002	Transportation Research Record	Y	108	USA
8	Hedonic price effects of pedestrian- and transit-oriented development	Bartholomew and Ewing (2011)	2011	Journal of Planning Literature	N	105	USA
9	Comparing transit-oriented development sites by walkability indicators	Schlossberg and Brown (2004)	2004	Transportation Research Record	Y	102	USA

Continued

Table 6 Fifteen most cited papers in the TOD research field.—cont'd

Rank	Title	Author	Year	Journal	Top TOD source?[a]	Citations	Country
10	Advance transit-oriented development typology: case study in Brisbane, Australia	Kamruzzaman et al. (2014a)	2014	Journal of Transport Geography	Y	97	Australia
11	Greenways: multiplying and diversifying in the 21st century	Walmsley (2006)	2006	Landscape and Urban Planning	Y	94	USA
12	Does TOD need the T?	Chatman (2013)	2013	Journal of the American Planning Association	Y	93	USA
13	Residential location and transit-oriented development in a new rail corridor	Olaru et al. (2011)	2011	Transportation Research Part A: Policy and Practice	N	92	Australia
14	Transit Oriented Development in Copenhagen, Denmark: From the Finger Plan to Ørestad	Knowles (2012)	2012	Journal of Transport Geography	Y	89	United Kingdom
15	Reasons for Living in a Transit-Oriented Development, and Associated Transit Use	Lund (2006)	2006	Journal of the American Planning Association	Y	80	USA

[a]See Table 8 for a list of the top cited sources for TOD articles.

Baker, the tenth most cited author listed in Table 5. This is due to not meeting the inclusion criterion of "at least 3 publications" for these authors. 12 out of the 15 top cited documents have been published more than 10 years ago. The most recent article that is listed in the top 15 citation category has been published in 2014 (Kamruzzaman et al., 2014a).

The 11 clusters are: Cluster 1 (Red, on the top right)—contains 11 papers focusing on Greenwald and Boarnet (2001) and Schlossberg and Brown (2004); Cluster 2 (Dark Green on the bottom right)—contains 9 documents focusing on (Sung and Oh, 2011) and (Olaru et al., 2011); Cluster 3 (Blue on the top left)—contains 9 papers focusing on (Chatman, 2013) and (Lund, 2006); Cluster 4 (Olive on the middle left)—contains 8 documents focusing on (Cervero, 2007); Cluster 5 (Violet on the bottom left)—contains 8 papers focusing on (Duncan, 2011) and (Bartholomew and Ewing, 2011); Cluster 6 (Aqua/Cyan in the middle)—contains 7 papers focusing on (Loo et al., 2010) and (Knowles, 2012); Cluster 7 (Orange on the center)—contains 7 documents focusing on (Papa and Bertolini, 2015); Cluster 8 (Brown on the upper middle)—contains 5 documents focusing on (Vale, 2015); Cluster 9 (Pink on the bottom left)—contains 5 items focusing on (Cervero and Duncan, 2002); Cluster 10 (Peach on the center)—contains 4 documents focusing on (Kamruzzaman et al., 2014a); and Cluster 11 (Light Green on the middle right)—contains 4 items focusing on (Cervero and Day, 2008). Papa and Bertolini (2015) and Vale (2015) are the only two papers that become the center of Orange, and Brown clusters, respectively but not listed as a top cited paper in Table 6. The cluster analysis identifies the lead document of each cluster and prevalent topics. As depicted in Fig. 6, there are 11 main citation networks centered on (mostly) the top cited documents listed in Table 6.

3.3.4 The most productive and influential sources in TOD research

The 677 research outputs were published in 272 different sources. The performance of these sources is measured by both the number of documents they published and the number of times these sources are citied. Tables 7 and 8, respectively show the top 15 productive and top 15 influential sources of the TOD literature. A network visualization of these sources is provided in Fig. 7. The figure shows how closely the different sources are related to each other in terms of citations (e.g., how many times Journal A cites Journal B or vice-verse). The visualization was conducted using only those sources that have at least five publications. Only 26 sources met the criterion.

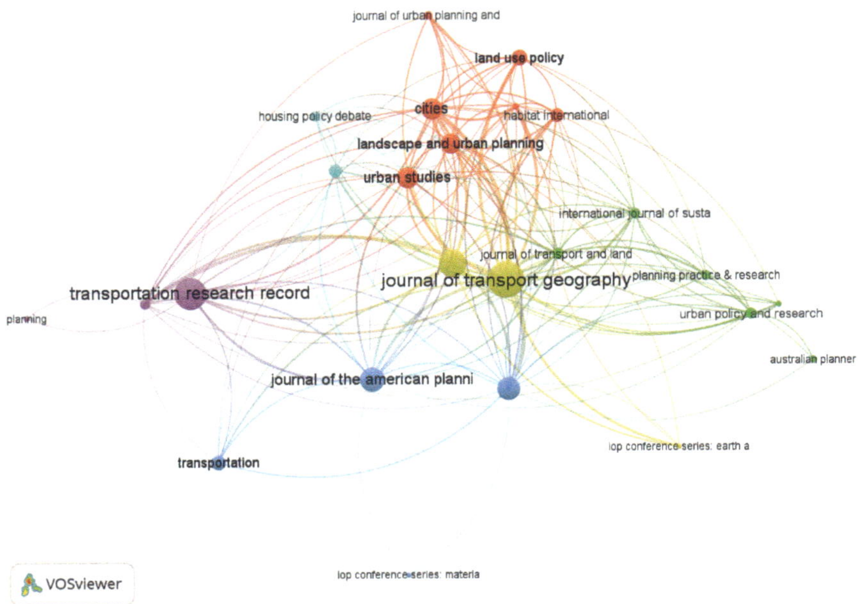

Fig. 7 Citation networks of sources (weight = citations).

Among them one source (Transit Oriented Development: Making it Happen) was not connected to the main network. This source is not visualized in Fig. 7.

Table 7 clearly shows that the two most productive sources of TOD research are Transportation Research Record (49 documents) and Journal of Transport Geography (40 documents). These two sources also have the greatest influence in the field in terms of the total number of citations they received. Transport Policy maintained its third position both in terms of the number of documents it produced (20) and the number of citations these documents received (522). A comparison between Tables 7 and 8 shows that there is a clear association between productivity of sources and their influence. Twelve of the 15 sources appear in both tables. It is also notable that some sources produced many documents but were not able to attract enough citations to be listed in the top 15 influential sources. This is particularly the case when a TOD paper is published in a conference proceeding (IOP conference, Australasian Transport Research Forum). Interestingly, there are few sources that have not published a higher number of documents, but each of the documents publish in these sources have the greatest influence in the TOD literature on average (e.g., Journal of the American Planning Association, Landscape and Urban Planning, Urban Studies).

Table 7 Top 15 productive sources in the TOD research field.

Rank	Source	Number of articles published
1	Transportation Research Record	49
2	Journal of Transport Geography	40
3	Transport Policy	20
4	IOP Conference Series: Earth and Environmental Science	20
5	Cities	19
6	Journal of Planning Education and Research	17
7	Journal of Transport and Land Use	14
8	Sustainability (Switzerland)	14
9	Transportation Research Part A	12
10	Australasian Transport Research Forum	12
11	Transit Oriented Development: Making it Happen	12
12	Urban Studies	11
13	Journal of The American Planning Association	10
14	Land Use Policy	9
15	Journal of Urban Planning and Development	9

The cluster analysis results as shown in Fig. 7 show that there are close citation enclaves among the top 15 influential sources. For example, Journal of Transport Geography and Journal of Transport and Land Use have close citation link. Similarly, Landscape and Urban Planning, Urban Studies, Cities, Land Use Policy, and Habitat International formed a citation cluster. Transportation Research Record is the dominant source with a little contribution from Transportation Research Part D of the Purple cluster, meaning that there is a strong self-citation link among the documents published in this journal.

3.3.5 The most productive and influential countries in TOD research

Table 9 lists the top 10 productive countries of TOD research in the world in terms of the number of documents originated from these countries. It also

Table 8 Top 15 cited sources in the TOD research field.

Rank	Source	Number of citations	Number of documents	Average citation
1	Journal of Transport Geography	914	40	22.85
2	Transportation Research Record	739	49	15.08
3	Transport Policy	522	20	26.10
4	Journal of the American Planning Association	396	10	39.60
5	Urban Studies	350	12	26.64
6	Cities	292	19	15.37
7	Landscape and Urban Planning	254	8	31.75
8	Land Use Policy	157	9	17.44
9	Transportation	153	7	21.86
10	Journal of Planning Education and Research	116	17	6.82
11	Habitat International	114	8	14.25
12	Transit Oriented Development: Making it Happen	97	12	8.08
13	Urban Policy and Research	84	7	12.00
14	Journal of Transport and Land Use	77	14	5.50
15	International Journal of Sustainable Transportation	76	8	9.50

outlines their influence in terms of the number of citations these documents received and average publication year of the countries. Clearly, the USA is leading the field not only by the number of research outputs it has produced (206) but also the number of citations these documents received (3505). On average, each document originated from the USA received 17 citations. Despite China is one of the top producers of TOD research outputs (126), they have little influence in the field with 5.6 citations per document. Australia, the Netherlands, South Korea have produced a moderate number of research outputs in TOD research field. Likewise, they have a moderate influence in the field as shown in their citation impacts in Table 9. Despite

Table 9 Most productive and cited countries in the TOD literature with average publication year.

Rank	Country	Number of documents	Total citation	Average citation	Average publication year
1	USA	206	3505	17.01	2013
2	China	126	705	5.60	2015
3	Australia	69	639	9.26	2013
4	Indonesia	40	33	0.82	2019
5	The Netherlands	36	478	13.28	2016
6	South Korea	30	436	14.53	2015
7	Canada	29	362	12.48	2015
8	Japan	21	91	4.33	2014
9	UK	20	258	12.90	2016
10	India	19	24	1.26	2018

Indonesia and India are among the top producer of research outputs, they have negligible impact on the field, perhaps due to their late involvement in TOD research.

3.4 Research cooperation/collaborative between different entities in the TOD literature

3.4.1 The collaborative networks of the authors of TOD publication

The co-authorship network was visualized to understand how different authors in the field of TOD collaborate/cooperate with each other. The investigation was conducted using authors with at least two research outputs which resulted in a total of 152 authors for analysis and is visualized in Fig. 8. The results show that there are many small clusters of co-authorship networks among the 152 authors, which mean that most of the authors were either working without any collaboration or even if they did, the size of their collaborative network is small. The largest connected co-authorship network comprised of 21 authors, located in the central part of Fig. 8. The main authors comprising this network include Carey Curtis, Luca Bertolini, John Renne, Robert Ewing, Dominic Stead, Dorina Pojani, Doina Olaru, R Thomas, S Hamidi, and G Tian. In addition, there are

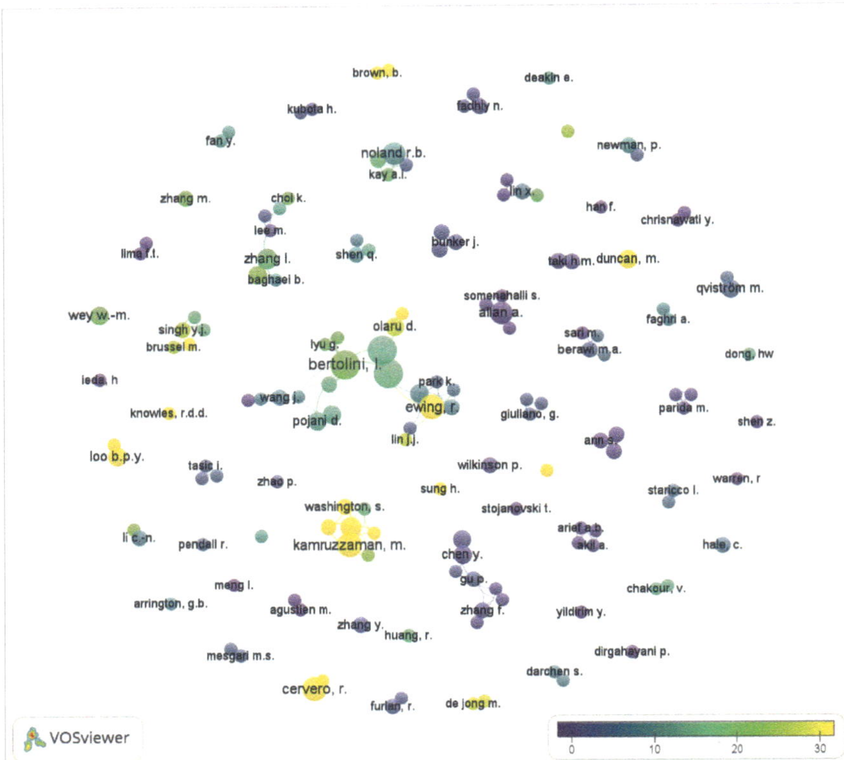

Fig. 8 Overlay visualization of co-authorship network (weights = documents, score = average citation).

few clusters of connected networks with seven or more authors and the central node of these networks are: (a) Md Kamruzzaman with Gavin Turrell, Douglas Baker, Simon Washington, Julian Hine, Farjana Shatu, and Billie Giles-Corti; (b) Y Wang with Y Chen, Y Jiang, Y Yang, J Zhou, F Zhang, J Zhang, and P Gu; (c) L Zhang with A Nasri, K Choi, M Lee, S Lee, J Lee, B Baghaei.

The size and color of the circles in Fig. 8, respectively represent the number of documents published by the authors and the average number of citations these publications received. Clearly, the number of documents form an important nexus between all the co-authors in the network as evident in the central cluster in Fig. 8. John Renne, Carey Curtis, Luca Bertolini, and Robert Ewing are the top most publishing authors within this cluster. Similarly, Md Kamruzzaman, Gavin Turrell, and Douglas Baker are the top publishers in the field. They have also attracted a high number of citations on average. Interestingly, Robert Cervero, Becky Loo, and Michael Duncan do not have a strong collaborative network, yet they have a higher citation rate on average.

3.4.2 The collaborative networks of countries in the field of TOD research

The collaborative networks of countries publishing TOD research are visualized in Fig. 9. The analysis is based on countries that have published at least 5 research outputs, which resulted in 23 countries for comparison. However, one country (Qatar) was found not to be connected with the remaining 22 countries—i.e., the authors from Qatar do not have co-authors from other countries. This finding also suggests that some degree of collaboration exists among the remaining 22 countries. This does not

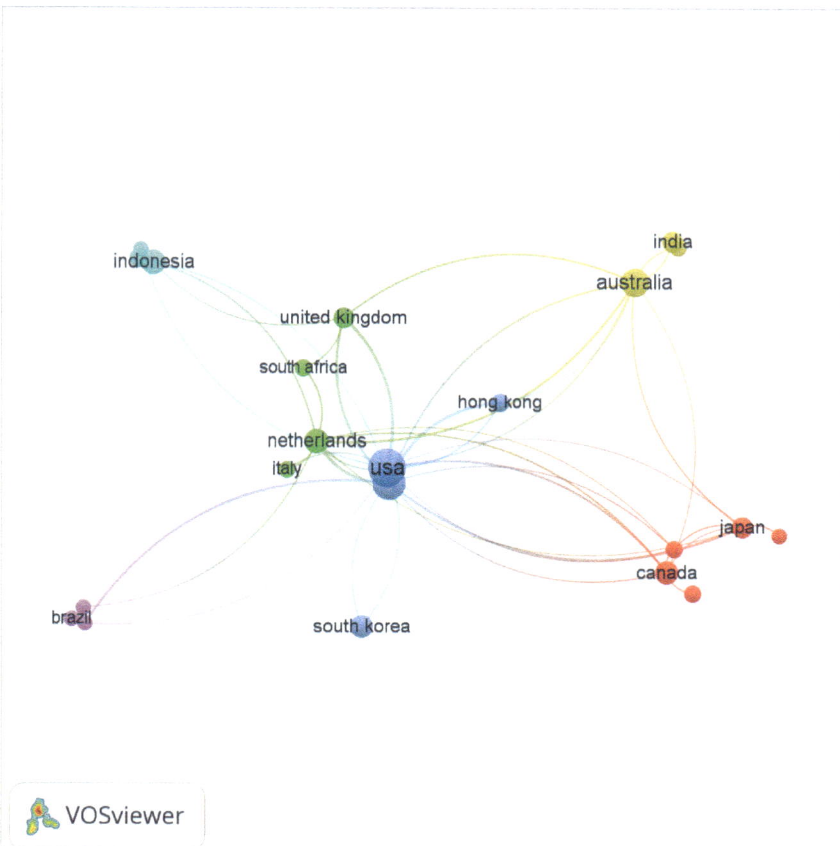

Fig. 9 Co-authorship networks of countries (weights = documents).

necessarily mean that all these 22 countries have a one-to-one collaboration, but may exist an indirect collaboration via co-authors located in a third country.

Fig. 9 shows that the co-authorship analysis of the 22 countries resulted in 6 clusters, which mean that some countries are linked closely in co-authorship compared to other countries. The size of the circles in Fig. 9 represents the number of documents these countries have produce (see also Table 9). Clearly, there is a strong co-authorship link between the USA and China, the top two publishing countries of TOD research. These two countries are located centrally in Fig. 9, which suggests that they act as a gateway having a direct link with almost every country. The green cluster comprises three European countries and South Africa, which is closely linked to the Netherlands. Australia has a stronger collaborative tie with India and Iran, and some weak links with the Netherlands and United Kingdom. India and Iran have a direct co-authorship link with only Australia (single-country link). France and Thailand also have a direct single-country link with Canada and Japan, respectively. The remaining 18 countries have a direct link with more than one country.

4. Discussion and conclusions

Transit oriented development (TOD) is one of the most influential neighborhood planning concepts, reflected by its acceptability and inclusion in city plan documents across the world (Kamruzzaman et al., 2016). The popularity of this concept in the policy arena, as a key response to urban sprawl, encourages many researchers to study TODs. The field has been maturing nearly 30 years now with hundreds of research outputs. However, to the knowledge of the authors, little attempt has been made to study the research field in its entirety in terms of what specific aspects of TODs were the focus of the researchers to study, which entities are driving the field with greater productivity and influence, and if a concerted effort is made by the entities to progress the field of research. This chapter is an attempt to address these gaps in the literature.

The research on TODs is maturing and enriching slowly but arguably at a comparable speed with other research fields in transportation and/or planning. The study found 677 research outputs on TODs since its inception in 1993. In a similar field, Wu et al. (2020) found 738 eligible research outputs on transport mode choice behavior in their bibliometric analysis. An increasing trend in publications on TODs was evident, which signifies an increasing research popularity of this neighborhood planning concept. It is likely that the upward trend will continue over some time given that 908 authors (about 86% of the total) have just begun publication on TODs with one output till now.

Broadly, the TOD research field has been evolved on nine thematic areas. Keywords reflect the core content of a publication (Xiang et al., 2017). Four themes were identified through an analysis of co-occurrence of keywords. These are: (a) TOD design and outcome; (b) broader policy priorities and goal of TODs; (c) TOD planning; and (d) Analytical methods in TOD research. The bibliometric coupling analysis identified five thematic structure of TOD research including: (a) Contextual effects of TODs; (b) TOD design and travel behavior outcome; (c) accessibility and typology of TODs; (d) economic effects of TODs; and (e) social impacts of TODs. These two types of analyses, therefore, complement our understanding of the underlying structure of TOD research. For example, the co-occurrence analysis identifies the "TOD design and outcome" theme, whereas the bibliographic coupling analysis reveals that such a broader theme can be sub-divided into various types of outcomes, e.g., economic, social effects, and travel. Both types of analyses also reveal unique theme which otherwise would not be possible to discern, e.g., TOD planning in the co-occurrence analysis and TOD typology in the bibliographic coupling analysis. The findings also show that the focus of investigation is a dynamic process with TOD design and outcome being the most recent focus.

TOD research outputs with the most frequently used keywords (e.g., land use) do not necessarily attract more citation, rather studies that focused on TOD outcomes were highly cited on average. The frequently used keywords reflecting the outcomes of TODs included "accessibility" and "travel behavior." Accessibility refers to the ability of people to access destination with relative ease. TODs are thought of a promoter of accessibility. On the other hand, travel behavior can be measured in many ways. However, in the TOD literature, travel behavior is mostly measured by mode choice behavior. Other outcomes of TODs, such as active transport and associated physical and mental health, equity, and affordability, were not found to be used frequently, suggesting a limited research on these topics (Sun et al., 2018).

Researchers often used very generic terms as a keyword to describe their studies (e.g., urban planning)—i.e., they do not reflect a specific focus/theme of research. The appearance of the word "urban" in frequently used keywords (e.g., urban planning, urban development, urban transportation, urban growth), as shown in Table 3, reflects a limited application of TOD research in a rural setting. An appearance of "public transport" as a keyword corroborates with the main goal of TODs—"to create settings which prompt people to drive less and ride public transit more" (Cervero et al., 2004, p. 8). Accordingly, keywords like "land use," "transportation development," "urban development," "sustainable development" and "built environment" reflect the notion of "settings" to promote public transport.

The performance analysis of TOD research entities (author, publication, source, country) shows that the two components of performance, productivity and influence, have a high degree of association. Although the causal direction is not known, the findings generally show that: (a) the most influential researchers (e.g., highly cited) have generally more research outputs such as Robert Cervero, Robert Ewing, Md Kamruzzaman, Luca Bertolini, John Renne, Carey Curtis; (b) the most influential sources (e.g., Journal of Transport Geography, Transportation Research Record, Transport Policy) produced more research outputs; and (c) more research outputs were generated from the most influential countries (USA).

Although the most influential authors generally have more research outputs, our investigation shows that additionally the authors usually have at least one influential publication to be the most influential. For example, Lei Zhang, Andrew Allan, and Robert Noland have been identified as one of the most productive authors, but they were not recorded in the top 10 influential author list. In contrast, Becky Loo, Michael Duncan and Douglas Baker were not identified as one of the most productive authors, but they are ranked within the top 10 influential author list because they have one influential document in the field. About 70% of the top cited authors have at least one top cited document.

Robert Cervero was identified as the most influential author in the TOD field. One of his publications, *Suburbanization and transit-oriented development in China*, was also identified to be the most influential document in the field, published in Transport Policy journal in 2008. Nevertheless, a lack of productivity and a lack of influence of authors do not restrict them to publish one of the highly influential documents in the field. Ample examples were evident in this study to show that researchers with overall low productivity and influence have authored one of the highly influential documents in the field, such as Michael Greenwald, Marlon Boarnet, Cynthia Chen, Eric Chan, Keith Bartholonew, Marc Schlossberg, Nathaniel Brown, Simon Washington, Anthony Walmsley, Daniel Chatman, Doina Olaru, Brett Smith, John Taplin, Richard Knowles, and Hollie Lund.

The influence of a TOD document increases with time, but the overall influence of authors is not determined by their maturity in TOD research. Our investigation found that most of the highly influential documents were published at least 10 years ago, with the exception of a document, *Advance transit-oriented development typology: case study in Brisbane, Australia*, published by Kamruzzaman et al. (2014a) in the Journal of Transport Geography in 2014. In contrast, the average publication year data of the most influential authors show that they have a wide range of variations in years of their TOD publication (Table 5), suggesting a mix of experience of authors in TOD research.

The Journal of Transport Geography forms the intellectual base of the TOD research field. It acts as a citation hub for articles published in other journals; which may be owing to its co-evolution with the concept of transit-oriented development. Interestingly, there are few sources that have not published a higher number of documents, but each of the documents published in these sources have the greatest influence in the TOD literature on average (e.g., Journal of the American Planning Association, Landscape and Urban Planning, Urban Studies).

The production of influential TOD research by affluent countries (USA, Australia, the Netherlands, UK, Japan, Canada) is consistent with western hegemony in the transport field (Derudder et al., 2019; Schwanen, 2018). The spatial balance of knowledge production in the field of TOD remains fairly constant over time, with only a slight trend toward more contributions from Global South countries (India, Indonesia) in more recent years. Schwanen (2017) suggests that a trend toward greater representation of the global south in transport knowledge production and influence, referred to as the decolonization of knowledge, is occurring. However, this trend is muted in the TOD literature. This may be due to the lack of suitability of TOD to the urban paradigms of the global south. However, it may also be due to the focus of this review on English-language publications.

The study reveals that there is limited collaboration among researchers studying TODs. Only a few clusters of collaborative networks of authors were identified in this study, suggesting that most of the authors are working of their own. The largest set of connected co-authorship network was formed by 21 authors when a minimum number of document threshold was set as 2. By comparison, a bibliometric network of pharmacological research found that 224 authors were connected in a co-authorship network even when the minimum number of document threshold was set as 5 (Romero and Portillo-Salido, 2019). Previous studies found that collaborations of different authors, institutes and countries have a measurable impact on citation behavior (Glänzel and Schubert, 2005). Our investigation also found that a higher degree of collaboration among authors increased their productivity and influence. John Renne, Carey Curtis, Luca Bertolini, and Robert Ewing, Md Kamruzzaman, Gavin Turrell, and Douglas Baker belong to large collaborative networks. They are also the top publishers with a greater influence in the field. Exception was found with Robert Cervero, Becky Loo, and Michael Duncan. They are influential despite not having a strong collaborative network. At the country level, a close collaborative link exists between the USA and China, which could be explained by volume of publications (they are the top productive countries), which in turn increases the opportunity for partnerships between authors in these two countries. International co-authorship involves multiple factors that influence the research, like the country size, economic and political conditions as well as mobility and technological advances at national level (Glänzel and Schubert, 2005).

The citation/co-authorship networks of different entities (author, document, country) are not randomly distributed, rather they are highly biased among certain entities, which were captured in the different clusters generated in this study. For example, an author does not cite randomly to all other authors; a document does not cite randomly to all other documents; an author of a country does not collaborate randomly with authors from all other countries. These findings signify that there are sub-groups of authors who intentionally/unintentionally cite the works of authors within their own sphere—perhaps due to topic similarity or due to familiarity of work through co-authorship. This biasness in citation/co-authorship networks enables the study to identify different themes of research in TODs and different collaborative enclaves.

References

Addison, C., Zhang, S.M., Coomes, B., 2013. Smart growth and housing affordability: a review of regulatory mechanisms and planning practices. J. Plan. Lit. 28, 215–257.

Aromataris, E., Munn, Z., 2020. JBI Manual for Evidence Synthesis. JBI. https://synthesismanual.jbi.global. https://doi.org/10.46658/JBIMES-20-01.

Aston, L., Currie, G., Delbosc, A., Kamruzzaman, M., Teller, D., 2021. Exploring built environment impacts on transit use—an updated meta-analysis. Transp. Rev. 41, 73–96.

Atkinson-Palombo, C., Kuby, M.J., 2011. The geography of advance transit-oriented development in metropolitan Phoenix, Arizona, 2000–2007. J. Transp. Geogr. 19, 189–199.

Bae, C.-H., 2002. Orenco station, Portland, Oregon: A successful transit oriented development experiment? Transp. Q. 56, 9–18.

Bartholomew, K., Ewing, R., 2011. Hedonic price effects of pedestrian- and transit-oriented development. J. Plan. Lit. 26, 18–34.

Bertolini, L., 1996. Nodes and places: complexities of railway station redevelopment. Eur. Plan. Stud. 4, 331–345.
Bertolini, L., Curtis, C., Renne, J., 2012. Station area projects in Europe and beyond: towards transit oriented development? Build. Environ. 38, 31–50.
Boarnet, M.G., Compin, N.S., 1999. Transit-oriented development in San Diego County: the incremental implementation of a planning idea. J. Am. Plann. Assoc. 65, 80–95.
Boschmann, E.E., Brady, S.A., 2013. Travel behaviors, sustainable mobility, and transit-oriented developments: a travel counts analysis of older adults in the Denver, Colorado metropolitan area. J. Transp. Geogr. 33, 1–11.
Broadus, R.N., 1987. Toward a definition of "bibliometrics". Scientometrics 12, 373–379.
Brown, B.B., Werner, C.M., 2008. Before and after a new light rail stop: resident attitudes, travel behavior, and obesity. J. Am. Plann. Assoc. 75, 5–12.
Calthorpe, P., 1993. The Next American Metropolis: Ecology, Community and the American Dream. Princeton Architectural Press, New York.
Canepa, B., 2007. Bursting the bubble: determining the transit-oriented development's walkable limits. Transp. Res. Rec. 1992, 28–34.
Cao, X., 2015. Heterogeneous effects of neighborhood type on commute mode choice: an exploration of residential dissonance in the twin cities. J. Transp. Geogr. 48, 188–196.
Cao, J., Cao, X., 2014. The impacts of LRT, neighbourhood characteristics, and self-selection on auto ownership: evidence from Minneapolis-St. Paul. Urban Stud. 51, 2068–2087.
Cao, X.J., Schoner, J., 2014. The influence of light rail transit on transit use: an exploration of station area residents along the Hiawatha line in Minneapolis. Transp. Res. A Policy Pract. 59, 134–143.
Carlton, I., 2009. Histories of Transit-Oriented Development: Perspectives on the Development of the TOD Concept. (Working Paper).
Carlton, I., University of California, B, Institute, U, Regional, D, 2009. Histories of Transit-Oriented Development : Perspectives on the Development of the TOD Concept: Real Estate and Transit, Urban and Social Movements, Concept Protagonist. University of California, Institute of Urban and Regional Development, Berkeley, CA.
Center for Transit-Oriented Development, 2010. Performance-Based Transit-Oriented Development Typology Guidebook. www.ctod.org.
Centre for Science and Technology Studies, L.U, 2020. VOSviewer, 1.6.15. Visualising Scientific Landscapes, The Netherlands.
Cervero, R., 1993. Transit-Supportive Development in the United States: Experiences and Prospects. University of California at Berkeley. Xvii 234, 94-08.
Cervero, R., 2007. Transit-oriented development's ridership bonus: a product of self-selection and public policies. Environ. Plan. A 39, 2068–2085.
Cervero, R., Dai, D., 2014. BRT TOD: leveraging transit oriented development with bus rapid transit investments. Transp. Policy 36, 127–138.
Cervero, R., Day, J., 2008. Suburbanization and transit-oriented development in China. Transp. Policy 15, 315–323.
Cervero, R., Duncan, M., 2002. Transit's value-added effects: light and commuter rail services and commercial land alues. Transp. Res. Rec. 1805, 8–15.
Cervero, R., Kockelman, K., 1997. Travel demand and the 3Ds: density, diversity, and design. Transp. Res. Part D: Transp. Environ. 2, 199–219.
Cervero, R., Sullivan, C., 2011. Green TODs: marrying transit-oriented development and green urbanism. Int. J. Sust. Dev. World 18, 210–218.
Cervero, R., Murphy, S., Ferrell, C., Goguts, N., Tsai, Y.-H., Arrington, G.B., Boroski, J., Smith-Heimer, J., Golem, R., Peninger, P., Nakajima, E., Chui, E., Dunphy, R., Myers, M., Mckay, S., Witenstein, N., 2004. Transit-oriented development in the United States: experiences, challenges, and prospects. Transp. Res. Board. TCRP Report 102.

Chakour, V., Eluru, N., 2016. Examining the influence of stop level infrastructure and built environment on bus ridership in Montreal. J. Transp. Geogr. 51, 205–217.
Chatman, D.G., 2013. Does TOD need the T? J. Am. Plann. Assoc. 79, 17–31.
Chen, Y., Yazdani, M., Mojtahedi, M., Newton, S., 2019. The impact on neighbourhood residential property valuations of a newly proposed public transport project: The Sydney Northwest Metro case study. Transp. Res. Interdiscip. Perspect. 3, 100070.
Choi, J., Lee, Y.J., Kim, T., Sohn, K., 2012. An analysis of Metro ridership at the station-to-station level in Seoul. Transportation 39, 705–722.
Chorus, P., Bertolini, L., 2016. Developing transit-oriented corridors: insights from Tokyo. Int. J. Sustain. Transp. 10, 86–95.
Cobo, M.J., Chiclana, F., Collop, A., de Ona, J., Herrera-Viedma, E., 2014. A bibliometric analysis of the intelligent transportation systems research based on science mapping. IEEE Trans. Intell. Transp. Syst. 15, 901–908.
Cole, S., Cole, J.R., 1967. Scientific output and recognition: a study in the operation of the reward system in science. Am. Sociol. Rev. 32, 377–390.
Crane, R., 2000. The influence of urban form on travel: an interpretive review. J. Plan. Lit. 15, 3–23.
Crowley, D., Shalaby, A., Zarei, H., 2009. Access walking distance, transit use, and transit-oriented development in North York City Center, Toronto, Canada. Transp. Res. Rec. 2110, 96–105.
Curtis, C., 2008. Evolution of the transit-oriented development model for low-density cities: a case study of Perth's new railway corridor. Plan. Pract. Res. 23, 285–302.
Curtis, C., 2012. Delivering the 'D' in transit-oriented development: examining the town planning challenge. J. Transp. Land Use 5, 83–99.
Curtis, C., Renne, J.L., Bertolini, L., 2009. Transit Oriented Development: Making it Happen. Ashgate Publishing Limited, Surrey.
De Vos, J., Witlox, F., 2013. Transportation policy as spatial planning tool; reducing urban sprawl by increasing travel costs and clustering infrastructure and public transportation. J. Transp. Geogr. 33, 117–125.
De Vos, J., Van Acker, V., Witlox, F., 2014. The influence of attitudes on transit-oriented development: an explorative analysis. Transp. Policy 35, 326–329.
Derudder, B., Liu, X., Hong, S., Ruan, S., Wang, Y., Witlox, F., 2019. The shifting position of the journal of transport geography in 'transport geography research': a bibliometric analysis. J. Transp. Geogr. 81, 102538.
Dill, J., 2008. Transit use at transit-oriented developments in Portland, Oregon, Area. Transp. Res. Rec. 2063, 159–167.
Dittmar, H., Ohland, G., 2004. In: Dittmar, H., Ohland, G. (Eds.), The New Transit Town: Best Practices in Transit-Oriented Development. Island Press, USA.
Dou, Y., Luo, X., Dong, L., Wu, C., Liang, H., Ren, J., 2016. An empirical study on transit-oriented low-carbon urban land use planning: exploratory spatial data analysis (ESDA) on Shanghai, China. Habitat Int. 53, 379–389.
Duncan, M., 2011. The impact of transit-oriented development on housing prices in San Diego, CA. Urban Stud. 48, 101–127.
Duncan, M., Christensen, R.K., 2013. An analysis of park-and-ride provision at light rail stations across the US. Transp. Policy 25, 148–157.
Ellegaard, O., Wallin, J.A., 2015. The bibliometric analysis of scholarly production: how great is the impact? Scientometrics 105, 1809–1831.
Ewing, R., Cervero, R., 2001. Travel and the built environment: a synthesis. Transp. Res. Rec. 1780, 87–114.
Ewing, R., Cervero, R., 2010. Travel and the built environment: a meta-analysis. J. Am. Plann. Assoc. 76, 265–294.

Falconer, R., Richardson, E., 2010. Rethinking urban land use and transport planning—opportunities for transit oriented development in Australian cities case study Perth. Aust. Plan. 47, 1–13.
Ferrell, C.E., Appleyard, B.S., Taecker, M., Allen, C., Armusewicz, C., Schroder, C., 2016. Livable Transit Corridors: Methods, Metrics, and Strategies. The National Academies Press, Washington, DC.
Fonseca, B.D.P.F.E., Sampaio, R.B., Fonseca, M.V.D.A., Zicker, F., 2016. Co-authorship network analysis in health research: method and potential use. Health Res. Policy Syst. 14, 34.
Garfield, E., 1970. Citation indexing for studying science. Nature 227, 669–671.
Glänzel, W., Schubert, A., 2005. Analysing scientific networks through co-authorship. In: Moed, H.F., Glänzel, W., Schmoch, U. (Eds.), Handbook of Quantitative Science and Technology Research: The Use of Publication and Patent Statistics in Studies of S&T Systems. Springer Netherlands, Dordrecht, pp. 257–276.
Goetz, A., 2013. Suburban sprawl or urban centres: tensions and contradictions of smart growth approaches in Denver, Colorado. Urban Stud. 50, 2178–2195.
Grant, M.J., Booth, A., 2009. A typology of reviews: an analysis of 14 review types and associated methodologies. Health Inf. Libr. J. 26, 91–108.
Greenwald, M.J., Boarnet, M.G., 2001. Built environment as determinant of walking behavior: analyzing nonwork pedestrian travel in Portland, Oregon. Transp. Res. Rec. 1780, 33–41.
Guo, Y.-M., Huang, Z.-L., Guo, J., Li, H., Guo, X.-R., Nkeli, M.J., 2019. Bibliometric analysis on smart cities research. Sustainability 11, 3606.
Hale, C., Charles, P., 2006. Making the most of transit oriented development opportunities. In: 29th Australasian Transport Research Forum, ATRF 06. The Australasian Transport Research Forum, pp. 1–19.
Handy, S., 2005. Smart growth and the transportation-land use connection: what does the research tell us? Int. Reg. Sci. Rev. 28, 146–167.
Hess, D.B., Lombardi, P.A., 2004. Policy support for and barriers to transit-oriented development in the inner city: literature review. Transp. Res. Rec. 1887, 26–33.
Higgins, C.D., Kanaroglou, P.S., 2016a. Forty years of modelling rapid transit's land value uplift in North America: moving beyond the tip of the iceberg. Transp. Rev. 36, 610–634.
Higgins, C.D., Kanaroglou, P.S., 2016b. A latent class method for classifying and evaluating the performance of station area transit-oriented development in the Toronto region. J. Transp. Geogr. 52, 61–72.
Higgins, C., Kanaroglou, P., 2018. Rapid transit, transit-oriented development, and the contextual sensitivity of land value uplift in Toronto. Urban Stud. 55, 2197–2225.
Holz-Rau, C., Scheiner, J., 2019. Land-use and transport planning—a field of complex cause-impact relationships. Thoughts on transport growth, greenhouse gas emissions and the built environment. Transp. Policy 74, 127–137.
Houston, D., Boarnet, M.G., Ferguson, G., Spears, S., 2015. Can compact rail transit corridors transform the automobile city? Planning for more sustainable travel in Los Angeles. Urban Stud. 52, 938–959.
Ibraeva, A., de Almeida Correia, G.H., Silva, C., Antunes, A.P., 2020. Transit-oriented development: a review of research achievements and challenges. Transp. Res. A Policy Pract. 132, 110–130.
Jamme, H.-T., Rodriguez, J., Bahl, D., Banerjee, T., 2019. A twenty-five-year biography of the TOD concept: from design to policy, planning, and implementation. J. Plan. Educ. Res. 39, 409–428.
Jang, S., An, Y., Yi, C., Lee, S., 2017. Assessing the spatial equity of Seoul's public transportation using the Gini coefficient based on its accessibility. Int. J. Urban Sci. 21, 91–107.

Jarneving, B., 2005. A comparison of two bibliometric methods for mapping of the research front. Scientometrics 65, 245–263.
Jones, C.E., Ley, D., 2016. Transit-oriented development and gentrification along metro Vancouver's low-income SkyTrain corridor. Can. Geogr. 60, 9–22.
Kamruzzaman, M., Baker, D., Washington, S., Turrell, G., 2013. Residential dissonance and mode choice. J. Transp. Geogr. 33, 12–28.
Kamruzzaman, M., Baker, D., Washington, S., Turrell, G., 2014a. Advance transit oriented development typology: case study in Brisbane, Australia. J. Transp. Geogr. 34, 54–70.
Kamruzzaman, M., Wood, L., Hine, J., Currie, G., Giles-Corti, B., Turrell, G., 2014b. Patterns of social capital associated with transit oriented development. J. Transp. Geogr. 35, 144–155.
Kamruzzaman, M., Baker, D., Turrell, G., 2015a. Do dissonants in transit oriented development adjust commuting travel behaviour? Eur. J. Transp. Infrastruct. Res. 15, 66–77.
Kamruzzaman, M., Shatu, F.M., Hine, J., Turrell, G., 2015b. Commuting mode choice in transit oriented development: disentangling the effects of competitive neighbourhoods, travel attitudes, and self-selection. Transp. Policy 42, 187–196.
Kamruzzaman, M., Baker, D., Washington, S., Turrell, G., 2016. Determinants of residential dissonance: implications for transit-oriented development in Brisbane. Int. J. Sustain. Transp. 10, 960–974.
Kasraian, D., Maat, K., Stead, D., van Wee, B., 2016. Long-term impacts of transport infrastructure networks on land-use change: an international review of empirical studies. Transp. Rev. 36, 772–792.
Kay, A.I., Noland, R.B., DiPetrillo, S., 2014. Residential property valuations near transit stations with transit-oriented development. J. Transp. Geogr. 39, 131–140.
Kessler, M.M., 1962. An Experimental Study of Bibliographic Coupling between Technical Papers. Massachusetts Inst of Tech Lexington Lincoln Lab.
Kim, S., Ulfarsson, G.F., Todd Hennessy, J., 2007. Analysis of light rail rider travel behavior: impacts of individual, built environment, and crime characteristics on transit access. Transp. Res. A Policy Pract. 41, 511–522.
Kimball, M., Chester, M., Gino, C., Reyna, J., 2013. Assessing the potential for reducing life-cycle environmental impacts through transit-oriented development infill along existing light rail in Phoenix. J. Plan. Educ. Res. 33, 395–410.
Knowles, R.D., 2012. Transit oriented development in Copenhagen, Denmark: from the finger plan to Ørestad. J. Transp. Geogr. 22, 251–261.
Knowles, R.D., Ferbrache, F., 2016. Evaluation of wider economic impacts of light rail investment on cities. J. Transp. Geogr. 54, 430–439.
Lang, W., Hui, E.C.M., Chen, T., Li, X., 2020. Understanding livable dense urban form for social activities in transit-oriented development through human-scale measurements. Habitat Int. 104, 102238.
Langlois, M., Wasfi, R.A., Ross, N.A., El-Geneidy, A.M., 2016. Can transit-oriented developments help achieve the recommended weekly level of physical activity? J. Transp. Health 3, 181–190.
Lee, P.-C., Su, H.-N., 2010. Investigating the structure of regional innovation system research through keyword co-occurrence and social network analysis. Innovation 12, 26–40.
Lee, S., Lee, S., Park, D., Lee, C., 2010. Analysis of travel patterns between road and transit-oriented development areas. J. Adv. Transp. 44, 3–10.
Lee, S., Yi, C., Hong, S.-P., 2013. Urban structural hierarchy and the relationship between the ridership of the Seoul Metropolitan Subway and the land-use pattern of the station areas. Cities 35, 69–77.
Lee, J., Choi, K., Leem, Y., 2016. Bicycle-based TOD as an alternative to overcome the criticisms of the conventional TOD. Int. J. Sustain. Transp. 10, 975–984.

Leydesdorff, L., 1987. Various methods for the mapping of science. Scientometrics 11, 295–324.
Leydesdorff, L., Park, H.W., 2016. Full and Fractional Counting in Bibliometric Networks. arXiv Preprint. arXiv:1611.06943.
Lin, J.J., Gau, C.C., 2006. A TOD planning model to review the regulation of allowable development densities around subway stations. Land Use Policy 23, 353–360.
Lin, J.J., Shin, T.Y., 2008. Does transit-oriented development affect metro ridership? Evidence from Taipei, Taiwan. Transp. Res. Rec. 2063, 149–158.
Liu, L., Zhang, M., Xu, T., 2020. A conceptual framework and implementation tool for land use planning for corridor transit oriented development. Cities 107, 102939.
Loo, B.P., du Verle, F., 2017. Transit-oriented development in future cities: towards a two-level sustainable mobility strategy. Int. J. Urban Sci. 21, 54–67.
Loo, B.P.Y., Chen, C., Chan, E.T.H., 2010. Rail-based transit-oriented development: Lessons from New York City and Hong Kong. Landsc. Urban Plan. 97, 202–212.
Loukaitou-Sideris, A., 2010. A new-found popularity for transit-oriented developments? Lessons from Southern California. J. Urban Des. 15, 49–68.
Lund, H., 2006. Reasons for living in a transit-oriented development and associated transit use. J. Am. Plann. Assoc. 72, 357–366.
Lyu, G., Bertolini, L., Pfeffer, K., 2016. Developing a TOD typology for Beijing metro station areas. J. Transp. Geogr. 55, 40–50.
Ma, X., Chen, X., Li, X., Ding, C., Wang, Y., 2018. Sustainable station-level planning: An integrated transport and land use design model for transit-oriented development. J. Clean. Prod. 170, 1052–1063.
Mathur, S., Ferrell, C., 2013. Measuring the impact of sub-urban transit-oriented developments on single-family home values. Transp. Res. A Policy Pract. 47, 42–55.
Meetham, A.R., Hudson, R.A., 1969. Encyclopaedia of Linguistics. Information and Control, London.
Merigó, J.M., Pedrycz, W., Weber, R., de la Sotta, C., 2018. Fifty years of information sciences: a bibliometric overview. Inform. Sci. 432, 245–268.
Moed, H.F., 2005. Citation Analysis in Research Evaluation. Springer, Dordrecht [Great Britain].
Mu, R., de Jong, M., 2012. Establishing the conditions for effective transit-oriented development in China: the case of Dalian. J. Transp. Geogr. 24, 234–249.
Nahlik, M.J., Chester, M.V., 2014. Transit-oriented smart growth can reduce life-cycle environmental impacts and household costs in Los Angeles. Transp. Policy 35, 21–30.
Nasri, A., Zhang, L., 2014. The analysis of transit-oriented development (TOD) in Washington, D.C. and Baltimore metropolitan areas. Transp. Policy 32, 172–179.
Olaru, D., Smith, B., Taplin, J.H.E., 2011. Residential location and transit-oriented development in a new rail corridor. Transp. Res. A Policy Pract. 45, 219–237.
Padeiro, M., Louro, A., da Costa, N.M., 2019a. Transit-oriented development and gentrification: a systematic review. Transp. Rev. 39, 733–754. <xocs:firstpage xmlns:xocs=""/>.
Padeiro, M., Louro, A., da Costa, N.M., 2019b. Transit-oriented development and gentrification: a systematic review. Transplant. Rev. 39, 733–754.
Papa, E., Bertolini, L., 2015. Accessibility and transit-oriented development in European metropolitan areas. J. Transp. Geogr. 47, 70–83.
Parsons Brinckerhoff Quade and Douglas Inc, Cervero, R., Howard/Stein-Hudson Associates Inc, Zupan, J., 1996. Part 2: commuter and light rail transit corridors: the land use connection. In: Transit Cooperative Research Program (Ed.), Transit and Urban Form. Transportation Research Board National Research Council.
Perianes-Rodriguez, A., Waltman, L., van Eck, N.J., 2016. Constructing bibliometric networks: a comparison between full and fractional counting. J. Informet. 10, 1178–1195.

Phani Kumar, P., Ravi Sekhar, C., Parida, M., 2018. Residential dissonance in TOD neighborhoods. J. Transp. Geogr. 72, 166–177.
Podsakoff, P.M., MacKenzie, S.B., Podsakoff, N.P., Bachrach, D.G., 2008. Scholarly influence in the field of management: a bibliometric analysis of the determinants of university and author impact in the management literature in the past quarter century. J. Manag. 34, 641–720.
Pritchard, R., Frøyen, Y., 2019. Location, location, relocation: how the relocation of offices from suburbs to the inner city impacts commuting on foot and by bike. Eur. Transp. Res. Rev. 11, 14.
Puello, L.L.P., Geurs, K., 2015. Modelling observed and unobserved factors in cycling to railway stations: application to transit-oriented-developments in the Netherlands. Eur. J. Transp. Infrastruct. Res. 15, 27–50.
Rayle, L., 2015. Investigating the connection between transit-oriented development and displacement: four hypotheses. Hous. Policy Debate 25, 531–548.
Renne, J.L., 2009. From transit-adjacent to transit-oriented development. Local Environ. 14, 1–15.
Renne, J., Hamidi, S., Ewing, R., 2016. Transit commuting, the network accessibility effect, and the built environment in station areas across the United States. Res. Transp. Econ. 60, 35–43.
Romero, L., Portillo-Salido, E., 2019. Trends in Sigma-1 receptor research: a 25-year bibliometric analysis. Front. Pharmacol. 10, 564.
Schlossberg, M., Brown, N., 2004. Comparing transit-oriented development sites by walkability indicators. Transp. Res. Rec. 1887, 34–42.
Schuetz, J., 2015. Do rail transit stations encourage neighbourhood retail activity? Urban Stud. 52, 2699–2723.
Schwanen, T., 2017. Geographies of transport III: new spatialities of knowledge production? Prog. Hum. Geogr. 42, 463–472.
Schwanen, T., 2018. Towards decolonised knowledge about transport. Palgrave Commun. 4, 79.
Singh, Y.J., Fard, P., Zuidgeest, M., Brussel, M., Maarseveen, M.v., 2014. Measuring transit oriented development: a spatial multi criteria assessment approach for the City Region Arnhem and Nijmegen. J. Transp. Geogr. 35, 130–143.
Singh, Y.J., Lukman, A., Flacke, J., Zuidgeest, M., Van Maarseveen, M., 2017. Measuring TOD around transit nodes-towards TOD policy. Transp. Policy 56, 96–111.
Sipe, N., Burke, M., 2011. Can river ferries deliver smart growth?: experience of CityCats in Brisbane, Australia. Transp. Res. Rec. 2217, 79–86.
Sivakumaran, K., Li, Y., Cassidy, M., Madanat, S., 2014. Access and the choice of transit technology. Transp. Res. A Policy Pract. 59, 204–221.
Stevens, M., 2017. Does compact development make people drive less? J. Am. Plann. Assoc. 83, 7–18.
Sun, G., Zacharias, J., Ma, B., Oreskovic, N.M., 2016. How do metro stations integrate with walking environments? Results from walking access within three types of built environment in Beijing. Cities 56, 91–98.
Sun, Z., Allan, A., Soltani, A., 2018. Scientometric Analysis and Mapping of Transit-Oriented Development Studies (1994–2018). Australasian Transport Research Forum.
Sung, H., Oh, J.-T., 2011. Transit-oriented development in a high-density city: identifying its association with transit ridership in Seoul, Korea. Cities 28, 70–82.
Sung, H.-G., Go, D.-H., Choi, C.G., 2013. Evidence of Jacobs's street life in the great Seoul city: identifying the association of physical environment with walking activity on streets. Cities 35, 164–173.
Surwase, G., Sagar, A., Kademani, B.S., Bhanumurthy, K., 2011. Co-citation analysis: an overview. In: Beyond Librarianship: Creativity, Innovation and Discovery. B.R. Publishing Corporation. Mumbai (India).

Tan, W.G.Z., Janssen-Jansen, L.B., Bertolini, L., 2014. The role of incentives in implementing successful transit-oriented development strategies. Urban Policy Res. 32, 33–51.

Thomas, R., Bertolini, L., 2014. Beyond the case study dilemma in urban planning: using a meta-matrix to distil critical success factors in transit-oriented development. Urban Policy Res. 32, 219–237.

Thorne-Lyman, A., Wampler, E., 2010. Transit corridors and TOD: connecting the dots. In: Ohland, G. (Ed.), Reconnecting America. The Center for Transit-Oriented Development.

Vale, D.S., 2015. Transit-oriented development, integration of land use and transport, and pedestrian accessibility: combining node-place model with pedestrian shed ratio to evaluate and classify station areas in Lisbon. J. Transp. Geogr. 45, 70–80.

van Eck, N.J., Waltman, L., 2010. Software survey: VOSviewer, a computer program for bibliometric mapping. Scientometrics 84, 523–538.

van Eck, N.J., Waltman, L., Dekker, R., van den Berg, J., 2010. A comparison of two techniques for bibliometric mapping: multidimensional scaling and VOS. J. Am. Soc. Inf. Sci. Technol. 61, 2405–2416.

Walmsley, A., 2006. Greenways: multiplying and diversifying in the 21st century. Landsc. Urban Plan. 76, 252–290.

Wang, Y., Yang, L., Han, S., Li, C., Ramachandra, T.V., 2017a. Urban CO2 emissions in Xi'an and Bangalore by commuters: implications for controlling urban transportation carbon dioxide emissions in developing countries. Mitig. Adapt. Strat. Glob. Chang. 22, 993–1019.

Wang, P., Zhu, F., Song, H., Hou, J., 2017b. A bibliometric profile of current science between 1961 and 2015. Curr. Sci., 386–392.

Wee, B.V., Banister, D., 2016. How to write a literature review paper? Transp. Rev. 36, 278–288.

Wey, W.-M., Chiu, Y.-H., 2013. Assessing the walkability of pedestrian environment under the transit-oriented development. Habitat Int. 38, 106–118.

Wey, W.-M., Zhang, H., Chang, Y.-J., 2016. Alternative transit-oriented development evaluation in sustainable built environment planning. Habitat Int. 55, 109–123.

Wood, D., 2009. Overview of briefing papers. In: Fostering Equitable and Sustainable Transit-Oriented Development. Vol. 1. Center for Transit-Oriented Development, pp. 1–3.

Wu, L., Wang, W., Jing, P., Chen, Y., Zhan, F., Shi, Y., Li, T., 2020. Travel mode choice and their impacts on environment—a literature review based on bibliometric and content analysis, 2000–2018. J. Clean. Prod. 249, 119391.

Xiang, C., Wang, Y., Liu, H., 2017. A scientometrics review on nonpoint source pollution research. Ecol. Eng. 99, 400–408.

Xu, T., Zhang, M., Aditjandra, P.T., 2016. The impact of urban rail transit on commercial property value: new evidence from Wuhan, China. Transp. Res. A Policy Pract. 91, 223–235.

Yang, J., Cao, J., Zhou, Y., 2021. Elaborating non-linear associations and synergies of subway access and land uses with urban vitality in Shenzhen. Transp. Res. A Policy Pract. 144, 74–88.

Zhang, M., 2007. Chinese edition of transit-oriented development. Transp. Res. Rec. 2038, 120–127.

Zhao, J., Deng, W., Song, Y., Zhu, Y., 2013. Analysis of metro ridership at station level and station-to-station level in Nanjing: an approach based on direct demand models. Transportation 41, 133–155.

CHAPTER ELEVEN

Corridor transit oriented development: Concept, practice, and research needs

Ming Zhang*
School of Architecture, University of Texas at Austin, Austin, TX, United States
*Corresponding author: e-mail address: zhangm@austin.utexas.edu

Contents

Abstract

Transit oriented development (TOD) as a land use-transit integration strategy has been widely adopted. This chapter focuses on the conception, practice, and research needs of corridor TOD (C-TOD). C-TOD builds on the premise of transit network effects generating synergies and potentials greater than the sum of individual TOD nodes. The chapter first introduces three exemplar C-TOD cases from Copenhagen, Denmark; Curitiba, Brazil; and Arlington, VA, of the United States. Next, the chapter defines C-TOD based on the concept of *transit travel shed* and introduces practical ways to delineate C-TOD. Various approaches for C-TOD analysis and planning exist and are summarized in two types here: typological approach and performance-based optimization approach. The chapter highlights three topical issues that warrant further research: (1) corridor level transit performance pertaining to C-TOD; (2) corridor-specific metrics and methods to capture the dynamic land use interactions between individual TOD nodes; and (3) corridor perspective and potential to address policy concerns such as housing affordability and transit displacement.

Keywords: Corridor transit-oriented development (C-TOD), Transit travel shed, Multi-objective optimization, Performance-based planning (PBP), Transit displacement

Advances in Transport Policy and Planning, Volume 9
ISSN 2543-0009
https://doi.org/10.1016/bs.atpp.2021.04.001

1. Introduction

Transit-oriented development (TOD) as Calthorpe (1993) conceived originally offers a scalable spatial framework for integrated land use design and mobility provision. The prototype TOD applies primarily at the local scale to the areas around transit stations. TOD can also scale up to create transit-oriented corridors along transit lines or to make a transit metropolis over regional public transportation networks. TOD promises communities a wide range of benefits, including personal health, land market efficiency, and socio-environmental sustainability (Cervero, 2004; FTA, 2019; HNTB, 2016). Such opportunities alongside TOD's application scalability have motivated various levels of governments and agencies to practice TOD and adopt plans and policy guidelines for TOD implementation (e.g., CoA (City of Austin), 2006; FDOT, 2009; City of Denver, 2014; ITDP (Institute for Transportation and Development Policy), 2017; The World Bank, 2018). Several countries have even released national guidelines to promote TOD (e.g., Ahamad, 2014; Zhou, 2016).

TOD principles are not entirely new. The practice of concentrating development around transit dates back more than a century in many European cities and in the streetcar-age communities of the United States. Prevailing car-oriented environments make contemporary TOD an attractive alternative, but the automobile's underlying market forces and its supporting institutional and regulatory structures also make TOD implementation challenging, particularly in North American cities where integrated land use-transit infrastructure has in contrast accumulated a rich asset, TOD has more readily gained popularity for the interest of achieving broader objectives such as environmental sustainability and social equity in addition to improving transit services and urban functions (Pojani and Stead, 2018). Many fast-growing Asian cities where major transit investments are underway have operated TOD as a spatial strategy to structure and guide urban expansion toward a desired pattern of concentrated decentralization (e.g., Fang and Xue, 2015; Mehta et al., 2016; Phuc, 2015).

The extent to which the TOD idea can turn into reality depends on many factors. Scholars have engaged in extensive research to investigate these factors and document the evidence of their effects on TOD performance outcomes. In an extensive review, Ibraeva et al. (2020) compiled more than 300 TOD-related studies and synthesized a rich body of knowledge concerning TOD effects on travel behaviors, real estate markets, residential location choices, urban forms, and community life. The *Journal of Planning Education and Research* recently published a special issue entitled "Twenty-Five Years in the Making: TOD as a New Name for an Enduring Concept" (Renne and Appleyard, 2019). The special issue contains eight articles in the TOD research front, addressing four thematic topics: the theoretical conceptualizations of TOD implementation, TOD and productivity of firms in the knowledge and creative industries, TOD-related housing and gentrification, and the relationship between pedestrian behavior and vehicle miles travel in the TOD setting.

With the meta-knowledge of TOD in the background, this chapter focuses on a specific topic, corridor TOD (C-TOD). The chapter stresses that C-TOD presents great yet not fully tapped potentials to augment the functional (land use and transit) and policy goals that the TOD idea has initially targeted. Transit systems present linear, corridor geometries inherent to their technological characteristics. Given the corridor nature of transit lines, one may assume that C-TOD would rise naturally as long as individual station areas along the line can develop to become TOD nodes. Many existing TOD plans do consider multiple TODs along transit lines in the corridor or regional scales. Nevertheless, adding up individual TOD nodes does not make a strong performing corridor automatically. Transit systems, like other transportation and communications systems, create network effects that grow increasingly along with the expansion of service size and coverage. Transit network effects provide access benefits greater than those of the sum of individual stations (Curtis and Schreurs, 2016). C-TOD analysis has an opportunity to devise corridor- and network-specific concepts, methods, and metrics to capture the network effects where the nodal TOD approach does not suffice. C-TOD planning should nurture and capitalize on the synergies brought by transit network effects between individual station areas (Huang et al., 2018). A C-TOD scope opens an array of research opportunities to such policy concerns as job and service accessibility of the mobility-disadvantaged, housing affordability, transportation emissions, value capture for transit financing, along with many others.

After this introduction, the chapter first presents three exemplar cases, highlighting their corridor TOD features. Next, the chapter conceptualizes C-TOD and elaborates on ways to delineate TOD corridors. In the subsequent section, the chapter reviews two types of approaches taken by the existing studies for C-TOD analysis and planning. The review is followed by the discussion of research needs concerning C-TOD. Finally, the chapter ends with concluding remarks.

2. Three exemplar cases of corridor/networked TOD

2.1 Copenhagen: The Finger Plan

Copenhagen, Denmark, is a transit metropolis featured with multiple transit-oriented "fingers" (Cervero, 1997). The Finger Plan is a regional plan created initially in 1947 for the Copenhagen metropolitan area in Denmark (Fig. 1). Danish town planners Steen Eiler Rasmussen and Peter Bredsdorff conceived the plan and used the shape of a hand to illustrate the proposed regional spatial framework. Five fingers of the hand correspond to the five rail corridors that stretch out from the "palm" (i.e., central Copenhagen). Rail stations along each finger function as focal joints where suburban communities develop with relatively high-density housing and its supporting shopping

Fig. 1 The Finger-Palm concept of Copenhagen, Denmark. *Modified from Map data @ OpenStreetMap contributors and available from https://www.openstreetmap.org.*

and service facilities. Then existing or proposed public transit, the S-train, connects the communities with one another along each finger "like beads on a string" (Knowles, 2012). Green wedges consisting of farmland and recreational spaces separate the fingers to prevent the region from sprawling growth.

The Finger Plan came out at the time when Copenhagen's private car ownership was low and public transit provided major mobility services to the city and its suburbs. In the 1950s and 1960s Copenhagen, like other European cities, experienced a post-war growth surge which led to a period of economic staggering and restructuring in the subsequent decades. The regional plan for Greater Copenhagen was updated six times after 1947 in response to the region's socioeconomic shifts. During this period, the agencies responsible for making the plans and their governing structures also underwent major changes. Despite these changes, the fundamental rail transit-based Finger-Palm frame has been retained (Sorensen and Torfing, 2019).

The Finger Plan existed decades before the term TOD was coined in the United States. Yet its planning principles resemble (or probably inspired initially) those underlying the contemporary TOD concept. At the same time the wide acceptance of TOD in the new century as a planning and policy strategy to counter sprawl (existing or potential in different country and city contexts) has helped strengthen Copenhagen's Finger-Palm frame. This is evident in the latest versions of Copenhagen's Finger Plan, although the term TOD itself never appeared in the plans explicitly (Denmark Ministry of the Environment, 2007, 2015, 2019).

The Finger Plan specifies a general rail network, along with other plan components, for the region and delimits station areas where development aims to meet the prescribed density thresholds and functional composition. For instance, residential areas were required to build at the minimum density of 40 units per hectare (~16 units per acre) for stations located in the core urban region or 25 units per hectare (~10 units per acre) for stations outside the urban core. The plan also specifies the minimum floor areas for office and services in each station area.

Copenhagen's Finger Plan history and implementation outcome demonstrate the effectiveness of integrated transit-land development, regardless it is termed TOD or not, to achieve livability and sustainability goals. The needed integration should happen between efforts at different spatial scales, including individual station areas, corridors, and the entire region.

2.2 Curitiba, Brazil

Curitiba, Brazil, offers an exemplar case for C-TOD practice based on a multi-tier bus rapid transit (BRT) system (Rodriguez and Vergel-Tovar, 2017; TCRP (Transit Cooperative Research Program), 2003). Curitiba is the capital city of the Brazilian state of Parana. In 2019, the city had an estimated population of 1.9 million, whereas its population combined with the greater Curitiba metropolitan area of 26 municipalities totaled over 3.6 million. Curitiba residents and visitors are well served by the region's multimodal transit networks consisting of BRT lines, the conventional bus routes that complement the trunk lines, and other feeder services. More than 80% of Curitiba residents use the bus-based transit services for their daily activities (ICLEI, 2016).

Curitiba's planning effort for integrated land use and transit development started in the 1960s. In the 1950s Curitiba experienced a population boom, prompting the city to seek long-term sustainable solutions to accommodate the past as well as the anticipated future growth. In 1964, the city launched a planning competition soliciting creative ideas to counter the development challenges facing the city. The winning team proposed a master plan for Curitiba in the form of a star with five structural axes radiating from the city center. Each axis would develop in high-density and mixed land uses along a transit corridor featuring a trinary road system. In the subsequent years the plan was refined and further strengthened during the 1972 Plan Reformation.

The concept of structural axis highlights Curitiba's innovative version of C-TOD (Fig. 2). Differing from Copenhagen's "beads on the ring" corridors, Curitiba's structural axis develops continuously with high-density and mixed land uses along each designated BRT corridor. This axial continuity is made possible by a unique trinary system of transit services and development specification. First, at the center of the trinary system, high-capacity BRT services operate on a dedicated two-way busway. In one city block on each side of the busway trunk line, a secondary one-way street runs in parallel to the trunk line on which intermediate bus services complement the truck line services. The land in the city block between the busway and the secondary street is zoned to develop at the highest allowable density. Furthermore, a tertiary road serves two-way traffic in another city block from the busway. Conventional bus services run on this road, providing more frequent stops than those on the trunk lines for local access. Land parcels between the secondary and the tertiary bus lines are zoned at lower intensity than those along the trunk lines but higher than the rest of the city.

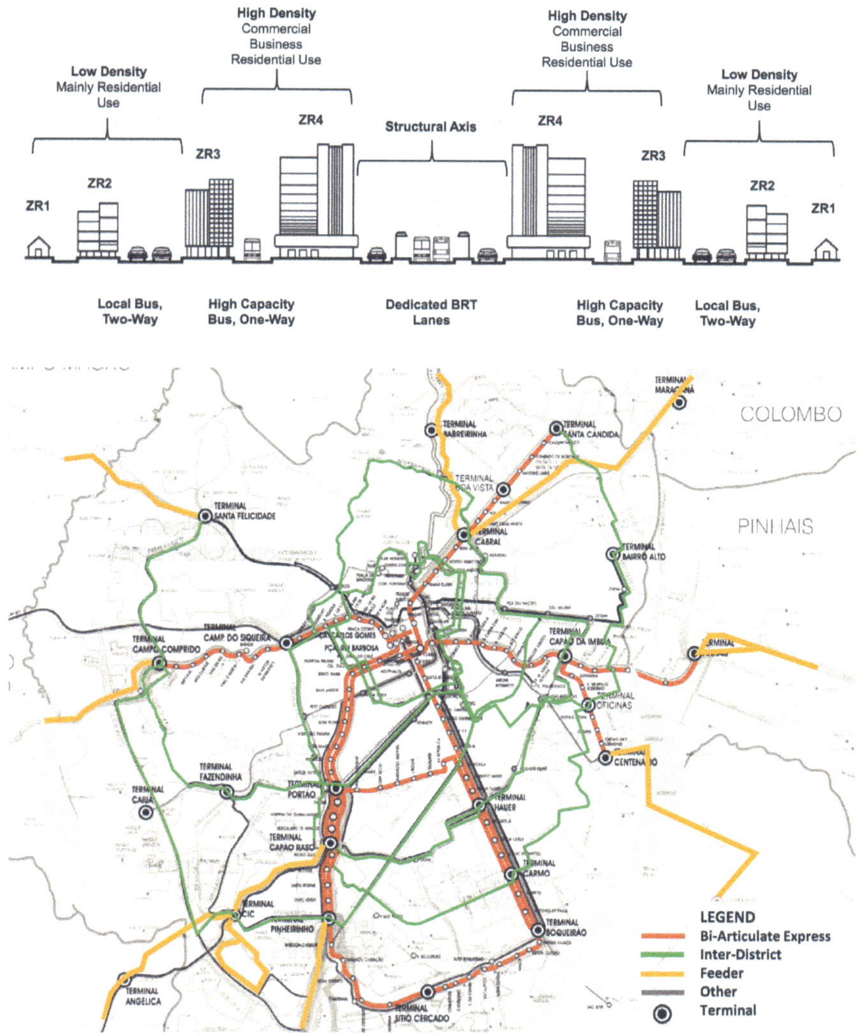

Fig. 2 The trinary road/transit system and structural axes of Curitiba, Brazil. *Source: Modified from ICLEI., 2016. Curitiba, Brazil: A Model for Transit Oriented Development. ICLEI Case Study, No. 190. Available at URL: https://sustainablemobility.iclei.org/wpdm-package/curitiba-brazil-a-model-of-transit-oriented-planning/.*

To ensure the mandatory implementation of the "star" master plan, the City of Curitiba adopted and has continually updated their 1972 zoning and land use regulations prescribing concentrated development along each axis. For instance, the 1972 zoning law designated high-density residential and commercial zones along the North-South and Northeast-West axes and required a FAR of six for these zones. The areas not on the main corridor but in close proximity to transit routes were regulated at the FAR of 4. By the zoning law, the ground and second floors of the buildings located in the transit corridors should devote a minimum of 50% floor spaces for retail and commercial services (ICLEI, 2016).

These supportive land use planning and zoning regulations were essential to the successful realization of Curitiba's structural axis model. Curitiba's practice of integrating transit and land development creates a unique region-wide corridor pattern not seen anywhere in the rest of the world.

2.3 Rosslyn-Ballston corridor

The Rosslyn-Ballston corridor located in Arlington, VA, is widely recognized as the best C-TOD example in the United States (Leach, 2004). The corridor contains five stations on the orange line of the metro system in the Washington, D.C. metropolitan area. In the 1960s when the regional metro agency was slated to expand its system network, Arlington planners and officials convinced the majority of the voters to embrace a new metro line for Arlington. Through bond financing, the city paid for relocating the line from its initially planned route on the Interstate 66 median to an underground alignment along Wilson-Fairfax Boulevard where Arlington's major retail and service business concentrated. A C-TOD style plan, known as the "bull's eye" plan, was prepared and adopted to integrate land use with the new metro line for the goal of revitalizing local retail and enhancing community economic development (Arlington, 2021).

The "bull's eye" plan contained five station areas within Arlington's city limits. For each station area, the city developed a "sector plan" (a *de facto* TOD plan), featuring high-density mixed uses in city blocks closer to the station and decreased densities in areas transitioning to the surrounding neighborhoods. Planning and development of the five station areas were well coordinated, with each having its unique identity. The Rosslyn station area, planned as a job center concentrates predominantly offices and hotel services. The Court House station area houses Arlington's county court, along with a mixture of offices and residential buildings. Clarendon station area, as an "urban village," hosts a retail center with nearby multifamily housing. The Virginia Square station area offers diverse uses of educational (George Mason University), office, and residential functions. Lastly, the Ballston station area serves as a major retail center surrounded by office, hotel, and apartment units. The sector plans for the five station areas have been updated several times and remain as guiding documents for the corridor today (Arlington, 2017) (Fig. 3).

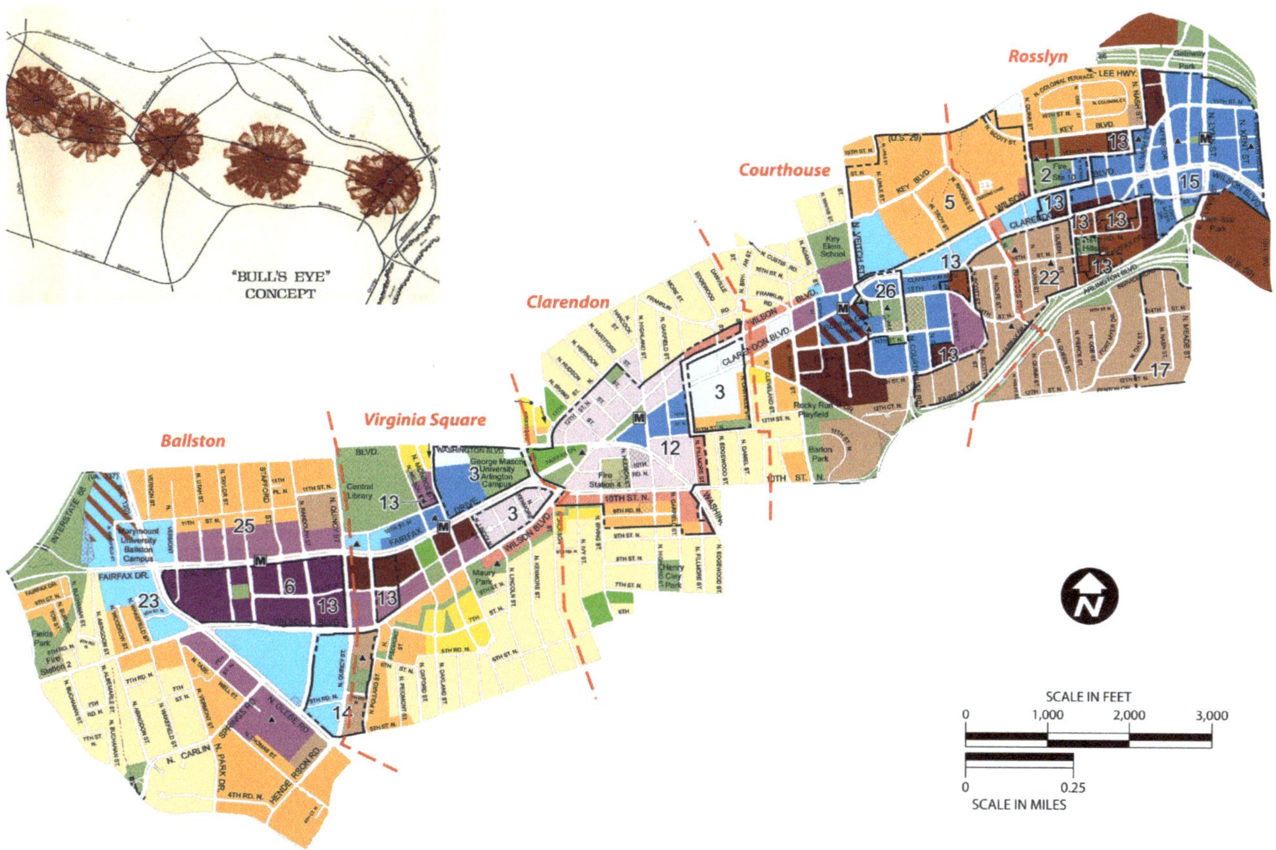

Fig. 3 The "bull's eye" concept and land use plan of the Rosslyn-Ballston corridor, Arlington, VA. *Source: Modified from Arlington, VA., 2017. General Land Use Plan: Adopted August 12, 1961 with Amendments Through June 30, 2018. Accessed on May 20, 2020 at URL: https://arlingtonva.s3.dualstack.us-east-1.amazonaws.com/wp-content/uploads/sites/31/2017/10/Booklet_June_2017.pdf.*

A number of indicators prove the success of the "bull's eye" plan. The corridor has kept a relatively balanced ratio of housing and jobs along the corridor. A high proportion of households living by the corridor owns only one car or none at all. Vehicle traffic on the streets in the corridor have grown in recent decades, but at a pace much slower than that on nearby streets and highways. Furthermore, Arlington has maintained the lowest tax rate for residential properties in the state of Virginia owing to the strong and vibrant retail and service businesses that largely concentrated in the corridor.

These three cases, Copenhagen's *Finger Plan*, Curitiba's *Structural Axes*, and Arlington, VA's *Bull's Eye* Corridor, differ in the transit technologies used, geographic areas served, along with many other aspects. Yet they exhibit a number of shared features. The three cities have pursued transit-centered multimodal mobility strategies to guide urban or regional development along designated corridors. To foster corridor development, the local and regional governments have provided transit-supportive zoning regulations and incentive policies through decades of persistent efforts. All of these efforts have resulted in corridor performance marked by popular acceptance and usage of transit services, reduced roadway congestions and vehicle emissions, and livable and vibrant places enjoyed by residents and business alike.

Departing from the case observations, the next section of the chapter conceptualizes C-TOD and discusses approaches to C-TOD analysis and planning.

3. Corridor-TOD: Definition, analysis, and planning

3.1 Corridor definition and delineation for TOD

Transportation systems such as highways, transit lines, and shipping channels typically display linear or curvilinear geometries focused along corridor spaces connecting networks of origins and destinations. This linear quality of transportation systems makes the corridor study a common practice in transportation system analysis and planning. The first step of which is to is to define the study area, delineating the corridor's length and width. Traditionally, transportation corridor studies have focused on system performance issues in the areas within the system's right-of-way (ROW) (ICF International, 2009). Increasingly, however, transportation agencies are taking on expanded responsibilities beyond improving system engineering and service performance, for example, enhancing economic development, strengthening environmental protection, and improving social equity. These new territories have motivated or forced the expansion of corridor study's scope to integrate the traditional ROW-based study with planning for land use activities adjacent to ROW (ICF International, 2009). A question of both conceptual and practical importance then arises: how far away from the system ROW should the corridor boundary be drawn?

The concept of travel shed provides a behavioral underpinning for corridor conception, definition, and delineation. A travel shed is analogous to a watershed; where a watershed includes all of the contributing areas draining runoff into a body of water, a travel shed includes all of the contributing areas directing people into a transportation network. At the corridor scale this describes an area where trips generally cluster in a linear pattern along trunk lines for longer distance trips along with the linked routes of feeder modes (Smith, 1999). When applied to nodal TOD planning and analysis, a travel shed denotes the area accessible by walking from the station center, also known as the pedestrian shed (PedShed, 2021). The threshold walking distance (or time) for a pedestrian shed may vary depending on people's willingness to walk, which is affected by personal characteristics and preferences, local walking environment, and other factors such as weather and culture. In the United States, a distance of ¼ mile (~400 m) or 5-min walk is commonly used. In Asian and European cities where walking is more popular than in the US cities, the threshold distance may be longer at 500, 600, or sometimes even 1000 m.

Transit travel sheds go beyond pedestrian sheds when other travel modes are considered for station access, and C-TOD analysis can define and delineate its spatial scope as that encompassed by the total transit travel shed area. Several studies have incorporated the concept of transit travel shed into their analytical methods, but operationalized it with various metrics. For example, when developing the Housing + Transportation (H + T) Index, Center for Neighborhood Technology (CNT, 2015) included an indicator "transit access shed" in its transportation cost model. The H + T Index operates at the Census block group level. CNT defines accordingly "transit access shed" on the aerial geography of block groups. Specifically, a transit access shed refers to "the total area that transit riders from the block group can access in 30 min with one or no transfers for all the transit stations within a ¼ mile of the block group" (page 7).

Bertolini (1999) in his node-place model (described below in further detail) for TOD assessment derived two out of a total 15 indicators, the number of stations within 20- and 45-min of travel, as two layers of the larger transit travel shed. Charlier et al. (2002) defined the rail transit travel shed as being the combinations of separate travel sheds associated with rail access modes, including pedestrians, bicycles, buses, and automobiles. The bus travel shed, according to the study, is "equal to the length of the bus route plus the walk access zone around bus stops" (page 14).

Liu et al. (2020) have adopted the concept of daily travel time budget to specify the spatial scope of the transit travel shed for C-TOD. Time-use and travel surveys from different cities and countries suggest that people spend approximately 60–90 min per day on travel (Schafer and Victor, 2000). In the case of rail transit, people can make their in-vehicle time less costly than driving because they can perform some productive activities or simply rest while onboard. The possibility of productive in-vehicle time with transit likely increases riders' travel time budgets (Mott MacDonald Limited, 2009). Accounting for these factors, Liu et al. (2020) estimated the transit travel shed in the range of a full journey time of 55–65 min by transit, including 5–10 min average access time between either end of the transit trip. For a typical rail transit that operates at an average speed of 30–45 miles per hour (including dwelling time), the transit travel shed specified by Liu et al. (2020) covers approximately 15–20 miles (or 15–20 stations) in length.

While the travel shed-based approach offers a sound behavioral basis to conceptualize and analyze C-TOD, practicing C-TOD often takes a purpose-driven approach to delineate the corridor space. Most commonly, the route alignment of a transit line is taken by default to determine corridor length. The World Bank (2018), for instance, refers to "the corridor scale for TOD planning as a finite public transit line within a transit network and the immediate area that benefits from the transit line." (page 23) Some transit routes may be very long. The resulting long corridors can be divided into segments for ease of planning as Ferrell et al. (2016) suggested. According to Ferrell et al. (2016), a corridor or segment for TOD should contain no less than three stations or stops. From the local community's perspective, a TOD corridor may include the portion of transit route and its vicinity within certain jurisdictional boundaries. This way of defining C-TOD helps with plan implementation, as shown by the Rosslyn-Ballston corridor example.

3.2 C-TOD analysis and planning

Scholars and practitioners have taken very diverse approaches to analyze and plan for C-TODs. This section categorizes and describes two types of approaches: the typological, and performance-based optimization. While the following characterization of two planning approaches for C-TOD focuses on the analytical and technical aspects of the work, it should be noted that this summary is not exhaustive of all elements of the process. In particular, public engagement, a critical element of all planning processes, is an essential piece to the making of a C-TOD but beyond the scope of discussion here. Furthermore, the two approaches are not mutually exclusive. Practicing C-TOD may apply either or combine the two approaches according to project needs and available resources.

3.2.1 Typological approach

C-TOD may contain multiple TOD nodes in a corridor and multiple corridors in a region. Very commonly analysts and planners first establish typologies of TOD nodes and corridors by considering sets of shared attributes and characteristics. They then develop planning and policy proposals corresponding to each type.

The study done by URS Corp (2011) represents a commonly practiced approach to assess TODs at the individual transit corridor level. URS Corp (2011) conducted a TOD corridor study for Durham-Orange County area, United States. The corridor consists of 19 light rail transit (LRT) stations. The study team composed a 19-indicator scoring scheme to assess the condition of each station area. They then juxtaposed the 19 stations' scores to create the corridor level assessment and five types of TOD nodes. Each station district falls into one of five TOD types, for which plan guidelines were proposed. Most existing C-TOD practices follow this node-based, typological planning approach.

For corridor level analysis, Center for Transit Oriented Development (2010) categorizes three TOD corridor types based on the functional characteristics of the locations each transit line serves: *Destination Connector*, *Commuter Corridor*, and *District Circulator*. Each corridor consists of multiple TOD nodes as well as the surrounding station areas reachable by walking and biking. *Destination Connectors* join residential neighborhoods to various job or service destinations such as commercial districts, business centers, and university or medical campuses. *Commuter Corridors* function mainly to link bedroom communities in suburbs with city center jobs. Typically, strong directional flows of work-related traffic occur along these corridors, with morning inbound and afternoon outbound travel highlighting daily peaks. *District Circulators* refer to the local circular corridors that link the points of interest within a district, for example, downtown districts, corporate components, and medical or university campuses. Access to various points of interest in the district can be achieved by means of walking, biking, and circular transit services.

Ferrell et al. (2016) created a different set of three corridor types based on the conditions of transit-land development in the communities where the corridors span. *Emerging Transit Corridors* refer to low-density, segregated-use communities with limited transit service. *Transitioning Transit Corridors* are in the process of transforming into high livability conditions with newly enhanced transit services. Finally, *Integrated Transit Corridors* contain both high-capacity and local transit services integrated with dense and diverse destinations. For each of the three types of corridor communities, Ferrell et al. (2016) specified elements for improvement considering factors that correspond to the livability principles published jointly by the U.S. Department of Transportation, the Environmental Protection Agency, and the Department of Housing and Urban Development.

In the European context, the node-place model developed by Bertolini (1999) is perhaps the most widely applied conceptual and analytical frame for assessing TOD, that is, the balancing of conditions between transportation and land use activities in transit station areas. The model conceives each station area having two kinds of value. One is *node value*, referring to the conditions of transportation supply in the station area. The other is *place value*, concerning the use functions that the station area offers. In his original conception, Bertolini specified a set of 15 indicators (nine for node and six for place) to operationalize the model. Based on the 15-indicator assessment, station areas are scored and grouped as node-place balanced, unbalanced nodes, or unbalanced places. For unbalanced nodes with surplus transportation supply, planning and policy interventions should aim to increase housing, shops, and other activity functions accordingly. The unbalanced places, on the other hand, would need further transportation improvement.

The node-place model is intuitively straightforward to interpret and can be scaled conveniently to different sizes of markets. The model has been widely applied and continues to be expanded and refined. Vale (2015) pointed out that a balanced node-place station area does not lead to a true TOD due to inadequate consideration of pedestrian accessibility (or the built environment quality in general) in the original set of 15 indicators. He then introduced the concept of pedestrian shed and proposed to combine the *pedshed ratio* with the node-place metric. As demonstrated through the case of Lisbon, Portugal, Vale also improved typological assessments classifying 83 station areas as either TODs or TADs (transit-adjacent development).

Although Bertolini's original node-place model touches on the realm of network conditions by considering stations within 20 and 45 min of travel, his work and refinements by others have primarily focused on the individual TODs. This limitation has motivated recent efforts to explore and incorporate new regional or network-wide attributes for TOD analysis. Huang et al. (2018) adapted the theory of network synergy to the study of TOD types. Synergy refers to the interactions between two or more individual entities that lead to the combined (synergetic) effects greater than the sum of the effects generated by each entity alone. The fact that individual station areas or TOD nodes are connected via transit lines suggests the existence of synergetic potential between the nodes. TOD analysis and planning should tap into and augment this synergetic potential. Through the Arnhem-Nijmegen, Netherlands case study, Huang et al. (2018) gained insights into the varying degrees of complementarity between TOD types when different policy or planning interests; for instance, residential housing price and building uses, are addressed.

Through further research into system scales of TODs, Papa et al. (2013) and Zhang et al. (2019) have explored the applications of network analytics to the regional network dimensions of the node-place model. Their premise states that a TOD node (i.e., a station area) may play a differentiated role between the local (station) scale and the transit network at the regional level. An individual TOD that shows poor performance based on nodal metrics could be critical to the entire network. The degree of individual TOD's network criticality cannot be fully captured by the analysis at the nodal level. To capture the network criticality for network TOD analysis, Papa et al. (2013) incorporated the Closeness Centrality index, a Graph Theory concept that characterizes how centrally each graph element (e.g., a station area) is located within the network. Zhang et al. (2019) used an index of weighted *Betweenness Centrality* to identify the relative positioning of a station area and to measure the extent to which it is connected in the regional network.

3.2.2 Performance-based optimization approach

Increasingly public agencies are practicing performance-based planning (PBP) as an alternative to the traditional, prescription-based planning (Baker et al., 2006; Grant et al., 2013). PBP helps deal with the growing complexity of planning challenges and increasing accountability of planning decisions. In the United States, the 2012 Federal surface transportation legislation, "Moving Ahead for Progress in the 21st Century Act" (MAP-21) requires incorporation of a comprehensive performance-based approach to statewide and metropolitan planning processes for decision-making. Planning for TOD aims to achieve multiple objectives under the umbrella of sustainability. The factors to be considered and assessed are complex, concerning impacts and performance in environmental (both the built- and natural-environments), economic/financial, and social realms. These challenges have motivated efforts to explore nontraditional, PBP-oriented alternatives for TOD analysis and planning. One specific PBP effort for TOD involves applications of multi-objective optimization techniques.

Lin and Gau (2006) developed a multi-objective programming model to determine the optimal level of floor-area ratios (FARs) by maximizing transit ridership and the living-environment quality (measured as the supply of residential and commercial spaces), and minimizing social inequality (measured as the density differential between transit station areas and non-station areas). This initial model, which applies only to individual TOD nodes, was expanded later (Lin and Li, 2008) for TOD planning (focusing on land use decisions) at the corridor and regional scales. In the expanded model, the authors introduced the concept of gray numbers (i.e., numbers taking a range of values rather than exact values) and applied the gray, multi-objective programming technique for decisions on allocating residential, employment, and recreational activities along transit corridors.

The optimization model for TOD planning developed by Li et al. (2010) and Ma et al. (2018) considered a set of variables representing the various dimensions of sustainability, including transit and land market efficiency (i.e., transit ridership and the real estate value of the land surrounding transit stations), proportion of affordable land supply, minimum cost of pollution control, maximum land use mixture, and functional compatibility of adjacent land parcels. Sahu (2018) incorporated the 3 D's (density, diversity, and design) of TOD attributes into the method she developed to assess land use scenarios for the proposed BRT line in Chhattisgarh, India. In this study, the author applied genetic algorithms (GAs) that enabled her to evaluate 30 TOD scenarios generated with four objective functions. Singh et al. (2015) also applied a spatial multi-criteria assessment method to evaluate TOD conditions in two regions in the Netherlands.

The aforementioned examples of TOD planning through multi-objective optimization applied mostly to individual TOD nodes (with an exception by Lin and Li, 2008). A recent study by Liu et al. (2020) expanded the nodal approach to transit corridors defined by transit travel sheds. This work developed the application of a novel C-TOD planning tool that incorporates data input at the parcel level as measured by the commonly used

5D variables of TOD planning: Density, Diversity, Design, Distance to Transit, and Destination Accessibility (Ewing and Cervero, 2010). Users (e.g., planners) can specify corridor level planning goals; for instance, total population, number of jobs, job-service-housing ratios, minimum or maximum FARs, and restrictions or permissions of land use functions. Where these variables are expressed across individual transit corridors containing up to hundreds or thousands of land parcels, the development options become thus literally infinite in terms of functional uses and the levels of development intensity. Liu et al. (2020) applied genetic algorithms to generate C-TOD scenarios permutating land use types and intensity for all changeable land parcels. The scenarios were then evaluated based on three sustainability indicators: sum of transit premiums; total accessibility to services and housing opportunities; and total emissions from buildings and household travel.

4. C-TOD research needs

Conceptualizing and practicing the corridor and network scales of TODs opens up opportunities and challenges beyond working with individual TOD nodes at the local scale. Three topical issues warranting further research and attention begin to emerge and are highlighted below.

The first issue pertains to the "T" in C-TOD, concerning how the network system could help improve transit service performance. It is expected and empirically confirmed that TOD helps increase transit ridership resulting from increased development intensity, along with other supply-side improvements in the station area. While corridor ridership will increase naturally when transit boarding at individual stations increases, C-TOD is expected to enhance transit performance beyond the sum of ridership from individual stations. From a corridor perspective, two indicators are important: ratio of directional flows along transit lines (Cervero, 2009) and internal rate of non-auto trip capture (Ferrell et al., 2016). Adding densities and increasing land use diversities in all station areas do not lead automatically to an even distribution between inbound- and outbound-rider flows on transit routes. A C-TOD approach should be able to capture the directional flow dynamics. A higher internal rate of non-auto trip capture means a greater share of trip origin-destination pairs falling within the corridor. The existing methods and metrics for nodal TOD are inadequate for this kind of corridor performance assessment.

Another "T" aspect of C-TOD pertains to corridor level multimodality. Multimodal consideration at the individual TOD node focuses on first-/last-mile connections between the trunk line transit and its access modes such as walking/biking, driving, and feeder transit services. For C-TOD, the multimodal connections at individual nodes remain critical. Route-level multimodal complementarity is also essential in order to make high-performance corridor TOD. Rail transit, whether light rail, metro rail, or commuter rail, provides reliable and fast service along designated routes but they are spatially constrained beyond that due to relatively distant station spacing (ranging from 1 to 10+ miles). Effective intermediate services to fill the gaps are essential to support C-TOD. The trinary bus/road systems in Curitiba reviewed earlier presents a continuous C-TOD example. Developing the high-performance C-TOD requires careful planning and coordination to avoid duplicated, intra-transit competition in the corridor while offering full coverage of transit services that meet the demand of diverse user segments by income, activities, time of day. Such work demands corridor-wide full integration, including scheduling, spatial data (route and stop locations), fare policy, and real-time information.

The second aspect is "D" (development) related. The commonly known 5D attributes of TOD may also apply to the corridor scale, yet the "corridor" keyword calls for corridor or network level concepts and metrics for C-TOD planning and assessment. From a system or network perspective, multiple local optimums for development do not necessarily add up to the global (system) optimum. A corridor or network perspective expects coordinated and integrated planning for development intensity and functional composition (i.e., density and diversity) at the corridor level in addition to the nodal level efforts. Staricco and Brovarone (2018) argues that TOD planning at the regional level should focus on establishing the overall spatial structure of TOD in terms of hierarchical distribution of transportation nodes, links, and activities, whereas TOD planning at the local level defines the precise contents of land use types and densities. This top-down, hierarchical approach, however, lacks direct feedback at the local, station level to inform corridor or regional level decisions with explicit consideration of inter-station land use interactions. The need for a dynamic approach to capture TOD nodal-corridor interactions warrants future research.

A transit line in most cases traverses multiple jurisdictions and communities. While transit lines link them together, their local interests do not necessarily work toward the same direction. In the United States or other countries where land use decisions are primarily local responsibilities, planning for C-TOD faces particular cross-jurisdictional challenges. Coordinating land use decisions among individual station areas to achieve broad objectives at the corridor or regional level requires tailoring analytical methods and tools as well as forging collective efforts among local stakeholders. Further studies are needed to document best practices and innovative coalition-building for successful C-TOD implementation.

In the third aspect of C-TOD research a corridor perspective offers more opportunities to address policy level concerns such as housing affordability and displacement that cannot be adequately addressed at the individual station level alone.

The Housing + Transportation (H + T) Index, developed by Center for Neighborhood Technology (CNT, 2015), offers one innovative approach in building on the corridor or network perspective capacity to address the affordability challenge. Conventionally, housing affordability considers only housing cost relative to income and sets 30% of household income as the affordability benchmark. However, an affordable housing unit does not offer any value to a needed household in need unless it is accessible by an affordable means of transportation. The H + T approach incorporates explicitly transportation affordability into the conventional housing affordability analysis, adding 20% of household income for transportation cost. This implies a spatial scope defined by the service area of affordable transportation. Affordability can be improved either by increasing the stock of affordable housing, or by improving transportation supply (lowering the unit cost of transportation), or both. For transit-based analysis, the H + T Index has been applied at the scale of transit corridors, as shown by the study of Mueller et al. (2018).

Many fast-growing cities are experiencing rapid depletion of affordable rental housing stocks, elevating the pressure on the elected city officials to seek solutions. Mueller et al. (2018) developed a corridor tool that assists city planners in prioritizing (re)development and transit improvement locations while minimizing displacement threats to low-income renters. The tool allows the user to calculate and evaluate three sets of metrics. The first measures accessibility to low-wage jobs by transit. The second assesses the existing stock of affordable rental housing vulnerable to loss by redevelopment or expiration of subsidies. The third metric considers redevelopment pressure and timing. The C-TOD encourages planners to explore many outstanding concerns of policy interest; for example, corridor transportation emissions and transit value capture (Fogarty et al., 2008).

5. Conclusions

TOD as a spatial concept has gained worldwide popularity in planning practice and academic research as well. There are ample examples of TOD plans and guidelines and voluminous output of scholarly research on TOD benefits and impacts. TOD in principle may apply to all geographic scales, ranging from project site level to metro/regional or state and country level. This chapter focuses on the intermediate scale at the corridor level, arguing that corridor TOD, C-TOD, presents a great deal of untapped potential.

The opportunity of C-TOD resides in the synergies brought by transit network effects. C-TOD analysis and planning should incorporate these network effects in order to achieve the corridor level gains that are greater than the sum of those from individual TOD nodes. C-TOD planning may be carried out for segments of a transit line, along the entire length of the line, or across multiple lines of the transit network. A corridor scope defined by the concept of transit travel shed offers sound behavioral underpinning for C-TOD analysis. The transit shed may extend to a spatial scope containing up to 20 miles (or 20 stations for a typical rail transit system) in length. This behavior-based delineation of corridor space opens up new opportunities to explore solutions to challenging issues such as job and service accessibility of the mobility-disadvantaged and housing affordability, for which nodal TODs offer very limited options.

C-TOD performance is closely related to that of nodal TODs yet there should be corridor-specific C-TOD methods and metrics. Examples of C-TOD metrics on transit performance include ratio of directional passenger flows and rate of corridor internal trip capture. Land use planning and environmental design for individual station areas are critical to make successful TOD nodes but insufficient to produce a strongly performing TOD corridor. Adopting innovative planning methods and new computing tools, for example, genetic algorithms for multi-objective optimization, can help deal with the increased complexity associated with corridor TODs.

Improving C-TOD analysis and planning does not guarantee a desired C-TOD outcome automatically. The experiences of Copenhagen, Denmark; Curitiba, Brazil; and Arlington, VA of the United States, demonstrate that C-TOD and regional TOD can succeed on the conditions of coordination across agencies and jurisdictions along with cooperation among all stakeholders.

References

Ahamad, Z., 2014. Planning for transit oriented development in Malaysia. In: Presentation at the Japan-OECD Policy Forum on Urban Development and Green Growth, Tokyo, October 14-16.

Arlington, V.A., 2017. General Land Use Plan: Adopted August 12, 1961 with Amendments Through June 30, 2018. Accessed on May 20, 2020 at URL https://arlingtonva.s3.dualstack.us-east-1.amazonaws.com/wp-content/uploads/sites/31/2017/10/Booklet_June_2017.pdf.

Arlington, V.A., 2021. Rosslyn-Ballston Corridor. Accessed on January 1, 2021 at URL https://projects.arlingtonva.us/planning/smart-growth/rosslyn-ballston-corridor/.

Baker, D., Sipe, N., Gleeson, B., 2006. Performance-based planning—perspectives from the United States, Australia, and New Zealand. J. Plan. Educ. Res. 25 (4), 396–409. https://doi.org/10.1177/0739456x05283450.

Bertolini, L., 1999. Spatial development patterns and public transport: the application of an analytical model in the Netherlands. Plan. Pract. Res. 14 (2), 199–210.

Calthorpe, P., 1993. The Next American Metropolis: Ecology, Community and the American Dream. Princeton Architectural Press, New York.

Center for Transit Oriented Development, 2010. Transit Corridors and TOD: Connecting the Dots. Accessed on October 10, 2018 at URL http://ctod.org/pdfs/tod203.pdf.

Cervero, R., 1997. The Transit Metropolis: A Global Inquiry. Island Press, Washington, D.C.

Cervero, R., 2004. Transit-Oriented Development in the United States: Experiences, Challenges, and Prospects. TCHRP Report 102, Transportation Research Board, Washington, D.C.

Cervero, R., 2009. Public transport and sustainable urbanism: global lessons. In: Curtis, C., Renne, J., Bertolini, I. (Eds.), Transit Oriented Development: Making It Happen. Ashgate, Farnham, pp. 39–47.

Charlier, J., Jacobsen, M., Hernandez, C., Herman, B., Ellis, L., 2002. Rail-Oriented Development: Strategies and Tools to Support Passenger Rail. CDOT-DTD-R-2001-19, Colorado Department of Transport.

City of Denver, 2014. Transit Oriented Denver: Transit Oriented Development Strategic Plan. City of Denver. https://www.denvergov.org/content/dam/denvergov/Portals/193/documents/TOD_Plan/TOD_Strategic_Plan_FINAL.pdf.

CNT, 2015. H+T Index Methods. Center for Neighborhood Technology.

CoA (City of Austin), 2006. Transit-Oriented Development (TOD) Guidebook. City of Austin, TX. http://www.austintexas.gov/department/transit-oriented-development.

Curtis, C., Schreurs, J., 2016. Planning for Public Transport Accessibility: An International Sourcebook. Routledge.

Denmark Ministry of the Environment. 2007, 2015, 2019. The Finger Plan. Denmark. Available at URL: www.naturstyrelsen.dk.

Ewing, R., Cervero, R., 2010. Travel and the built environment: a meta-analysis. J. Am. Plann. Assoc. 76 (3), 265–294.

Fang, W., Xue, L., 2015. How a Chinese Megacity is Innovating Finance for Transit-Oriented Development. TheCityFix. Accessed on December 20, 2020 at URL https://thecityfix.com/blog/how-chinese-megacity-innovating-finance-transit-oriented-development-tdm-wanli-fang-lulu-xue/.

FDOT, 2009. Transit Oriented Development Design Guidelines. Florida Department of Transportation.

Ferrell, C., Appleyard, B., Taeckr, M., Allen, C., Armusewicz, C., Schroder, C., 2016. Livable Transit Corridors: Methods, Metrics, and Strategies. TCRP Research Report 187, Transportation Research Board, Washington, D.C.

Fogarty, N., Eaton, N., Belzer, D., Ohland, G., 2008. Capturing the Value of Transit. Center for Transit-Oriented Development. Accessed on May 31, 2020. Available at URL http://www.reconnectingamerica.org/assets/Uploads/ctodvalcapture110508v2.pdf.

FTA (Federal Transit Administration), 2019. Transit Oriented Development. Accessed on January 1, 2021 at URL https://www.transit.dot.gov/TOD.

Grant, M., D'Ignazio, J., Bond, A., McKeeman, A., 2013. Performance Based Planning and Programming Guidebook. U.S. FHWA. https://www.fhwa.dot.gov/planning/performance_based_planning/pbpp_guidebook/page00.cfm.

HNTB, 2016. America THINKS Transit Oriented Development. Accessed on January 10, 2021 at URL https://ww1.prweb.com/prfiles/2016/05/24/13438543/AThinks_TOD_Factsheet_516.pdf.

Huang, R., Grigolon, A., Madureira, M., Brussel, M., 2018. Measuring transit-oriented development (TOD) network complementarity based on TOD node typology. J. Transp. Land Use 11 (1), 304–324.

Ibraeva, A., de Almeida Correia, G., Silva, C., Antunes, A., 2020. Transit-oriented development: a review of research achievements and challenges. Transp. Res. A Policy Pract. 132, 120–130.

ICF International, 2009. Corridor Approaches to Integrating Transportation and Land Use. NCHRP 8-36-86. Washington, D.C.

ICLEI, 2016. Curitiba, Brazil: A Model for Transit Oriented Development. ICLEI Case Study, No. 190. Available at URL https://sustainablemobility.iclei.org/wpdm-package/curitiba-brazil-a-model-of-transit-oriented-planning/.

ITDP (Institute for Transportation and Development Policy), 2017. TOD Standard 3.0. ITDP: New York. Accessed on January 20, 2020 at URL https://www.itdp.org/publication/tod-standard/.

Knowles, R.D., 2012. Transit oriented development in Copenhagen, Denmark: from the finger plan to Ørestad. J. Transp. Geogr. 22, 251–261.

Leach, D., 2004. The Arlington County case study: Rosslyn-Ballston corridor. In: Dittmar, Ohland (Eds.), The New Transit Town: Best Practices in Transit-Oriented Development. Island Press, Washington, D.C, pp. 131–154.

Li, Y., Guo, H.L., Li, H., Xu, G.H., Wang, Z.R., Kong, C.W., 2010. Transit-oriented land planning model considering sustainability of mass rail transit. ASCE J. Urban Plann. Dev. 136 (3), 243–248.

Lin, J., Gau, C., 2006. A TOD planning model to review the regulation of allowable development densities around subway stations. Land Use Policy 23, 353–360.

Lin, J., Li, C., 2008. A grey programming model for regional transit-oriented development planning. Pap. Reg. Sci. 87 (1), 119–139.

Liu, L., Zhang, M., Xu, T., 2020. A conceptual framework and implementation tool for land use planning for corridor transit oriented development. Cities 107. December 2020. https://doi.org/10.1016/j.cities.2020.102939.

Ma, X., Chen, X., Li, X., Ding, C., Wang, Y., 2018. Sustainable station-level planning: an integrated transport and land use design model for transit-oriented development. J. Clean. Prod. 170, 1052–1063.

Mehta, P., Mungekar, N., Mathew, M., 2016. Transit Oriented Development Manual: Delhi TOD Policy and Regulations Interpretation. The Hub. Accessed on December 20, 2019 at URL https://wricitieshub.org/publications/transit-oriented-development-manual-delhi-tod-policy-regulations-interpretation.

Mott MacDonald Limited, 2009. Productive Use of Travel Time and Working Time Savings for Rail Business Travellers (Draft Final Report). Department for Transport, UK.

Mueller, E., Hilde, T., Torrado, M., 2018. Methods for counter spatial inequality: incorporating strategic opportunities for housing preservation into transit-oriented development planning. Landsc. Urban Plan. 177, 317–327.

Papa, E., Moccia, F.D., Angiello, G., Inglese, P., 2013. An accessibility planning tool for network transit oriented development: SNAP. Planum J. Urban. 27 (2), 1–9.

PedShed, 2021. What Is a Ped Shed? Accessed on January 1, 2021 at URL: http://pedshed.net/?page_id=5#:~:text=A%20ped%20shed%20is%20the,feet%2C%20or%20400%20meters.

Phuc, L.M., 2015. Transit-oriented development in Ho Chi Minh city: opportunities & challenges. In: Presentation at the Knowledge Sharing Seminar on Good Practice on TOD. Online Conferences Organized by the World Bank. Accessed on October 1, 2020 at URL https://www.jointokyo.org/files/cms/news/pdf/Agenda_TOD-Seminar_FINAL.pdf.

Pojani, D., Stead, D., 2018. Past, present and future of transit-oriented development in three European capital city-regions. In: Shiftan, Y., Kamargianni, M. (Eds.), Preparing for the New Era of Transport Policies: Learning From Experience. Elsevier, Amsterdam, pp. 93–118.

Renne, J., Appleyard, B., 2019. Twenty-five years in the making: TOD as a new name for an enduring concept. J. Plan. Educ. Res. 39 (4), 402–408.

Rodriguez, D., Vergel-Tovar, C.E., 2017. Urban development around bus rapid transit stops in seven cities in Latin-America. J. Urban. 11 (2), 175–201. https://doi.org/10.1080/17549175.2017.1372507.

Sahu, A., 2018. A methodology to modify land uses in a transit oriented development scenario. J. Environ. Manag. 213, 467–477.

Schafer, A., Victor, D.G., 2000. The future mobility of the world population. Transp. Res. A 34 (3), 171–205.

Singh, Y., He, P., Flacke, J., Maarseveen, M., 2015. Measuring TOD over a region using GIS based multiple criteria assessment tools. SPA J. School Plan. Archit. 19 (1–2), 1–22.

Smith, S., 1999. Guidebook for Transportation Corridor Studies: A Process for Effective Decision-Making. NCHRP Report 435, National Academy Press, Washington, D.C.

Sorensen, E., Torfing, J., 2019. The Copenhagen metropolitan 'Finger Plan': a robust urban planning success based on collaborative governance. In: Compton, M., Hart, P. (Eds.), Great Policy Successes: Or, A Table About Why It's Amazing That Governments Get So Little Credit for Their Many Everyday and Extraordinary Achievements as Told by Sympathetic Observers Who Seek to Create Space for a Less Relentlessly Negatively View of Our Pivotal Public Institutions. Oxford University Press.

Staricco, L., Brovarone, E.V., 2018. Promoting TOD through regional planning: a comparative analysis of two European approaches. J. Transp. Geogr. 66, 45–52.

TCRP (Transit Cooperative Research Program), 2003. Curitiba Brazil BRT Case Study, TCRP Report 90. vol. 1 Published by the Transportation Research Board, Washington, D.C.

The World Bank, 2018. TOD Implementation Resources & Tools. The World Bank, Washington D.C.

URS Corp, 2011. Durham-Orange County Corridor Alternatives Analysis. vol. 4. TOD Assessment Report. Morrisville, NC.

Vale, D., 2015. Transit-oriented development, integration of land use and transport, and pedestrian accessibility: combining node-place model with pedestrian shed ratio to evaluate and classify station areas in Lisbon. J. Transp. Geogr. 45, 70–80.

Zhang, Y., Marshall, S., Manley, E., 2019. Network criticality and the node-place-design model: classifying metro station areas in Greater London. J. Transp. Geogr. 79, 102485.

Zhou, J., 2016. The transit metropolis of Chinese characteristics? Literature review, interviews, surveys and case studies. Transp. Policy 51, 115–125.

CHAPTER TWELVE

Big and/or open data and transit-served area research

Jiangping Zhou*
Department of Urban Planning and Design, Faculty of Architecture, The University of Hong Kong (HKU), Pok Fu Lam, Hong Kong SAR, China
*Corresponding author: e-mail address: zhoujp@hku.hk

Contents

Abstract

This chapter looks at how big and/or open data (BOD) can be used to facilitate the transit-served area (T-SA) research and practices. It considers T-SA, or areas within a comfortable walking/biking distance/time (e.g., 800 m or 10 mins) to a transit station or stop, as consisting of two components: TOD-ness and T-SA performance. TOD-ness measures the extent to which the existing conditions of a T-SA meet (ideal) transit-oriented development (TOD) standards deemed as important by TOD advocates. T-SA performance can be quantified or qualified by indicators or phenomena such as increased transit ridership, improved air quality, neighborhood revitalization, enhanced mobility and environment, public safety, alternative lifestyle, and sense of community. These are the benefits and hopes that people have for performing T-SAs. This chapter revisits what existing studies have informed us concerning T-SAs, TOD-ness, and T-SA performance. It attempts to show how BOD can be used to improve the existing studies. Specifically, it synthesizes what data have been used in the existing studies. It also illustrates how BOD have improved our understanding and evaluation of T-SAs, in particular, how BOD can be used to (a) formulate indicators measuring TOD-ness and T-SA performance

Advances in Transport Policy and Planning, Volume 9
ISSN 2543-0009
https://doi.org/10.1016/bs.atpp.2020.08.003

and (b) verify/produce existing/new evidence and knowledge about the relationship between TOD-ness and T-SA performance. Finally, it outlines how BOD and traditional data can supplement each other to improve future studies on T-SAs. It stresses that four areas could be improved to best utilize and fuse BOD and traditional data.

Keywords: Transit-served area, Big data, Open data, Traditional data, Scholarship

Many developed countries or cities are in the so-called "Freeway Era," which is characterized by spread-out urban form, heavy dependence on private cars, and abundant supply of parking lots and highways (c.f., Muller, 2017; Shoup, 2011). On the one hand, residents can enjoy benefits such as large single family homes, high motorized mobility, and tranquil suburban lifestyle; on the other hand, they also experience enormous multidimensional costs such as traffic congestion, excessive petroleum consumption, degraded air quality, shrinkage of natural landscapes, dwindled sense of belonging/community, and loss in social capital (Bernick and Cervero, 1997; Calthorpe, 1993; Newman and Kenworthy, 1999; Putnam, 2001). Transit-oriented development (TOD), which was pioneered by Calthorpe (1993), provides a suite of (new) strategies and development models to minimize those costs and to optimize the positive effects of transit-land use integration, thus benefiting for the society at large.

Transit-served areas (T-SAs) are irregular polygons within a comfortable walking/biking distance/time (e.g., 800 m or 10 mins) to a transit station or stop. T-SAs can also be called "transit-served neighborhoods," "transit-served subcity nodes," "transit served real estate development," "transit-rich neighborhoods," "transit-served nodes and corridors," "station areas," "station precincts," to name a few (Bertolini et al., 2012, p. 31; Cervero et al., 2002, p. 75; Cervero et al., 2004, p. S10, S13, 139, 177, 322, 349; Carlton, 2007 p. 1; Olaru and Curtis, 2015, p. 6; Renne, 2009, p. 3; Wang and Woo, 2017, p. 183). They are crucial venues where TOD should be implemented or enhanced.

Quality and performance of T-SAs are imperative to the TOD success. TOD-ness[a] is a term coined by TCRP (2007) to denote quality of T-SAs and measures the extent to which the existing conditions of T-SAs meet (ideal) TOD standards proposed or deemed as important by TOD advocates. Commonly seen TOD-ness narratives include but are not limited to Density, Diversity, Design, Distance, and Destination, i.e., 3-Ds or 5-Ds (e.g., see Bertolini et al., 2012; Carlton, 2007; Cervero and Kockelman, 1997;

[a] Hereafter, I treat "TOD-ness" as both singular and plural to simplify.

Cervero et al., 2002, 2004; Olaru and Curtis, 2015; Renne, 2009; Wang and Woo, 2017). Explicitly or implicitly, decision-makers who enthusiastically promote TOD believe or assume that good TOD-ness can improve the performance of T-SAs. Such performance can be quantified or qualified as indicators or phenomena such as increased transit ridership, improved air quality, neighborhood revitalization, enhanced mobility and environment, public safety, alternative lifestyle, sense of community, and public safety/celebration (Bernick and Cervero, 1997).

In this chapter, we aim to accomplish two tasks: first, synthesizing sporadic evidence or knowledge concerning TOD-ness and its impact on T-SA performance in existing literature; second, describing and discussing how BOD can provide extra evidence and knowledge in that regard. The argument is that BOD can be used to quantify both TOD-ness and T-SA performance. We illustrate that BOD can help fill in some information/knowledge gaps concerning the relationship between TOD-ness and T-SA performance and can produce insights that traditional data alone could not offer. In other words, BOD, alone, or in combination with traditional data, can improve the existing T-SA or TOD scholarship and practices.

1. TOD-ness and T-SA performance: What we know

1.1 The "big picture"

To get a big picture on the existing literature around the relationship between TOD-ness and T-SA performance, a forward reference search was performed, a method that identifies refereed articles, reports, and books touching on the relationship. To implement the method, two classics on the topic were chosen as the starting point: Calthorpe (1993) and Cervero and Kockelman (1997). Studies citing them and their derivatives were identified, collected and read, yielding 100 + studies. Then, the 5-Ds mentioned above were used as references to reclassify and count variables or concepts in these studies. Also categorized was the degree to which T-SA performance measures these variables or concepts are correlated. Fig. 1 presents the overall findings in a diagram.

Several findings can be drawn from Fig. 1. First, among the 5-Ds, Density and Design are considered more frequently than the other Ds: Distance, Diversity, and Destination. Compared to other Ds, Destination is the least frequently examined. This does not mean that Destination will not influence T-SA performance to a similar degree as the other Ds.

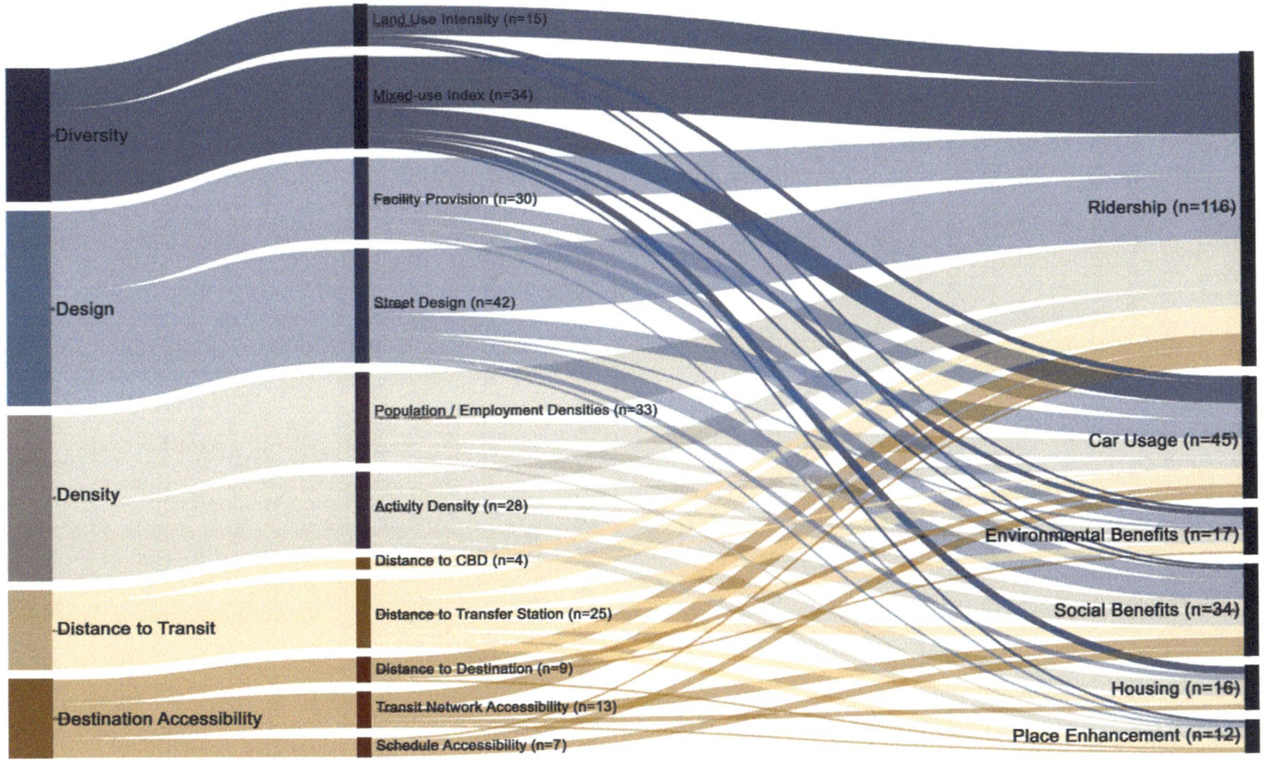

Fig. 1 "Big picture": TOD-ness and T-SA performance. Notes: The leftmost column shows which are the 5-Ds and how many studies (the numbers in the parentheses) consider these Ds respectively. Five bars are used to represent these Ds too. The height of these bars is proportional to the number in the parentheses, i.e., how many of the existing studies consider each of the 5-Ds. The middle column reflects the most typical indicators the existing studies employ to operationalize each of the 5-Ds. As with the 5-Ds, bars are used to represent these indicators and the height of these bars is proportional to the number in the parentheses, i.e., how many of the existing studies use each of those indicators. The rightmost column shows the most frequently mentioned T-SA performance in the 100+ studies that were identified. Between any two neighboring columns, curves of different width show how the 5-Ds, indicators, and T-SA performance are related, and how strong is the relationship.

Actually, based on the curve between columns/bars, Destination can still predict T-SA performance in aspects such as ridership, environmental benefits, place enhancement, social benefits, and car usage.

Second, different indicators can be formulated to measure the 5-Ds. Except for Destination, it seems that at least two indicators can be developed to quantify other Ds. In other words, there have not been universally accepted indicators to operationalize the 5-Ds (or more accurately four out of the 5-Ds) with empirical data. The middle columns/bars show some of the often-used indicators in the existing studies, e.g., activity densities, mixed-used index, and distance to transfer station.

Third, T-SA performance can be multidimensional, which ranges from (transit) ridership to environmental benefits. However, ridership is the most dominant among all those indicators or concepts that the existing studies have developed to quantify or qualify T-SA performance. This might not be surprising: increased transit ridership is the primary goal and hoped-for benefit of TOD and other benefits can be spinoffs, as Bernick and Cervero (1997) pointed out.

1.2 Claims, evidence, and knowledge

After defining and measuring different Ds and aspects of T-SA performance, authors have made many claims, presented much empirical evidence, and produced rich knowledge concerning the relationships between TOD-ness and T-SA performance. At some risk of oversimplifying the existing studies, 37 out of the 100+ articles identified above were selected and synthesized to provide a snapshot of the kind of claims, evidence, and knowledge concerning the relationships between TOD-ness and T-SA performance that are in place in the existing studies (Table 1). The 37 articles were selected based on both subjective and objective criteria:

- How seminal they are in terms of advancing new concepts or ideas about TOD, TOD-ness, and the T-SA performance, respectively;
- How many citations they generated respectively—especially those articles published 5 or more years ago that are not cited 10 or more times in Google Scholar are weighted less and even totally excluded;
- Who is/are the author(s)—articles by leading professional entities or academics are preferred;
- Impact factor and fame of the outlet where an article is published.

What is meant in terms of "claims" in the articles is that the author(s) did not collect empirical data, fit models, and/or present verifiable results about

Table 1 Existing claims, evidences, and knowledge about TOD-ness and T-SA performance.

Source	Claims (C), evidence (E), and/or knowledge (K)	Notes
Calthorpe (1993)	C: TOD-ness such as Distance, Density and Diversity can reduce car ownerships, auto trips, etc	He did not propose the "Ds" concept but described them as something like "comfortable walking distance" and "mixed-use" (p. 56)
TCRP (1995)	E: Population density, distance to CBD, and employment size at CBD can all boost transit ridership at T-SAs	T-SAs were 216 rail-served station areas across the US
Cervero and Kockelman (1997)	E: Density, land-use diversity, and pedestrian-oriented designs generally reduce trip rates and encourage non-auto travel in statistically significant ways, though their influences appear to be fairly marginal	The 3-Ds were first proposed therein
Bernick and Cervero (1997)	E: Proximity to rail is associated with employment, population and residential building growth; Residential/retail attributes (e.g., housing density) and rail station areas' street patterns influence mode split	They called T-SAs "transit villages"
Boarnet and Crane (1998)	E: Proximity to the rail station may entice other land uses rather than residential housing	Supply of transit-based housing was considered as a good T-SA performance indicator
Cervero et al. (2002)	E/K: TOD can increase transit ridership and rent premium	The knowledge was based on evidence from secondary sources
Caltrans (2002)	C: TOD has a wide range of positive outcomes	This is a document focusing on TOD promotion
Wells and Renne (2003)	C: T-SAs meeting certain criteria would have good performance, which can be measured using indicators	More information concerning those criteria can be found at: https://goo.gl/Do9tEP
Cervero et al. (2004)	E/K: TOD has a wide range of positive outcomes	The knowledge was based on evidence from secondary sources
Dittmar and Ohland (2004)	C/E: Density, walkability, Diversity, location-efficient development and convenient transit services at T-SAs can improve quality of life and metro economies	Some evidences were presented in case studies

NCHRP (2005)	C: TOD can mitigate sprawling developments, preserving land, reducing traffic congestion, etc	Governments need to invest into TOD-related data and update them "yearly or less frequently" (p. 2)
Renne (2007)	C: TOD can yield many benefits and evaluation of them is subjective. But the evaluation should be cross-sectional and longitudinal	Official data plus ad-hoc surveys were used to develop indicators for both TOD-ness and T-SA performance
TCRP (2007)	E/K: TOD-ness such as Density, land use mix, site layout and pedestrian-friendly design can have effects on travel demand	It was based on information from secondary sources
Kahn (2007)	E: Proximity to rail transit can increase gentrification at station areas	Indicators for T-SA performance based on census data: Average housing prices; ratio of college graduates in a census track
Dill (2008)	E: Distance to rail transit and parking pricing influence commute mode choice	Evidence was based on survey data
Cervero and Murakami (2009)	E: Rail + Property Development increases ridership and housing prices	Evidence was based on local official statistics and transit agencies' reports
Renne (2009)	E/K: TOD-ness such as Density, Design, and Distance can increase transit ridership	Censuses and a special TOD database were used
Loo et al. (2010)	E: Station characteristics have the most significant impacts on rail ridership	Station characteristics were Total commercial/ residential floor area; parking area; location of the station (dummy); mixed land use (dummy); generalized travel cost to Midtown; major interchange station (dummy); number of bus stops
Sung and Oh (2011)	E/K: TOD-ness such as Density, Diversity and Design has significant impacts on transit ridership	In Seoul, some factors can be more influential, e.g., transit service network, land use mix and urban design

Continued

Table 1 Existing claims, evidences, and knowledge about TOD-ness and T-SA performance.—cont'd

Source	Claims (C), evidence (E), and/or knowledge (K)	Notes
Chatman et al. (2014)	E: The combination of more concentration of jobs and population and more expensive CBD parking costs can increase ridership at T-SA. A higher value of population, jobs, and congestion score increases passenger miles at the metropolitan level, especially high-wage jobs and leisure jobs	Databases from transit agencies, local governments and censuses were assembled and used
Nasri and Zhang (2014)	E: Households in T-SA with good TOD-ness have less car usage and vehicle miles traveled	Household travel surveys were used. TOD-ness is measured by employment/bus stop densities, rail access, distance to CBD, and block size
Singh et al. (2014)	C: TOD can stimulate sustainable development by encouraging better land use and transport integration, which can be measured by a TOD index	TOD-ness and T-SA performance can be simultaneously measured by an index
Noland et al. (2014)	E: Presence of a train station and redevelopments near train stations can have many beneficial effects, e.g., increased share of non-auto trips and cost of travel	Data from interviews, focus groups, and surveys were used
Papa and Bertolini (2015)	C: Proximity to the transit station and regional rail accessibility of a station could deliver multiple benefits, e.g., shaping polycentricism, mitigating sprawl, boosting transit ridership, etc	Regional rail accessibility (to jobs and population) of a T-SA might affect its performance
Lyu et al. (2016)	E: Different T-SAs can be categorized according to morphological characteristics, carrying capacity used, benefits produced, etc	In other words, different TOD-nesses can lead to different levels of T-SA performance
Renne et al. (2017)	E: Network accessibility to jobs and population within station areas yield an increase in transit commuting at all fixed-guideway transit stations in US. Besides, factors such as socioeconomics, walkability, land-use diversity, and transit service contribute to the increase of transit commuting	Again, regional rail accessibility of a T-SA might affect its performance. Also, socioeconomic factors could influence T-SA performance

Cervero et al. (2017)	C/E: TOD, together with other strategies, can create better communities, environments, and economies	TOD-ness can be measured by indicators such as densities of residents and employees, average block size, availability and quality of urban living infrastructure, access to and connectivity of bikeways and sidewalks, transit service frequency and place identity
Griffiths and Curtis (2017)	E: Increasing housing density in T-SAs can reduce car trips	Survey data were used
Loo and du Verle (2017)	E: T-SA performance can be more than just transit ridership. It should include other benefits, e.g., the share of walking, greenery and vibrancy	TOD-ness was measured by metro/bus access, gross floor areas of different land uses, Simpson index of land uses, road length/total area, share of built open space, total number of station exits, presence of covered walkways, number of retail shops, and population/employment densities
Rodriguez and Vergel-Tovar (2017)	E: TOD-ness at bus rapid transit station areas can boost ridership	Self-collected primary data and secondary data from local transit agencies were used. Used as many as 38 variables to measure TOD-ness
Singh et al. (2017)	E: Different T-SAs can have different levels of TOD-ness and performance	A TOD index can be used to quantify TOD-ness and T-SA performance simultaneously
Renne (2018)	E: T-SAs in proximity to ports have high levels of population, housing, job density, transit usage and walking and lower level of car ownership	TOD-ness was measured by job density, percentage of professional jobs, and walkability scores
Gu et al. (2019)	E: TOD-ness can improve air quality of cities	TOD-ness and different Ds were measured by indices, which were based on different variables concerning built environment, e.g., job-housing mix, population density, density gradient, (average) distance to municipal public services and facilities or passenger transport terminal(s)

Continued

Table 1 Existing claims, evidences, and knowledge about TOD-ness and T-SA performance.—cont'd

Source	Claims (C), evidence (E), and/or knowledge (K)	Notes
Zhao and Li (2018)	E: TOD-ness can encourage people to live and consume in or around transit stations. (In addition to land use near stations, available transport services and individual preference influence T-SA performance, e.g., mode choice)	Survey data were used
Zhou et al. (2018)	E: Points of interest and the active smartphone population in a T-SA per hour is correlated	BOD were used to measure both TOD-ness and T-SA performance. Station characteristics were measured by indicators such as special neighborhoods, specific metro lines, and age of the district
Zhou et al. (2019)	E: TOD indices by Gu et al. (2019) would predict T-SA performance	
Zhou et al. (2020)	E: Centrality of T-SA, Ds, and station characteristics all influence T-SA performance	

Notes: Sources: Adapted from Zhou, J., Wang, Q., and Liu, H., 2018. Evaluating transit-served areas with non-traditional data. J. Transp. Land Use 11 (1), 1323–1349, Zhou, J., Yang, Y., Gu, P., Yin, L., Zhang, F., Zhang, F., and Li, D., 2019. Can TODness improve (expected) performances of TODs? An exploration facilitated by non-traditional data. Transp. Res. D 74, 28–47, Zhou, J., Yang, Y., and Webster, C., 2020. Using big and open data to analyze transit oriented development: new outcomes and improved attributes. J. Am. Plann. Assoc. 86 (3), 364–376.

what they wrote. With regard to "evidence," it means that the author presents verifiable results derived from case studies and statistical models with empirical data as input. Regarding "knowledge," it is treated as something that at least several authors recurrently believe in or validate.

Several findings can be drawn based on the articles in Table 1. First, many existing studies after Calthorpe (1993) indeed provide more and more evidence in different cities and contexts concerning how TOD or TOD-ness can improve T-SA performance. This can be measured using a wide array of indicators.

Second, largely because different indicators and a wide variety of data were used to measure TOD, TOD-ness, and T-SAs, there is still little agreement concerning the relationship between TOD-ness and T-SA performance. We at best have some generic knowledge such as: TOD can increase transit ridership and rent premium (Cervero et al., 2002), TOD has a wide range of positive outcomes (Cervero et al., 2004), and TOD-ness such as Density, land use mix, site layout, and pedestrian-friendly design can influence travel demand (TCRP, 2007). Often there is only some context-sensitive evidence such as T-SAs in proximity to ports have high levels of population, housing, job density, transit usage and walking and lower levels of car ownership (Renne, 2018), TOD-ness can improve the air quality of cities (Gu et al., 2019), and TOD-ness can encourage more people to live and consume in or around transit stations (Zhao and Li, 2018).

Third, authors have attempted to "standardize" indicators and indices (and even data) used to measure both TOD-ness and T-SA performance. Gu et al. (2019), in particular, demonstrated that TOD-ness across 37 Chinese cities could be measured by the same indices concerning Density, Diversity, Design, and accessibility with a common set of conventionally available BOD and traditional data:

- Official statistics by different governmental agencies, e.g., China City Statistical Yearbook;
- Open data available to the public and compiled by not-for-profit entities, e.g., Beijing City Lab (www.Beijingcitylab.org) and the Worldpop (www.worldpop.org.uk);
- Open data (e.g., Baidu Map) prepared by for-profit companies (e.g., Baidu) but allowed for the public to access or crawl via Application Programming Interface (API).

Zhou et al. (2018, 2019, 2020) showed that anonymous and aggregated digital traces left by smartphone users with location-based service (LBS) providers such as Google Map and Baidu Map could be used to standardize and monitor population estimates across various spatiotemporal granularities.

Based on those estimates, one could develop (new) indicators to measure T-SA performance such as people per hour in a T-SA on weekdays and people per weekday or weekend, which have rarely been seen before prior to the advent of the smartphone technology and related digital traces and open data.

Fourth, standardized and/or new indicators or indices measuring TOD-ness and T-SA performance can facilitate the production of new knowledge concerning T-SAs. Based on these indicators, we can expect more knowledge about which TOD-ness might influence which T-SA performance across cities and which TOD-ness impact might be most context sensitive. This would be of great interest to decision-makers or policy analysts who want to lay down technical and policy guidelines to promote TOD across cities. Based on Gu et al. (2019), notably, the average TOD-ness quality across different T-SAs in a city was found to be positively associated with the ambient air quality in the city. This could mean that improving TOD-ness should be of growing consideration in public policies concerning ambient air quality at the city level.

Last but not least, BOD might enable us to (1) redefine TOD-ness and T-SA performance in a manner that traditional data such as surveys and censuses cannot accomplish, (2) measure TOD-ness and T-SA performance more exclusively and efficiently with existing indicators and new indicators and across more spatiotemporal resolutions (e.g., see Zhou et al., 2018, 2019), and (3) produce new evidence and knowledge concerning TOD-ness and T-SA performance. The following subsection describes these in more detail.

2. TOD-ness and T-SA performance: What we could/should know more with BOD

Several existing studies have already demonstrated the great potential of BOD in shedding new light on the relationship between TOD-ness and T-SA performance. This subsection revisits the basics of BOD and synthesizes what BOD can augment in the T-SA scholarship and practices, especially in the study of the relationship between TOD-ness and T-SA performance.

2.1 BOD ABCs

With the advent of new technologies and devices such as the Internet of Things (IoT), smartphones, smartcards, LBS, and cloud-based services,

BOD have been increasingly available and accessible, continuously produced and updated, and widely distributed and utilized. BOD consist of three types of data: big data, open data, and big and open data. In other words, big data might not necessarily be open data and open data might not necessarily be big data. Only the data that meet a certain level of criteria can be considered both "big" and "open."

In the existing studies listed in Table 1, one popular source of open data used by authors is OpenStreetMap (OSM) data. OSM can be used as an example for us to better define "open data." They should have at least the following characteristics:

First, they are not proprietary, which means that (1) no specific person or entity hoards them for whichever reason and one does not need an official permission from the owner or creator to use and distribute them and (2) they are available at no cost to users—to help users get them, they are usually stored somewhere online and accessible over the Internet and can be downloaded virtually by any Internet user.

Second, the production and maintenance costs of open data are often not borne by the end-users. Either the general tax revenue from the government or the donations from individuals or entities cover those costs.

Third, unless they are produced on a regular basis by the government (e.g., census data), the quality and reliability of open data are often not as strictly controlled as those of proprietary data, especially when they are crowd sourced or produced—i.e., anyone can (partially) produce and update them.

Fourth, the frequency of being updated and the spatiotemporal coverage of open data can be volatile. This could be a natural consequence of the above-mentioned characteristics, e.g., the production and maintenance costs of open data are partially and often fully reliant on private donations and they are crowd produced.

In the existing studies listed in Table 1, one popular big data set used by authors is smartcard data. The characteristics of such data have been intensively discussed in the literature, which include but are not limited to:

- Huge in volume—big data consist of a much larger size of data than small data, usually in magnitudes of terabytes or petabytes;
- High in velocity—unlike the small data, big data can be generated in or near real-time;
- Diverse in variety—big data can be either structured or unstructured in nature and can contain both temporal and spatial information;
- Exclusive in scope—big data can capture even the whole population or at least in a sample size that is much larger than small data;

- Fine-grained in resolution—big data can hold much more detail about the subjects that scholars or administrators might want to have than small data;
- Relational—big data can have many more common fields even more when a large number of diverse datasets can be joined together;
- Flexible and scalable—big data can add new fields and expand in size efficiently (Boyd and Crawford, 2012; Dodge and Kitchin, 2005; Kitchin, 2013; Marz and Warren, 2012; Mayer-Schonberger and Cukier, 2013; McKinsey Global Institute, 2015).

Not surprisingly, BOD have characteristics of both big data and open data mentioned above. Baidu Population Heatmaps used by Zhou et al. (2018, 2019, 2020) are a type of BOD. On the one hand, one of their dominant features is that they can be downloaded at no cost to end-users, although those Baidu Population Heatmaps that can be downloaded by end-users might not be of the highest quality. On the other hand, they are derived from millions or even billions of smartphone users' usage of various LBSs underpinning their smartphone apps.

2.2 Better defined T-SA, TOD-ness, and T-SA performance with BOD

Given the above characteristics of BOD, T-SA, TOD-ness, and T-SA performance can be better defined and even redefined with BOD. In existing studies such as Bertolini et al. (2012), Carlton (2007), Cervero et al. (2002, 2004), Olaru and Curtis (2015), Renne (2009), and most notably Wang and Woo (2017), T-SA and its analogs are often nebulously defined as an area around a transit station or stop. Some regard T-SAs as areas within a comfortable walking distance to a transit station or stop. Others quantify the range of the distance, e.g., 800 m' or 10 mins' walk for most people. But even if we can operationalize those areas with some empirical data, we might only be able to do that for a limited number of samples and T-SAs. Then we usually assume that all the T-SA geographical boundaries can be defined based on what we have learnt from the samples, e.g., if most residents in a few T-SAs are willing to walk up to 10 mins to and from the primary transit station therein, we assume that most residents in all the T-SAs would do likewise. But there could often be cases that residents in T-SAs where most residents are youths are willing to walk longer than 10 mins to and from a transit station.

The availability of BOD can challenge and even revolutionize this long-standing practice. We could, for instance, divide areas around a transit station into grids, which would be as small as 50×50 m. Within each grid,

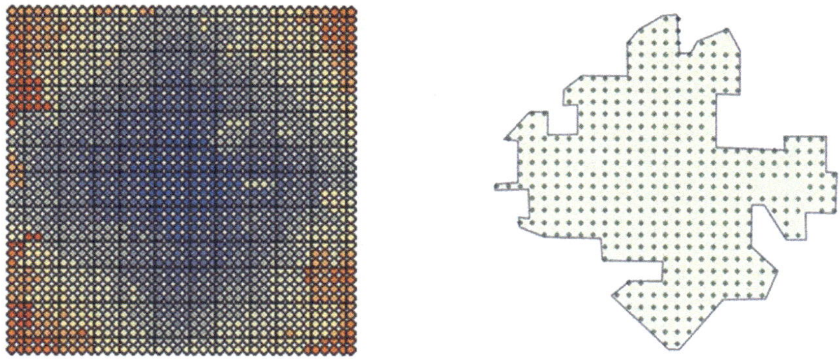

Fig. 2 Defining T-SAs with BOD: An illustration.

there are multiple probable origins or destinations where residents or visitors can travel to and from. It is represented by tiny circles in the left panel of Fig. 2. Then based on either open data from OSM or a combination of OSM and navigation records of LBS users, computer programs can be written to derive a polygon, within which it would only take people or 90% of LBS users say 10 mins or less to travel between the tiny circles and the transit station. Such polygon can be derived efficiently for each T-SA of interest to us. It can also continuously be updated as new navigation records are produced and collected.

By connecting those navigation records to other open data, e.g., point of interest (POI) data from Baidu, the IT Giant of China, we can also better quantify which origin or destination would be the most popular among residents or visitors in each T-SA. We can comparatively monitor how the popularity of different POIs evolves as those navigation records and POI data are constantly and passively produced or updated, either by millions of LBS users or LBS providers such as Baidu. Zhou et al. (2018, 2019), for instance, have already demonstrated how similar BOD can be exploited to define and monitor T-SA performance and how such performance was influenced by TOD-ness, which can also be quantified with BOD and station (area) characteristics, such as when a station was built and which subarea the station is in a city. In other words, BOD have provided us with new opportunities to refine or even overhaul our understandings of T-SA, TOD-ness, T-SA performance, and their relationships.

2.3 New/improved indicators with BOD

In spite of the above-mentioned characteristics and potentialities of BOD, few authors (or entities) have utilized them to develop TOD-ness and T-SA performance indicators (or indices). Based on our professional network, Google, and several popular academic databases (e.g., Web of Science), we only identified several studies or reports that contain BOD-based indicators for TOD-ness and T-SA performance (see Table 2).

Several findings can be drawn from Table 2. First, most existing studies or reports simply replaced traditional data with BOD when calculating TOD-ness and T-SA performance indicators, which have been defined or used before. This might be due to two reasons:

(1) Most BOD are not produced for the purpose of quantifying TOD-ness and T-SA performance—e.g., smartcard data are produced primarily because transit agencies want to better charge and validate fares while reducing the costs or inconvenience of handling cash payments (e.g., see Pelletier et al., 2011);

(2) Access to, processing and the analysis of many big data might still be a challenge to T-SA scholars or analysts, and they still have difficulty in obtaining big data and/or are still in the process of exploring how big data can be best utilized.

Second, BOD can be exploited to refine long-existing TOD-ness and T-SA performance indicators or related concepts. In particular, Zhou et al. (2018, 2019, 2020) have used Baidu Population Heatmaps to estimate the number of active smartphone users in a T-SA per hour, which can be a good proxy of the population in a T-SA. The latter has long been an indicator (or a component of the index) for TOD-ness or both TOD-ness and T-SA performance simultaneously (e.g., see Singh et al., 2014, 2017; TCRP, 1995). But it has rarely been measured in small temporal units such as day of the week and hour of the day. In addition, Zhou et al. (2020) demonstrated that smartcard data can enable analysts to differentiate frequent and non-frequent metro riders. This could help decision-makers to fathom how different TOD-ness influence two groups of metro riders.

Third, BOD can be used to produce new indicators that measure TOD-ness and T-SA performance, which did not exist before the advent of BOD and new phenomena such as social media based on smartphone apps, LBS, and corresponding data generated because of them. Weibo check-in's, which reflect where smartphone app-based social media users are active and how active they are in different locations (including POIs) can be used to develop new indicators for both TOD-ness and T-SA performance. Zhou et al. (2018), for instance, used POIs with at least one Weibo check-in to measure the overall supply and distribution of POIs in a city and the density of POIs in a T-SA. Those measurements are unlike any existing TOD-ness indicators in granularity.

Table 2 Existing BOD-based indicators for TOD-ness and T-SA performance.

	TOD-ness		T-SA performance	
Source	**Input**	**Indicator**	**Input**	**Indicator**
Sung and Oh (2011)[a]	n/a	n/a	Smartcard data	Transit ridership
Papa and Bertolini (2015)[a]	OpenStreetMap	Rail-based accessibility	n/a	n/a
Lyu et al. (2016)[a]	Google Map	Number of stations within 20 mins of travel by metro	n/a	n/a
	OpenStreetMap	Average block size; length of paved footpath per acre	n/a	n/a
	Walk scores	Walk scores of each station area	n/a	n/a
	Baidu Map[b]	Number of POIs by category; average distance to jobs; degree of the functional mix; car parking capacity; travel times to major employment and activity centers by metro; the average distance from a station to residents	POIs from Baidu Map	Number of workers by sector

Continued

Table 2 Existing BOD-based indicators for TOD-ness and T-SA performance.—cont'd

	TOD-ness		T-SA performance	
Source	**Input**	**Indicator**	**Input**	**Indicator**
Caijing (2017)[a]	Meituan[c]	Entertainment and leisure POIs: Number and size; shopping and retailing POIs: Number, size and class; catering POIs: Number and size	Gaode Map[b]	Level of congestion
	Centa Data[d]; Baidu Map	Residential POIs: Size, class and convenience	Baidu Map	Starbuck preference
	IfChange[e]; Baidu Map	Business POIs: Size, class	IfChange	Business POIs: Purchasing power
	Gaode Map; Baidu Map	Transport friendliness	Meituan	Entertainment and leisure POIs: Vitality and purchasing power; shopping and retailing POIs: Purchasing power
Gu et al. (2019)	Official statistics of different governmental agencies; open data from non-for-profit entities, e.g., Beijing City Lab; open data from for-profit companies, e.g., Baidu	Indices for TOD-ness as a whole and different Ds, i.e., different aspects of TOD-ness	Air quality indices by different governmental agencies	Air quality indices

Zhou et al. (2018)	Weibo check-in's; Weibo POI data	POIs with at least one Weibo check-in	Baidu Population Heatmaps	Active smartphone users in a T-SA per hour
Lyu et al. (2020)	OpenStreetMap; Google Map; Baidu Map; Walk Score	Six indicators measuring three components of TOD: level of transit services ("T"), level of integration of transit services and land uses ("O"), and level of development ("D")	n/a	n/a
Zhou et al. (2019)	Weibo check-in's; Weibo POI data; OpenStreetMap	Indices by Gu et al. (2019); regional-level TOD-ness indicators measuring three components of TOD, similar to Lyu et al. (2020)	Baidu Population Heatmap; smartcard data	Active smartphone users in a T-SA per hour; metro ridership into a T-SA per hour
Zhou et al. (2020)	Weibo check-in's; Weibo POI data; OpenStreetMap; shared-bike usage records	The regional centrality of a station within the local metro network; destination density (all and category-specific); destination diversity; walkability; bikeability	Baidu Population Heatmap; smartcard data	(a) Active smartphone users in a T-SA per hour; (b) Metro ridership into a T-SA per hour; (c) Frequent metro riders, (d/e) Net/gross ratios of frequent metro riders, i.e., c/b and c/a; (f) The ratio of metro riders, i.e., b/a

[a]Authors did not differentiate indicators between the features and behaviors. Their indicators were categorized based on the definitions of this study.
[b]Google Map's peers in Mainland China.
[c]A Yelp's peer in China.
[d]One of the largest on-line realtors in China.
[e]On-line talent recruiter.

2.4 New/expected evidence and knowledge

When BOD are used to refine existing and produce new indicators for TOD-ness and T-SA performance, we can expect better and new evidence and knowledge about T-SAs. Of course, this does not necessarily mean nor preclude that traditional data such as censuses and travel surveys cannot be used in the refinement and production of existing and new indicators for TOD-ness and T-SA performance. Table 3 shows the relationships between traditional data, BOD, and refined and new indicators for TOD-ness and T-SA performance.

2.4.1 Refined/new indicators because of BOD

Each cell in the lower right corner of Table 3 represents one possible relationship between data (BOD, traditional data, or the combination of the two) and indicators (defined or used before vs. never defined or used before). BOD have more possibilities than traditional data to be deployed in the development of refined or new indicators for T-SA research, either alone or together with traditional data. In theory, with these refined or new indicators plus appropriate methods and tools to analyze or visualize them, we can expect better and new evidence and knowledge concerning T-SAs. In reality, Kim et al. (2017), Tao et al. (2014), and Zhou et al. (2018, 2019, 2020) have illustrated how Indicators (1) to (6) in Table 3 can be formulated to facilitate T-SA scholarship and practices.

Indicators (1) to (4): The relationship between any pair of T-SAs and the attractiveness of a T-SA can both be reflected by passenger flows to and from corresponding T-SAs. Prior to the advent of smartcard-based passenger counts, researchers had to rely on traditional data from sources such as onboard surveys or manual counts at different transit stations or stops to quantify passenger flows. For a relatively small transit network, say, a transit

Table 3 Traditional data, BOD, and new/refined indicators.

	Indicators defined or used before?	
Input	**Yes**	**No**
Traditional data	(1) Old indicators	(2) New/refined indicators
BOD	(3) Old/refined indicators	(4) New/refined indicators
Combination of the above	(5) Old/refined indicators	(6) New/refined indicators

network with a few bus routes and a dozen bus stops, the labor and monetary costs of traditional data collection are still not prohibitive. However, for a transit network with hundreds of bus and subway routes and thousands of stations and stops, the labor and monetary costs can be surprisingly high. Tao et al. (2014) demonstrated that smartcard data can be exploited to quantify and geovisualize passenger flows between different bus stops for Brisbane, Australia, a city with 170 bus routes and 12,792 bus stops. Passenger flows between a pair of bus stops per day, for instance, can be derived from either traditional data or BOD. They represent Indicators (1) and (3) in Table 3. In theory, passenger flows between any pairs of bus stops per hour can also be derived from traditional data. But such (refined) indicators, however, have rarely been defined or used prior to the advent of BOD. It is simply too costly and time consuming to develop them. Thus, they can be largely considered as Indicator (2) in Table 3. In Tao et al. (2014), BOD were used to quantify indicators such as passenger flows between any pairs of bus stops across multiple temporal resolutions. These indicators and their geovisualization, e.g., actual bus flows based on smartcard data covering 80% or more riders, would not been possible if they had relied solely on traditional data. They represent Indicator (4) in Table 3.

Indicators (5) and (6): Compared to Tao et al. (2014), Kim et al. (2017) better illustrated how the combination of traditional data and BOD can be used to develop Indicators (5) and (6) in Table 3. In the four-step travel demand forecast model, traditional data such as land use maps and censuses can be used as input to estimate and predict passenger flows by transit between any pairs of traffic analysis zones for the present or the future. By completing the traffic assignment procedure, the modeler can then allocate predicted flows along different transit routes. With the availability of smartcard data, the modeler can get nearly real-time passenger flows derived from smartcard data along different transit routes (i.e., Indicator (3) in Table 3). She/he can also simply use archived smartcard data as input to predict the future passenger flows, which represent Indicator (5) in Table 3. Kim et al. (2017) went a step further. They showed that smartcard data, coupled with traditional data such as transit network maps, can be used to derive trip trajectories of each individual rider. The derived trajectories and the known transit services between the origin and the destination of those trajectories can then used to compute a "stickiness index." The index measures to what degree a rider sticks to one or two specific routes of bus services across months. It represents Indicator (6) in Table 3.

2.4.2 BOD-based indicators and T-SA scholarship

Zhou et al. (2018, 2019, 2020) illustrated how BOD-based indicators can help advance the T-SA scholarship, especially in quantifying TOD-ness, T-SA performance, and their relationship. Zhou et al. (2018), for instance, used Baidu Population Heatmaps to estimate the number of active smartphone users in a T-SA. As compared to the population in a T-SA based on traditional data such as censuses or surveys, the number of active smartphone users in a T-SA can be regarded as representative of Indicator (2) in Table 3. Compared to long-established indicators such as the population or estimated incoming workers in a T-SA based on censuses or surveys, the number of active smartphone users in a T-SA has the following characteristics and/or advantages:

- The population in a T-SA is only a static snapshot of the residents whereas the number of active smartphone users in a T-SA can consider both residents in, and incoming visitors to a T-SA;
- The number of active smartphone users in a T-SA can be (dis)aggregated into more spatiotemporal units, for instance, the number of active smartphone users in a T-SA per hour, the number of active smartphone users in a T-SA per weekday, and the number of active smartphone users in a T-SA per week.
- With some effort, the number of active smartphone users in a T-SA can be broken down into other categories such as the number of active smartphone users who do not reside in a T-SA, the number of active smartphone users in a T-SA that are all from another T-SA, and the number of active smartphone users in a T-SA that all go to another T-SA after regular office hours.
- The number of active smartphone users in a T-SA can be constantly updated as it is based on a type of BOD that are continuously collected and updated by Baidu, which relies on the BOD to ensure and improve its various products and services.

Taking advantage of the temporal continuity and wide geographic coverage of smartcard data, Zhou et al. (2019) examined whether the same set of TOD-ness variables influence metro ridership into a T-SA on weekdays and weekends and if not, which TOD-ness variable would have the biggest impact on weekdays and on weekends, respectively. Their study covered all the 167 T-SAs in Shenzhen served by metro as of 2017. It would have been costly if not challenging to do so if the study had solely depended on surveys or interviews. Getting the metro ridership into each of the 167 T-SAs by day of the week in the city can be a demanding task even if we overlook the data collection costs via traditional means such as manual counting and surveys. In addition, to continuously update the number, the same demanding task would have to be undertaken again and again. One can, however, reuse a similar computer program to update the metro ridership by day of the week and even by hour of the day through continuously and automatically collected and updated smartcard data as input.

Zhou et al. (2020) advanced Zhou et al. (2019)'s approach in terms of further categorizing metro ridership by riders' frequency of usage and exploring what kind of TOD-ness and other factors affected the numbers of frequent and occasional riders. Specifically, they categorized metro riders by T-SA into two groups: frequent riders and non-frequent riders. Frequent riders are those who leave a T-SA for another destination at least twice in five consecutive weekdays whereas non-frequent riders are the remaining riders. They found that the metro ridership and the frequent riders at the T-SA level in Shenzhen were influenced by a similar set of independent and TOD-ness variables. Interestingly, metro station areas with more metro stations could expect fewer frequent riders. In other words, the more metro stations in a metro station area the less likely that (frequent) metro riders would stick to one of them. In addition, they developed another new indicator: the ratio of frequent riders and metro ridership by T-SA. They showed that this indicator was positively associated with the number of bus stops, walkability, and network directed-ness. They found that the lower the network directed-ness, the higher the proportion of frequent riders. They speculated that this was because many frequent riders resided in communities in comparatively remote locations, as they were attracted by the lower housing prices.

2.5 Limitations of BOD

Indicators and studies purely based on BOD do have several drawbacks too, which can prevent them from generating all-rounded evidence and knowledge. First, it could still be costly and challenging for analysts to acquire and process BOD, as mentioned above. In the US, for instance, archived cellular network data are so expensive that few planning professionals and academics have used them for their analyses. This could mean that the active smartphone users in a T-SA indicator developed by Zhou et al. (2018, 2019, 2020) might not be replicable among T-SA researchers outside the contexts of Shenzhen/China.

Second, BOD may only provide a partial picture. For example, smartcard data collected by most transit agencies only contain information on rider's origin, destination, start/end time of her/his trip, fare payment, and route choice. We do not know who the rider is, why she/he rides transit, and whether/how her/his socioeconomic attributes affect her/his mode choice, locational choices, and perception of travel.

Third, BOD might not be representative of the whole population. Smartphone data, for instance, overlook those users who do not own a smartphone. Thus, if we use indicators such as the active smartphone users in a T-SA as a proxy of the workers or residents in a T-SA, they could be biased.

Understandably, the combination of BOD and traditional data can help overcome the above drawbacks. In this regard, Zhou et al. (2018) provide some good examples. Their studies first quantified T-SA performance with the number of active smartphone users in a T-SA per hour based on Baidu Population Heatmaps and then measured TOD-ness by the number of POIs with at least one Weibo check-in. They then categorized 167 T-SAs into four groups and quadrants by the means of the two measurements (see Fig. 3). In Fig. 3, each circle represents one T-SA. The size of circle is proportional to how many metro riders are generated by a T-SA per hour. In Quadrant I, all the T-SAs herein have more POIs (or other TOD-ness indicators) and active smartphone users ("co-presences" in the figure) than

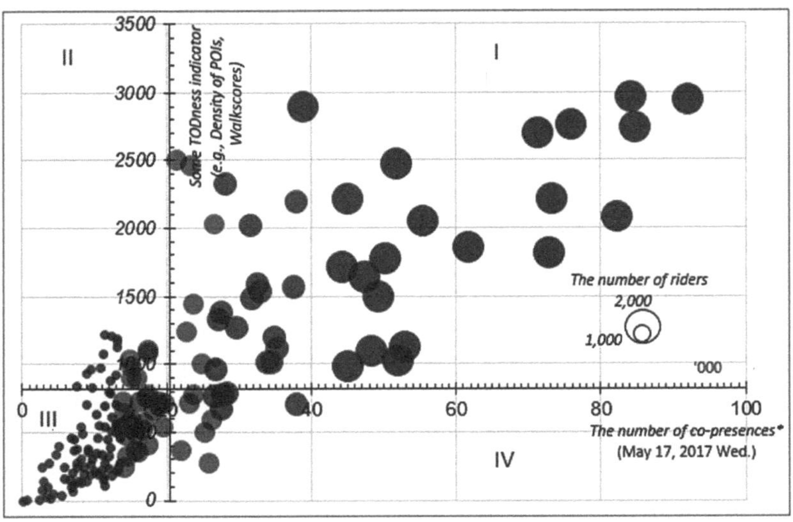

Fig. 3 Categorizing/evaluating T-SAs with BOD.

the mean. In Quadrant II, all the T-SAs herein have more active smartphone users than the mean but fewer POIs than the mean. In Quadrant III, all the T-SAs herein have fewer active smartphone users and POIs than the mean. In Quadrant IV, all the T-SAs herein have more POIs than the mean but fewer smartphone users than the mean.

After consulting local urban planners and decision-makers, the researchers selected one representative T-SA from each group/quadrant to conduct case studies, in the hope of better understanding why different T-SAs varied in TOD-ness (measured by the number of POIs) and T-SA performance (measured by the number of active smartphone users). The extra data and information they collected in support of their case studies were "traditional," i.e., they were from sources such as site audits, interviews, refereed publications, on-line searches, and governmental reports. The case studies enabled the researchers to know what BOD had not allowed them to address such as: why does a T-SA have fewer POIs than the mean but more active smartphone users than the mean, who are most likely to be these smartphone users, and how local urban master plans and land use planning might have affected the TOD-ness and T-SA performance of those representative T-SAs, respectively. In short, BOD enabled them to effectively categorize 167 T-SAs into four meaningful groups/quadrants. Case studies helped them answer why a particular T-SA fell into one of the groups/quadrants. Of course, following the same procedures, their methods also allowed the researchers to evaluate the performance of the 167 T-SAs, where the number of active smartphone users in a T-SA per POI and per hour would be an indicator. Here, it is assumed that each POI in a T-SA requires notable investment and its efficiency is positively correlated to the active smartphone users in the T-SA.

3. Discussion and conclusions

Many cities in developed countries like the US and Australia have been characterized by car dependence and urban sprawl. Subsequently, these cities are faced by consequences such as recurrent traffic congestion, excessive fuel consumption, sedentary lifestyle, prevalent obesity, wasteful land consumption, loss of natural landscapes, and decreasing social capital. To address those issues, TOD has been advanced as a strategy and as a model for urban development. One indispensable ingredient of TOD success is performing T-SAs that are well connected to one another by fast, reliable, and comfortable transit services.

For performing T-SAs, TOD advocates have many to-do's in mind and hoped-for benefits. As mentioned above, the typical to-do's for a performing T-SA are Density, Diversity, Design, Distance, and Destination, i.e., 3-Ds or 5-Ds whereas typical hoped-for benefits for a performing T-SA include but are not limited to decreasing car ownership, reducing auto trips, increasing public transit ridership, and improved quality of life.

This chapter treats the to-do's as TOD-ness and the hoped-for benefits as T-SA performance. Much of what we know about TOD-ness, T-SA performance, and their relationship is largely based on and subsequently constrained by traditional data. Due to this fact, we can see that most indicators we formulate for TOD-ness and T-SA performance have the following attributes:

First, they tend to focus on T-SA performance at the aggregate level, e.g., overall ridership to and from a T-SA. In actuality, the trips to and from a T-SA can be further broken down into those made by frequent riders and occasional riders. These two groups of riders can also be sensitive to different types of TOD-ness. Thus, depending on the kind of ridership, i.e., frequent ridership or occasional ridership, that a policy aims to increase, different types of TOD-ness improvements are warranted.

Second, they provide a snapshot of the past rather than an up-to-date and even a real-time picture about T-SAs. TOD-ness indicators based on local land use maps, for instance, only reflect situations when the maps were last updated. They cannot show changes between two versions of corresponding maps. Usually, the temporal interval of the two versions are months and even years. Similarly, T-SA performance indicators based on censuses might only reflect recent situations as two waves of censuses can be 5–10 years apart.

Third, their geographic coverage and sample sizes can be limited. In the case of Shenzhen, it was simply too expensive or even impossible to formulate T-SA performance indicators such as hourly frequent ridership to and from a T-SA based on data from traditional sources such as surveys and interviews. Thus, most of the existing studies use T-SA performance and TOD-ness indicators formulated and based on a relatively small geographic coverage and sample size.

Given their characteristics such as volume, velocity, variety, and exclusiveness, BOD can be used to supplement and even replace traditional data when we attempt to develop indicators to measure and monitor TOD-ness and T-SA performance across a large number of T-SAs exclusively, timely, and continuously. As illustrated in existing studies such as Kim et al. (2017), Tao et al. (2014), and Zhou et al. (2018, 2019, 2020), BOD can even enable us to produce refined and new indicators measuring TOD-ness and T-SA performance. Based on these refined and new indicators, we can generate more and newer evidence and knowledge concerning T-SA, TOD-ness, and T-SA performance.

In the future, much more breakthroughs concerning the above evidence and knowledge can be expected should BOD be better exploited and should BOD be better fused with traditional data. In terms of exploiting BOD and fusing BOD and traditional data to improve the T-SA scholarship, several areas are worth of more attention based on the author's experience and knowledge concerning BOD and the T-SA scholarship.

First, for T-SA researchers in different contexts, there should be a tailored inventory of BOD that are available and accessible to them. Only when T-SA researchers have that kind of inventory can they know best (a) what BOD they can actually acquire and analyze and (b) what they can and should do to with other stakeholders as early as possible and as collaboratively as possible to improve the quality and relevance of BOD for T-SA scholarship and practices. In the context of Shenzhen, the author initially had access to only Baidu Population Heatmaps, OpenStreetMap data, and Weibo check-in data. But after he and his students illustrated in Zhou et al. (2018) that they could make sense of those BOD, other scholars started approaching them to see how Baidu Population Heatmaps could be supplemented by a local transit agency's smartcard data. These scholars later became the author's collaborators and co-authors in Zhou et al. (2019).

Second, pilot studies should be conducted to demonstrate to key stakeholders the significant value of BOD in T-SA scholarship and practices. Pelletier et al. (2011) has rightly pointed out that BOD such as smartcard data are often only collected for a special business purpose. This can mean that BOD, by default, might rarely be considered in its full potential and application. Thus, people might under-appreciate the value of BOD. When this is the case, it can be challenging for BOD owners to do more than business as usual. Over time, this results in the absence of a good ecosystem and culture of sharing BOD and improving BOD so that the greater benefits that can be produced than what is achieved in the business as usual scenario are absent too. To change this, it is crucial that T-SA researchers proactively and strategically exploit whichever BOD that they can have access to. Only by doing so can they better persuade other (key) stakeholder to keep sharing and improving BOD.

Third, both BOD and traditional data have their respective pros and cons. Fusion of BOD and traditional data can help enlarge their respective pros and overcome their respective cons. Creative ways should be explored to facilitate data fusion. When collecting smartcard data, for instance, contributors can be encouraged to share as much as possible sociodemographic information as they are willing to share so long as they do not violate any privacy protocol. For those individuals who do share that information, they should be rewarded by incentives such as anonymous prepaid credit card and discounted fares based on random drawing. Similar actions can also be undertaken when census and surveys are conducted, for instance, interviewees can voluntarily share their smartcard ID number and their cellphone number. Later, those numbers can be used to link corresponding smartcard, cellphone, and census/survey data. Of course, in addition to the fusion of BOD and traditional data, more should also be done to improve the fusion of different types of BOD or traditional data.

Lastly, even though the fusion of BOD and traditional data has great potential in advancing quantitative studies in the realm of T-SA scholarship, it should still be enhanced by qualitative methods, including the case study method. Apart from TOD-ness that can be easily quantified, other subtle factors such as history, culture, preference, and tradition can also profoundly contribute to performing T-SAs. As shown in Zhou et al. (2018), qualitative methods such as interviews, focus groups, and case studies can help us understand how these factors shaped and keep reshaping a T-SA.

References

Bernick, M., Cervero, R., 1997. Transit Villages for the 21st Century. McGraw-Hill, New York.

Bertolini, L., Curtis, C., Renee, J., 2012. Station area projects in Europe and beyond: towards transit oriented development? Built Environ. 38 (1), 31–50.

Boarnet, M., Crane, R., 1998. L.A. story: a reality check for transit-based housing. J. Am. Plann. Assoc. 63 (2), 189–204.

Boyd, D., Crawford, K., 2012. Critical questions for big data. Inf. Commun. Soc. 15 (5), 662–679.

Caijing, D.T., 2017. Rediscover Shenzhen on the rail 2017: Shenzhen urban big data vitality report. DT Caijing, Shanghai.

California Department of Transportation (Caltrans), 2002. Statewide Transit-Oriented Development Study: Factors for Success in California. Caltrans, Sacramento, CA.

Calthorpe, P., 1993. The Next American Metropolis: Ecology, Community, and the American Dream. Princeton Architectural Press, Princeton, NJ.

Carlton, I., 2007. Histories of Transit-Oriented Development: Perspectives on the Development of TOD Concept (WP-2009-02). University of California, Institute of Urban and Regional Development., Berkeley.

Cervero, R., Kockelman, K., 1997. Travel demand and the 3Ds: density, diversity, and design. Transp. Res. D 2 (3), 199–219.

Cervero, R., Murakami, J., 2009. Rail and property development in Hong Kong: experience and extensions. Urban Stud. 46 (10), 2019–2043.

Cervero, R., Ferrell, C., Murphy, S., 2002. Transit Cooperative Research Program, Research Results Digest Number 52. Transportation Research Board, National Research Council, Washington, D.C.

Cervero, R., Murphy, S., Ferrell, C., Goguts, N., T-SAi, Y., Arrington, G.B., Boroski, J., Smith-Heimer, J., Golem, R., Peninger, P., Nakajima, E., Chui, E., Dunphy, R., Meyers, M., McKay, S., Witenstein, N., 2004. Transit-Oriented Development in the United States: Experiences, Challenges, and Prospects. Federal Transit Administration, Washington D.C.

Cervero, R., Guerra, E., Al, S., 2017. Beyond Mobility: Planning Cities for People and Places. Island Press, Washington D.C.

Chatman, D.G., Cervero, R., Moylan, E., Carlton, I., Weissman, D., Zissman, J., Guerra, E., Murakami, J., Ikezoe, P., Emerson, D., Tischler, D., Means, D., Winkler, S., Sheu, K., Kwon, S.Y., 2014. Making Effective Fixed-Guideway Transit Investments: Indicators of Success. The National Academies Press, Washington, DC.

Dill, J., 2008. Transit use at transit-oriented developments in Portland, Oregon, area. Transp. Res. Rec. 2083, 159–167.

Dittmar, H., Ohland, G., 2004. The New Transit Town: Best Practices in Transit-Oriented Development. Island Press, Washington, D.C.

Dodge, M., Kitchin, R., 2005. Codes of life: identification codes and the machine-readable world. Environ. Plan. D 23 (6), 851–881.

Griffiths, B., Curtis, C., 2017. Effectiveness of transit oriented development in reducing car use: Case Study of Subiaco, Western Australia. Urban Policy Res. 35 (4), 391–408.

Gu, P., He, D., Chen, Y., Zegras, P.C., Jiang, Y., 2019. Transit-oriented development and air quality in Chinese cities: a city-level examination. Transp. Res. D 68, 10–25.

Kahn, M., 2007. Gentrification trends in new transit-oriented communities: evidence from 14 cities that expanded and built rail transit systems. Real Estate Econ. 35 (2), 155–182.

Kim, J., Corcoran, J., Papamanolis, M., 2017. Route choice stickiness of public transport passengers: measuring habitual bus ridership behaviour using smart card data. Transp. Res. C 83, 146–164.

Kitchin, R., 2013. The Data Revolution: Big Data, Open Data, Data Infrastructures and Their Consequences. Sage, London, UK.

Loo, B.P.Y., du Verle, F., 2017. Transit-oriented development in future cities: towards a two-level sustainable mobility strategy. Int. J. Urban Sci. 21, 54–67.

Loo, B.P.Y., Chen, C., Chan, E.T.H., 2010. Rail-based transit-oriented development: lessons from New York City and Hong Kong. Landsc. Urban Plan. 97, 202–212.

Lyu, G., Bertolini, L., Pfeffer, K., 2016. Developing a TOD typology for Beijing metro station areas. J. Transp. Geogr. 55, 40–50.

Lyu, G., Bertolini, L., Pfeffer, K., 2020. How does transit-oriented development contribute to station area accessibility? A study in Beijing. Int. J. Sustain. Transp. 14 (7), 533–543. https://doi.org/10.1080/15568318.2019.1578841.

Marz, N., Warren, J., 2012. Big Data: Principles and Best Practices of Scalable Realtime Data Systems, MEAP ed. Manning, Shelter Island, New York.

Mayer-Schonberger, V., Cukier, K., 2013. Big Data: A Revolution that Will Transform How We Live, Work, and Think. Houghton Mifflin Publishing House, New York.

McKinsey Global Institute, 2015. Open Data: Unlocking Innovation and Performance With Liquid Information. available at: http://goo.gl/IavBty. Accessed 13 February 2015.

Muller, P.O., 2017. Transportation and urban form: stages in the spatial evolution of the American Metropolis. In: Giuliano, G., Hanson, S. (Eds.), The Geography of Urban Transportation, fourth ed. Guilford, New York, pp. 57–112.
Nasri, A., Zhang, L., 2014. The analysis of transit-oriented development (TOD) in Washington D.C. and Baltimore metropolitan area. Transp. Policy 32, 172–179.
National Cooperative Highway Research Program (NCHRP), 2005. Transit-Oriented Development: Developing a Strategy to Measure Success. The National Academies Press, Washington D.C.
Newman, P., Kenworthy, J., 1999. Sustainability and Cities: Overcoming Automobile Dependence. Island Press, Washington D.C.
Noland, R.B., Ozbay, K., DiPetrillo, S., Lyer, S., 2014. Measuring Benefits of Transit Oriented Development. Mineta National Transit Research Consortium, San Jose State University, San Jose, CA.
Olaru, D., Curtis, C., 2015. Designing TOD precincts: accessibility and travel patterns. Eur. J. Transp. Infrastruct. Res. 15 (1), 6–26.
Papa, E., Bertolini, L., 2015. Accessibility and transit-oriented development in European metropolitan areas. J. Transp. Geogr. 47, 70–83.
Pelletier, M.P., Trepanier, M., Morency, C., 2011. Smart card data use in public transit: a literature review. Transp. Res. C 19 (4), 557–568.
Putnam, R.D., 2001. Bowling Alone: The Collapse and Revival of American Community. Simon & Schuster Ltd., London, UK.
Renne, J.L., 2007. Measuring the Performance of Transit-Oriented Developments in Western Australia. Planning and Transport Research Centre. The Government of Western Australia, Perth, Australia.
Renne, J.L., 2009. Measuring the Success of Transit Oriented Development. Institute for Sustainability and Technology Policy, Murdoch University, Perth, Australia.
Renne, J.L., 2018. Transit-oriented development and ports: a national analysis in the United States. J. Transp. Land Use 11 (1), 297–304.
Renne, J.L., Hamidi, S., Ewing, R., 2017. Transit commuting, the network accessibility effect, and the built environment in station areas across the United States. Res. Transp. Econ. 60, 35–43.
Rodriguez, D.A., Vergel-Tovar, E., 2017. Urban development around bus rapid transit stops in seven cities in Latin-America. J. Urban. 11 (2), 175–201.
Shoup, D., 2011. The High Cost of Free Parking, Updated ed. Taylor & Francis Inc., Chicago, US.
Singh, Y.J., Fard, P., Zuidgeest, M., Brussel, M., van Maarseveen, M., 2014. Measuring transit oriented development: a spatial multi criteria assessment approach for the City Region Arnhem and Nijmegen. J. Transp. Geogr. 35, 130–143.
Singh, Y.J., Lukman, A., Flacke, J., Zuidgeest, M., van Maarseveen, M.F.A.M., 2017. Measuring TOD around transit nodes-towards TOD policy. Transp. Policy 56, 96–111.
Sung, H., Oh, J.T., 2011. Transit-oriented development in a high-density city: identifying its association with transit ridership in Seoul, Korea. Cities 28 (1), 70–82.
Tao, S., Corcoran, J., Mateo-Babiano, I., Rohde, D., 2014. Exploring bus rapid transit passenger travel behaviour using big data. Appl. Geogr. 53, 90–104.
TCRP, 2007. Transit oriented development traveler response to transportation system changes, report 95. Federal Transit Administration, Washington D.C.
Transit Cooperative Research Program (TCRP), 1995. Regional Transit Corridors: The Land Use Connection. TCRP, Washington D.C.
Wang, K., Woo, M., 2017. The relationship between transit rich neighborhoods and transit ridership: evidence from the decentralization of poverty. Appl. Geogr. 86, 183–196.

Wells, J.S., Renne, J., 2003. Transit Villages in New Jersey: Recommendations for Assessment and Accountability. Alan M. Voorhees Transportation Center, Rutgers University, New Brunswick, New Jersey.

Zhao, P., Li, X., 2018. Suburbanization, land use of TOD and lifestyle mobility in the suburbs: an examination of passengers' choice to live, shop and entertain in the metro station areas of Beijing. J. Transp. Land Use 11 (1), 195–215.

Zhou, J., Wang, Q., Liu, H., 2018. Evaluating transit-served areas with non-traditional data. J. Transp. Land Use 11 (1), 1323–1349.

Zhou, J., Yang, Y., Gu, P., Yin, L., Zhang, F., Zhang, F., Li, D., 2019. Can TODness improve (expected) performances of TODs? An exploration facilitated by non-traditional data. Transp. Res. D 74, 28–47.

Zhou, J., Yang, Y., Webster, C., 2020. Using big and open data to analyze transit oriented development: new outcomes and improved attributes. J. Am. Plann. Assoc. 86 (3), 364–376.

FSC
www.fsc.org
MIX
Papier | Fördert gute Waldnutzung
FSC® C083411

Kolibri 360 GmbH
Ferdinand-Jühlke-Straße 7
99095 Erfurt, Deutschland
produktsicherheit@kolibri360.de